Ten Yards Beyond the Finish Line

Coach Roy Griak: A Journey in Maroon and Gold

By Don Timm with Lindsay Nielsen
Foreword by Garry Bjorklund

Minneapolis

Minneapolis

FIRST EDITION MAY 2018
TEN YARDS BEYOND THE FINISH LINE
Roy Griak: A Journey in Maroon and Gold
 Calumet Editions is an imprint of Calumet Editions, LLC.

For information, contact Calumet Editions at info@calumeteditions.com.

Printed in the United States of America.

10 9 8 7 6 5 4 3 2 1

ISBN: 978-0-9987319-4-0

Book and cover design: Gary Lindberg

To Coach
Your inspiration and guidance has carried thousands to the finish line and beyond.

"When I was a young man, I would have loved to have had the
opportunity to compete for Coach Griak."
(Jim Bush whose UCLA teams won 5 NCAA Track and Field championships)

"Coach Bush, I had that opportunity."
(Don Timm)

Acknowledgements

This book has been a work in progress for many years and would not have been possible without the assistance of a host of people. Thanks to co-author, Lindsay Nielsen, for her work concerning Coach's early life and his last days and for her continued advice and encouragement throughout the project. Thanks to Kay Richardson for allowing me to spend so much time with Coach in their home and also for the countless meals and snacks she provided. Thanks to Seth and Jason and their mother, Rose-Mary, for giving me access to family pictures and records that documented Coach's career and for their support in writing the history of his life. Countless athletes over more than a half-century thank the entire Griak family for sharing him with us for so many years. I am grateful for Seth and Jason's willingness to share the cost of publishing this book. We will honor their father's desire that all proceeds will go to the Roy Griak Endowment Fund to award scholarship aid to future Gopher cross country and track and field athletes. Thanks to all those who shared their memories of Coach and to those who helped in any way to tell the story of Coach's life.

Patrick Mader has been a great help both in his enthusiasm for this project of Coach's life and for his assistance concerning grammar and usage. Any grammatical errors that remain are mine not his. Thanks to those who provided pictures, and to Jaimie Huntress and Coach's niece, Patti Petrich, for their technical expertise.

I would like to thank Jeff Renlund for sharing his vast knowledge of high school cross country and track and field and for the pictures he shared. Thanks also to Calumet Edition's Gary Lindberg for his work in enhancing and cropping the pictures and for his patience with this author.

I am grateful to Tom Stuart, Richard Simonsen and the late Steve Hoag for sharing their memories of the 1968 Gopher Big Ten Track and Field Championship, to Steve Hoag for recounting the 1968 NCAA cross country meet and to Tom Heinonen and Norris Peterson for recalling their championship cross country team of 1964. I am deeply indebted to my teammates from the 1969 Big Ten Championship cross country team, especially Garry Bjorklund, Tom Page, Mike Hanley, Terry Thomas, Gene Daly and Pat Kelly not only for sharing their memories of that day and year but, as Yogi Berra would have said, "for making it necessary" by the way they competed in the Conference Meet. Thanks to Garry for providing the Foreword.

I am thankful for the patience and encouragement my wife Bonnie has given me in what has seemed like the longest distance run of my life. Without her support this project would not have been possible. I am also grateful to our son, Andy, daughters Liz and Katie and to our son-in-law, Dan, who offered their considerable computer skills to this acknowledged Luddite. Special thanks to Liz, who typed the tributes into a workable format.

I deeply cherished my time with Coach Griak, both as an athlete and in the 45 years since I competed for the Gophers. My retirement from teaching and coaching coincided with the last years of his life and this was a blessing and privilege that allowed me to spend a great deal of time with him. This book was a result but the memories, the laughter, the wisdom he imparted, the sentiments he expressed, the tears we shared…these were the most important rewards from our time together.

Don Timm, 2018

Contents

Ten Yards Beyond the Finish Line

Coach Roy Griak: A Journey in Maroon and Gold

By Don Timm with Lindsay Nielsen
Foreword by Garry Bjorklund

Foreword

Garry Bjorklund

Growing up in Twig and attending Proctor High School I had no idea what I was getting myself into when I signed up to attend the University of Minnesota and to run for the Golden Gophers. The decision certainly wasn't about facilities or equipment. It was about Roy Griak and his challenge to me, and to all of his runners, that we should aspire to be good enough to earn the right to wear Maroon and Gold. Back in Twig, my highest aspiration was running six miles without stepping in cow manure.

Coach Griak's recruiting letters talked about team success, individual progress and friendship. As our coach, he made no promises but instilled in us well-worn traditions that have been part of University of Minnesota Cross Country for over 100 years. Every day he reinforced a mind-set that we could take to the starting line with anyone whatever the competition: a dual meet, Big Ten Championship, NCAA Championship…life in the real world. He would say, "We are as good as anybody here."

Everyone wanted to be one of his "Pumpkins" and conversely each of us at one time or another performed so poorly that we looked like a "Manure Pile." Either way, you got a Griak hug and reassurance that you would always be one of his Boys. Not everyone who came to the University arrived brimming with talent, self-confidence and clarity of purpose. Coach called us his Boys, but his intention was to help us become men.

There were no stars on Griak teams. Everyone, including Coach, got an oversized T-shirt, baggy white cotton shorts, a jock strap that could cut metal, knee high tube socks (that doubled as race mitts), a green towel and a locker in the basement of Cooke Hall. Privacy to shower or to do your business was nonexistent. Our weight room was an exercise bike, chin-up stand, and one set of bar bells in a corner of the field house. Our indoor and outdoor tracks were dirt. Our cross country course (Les Bolstad Golf Course) was incredible as were various training sites around Minneapolis / St. Paul. All in all, I don't remember anyone suggesting that our situation was deficient.

Every time I visit the Griak Invitational I go over and stand where the old starting line was located. Just remembering events that happened almost 50 years ago causes me to reflect and compare then to now. The course may have changed and certainly there is more pomp and circumstance (70 port-a-johns, really!!). The runners today are faster than we were, but not tougher. Don Brown was the greatest track / cc announcer I've ever heard. As the father of two daughters, I believe the addition of women has improved the sport. Bottom line, "Is the running experience today better than it was in the 1960s?" In my mind the answer is clearly, not any better – different, but not better.

The individuals I aspired to emulate from teams before my time are still my heroes as are my teammates from my four years at Minnesota. The shared aims of our team in '69 was like nothing I have experienced before or since as an athlete or a coach. Most importantly, we were blessed to have Roy Griak as our Coach and life-long friend. I truly hope that the kids of today have as much to look forward to as we experienced when we were their age.

Garry Bjorklund
University of Minnesota Track and Cross Country
1969-1974

Introduction

Don Timm & Seth Griak and Jason Griak

In 1909, the Minnesota Gophers won their first conference title in cross country. Five years later in 1914, as World War I was breaking out in Europe, they won another cross-country title. The Gophers would not win another conference cross country championship for fifty years. That title came in 1964 just a year after Coach Roy Griak began his long tenure coaching at Minnesota. Ironically, there would be another five-year span before the Griak-led Gophers would win their next Big Ten championship in 1969. The 1969 team remains the most recent University of Minnesota (U of M) team to claim a conference cross country title. I was privileged to have been a member of that team.

Coach Griak and the seven runners who would represent Minnesota arrived at the golf course used by the University of Indiana to preview the course on the eve of the November 15, 1969 Big Ten Championship.

We were a young and inexperienced team. Only two of our runners, Pat Kelly and Tom Page, had previous experience running in a conference championship meet. There was a cold, light rain falling on the golf course in Bloomington that afternoon and it was already getting dark as Coach Griak gave us a tour of the course we would run the next day. There were some runners from the other schools on the course, but we were focused on the coming race and did not make any contact with them. I saw no other coaches on the course. I suspect the other coaches were warm, dry and being well fed at a banquet the University of Indiana had provided in their honor. Coach Griak remembered that he arrived late to the banquet and coaches meeting and that he was dripping wet. He had passed up the banquet to be with us on one of the coldest, wettest evenings we had practiced in all year.

Minnesota's 1969 Big Ten Championship Cross Country Team. Front Row (L-R): Tom Page, Mike Hanley, Gene Daly, Pat Kelly. Back Row (L-R): Coach Griak, Terry Thomas, Garry Bjorklund, Don Timm

Coach had chosen to be with his runners. At the time, we didn't realize how important this tour would be to our success the next day. The well chalked route was no longer visible the morning of the race because the rain had turned to snow during the night and the course was blanketed in two inches of whiteness. During our preview of the course Coach had calmly discussed with us the need for tying the laces of our spikes tighter because they would be wet the next day and wet laces and shoes would expand. He talked to us about areas on the course where sharp turns would likely become slippery. We listened to his suggestions on what we should wear. We made no concessions to the predicted 25-degree temperature other than wearing socks on our hands. Unlike the runners from the University of Illinois, our team chose not to wear tights underneath our usual lightweight shorts and uniform tops. The morning of the race Coach told us that the "Fighting Illini" must have thought that it was cold. I think he was telling us that we were tougher than they were as he simply stated, "Your heat will come from running fast." He told us, "This is our kind of day." Coach also had a special concoction of "hot stuff" he put on the small of our backs before we went to the starting line on race day. It made us feel warm even if the temperature was not. Coach discussed our strategy, "Stick together in a pack; draw strength from each other." Nothing was left to chance. With his advice and his presence, he calmed our nerves, boosted our confidence and assured us that we were ready to run our best race of the year. I believe that because of Coach Griak's faith in us and ours in him we were better prepared mentally for the race than any other team in the meet.

EACH OF YOU MUST ESTABLISH A GOAL FOR YOURSELF COME THE BIG TEN CROSS COUNTRY CHAMPIONSHIP THIS SATURDAY -- ANY HALF HEARTED EFFORTS WILL RESULT LITTLE IN THE WAY OF ANY SELF SATISFACTION. WE CAN DO IT – I REPEAT – WE, AS A TEAM CAN ACCOMPLISH MUCH ON SATURDAY... HAVE THE SELF-CONFIDENCE TO HAVE YOUR ULTIMATE EFFORT AND THE REST WILL TAKE CARE OF ITSELF. BE SURE OF YOURSELF, AND WHAT GOALS YOU ARE AFTER – YOU CAN DO IT – WE CAN DO IT – THE TEAM CAN DO IT – WE, WE, WE, WE, YES, WE CAN.

Example of a Coach Griak bulletin board message

Coach Griak was the kind of man who engendered respect and trust. We never doubted him, and we did run our best race that day. Coach Griak's coaching went far beyond our physical training. As much as he could control the outcome of a season or a meet he left nothing to chance. A day did not go by without him encouraging us, building us up, challenging us and prodding us to work hard. He set an example of personal fitness that inspired us. Few could keep up with him in the calisthenics part of our workouts. He was a psychologist and subtle cheerleader who instilled in us a belief that as a group we could do great things. Throughout the season he had told us to respect all of our opponents but not to be afraid of any of them. To the left, in Coach's own printing, is an example of the type of message that we would find on the locker room bulletin board in the days before a big meet.

The Minnesota Gopher cross country team of 1969 exemplified several characteristics that were trademarks for Coach Griak's teams. All seven runners on the conference meet team were native Minnesotans. Many other collegiate teams were made up of runners from various states or countries. Like our coach, we had deep pride in representing our state and the University of Minnesota.

Pat Kelly and Coach

Another characteristic of Coach Griak's teams was the determined attitude of his runners under difficult conditions. When we encountered snow and frigid temperatures at the conference meet we saw it as a challenge and maybe even an advantage rather than an obstacle. We had been told by Coach that we were "Minnesota tough" and we believed him. We knew that we had an edge on teams that might be thinking negatively about the weather. Freshman Garry Bjorklund attributed part of the Gopher success that day to being prepared. He said, "One of the nice things about living in Minnesota is that you have to be ready for anything and can't take the weather for granted." We had also been taught that we needed to be able to adjust to any problems that might occur during a race and that no matter what happened we should never lose heart or give up.

Our Captain in 1969, Pat Kelly, was struggling greatly from the effects of a hip injury that had sidelined him for much of the season. Just his presence on the starting line was an encouragement for the rest of us. Pat struggled in the conference meet but finished the race. Another Gopher, Terry Thomas, was spiked midway through the five-mile race and finished the last 2 1/2 miles of snow and mud running with one spiked shoe and one bare foot. He didn't back off and managed to claim 26th place as our vital fifth runner. Near the end of the race, Coach was positioned on a downhill just before the last climb to the finish line. Concerned about the treacherous footing and not wanting us to fall, Tom Page remembered him yelling, "Keep your composure," as we went by him.

Coach Griak had a way of getting the very best from his runners by respecting each of us, giving his best, and expecting that we would give him our best in return. He had told us, "If you take a chance in life sometimes good things happen, sometimes bad things happen, but if you don't take a chance, nothing will happen."

I know from personal experience that Coach had no favorites among his athletes. The 1969 Gophers had a number of runners who had excelled in high school and were highly recruited by many colleges. Tom Page was a Minnesota high school state cross country champion from Edina. Mike Hanley was a

4:13 miler from Anoka High School. Garry Bjorklund was a state champion in cross country from Twig, Minnesota and Proctor High School, who had also won three state mile titles in track. In the spring of 1969 he had run a Minnesota state record 4:05 mile.

Gopher runners at Thomas Beach on Lake Calhoun in the late summer of 1970: (L-R) Terry Thomas, Garry Bjorklund, Mike Hanley, Greg Nelson, Don Timm, Carter Holmes and Tom Page

Garry was heavily recruited by many elite distance programs in the nation. One of the reasons he chose Minnesota, beside the fact that he and Coach were both from the Duluth area, was that while most of the other eager and hopeful coaches told Garry that he would be the best runner on their team, Coach Griak had challenged him by saying, "IF you can make our team."

Minnesota placed four runners in the top eight spots in the Big Ten Meet in 1969. The Gopher places of 1, 2, 3, 8 and 26 added up to 40 points and the team title. Tom Page summed up the feeling the Gopher runners had that day about the race and about our Coach when he said, "I was proud to be a member of such a great bunch of guys and to accomplish this for a man who was not only our coach but our friend." Recalling that day 45 years later in the summer of 2014, Coach talked of the sheer excitement he felt at the "beautiful sight" of three Minnesota Gopher runners coming over the last hill and holding the top three spots in the meet. "Holy cow, that was pretty special." In a letter written to me two decades ago, Garry Bjorklund said, "I'd give every time, title, honor, etc. to relive the fall of 1969. Winning was important but I think the best part was for a bunch of pumpkins believing that magic could happen. Even if we hadn't won, that would still be the best time of my life as an athlete."

Three of the first four Gopher placers are mentioned in the paragraphs above. I was the fourth and I was treated exactly like the prized recruits even though I was an unheralded walk-on. I came to the University of Minnesota in the fall of 1969 having never met Coach Griak. I had done little athletically in high school that would have caused him to know my name and I certainly was not recruited by Minnesota or any other school.

On my first day of classes that fall I located Coach Griak's office which was in room 221 of the athletic department in Cooke Hall. I introduced myself and asked if I could try out for his cross-country team. He didn't laugh at my high school times and he didn't tell me that his team had been practicing twice a day for the last month and that I was too late. Instead, he stopped what he was doing, took me to the equipment room, gave me practice gear (shoes, white shorts, gray t-shirt, socks, jock and a green towel) and welcomed me to the team. Coach had never seen me run a step and yet he made me feel that I was important.

He has probably welcomed a thousand young men this way and this was one of the many reasons why people loved him. He had a way of making everyone feel that they were the most important person in his world at that moment. In my years at Minnesota, I experienced first-hand

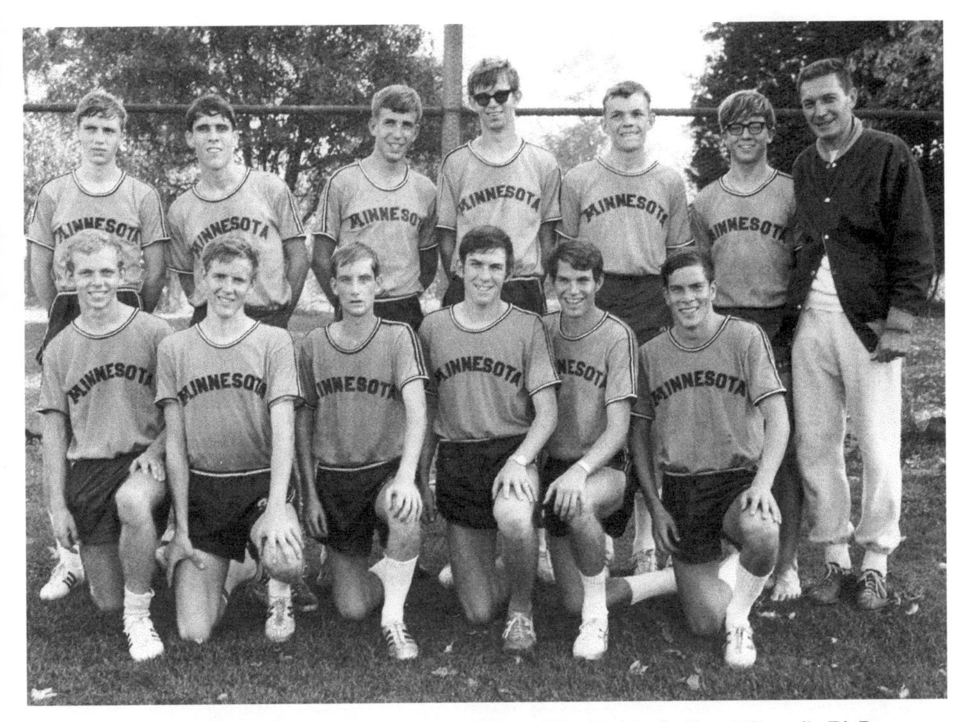

1969 Minnesota Gopher Cross Country Team (Top Twelve): Front Row (L-R) Dean Swanson, Carter Holmes, Gene Daly, Mike Hanley, Tom Page, Greg Nelson. Back Row (L-R) John Hopko, Pat Kelly, Garry Bjorklund, Terry Thomas, Don Timm, Mike Lawless, Coach Griak

that we were all Coach's boys and that, as long as we gave our best in practice and competition, we were all treated to the same praise, kicks in the backside when deserved, encouragement, understanding in tough times, bad jokes, concern for our schoolwork and families, fatherly advice and finally, his love.

Along the way we were introduced to Coach Griak's philosophy of life. Coach did much more than help his athletes, whether they were runners, throwers, vaulters or jumpers, to discover their physical limits. His teachings molded us and changed us forever. The title "Coach" when applied to Coach Griak, became an address of ultimate respect.

In the pages that follow, Coach Griak's philosophy and the way he treated his athletes, colleagues and friends, will be reflected in the words of those whose lives he helped to shape and in what co-authors, Lindsay Nielsen and Don Timm were able to pry from Coach himself. In addition to the 1969 team described in this introduction, Coach's two other Big Ten championship teams, the 1964 cross country team and the 1968 track and field team will be also highlighted as well as the 1968 cross country team that gave Coach his highest NCAA place when they finished fourth.

When first approached about this book, Coach Griak had said that he would help as long as the book wasn't about him. However, over the last five years of his life he graciously revealed a great deal about the unique life he led. At the time that I was a member of his teams I knew how special he was to the Gopher student / athletes who had the good fortune to call him "Coach." However, my research for this book revealed that the qualities that made him so special were already present in his youth when he bore great responsibility in helping his mother and siblings after the death of his father. At Morgan Park High School, he stood out not only as an excellent student and gifted athlete but one who held the respect of his peers as their elected senior class president. During World War II he demonstrated his patriotism and willingness to serve while gaining a deeper appreciation for his family and country. Like many who survived the war he returned to the United States with special goals and a great hope for the future. His Gopher teammates remembered him as an enthusiastic and hardworking athlete. He carried that work-ethic and enthusiasm into his teaching and coaching. In reading the tributes of those who competed for Coach at St. Louis Park High School, I realized that they knew him to be very special long before he coached at the U of M. Family members, co-workers, rival coaches and fans all knew that Roy Griak was special. World-class athletes, who had been tutored by some of the top coaches in the nation saw Coach as uniquely special when they met him as a member of one of the many United States international teams he coached or managed. In their own words, those who have submitted letters about Coach Griak will attest to the many lives he has influenced. Coach would have been quick to add about these people, "They have given me much more than I have given them." Once you have read the book, you can judge for yourself the validity of that statement.

Note to the reader: Coach Griak was perhaps the most organized person I have even known. He kept 3 X 5 notecards with records of every workout each of his athletes had ever done and the results of each of their competitions. He gave me a copy of my complete record two decades after I had completed my eligibility. Every tool in his garage had a place and he expected it to be returned there when its job was done. He had the name, address and phone number of almost every athlete he had ever coached and in 2015 was still seeking information on those who had moved or somehow fallen off his RADAR. He wrote personal letters to any and all who had contributed in any way to his endowment fund or to the University of Minnesota. He was very organized in almost everything he did.

However, in relating the story of his life, Coach's organizational skills were often difficult to follow. To ask him a question about one area

Coach Griak with a stopwatch at the Bierman Track

of his life would lead to the desired result but usually included many side stories. The side stories sometimes did not seem to relate to the original question; however, Coach knew where he was going and the story always returned to the topic at hand. Although the story may seem disjointed or circuitous, I have tried to remain faithful to the report as it was told me by Coach. *Be patient and Coach Griak will get you to the finish line (and beyond).*

Coach Griak

While competing for the Gophers and training under Coach Griak's guidance, I was aware that he seemingly knew everything about track and field. Although I was focused on distance running as a cross country runner and steeplechaser / 3-miler, I was always amazed at his versatility and the depth of his knowledge and expertise in all areas of the sport. Having taken his track and field class at the University, I knew that he could analyze and discuss the specifics and mechanics of any event whether it was the high jump, the shot, the hurdles, sprinting and starting out of the blocks, baton exchanges in the relay events, the horizontal jumps, the pole vault and the discus as well as middle and distance running. He was an expert on the precise body mechanics that would lead to the best results in each discipline. Coach had studied the philosophies and training methods of all the famous coaches. He could discuss the logic of certain established training schedules and also suggest things he had discovered that would work even better. When I ran for Coach he had few assistants (usually one and that was a volunteer). In the years I was at the University of Minnesota, Dick DeSchriver and Gil Weingarten were the assistant coaches I remember. I was always amazed that Coach Griak could direct the workouts of so many different events that were taking place simultaneously in the field house or on the outdoor track. I can still envision him standing in the middle of the track holding 3-4 running stop watches (at that time everything was timed with stop watches). He could time sprinters, middle distance runners and distance runners at the same time in their different workouts and still give all of us our splits at every 110 yards. Although my race, the 3,000-meter steeplechase, was run in meters, all the other races were still measured in yards.

Coach Griak was an unquestioned authority on the track, the field and in cross country. Without a doubt, we knew that what he had planned for us each day had been meticulously calculated based on the stage of the season, what we had done in the workouts the day before, our short term and long term goals, if a runner was injured or ill, and the weather (although he always said that cold and wind were opportunities to become "Minnesota tough"). Hard workouts and easy days ("active rest") were interwoven to create an overall plan to bring Minnesota runners to their peak for the biggest meets. We had faith in his plan and ran, jumped, vaulted or threw believing that we would be at our best for the toughest competitions.

What I did not realize about Coach Griak until recent decades was the depth of his knowledge in areas other than track and field. I was a history teacher for nearly four decades and still consider myself both a history teacher and a lifelong student of history. Listening to Coach Griak's account of growing up in Duluth during the Depression or to his account of his Army service in the Pacific during WW II was better than reading a history book. Coach had a genuine interest in and love for history. He had a great devotion and respect for his country and tremendous pride in representing the United States both during WW II and as a coach of American teams in international competitions.

We often exchanged history books and enjoyed discussing them together. When we visited, Coach would often inquire about the books I was currently reading and would ask me to give him a report on them when I finished. I came to admire not only how well versed he was in certain historical topics but also his desire to broaden his knowledge. Where many people who have reached the age of 90 would see their focus of interests shrink, Coach's mind was like a sponge seeking to soak up knowledge and expand into new areas of learning. He told me early in 2013 that he had spent so much time focused on track and field that he now wanted to explore areas that he had glossed over for many years. Coach subscribed to several news magazines and read them so that he was aware of current happenings throughout the United States and the world. While having lunch with him in 2012 at the Mayo Clinic, I witnessed him giving more than he took in a discussion with a stranger who happened to sit at our table and proceed to badmouth the government and a particular political party.

Coach in front of his Plymouth home

Coach's Character

Coach Griak truly believed the adage that, "It is more blessed to give than to receive." Anyone who ever lent him a hand or did any simple kindness for him was repaid many times over. Coach had tremendous neighbors and they were very helpful to him. It was interesting to see them decked out in University of Minnesota clothes. I know where they got those items because I have also been the recipient of many a sweatshirt, stocking cap, jacket or shirt. Coach usually gave away his new Minnesota gear while he continued to wear garments that were several decades old.

Although he was the longest tenured coach at the University of Minnesota, and probably should have been granted a lifetime pass to all Gopher contests, to the very last year of his life Coach Griak continued to buy four Gopher season tickets for football, basketball and hockey. However, most of those tickets were given away to his friends and neighbors. When health issues made it difficult for Coach to attend the games he continued to buy the tickets to support the Gopher programs and so that his friends could enjoy seeing the games at the stadium or arena. He continued to watch the contests but from his home. Coach loved to watch Minnesota athletes in every sport when they competed on the Big Ten network. A more ardent supporter of Gopher athletics did not exist.

In addition to a lifelong admiration for my Coach, the idea of collecting stories (tributes) about him and putting them into a book about his life was prompted by several factors. One was Coach's advancing age and the fear that an account of parts of his amazing life might be lost if it was not documented. Another factor was that in this age of highly publicized athletic scandals, collegiate programs rated mainly on their won-lost records and coaches with less than permanent allegiance to the traditions and standards of their school, I felt that there was a need to honor a coach who not only developed successful teams but who had never been in trouble with the NCAA or the University of Minnesota, who faithfully represented the University for 52 years and who cared deeply about those on his team not only as athletes but as people. Coach Griak did not see a young athlete as someone whose value in four years as a Gopher rested solely on what they could do on the athletic field but as someone whose time representing the University of Minnesota was just a part of an education that would make them a better person and a citizen who would contribute to society. Those who were privileged to have competed on his teams knew that Coach's interest in them, and their careers and families, continued long after they had completed their collegiate eligibility. Although Coach's memory retained the exact time or distance that was the personal best for each of his athletes, it seemed that his perception of their contribution to his team only grew with the passage of time. He was very proud of what they accomplished while they were at the University and later, in their chosen careers.

There were a number of observations in recent years that also prompted me to ask Coach for permission to write about his life. After taking his track and field class while in college, I knew the number of events that made up a track meet. However, I witnessed an additional event whenever I would attend a meet at the field house or at the Bierman track. I would watch Coach Griak and keep track of the number of people who would approach him before, during and after a meet. Until recent years, trying to find Coach Griak stationary at the meet was virtually impossible as he was not just a spectator, but coach, meet director and jack-of-all-trades. He was always busy but he never brushed aside those who approached him with statements like, "Coach, I ran for you twelve years ago but I just wanted you to meet my son," or "Coach Griak, thanks for all that you did for my son when he was in school here," or "Coach, I want to introduce you to my fiancee." No matter how long it had been since the athlete had been on his team or how "successful" they had been athletically, Coach not only took the time to inquire about their post collegiate career and where life had taken them but he seemed to revel in those contacts and had a way of making that athlete, parent or family member feel more important.

Seeking tributes about Coach was definitely not his idea. The decision to do this came from me and with his reluctant permission. It evolved after years of hearing his stories and thinking that someone should write this down. I realized that Coach was too humble to boast about the many lives he had touched and that, even though he had told me many interesting stories, there had to be more. I witnessed Coach making a strong impression on my runners and their parents each time he spoke at one of our banquets. He did not talk about his athletic and coaching success. Instead, he told the runners that if there was one thing he would like to have the chance to do again it would be to tell his mother that he loved her. He stressed how important it was for the young athletes to take advantage of every opportunity to tell the people in their lives (mother, father, teachers and coaches) how much they were loved and appreciated.

The decision to actively seek tributes about Coach Griak came to a head several years ago when I was privileged to have Coach tell me about one of the incidents listed below and then was a witness to the other. At that point, I began collecting and writing down stories about his amazing life and the impact he has had on so many people. The two stories below initiated the documentation process and eventually led to this book.

Coach told me a story several years ago about an encounter he had while out shopping. As Coach went from one part of a store to the next he noticed that he had seen the same man in each area and that the man seemed to be staring at him. The man appeared to be following him. Finally, the man came up to him and asked him if he was Mr. Griak. Coach was not sure just who was asking the question until the man volunteered that he remembered Coach from a junior high physical education class four decades earlier. He said that he had not been very athletic and that the other students had often laughed at him and his efforts to run, jump or do calisthenics. The man related that Coach had encouraged him and told him to just do his best and then had given him a pat on the back when he began to improve. He told Coach, "I just wanted you to know that your encouragement in that class gave me the confidence to be successful in other areas of life." Coach asked him where his life had taken him and he replied that he had been a decorated fighter pilot during the war in Vietnam.

In 2012, I accompanied Coach to the Home Depot to help with an errand. He said that he wanted help with some fertilizer for his lawn. He bought twice as much as he needed. I did not realize until later that one bag was for me and my lawn. When he paid for the fertilizer, the clerk at the check-out counter looked at him quizzically. As Coach left and began to slowly walk out, I was behind him with the cart. The clerk asked me, "Was that Roy Griak?" When I told her yes, she said that Coach had been her junior high physical education instructor in St. Louis Park. Although Coach had walked, with great effort, all the way to his car by the time that I got there and told him what the clerk had said, he immediately walked all the way back to the store so that he could talk with her. They talked pleasantly for several minutes. Later, I asked Coach if he had remembered her from so long ago and he said no he had not but that if she remembered him he wanted to greet her and ask how life had treated her.

When I realized that these acts of kindness were only two of the ones I had witnessed or that he had casually mentioned, I knew that they were just the tip of the iceberg. Having stumbled upon numerous unsolicited examples of Coach's unique character I came upon the idea of actively seeking tributes from his friends, coaching peers, co-workers and athletes. Coach Griak was far too humble to have entertained this idea but, with a great deal of prompting, he agreed to allow me to begin this process. Coach Griak's life was one of befriending and caring for others. I am sure that he was not even aware of all the people he had encouraged and aided. Offering compliments, words of thanks, sincere concerns and positives about others and about each day were as much a part of Coach Griak's life as breathing.

The letters contained in this book, though numerous, wonderful and heartfelt, reflect only a small fraction of the lives altered by their association with Coach. If, as you read through them find yourself thinking, "Hey, I have a story to tell," please tell it. Coach Griak's family would love to hear from you because, as we all have been made to feel, we were each his favorite.

Don Timm

Author's Note: Seth and Jason Griak are the sons of Roy and Rose-Mary Griak. Thanks to both Seth and Jason for sharing the following memories of their father. These memories add a dimension to the book that would otherwise be missing for those who knew their father only as their Coach, mentor and friend or as their co-worker, mentor and friend. Although Coach had a multitude of athletes who he treated as his "sons," only Seth and Jason could call him Dad. Thank you for sharing your father with so many of us. It is great to know that Coach created wonderful memories for you even though so much of his time was spent with his University duties and his Gopher athletes.

By Seth Griak

First of all, I would like to thank Don Timm and Lindsay Nielsen for taking on this project. Don and Lindsay have worked very hard in completing this book and deserve much thanks. I also would like to say thank you to all the people who helped my father become the man that he was. Athletes, students, friends and family all gave him the opportunity to share his passion for track and field and for life. As the saying goes, you reap what you sow. Thanks for giving back to him, throughout his life, the energy to do what he loved.

Growing up, I didn't think of my Dad as being anything but my father first and coach second. As youngsters, he took us down to the "U" and we got to shoot hoops in the field house on the weekends during track practices, skate in the old Mariucci, shoot hoops in the "Barn," run through the dark tunnels under Cooke Hall, etc. All just normal stuff we thought at the time, but as we got a bit older, we realized how lucky we were. He coached our church basketball teams and tried to attend as many of our sporting events as possible. He was a great Dad!

Back then, he was the Track and Field Coach, Cross Country Coach, recruiter, travel coordinator, etc. He had some help, but in the early days, he pretty much did it all. He was extremely dedicated and as they say, "all in" when it came to his sport and his athletes. He bled maroon and gold. It didn't matter what sport or cause that needed a booster at the "U," he was passionate about supporting the University. I started to realize as a young adult that his passion for coaching and the "U" were very, very important to him and were a large part of his identity. I called him Dad. Many people called him Coach. I really think he was more of a teacher than anything. He taught us to give our best effort, respect people, be snotty nose tough, etc. All of these are life lessons Jason and I will hopefully follow and pass on to others. Thanks Dad.

Here is a funny story about my Dad:

I came by the track office at Bierman to say hello to Dad a few years ago just before Halloween. He was retired and sharing an

Bob Wagner, Seth Griak, Coach Griak, Lefty Wright and Jason Griak at the Griak CC Meet – Coach and Lefty are in the golf cart

office with Lynden Reder. He was doing his fund raising and assisting Steve Plasencia and working with Jo Rider. I ran into Steve in the hallway and he said Dad was down in the locker room doing something. He also mentioned that they had to keep the doors to the offices shut as they were having trouble with people walking into the building and stealing laptops and such.

Vincent with "Papa" Griak in his Bierman office

They had experienced a recent theft and were on the lookout for suspicious characters. I immediately saw my opportunity to mess with my Dad but needed a co-conspirator. I asked Steve to go downstairs and tell Dad that there was some strange looking dude walking around Bierman and that he was worried it might be the computer thief. I knew that my Halloween costume was in the car and I hustled out to grab it before Dad emerged from the locker room. I was going to an upcoming party as Kid Rock, a long-haired, grungy rocker. I quickly threw on the green army hat with the long stringy hair sewn into it. I put on an old, worn army jacket of Dad's and some wrap-around sunglasses. Dad came up from the locker room to intercept the criminal, hustling as fast as he could with a cane he was using as the time. I had grabbed Steve's laptop and had tucked it under my arm. I timed my passing with Dad perfectly at the front door of Bierman. The long-haired hippie dude with the laptop was exiting as he was coming up the stairs. From the top of the stairs, Steve yelled at Roy, "GET HIM. GET HIM." I kind of bumped into him with the loot as he was yelling at me to drop it. At the same time, he was whacking me with his cane. He wasn't messing around and I realized that I better call off the charade before he had a heart attack. I yanked off the hat with the hair and ripped off the glasses. Dad was still swinging away. When he realized what had happened, his jaw dropped to the floor. He wasn't happy that we had got him. Steve and I were laughing so hard that we were crying. I had bruises all over my arms but it was worth it. Dad was probably around 85 at the time and putting a beat down on a perceived criminal; that was Dad.

By Jason Griak

My father was captivated by our young son, Vincent. Nikki and I enjoyed watching Dad's fascination with his grandson as he loved to watch Vince run and play. He had plans to set up an agility station in our basement as an early exercise program. Always the teacher, Dad had a whole workout program where Vince would hop on one foot, then two, and so on. He would call Vincent "Brkovi" which means "whiskers" in Serbian. Vince loved going to Papa Griak's office to explore and to just to hang out and crawl between Dad's legs at his desk.

This reminded me of when my brother Seth and I were children and explored the tunnels under the field house and the William's Arena area. I have fond memories of my Dad hauling my brother and me off to bed while whistling the *Colonel Bogey March* from one of his favorite movies, *Bridge on the River Kwai*. The bedtime whistling is a ritual I have continued with Vince.

I talked with my Dad almost every day on the phone. I felt like I had a special relationship with him. He would call me or I would call him. It was usually a short conversation but we just wanted to say that we loved each other. He always checked to say that he was thinking about us and to make sure that we had made it safely home from a trip or just to ask if we had a good day.

In 1984, the summer Olympics were held in Los Angeles. My father was head manager for the track and field squad. The staff was the same one that had been chosen for the 1980 Moscow games that were eventually boycotted by the United States. Seth and I were also able to go to Los Angeles where my Dad had arranged for us to stay at a rental home several miles from the Coliseum. My brother and I would travel to the Coliseum on our roller blades. Our Dad took good care of us by meeting us for lunch outside the Olympic Village. Whenever he could, he provided us with steaks he had stuffed under his shirt after visiting the training table. Even with all of his duties, he had his boys in mind. Seth and I had usually set out on our adventure with some tickets in hand and we sometimes made a few bucks scalping them outside the Coliseum. We were on our roller blades and were prepared for a quick get-away if necessary! Being at the Olympic Games and spending time with Dad was great and created memories for a lifetime.

My father was a great promoter of track and field his whole life. As we were growing up, Seth and I went to quite a few all-comers meets and we loved going to the track with Dad and running a few sprint races. Often we would accompany him on weekends to competitions or practices. I didn't realize until later how special it was see track meets close up and to rub shoulders with the Gopher athletes. I can remember running victory laps with Garry Bjorklund after one of his numerous triumphs. Like my Dad did with so many people, Garry had a way of making me feel like I was the one who had accomplished something great!

When I was competing in high school for St. Louis Park I often didn't want my parents to attend my sporting events. One time in particular though, my Dad did attend a region meet that led to qualification for the Minnesota state meet. Dad was there with some other Gopher coaches. They were on their way to a William's Fund gathering in Hutchinson but Dad made sure that they stopped at the meet to see me run. I respected Dad's knowledge and experience but appreciated that he didn't give me too much advice. He knew when to talk with me and when not to and his words were always wise. All he told me that day was to stay on the leader's outside shoulder and not to let him go. I followed Dad's advice until the final curve. The leader went wide and I slipped into lane one and battled it out to a photo finish where I got him on the lean. I was grateful for my Dad's easy way of giving advice and happy that I let him attend the meet.

Author's Note: Jason placed second in the 1979 Minnesota State Track and Field Meet when he ran 3200 meters in 9:16.77 for St. Louis Park High School. He placed just ahead of one of Coach Griak's future All-Americans, Dave Morrison of Lakeville.

My Dad developed some pretty good kitchen skills over time. One of his specialties was making crockpot meals as they were ready to be eaten when practice might go long. Our dog, Heinie, was getting long in the tooth and had become somewhat of a food and garbage hound.

One day, Heinie had gotten up on the kitchen counter and had eaten an entire roast and all the potatoes. He left only a few carrots. My Dad could have had his hide when he discovered him, bloated and lying on the kitchen floor! He often called him a "dumb dog" but I think he really liked him.

One of our last trips to Duluth together came with his induction into the Duluth Hall of Fame. Dad's brother, Steve, Dad, Seth and I all rode in Uncle Steve's car. After the banquet and on our way out of town we decided to stop by the old neighborhood in Gary-New Duluth. Dad had told us many times about a sidewalk in front of his boyhood home that had all the names of the kids etched in the cement. That night, as we explored, sure enough it was still there after all those years. Seth thought it would be a good idea to keep the slab for posterity and, as that section was already broken off, we decided to give it a go. This was against the advice of the older two occupants of the car. Seth told Uncle Steve to leave the back of his van open and to wait for us. Soon, we had piled a 100-pound slab into the back of his mini-van. Shortly thereafter, we stopped for gas. Sure enough, a police car happened to pull in. With a wry smile, Seth told Steve and Dad, "The cops are here!" My uncle emphatically said, "I knew it." However, our cargo was not discovered and we made it safely out of Duluth with our keepsake.

In his later years, my Dad inspired me with his determination and optimism. In the months before his death I can still envision him in the hospital doing standing push-ups, squats and arm circles as he prepared to return to his home. Dad was a fighter to the very end of his time on earth and even though he had lived a long, productive life, and was limited by a body that was wearing down, he still had things he wanted to accomplish. For decades, he had told his athletes to never give up and he practiced what he preached. Even in his last year of life, he would sometimes stay up very late doing research to prepare for meetings with potential donors to his endowment fund. He was always planning for the future. Although it was nearly two decades since he had been the head coach at Minnesota, he wanted to do everything he could to see that the program continued at a high level and that there would be opportunities for the student/ athletes of the future who he might never know. Dad dedicated his life to the University of Minnesota and his athletes but I never felt neglected. I am very proud of him and miss him every day. He was a great dad in every way.

Coach Griak's Philosophies on Life and Coaching

Coach Griak knew so many people from so many periods of his life that attempting to categorize the 140 tributes accumulated for this book posed a problem. There were tributes from high school friends and teammates, collegiate teammates, wartime buddies, teaching peers and athletes from St. Louis Park, as well as fellow coaches, Olympic athletes, U of M administrators and a myriad of Gopher athletes and their contemporaries. Rather than listing the tributes chronologically or by how they knew Coach, they were arbitrarily placed in groupings based on some of Coach's favorite sayings. The placements were purely subjective but some aspect of each tribute pointed toward a particular category. Many of the tributes were so universal in their praise of Coach that they could have fit into almost any of the categories. The last two groupings are not from Coach's sayings but fell under the frequent theme that Coach Griak had created a legacy or that Coach Griak had altered the life of the writer.

Most of the tributes were written in the two years before Coach's death in July of 2015. For those tributes, Coach was asked to comment on the first thing that came to his mind when the name of the writer was given. Those comments are found just before each tribute.

The personal tributes to Coach found in this book are categorized by some of his philosophies and favorite and most used sayings:

"Snotty-nosed tough."

"Minnesota tough."

You are never tired."

"The hills are our friends."

"Positive attitude and determination."

"Believe in yourself."

"10 yards beyond the finish line."

"Run through the finish line in everything you do."

"Give your best effort and the best will come back to you."

"Have a sense of humor."

"You can work hard and still have fun doing it."

"I have a ninety-eight-year-old grandmother who can run faster than that!"

"You are only as good as your last runner."

"Camaraderie and pride."

"Your books are your lunch pail"

"Hit the books."

"Be a competitor in the classroom as well as on the athletic field."

"Stay focused."

Commitment.

"Everyone needs someone at sometime (a helping hand). It makes a world of difference if that helping hand is there or if it is not there!"

"Console the person having a difficult time. The leader doesn't need the attention; they already have it. Gravitate to those in greatest need."

"That young athlete needs a hug."

"Everyone matters."

"Love them all."

"Be interested in them as human beings. The younger ones are the most impressionable."

"I tried to put myself in the athlete's shoes. How do they feel?"

"You can do more with a pat on the back than a kick in the pants."

"My athletes are my heroes."

Coach does not forget his athletes nor anyone in his St. Louis Park and University of Minnesota families.

His loyalty is legendary.

"Gol darn it."

"Malo po malo." ("Little by little," in Serbian)

Everyone Needs Someone at Sometime

A Collection of Roy Griak Tributes

Glenn Amundsen

Coach Griak: *Glenn is one of the University of Minnesota's biggest fans. I met him at an all-comer's meet at the University.*

Thanks very much indeed for allowing me to share with you a moment which involved my young daughter and Coach Griak.

My daughter, Michele, was with us (my wife and me) as we went to an outdoor all comer's meet at the U of M. It was a great chance to try a lot of events, which Michele did.

One particular event was the 220 (200 meters maybe). Roy got all the competitors lined up at the starting line. He ran eight girls in each race and all the participants received a ribbon. My daughter got to the finish line last but kept on running, not aware the event was over.

Roy saw what was happening and ran after her. He caught her in short order. He very gently patted her head to tell her that the race was over, adding, "Great race young lady, you ran farther than all the other girls in the race!" Michele remembered getting such a nice compliment from the Great Roy Griak.

Thanks coach Griak.

Glenn Amundsen
Rochester, Minnesota

Tom Christenson

Coach Griak: *Tom was a quarter-miler for me on the 1968 Big Ten Gopher Track and Field Championship team. He had also run for Oscar Yngve at Minneapolis Roosevelt.*

I was a member of your track and field team at Minnesota from 1964-1968. I will always remember and be grateful to you for treating all the members of the team with equal concern and time regardless of our relative abilities and value to the team. You always carried yourself as a gentleman with your team members and your competitors. I tried to duplicate that role modeling as I proceeded through my teaching and coaching career at Osseo High School. You are a Minnesota treasure and I am fortunate to have known you for these 49 years. I wish you many more years of a great life.

Tom Christenson
Class of 1968, U of M 1964-68

Gene Daly

Coach Griak: *Gene was a St. Cloud Tech athlete who was a varsity member of the 1969 Big Ten Championship CC team. Gene was an outstanding athlete and leader who is still devoted to the cause of the Gopher program.*

My father passed away unexpectedly in February of my junior year at the U. I got the call from home very early in the day and went over to see Coach Griak later that morning and he insisted on driving me home to St. Cloud. We left later that morning and got to my home around noon. Coach sat with my mother, brothers, and sisters for an extended period of time listening to and sharing stories of my father. He spent most of the day with my family prior to going back to the U that day. I will never forget the time Coach took to be with me and my family on a very hard day.

I ran on the 1969 Big Ten Champion Gopher Cross Country team. The meet was at the University of Indiana golf course. We arrived at the course very late in the afternoon, the day before the meet, to do some jogging and to get familiar with the route we were to run the next day. Coach ran the course with us, directing us through the entire route, pointing out critical turns, straight-aways, hills and valleys and talking through possible race strategies for the next day. We completed our workout in the dark and then we found out that Coach had missed the pre-meet coaches' meeting and social to be with us at the course. Our main competition for the championship that year was Michigan State and they arrived at the course later than we did that Friday afternoon and I remember their runners saying that they had no understanding of the course layout or route for the race in the morning. Their coach was not with them. We woke up the day of the race to snow on the ground, wind, and very cold temperatures, but confident that we were well prepared and ready for the competition. Prior to the race, Coach said it was a "Minnesota Day" and it truly was!

Gene Daly
U of M athlete 1970-1974

Doug Edmonson

Coach Griak: *Doug was from Richfield High School and ran cross country and track at Minnesota. He was a student of the game and a good worker.*

I met Roy Griak as a senior in high school when he approached me, after the Region V track meet, to come to the University of Minnesota. While I had the fourth fastest 880 time in the state, I had just missed qualifying for the state meet. Despite my disappointment, it didn't take much convincing me to come to the U as I had always wanted to be a Gopher. I walked on to the team, and after a strong red-shirt freshman season, Roy offered me a partial scholarship. I didn't have stellar college track career, but Roy was always there to support me, as he did with every athlete, regardless of performance or ability.

Our son Zach, who had been the Missouri high school 800-meter champ, decided to accept a partial ride to the U in 1998. It was an even greater pleasure having Roy coach the incoming freshman, thirty plus years after I had attended. Roy's first meeting with Zach included pulling out my performances on a 3x5 card file that Roy kept on every athlete he had ever coached. Roy told Zach "that his Dad couldn't hide the truth" because he had statistics to prove it! We had a good laugh about that. What Roy didn't have on that card was the story Roy had never caught wind of during my junior year.

While running indoor in 1969, I joined a group of Iron Rangers on an intramural hockey team that only had six guys. If someone didn't show up, they played the whole game short-handed. Being very fit, I could skate the whole game, alternating defense and wing. We made it to the championship intramural game, and while losing 8-1, all hell broke loose. Our goalie started a fight and everyone dropped their gloves (except for me and a player on the other team). While we were watching this, my captain skated across the ice and struck me over the head with his stick, leaving me dizzy and dumbfounded in a pool of blood on the ice. The worst part of the night was a shaved head and six stitches.

The worst part of the next day was going to track practice and explaining to Roy that I was playing intramurals during indoor season. Instead, I wore a maroon and gold stocking hat throughout practice (and some 85 degree March weather) for about a week until my hair started growing out. You wouldn't believe the ribbing I got as I headed to the shower with the cap on, as Roy walked through the locker room! So when I told Roy the story, thirty years later, he had no idea that I was skating around Williams Arena, getting some extra leg conditioning and a few scars to boot.

Roy was a great coach and a good man. He treated us with full respect, celebrated our successes and agonized over our disappointments. It was a great privilege to run for the U of M under his tutelage and an even greater experience to have my son work with him thirty years later.

Doug Edmonson
Cross Country and Track 1966-70

Scott Landes

Coach Griak: *Scott was a member of my Gopher cross country and track and field teams in the mid 1970s.*

Coach, you paid just as much attention to me as a JV runner as you did to the superstars. Thanks for everything.

Scott Landes,
Gopher CC and T & F (1974-1976)

Gerald Metzler

Coach Griak: *Gerry is an ex-Marine who ran the mile for Minnesota. He ran like a duck. He looked like a duck but he ran much faster than a duck. Gerald Metzler was not a good looking runner but he was one of the toughest.*

We were on the starting line at the Ohio State University golf course for the Big Ten Cross Country Championships. The date was November 5, 1979, and it was a beautiful crisp fall morning. My teammates and I were excited but not as excited as the late John Griffin. John was a senior from Detroit, Michigan and a transfer from Wayne State University. The starter said through his bullhorn, "Gentlemen, sweats off!" John went right into action. Pulling the bottoms of his sweat suit off, he then looked down and realized along with the laughing crowd that he was standing there wearing only a jockstrap, white socks and spikes. John yelled out, "Wait, Coach, I forgot my shorts!" then proceeded to dance around on one leg while rapidly trying to get his other leg through the sweat suit bottoms. The officials delayed the race so that John and Coach Griak could run down a small hill behind the large crowd. The modest Coach Griak took off his sweats, then his running shorts, and tossed them at John. With the crowd laughing, there was Coach Griak standing for all to see in his warm up top, underwear, socks, and shoes. John immediately took care of his little problem while Coach took his sweet time pulling on his warm up bottoms. Coach Griak gave a new twist to the saying, "Giving the shirt off your back."

Gerald T. Metzler
U of M runner
1970's

Ray Miller

Coach Griak: *Ray went to Minneapolis Edison High School. He won the Minnesota State CC Champion in 1957 by defeating Archie Patterson of St. Louis Park. The following spring Ray was narrowly defeated by Archie for the state 880-yard title in track. Ray was on the team when I came to the U of M. He was a tough little guy who was appreciative of everything done for him.*

In 1962, I was a walk-on at Minnesota after being discharged from the Navy. Jim Kelley was the coach at that time. When Roy became Coach in 1963, he got me a scholarship for the time I was at the U of M.

Roy was very organized and prepared for each track and cross country meet. I have great appreciation for his coaching. Most of all… he is my friend.

Raymond Miller
U of M athlete
1962-1963

Van Nelson

Coach Griak: *Van became a United States Olympian in the 10,000-meters at Mexico City in 1968. Van's brother Greg ran mile for me at the University. Van ran at St. Cloud State.*

Even though I was not going to attend the University of Minnesota, Coach Griak let me run in the field house when I was a senior at Washburn. Thanks, Coach for your continued support.

Van Nelson
1968 U.S. Olympic team

Mark and Stacy Plencner

Coach Griak: *Joe Plencner was a gifted pole vaulter. His parents (Mark and Stacy) drove from the Dakotas to watch him nearly every meet. Joe is a young man who is very grateful for what the University did for him.*

In the spring of 2005 our son, Joseph Plencner, competed in several events for the Fargo South High School track and field team in Fargo, North Dakota. His success in the pole vault resulted in a state championship and, ultimately, a call from Coach Phil Lundin. Shortly thereafter, Joe submitted his letter of intent to compete for the Gophers. As a parent, this was a shining moment – to be offered an opportunity to compete in the Big Ten was an offer too good to pass up. Soon we would begin to meet other Gopher parents and form an amazing band of traveling parents that followed the Gophers all over the United States: east to Penn State, south to Arizona, west to Oregon, and to many other Big 10 campuses. All of these were fantastic experiences for parents and memories to be cherished for a lifetime. Yet, one individual, who initially appeared as a soft spoken friend of the team, became to us, an iconic bond to the past and the future of Gopher athletics unlike anything we had known, or anything we may ever know.

Roy Griak was a stabilizing force for athletes and parents. Competition brings out the best in athletes, but can also bring out the worst. One bad performance can ignite a powder keg of inconsistency and poor performance. Athletes have egos that are as fragile as anyone's, and there must be a stabilizing force in their midst to bring them back on course. Roy Griak was the one. His long history in dealing with triumph and tragedy could quickly refocus and convince athletes that they were champions in the past and would be champions again. Most importantly, the message was that their great championship may not be on the field, but rather, it may occur further down the road. This is the message he so eloquently delivered to not only the athletes, but the parents as well. With every great victory, Roy was there to congratulate, and with every disappointment, he was there to console. Every Gopher was so fortunate to have Roy in their corner.

Joe had wonderful success as a Gopher and was a part of four straight Big 10 Championships, but several injuries blunted his senior season. Joe recalled his final vault as a Gopher at the Big Ten outdoor championships in Bloomington, Indiana. He told us that as he ran down the runway, knowing he would not win, and as his five years of competition funneled to this one final attempt, his thoughts turned to Roy Griak, and the feeling of letting this great warrior down. Who was one of the first to console him at the end of a fine career? Roy Griak. Who wrapped an arm around the parents who had tears in their eyes as they lamented the end of their days as traveling Gopher parents? Roy Griak.

Each year, we try to get back to the Jack Johnson indoor to watch the athletes compete and to meet with our track friends from the past. Among the attendees, we often see the Storvicks and Silovichs whom we bonded with so greatly. When we all arrive, one of the first people we hope to see is Roy.

Coach Roy Griak. Fifty years of athletes have called your name. Fifty years of parents and fans have heard your voice. All have listened and all have benefited from your wisdom. You are truly a remarkable coach and friend. Thank you for everything you have done – for the University, for the program, and for the student athletes.

Mark and Stacy Plencner
Parents of Joseph Plencner – pole vault – '05-'10

Tom Poliseno

Coach Griak: *Tom was a soft spoken, smooth, efficient runner. He had better than average talent and tremendous enthusiasm. He ran cross country and was a miler in track at Minnesota.*

I ran for Coach Griak from the fall of 1977 (Cross Country) through spring of 1981 (Track) and was fortunate enough to captain the '81 track squad.

I'll never forget my first meeting with Coach Griak. I met him for lunch at the Italian restaurant just off campus on 4th Street (Vescio's). I instantly knew that selecting the University and joining the cross country and track teams would be just the right mix for me. He had a twinkle in his eye and you just knew he was going to treat you fairly and with respect during the next four years. I'm sure I second guessed myself that next August as I was staring up at the sky while doing gut busters down at the lakes and hearing Coach bark, "Keep those legs up Poliseno." But even at age eighteen you knew the bark wasn't accompanied by a bite.

Coach made us tough and strong competitors. Coach made us good student-athletes. And Coach made us good men by example. When you did well he was there to congratulate you. When you didn't do so well, he was there to put an arm around you and offer encouragement for the next time out.

Everyone who participated in track and cross country at the U should consider himself fortunate. There are times in life when you have a mentor to teach and lead you through the pitfalls of life – to share their experiences with you in the hopes that you will learn and thereby become a better human being. I'm fortunate enough to have had a few of these great men to learn from. I'm proud to say my father was one of those people. And Roy is another one – he certainly had a positive impact on my life and when I look back on the successes I've had in my family life and business life I know a lot of it is because of the time spent under his guidance during those four years at the U.

Tom Poliseno
U of M runner 1977-1981

Ken Popejoy

Coach Griak: *Ken was a tremendous miler at Michigan State in the late 1960s and early 1970s. He was the first MSU runner to break 4:00 in the mile and was an NCAA indoor mile champion in 1972. He was also a very good cross country runner. Once after a dual meet between Minnesota and Michigan State, he had been left behind at the MSU golf course and our Minnesota team befriended him. I think that if he could have he would have transferred to Minnesota that day.*

In the fall of 1972, I had started out the season as one of the favorites to maybe win the Big Ten CC individual championship. My friend, Garry Bjorklund, had won it in his first three years but was injured in his senior season.

By the time Minnesota came to my course for the Michigan State dual meet, I was pretty badly injured with shin splints in both legs and my season was basically over. Nonetheless, I ran the 6-mile race and was well into last place with two miles to go. My coach yelled at me to drop out as I was "an embarrassment to me, him and my school." Well, I refused to drop out and when I came to the finish straight, the chute and timing was being removed! As I crossed what was the finish line area, my coach had packed the rest of the team into a van and was leaving the course. I was left to find my own way way... with sore shins, two miles from campus.

As I sat on the bench, pondering my current misfortune and my potentially dismal future in the sport, the Minnesota team ran by on their warm down. Coach Griak stopped and asked why I was sitting by myself without a team or a coach. As I told him, he put his arm around me, just like a father and after an amazing and encouraging conversation, he invited me to go with him and the Minnesota team to get a steak dinner before they left town. Both he and all the team members took me in as if I was one of their own!!!!

I truly don't know if I would have had any future in running without the kindness and support of this warm and gentle man. Minnesota, the Big Ten and the sport itself has lost a role model, a mentor and a friend.

There will never be another Roy Griak...he will continue to live in all of us who were so fortunate to be touched by his goodness.

Ken Popejoy
Michigan State runner

Author's note: In a conversation with Ken Popejoy on Feb. 2, 2016, he told me that his MSU coach, Jim Gibbard, had been an Army tank gunner with the 20th Armored Division in WW II and that on four occasions he had climbed out of burning tanks as the sole survivor. He had twice been a prisoner of war. Ken speculated that Coach Gibbard's wartime experiences may have had something to do with the peculiar treatment of his athletes. Magnanimously, Ken agreed to honor one of Coach Gibbard's dying wishes, that Ken deliver the eulogy at his funeral. Not only a great runner but a forgiving man, Ken did this when Coach Gibbard died in 2011. Ken still holds the Michigan State outdoor records for the mile (3:57.0) and 800 meters (1:47.2). In a letter to Ken Popejoy on May 24, 2002 Coach Griak wrote, "Hi, Ken - my favorite opponent and friend. Hope all is well with you - you still own the Minnesota state best mile record. You are a very special person and memory. R. G."

UNIVERSITY OF MINNESOTA

Twin Cities Campus — *Men's Intercollegiate Athletics* — *226 Bierman Field Athletic Building, 516–15th Avenue S.E., Minneapolis, MN 55455, 612-625-4838, Fax: 612-626-7859*

May 24, 2002

Ken Popejoy
1707 S. Thompson Dr.
Wheaton, IL 60187

Dear Ken,

For nearly 100 years, the competitive success of the University of Minnesota Men's Track and Cross Country teams has been unquestionable both athletically and academically. Thanks to friends like you, we plan to continue this success for another 100 years, but we need your continued support.

Last year, more than $225,000 in financial aid was awarded to 42 track and cross country student-athletes. Many of these young men, just like many of you, would not be able to attend the University and work toward their degree without the financial aid made available for them. To remain competitive, our program relies largely on the generosity of donors who support our scholarship fund.

In 1998, we established the Roy Griak Endowment Fund to provide permanent financial aid to student-athletes. In light of recent budget cuts and possible elimination of non-revenue sports, it is important that all of our former athletes and friends of the program partner with us by making an investment in the lives of our student-athletes.

The survival of our track and cross country teams depends on the on-going, generous support of friends like you. To that end, we ask you to consider making an investment of $100, $250, $500 or $1,000 to provide financial aid assistance to our student-athletes. Please know that whatever level of gift you are able to give will be greatly appreciated by us as well as our student-athletes.

Enclosed, you will find a brochure outlining our efforts, a commitment card and reply envelope. If you have any questions, please don't hesitate to call any one of us at 612-625-6063.

Gratefully,

Roy Griak — Phil Lundin — S. Plasencia

Coordinator Roy Griak — Coach Phil Lundin — Coach Steve Plasencia

P.S. A special thanks to our past donors who are listed on the other side.

Hi Ken — my favorite opponent & friend. Hope all is well with you – you still own the state best mile record. You are a special person & memory. R. G.

Note from Coach to Ken Popejoy

Coach was referring to Ken's 3:59.20 which is the all-time mile record for the Big Ten Conference Meet. Ken ran 3:58.4 to defeat Dave Wottle (3:58.6), Marty Liquori (3:58.7), Bob Wheeler (3:59.3) and Michael Boit (4:00.2).

Ken Popejoy running against Wottle, Liquori, Wheeler and Boit – 1973

The picture was taken on May 27, 1973. The race was one week after Ken had run 3:59.2 in the Big Ten Meet run at Minnesota and six months after Coach had befriended him after the Minnesota-MSU dual cross country meet in October of 1972.

Jim Reece

Coach Griak: *Jim was a distance runner from Edina and a friend of Tom Page. He ran cross country for the Gophers. He was industrious and all business.*

I wasn't in the same league as the runners on the 1968 University cross country team. I knew Tom Page who was a year ahead of me at my high school and he encouraged me to walk on. The freshman class only had about eight runners and more than half were the best runners in Minnesota my senior year in high school. And the rest of the team was similarly made up of high school, Big Ten and NCAA top performers.

Coach could not have been nicer in letting me join the team. He treated me identically to everyone else. I was often with the guys in Coach's car when we traveled to some meets and he was always encouraging me. To this day, I remember those (rare) days when I kept up with my teammates on a long run and how he congratulated me.

Decades later, I was watching an indoor meet at the field house because my college age daughter had a friend on the track team. We saw Coach and my daughter encouraged me to say hi. I had admired Coach and his athletes over the years, but I felt a little shy about saying hello since I only ran for one year decades ago and did nothing remarkable while on the team. To my utter amazement, Coach not only thanked me for coming up to see him, but he immediately placed me, mentioning Tom Page and our high school coach, Ed Hendrickson. I was astounded. I have tried to keep in touch ever since.

Coach taught me a lot that I have applied in my business and professional life – practice and hard work is necessary to improve, but you should have fun doing it and you should treat others with respect – and help those who might need a little more encouragement or assistance than others.

I feel very grateful and fortunate that I was on one of Coach's teams.

With admiration and many thanks to Coach Griak,
Jim Reece, freshman class of 1968

Jim Richard

Coach Griak: *Jim was a walk on at Minnesota who always tried very hard. He and his wife Janet are big supporters of the program.*

Coach Griak's HUGE Impact on Me, by Jim Richard (Minnesota '80 B.S. Business)

Coach Griak had a hugely positive and life changing impact on me! We have stayed friends for almost 40 years. Beginning in 1975, Coach changed the trajectory of my life – I am grateful beyond words.

Because of Coach, I had the opportunity to be a Minnesota student athlete, make lifelong friends in CC/Track, get a great degree at the Carlson Business School, and then have a great career with Fortune 500 companies. My family (wife Janet and three daughters) and I have been blessed in so many ways, by Coach's support for the past 38 years.

In 1975 Coach Griak recruited me as a walk-on for CC/Track from Ramsey HS. I wasn't fast enough for one of the few scholarships and I was in a position where I had to pay 100% of my education on my own. Coach Griak went out of his way to secure an on-campus job for me that ultimately funded my Minnesota Gopher education AND allowed me to be a student athlete.

Coach and his positive leadership were, and are even today, a game changer for me in so many ways. As my career progressed, out of appreciation for Coach Griak, my wife and I decided to fund an endowed Gopher CC/Track scholarship. My hope is that others can have the good fortune that Coach helped me achieve at Minnesota and in my life.

The best leaders make everyone around them better - they take them to a new level. Coach Griak unselfishly did that for me and countless others at the University of Minnesota.

Coach Griak is The Best,
Jim Richard and family

Dick and Dora Riter

Coach Griak: *The Riter's have two sons who ran for the Gophers (Tony and Trent). Dick is a track and field enthusiast. He and Jack Mayeron have taken over the indoor high school meet held at the field house each year. It is in good hands. I will leave this earth knowing that the meet will go on.*

There are many things that we can thank Roy for but one is making us all better people.

I would like to thank Roy for running all the different all comer and high school meets throughout the years. Many of us just loved to compete during youth, high school, collegiate, post-collegiate, and master years. The meets you ran on your own time helped all levels of athletes have a chance to test how good they were or could be. It started in the summer with all-comer meets at the local high schools, the U of M, and any place there were cinders. Then in the winter you opened the field house many nights to give athletes a chance to get out of the cold and let legs run free of winter clothing. You would be in the field house alone and grab coaches, parents, and athletes to help time everyone. You started the Northwest Open and the High School Indoor Meet to give everyone a chance to compete after a long winter. The field house in the early years was the only indoor track in the five state area. Athletes came from all over the five state area and Canada. You helped run Intramural meets during spring. I competed in all of them and thank you for helping me fall in love with the sport. Your efforts continued after I quit competing and they became even more important when I started coaching. It was very important for my athletes to be able to run indoors during the winter. Those meets were and still are very motivating. No one else throughout the years SELFLESSLY has done more to motivate athletes.

I would also like to THANK YOU for allowing Tony to run for you and the University of Minnesota. (Trent competed after Coach had retired).

Your admirer,
Dick Riter
parent of Tony & Trent Riter, Gopher runners
Mounds View Coach / Track Official

Mike Rogalski

Coach Griak: *Mike was a very good Gopher long jumper. He was a real good athlete who always worked hard to get better.*

I came to the U of M track program in 1987 after being recruited out of Marshall, MN as a long jumper who won the Minnesota AA event as a junior in 1986 and was runner-up as a senior in 1987. I was thrilled to be given the chance to compete at the D-1 level and in the Big Ten having come from a relatively smaller school in southwest Minnesota.

"Observations while an Athlete"

- "Hard Ass" – as a freshman, my first impression of Coach Griak was that he was a tough son-of-a-gun. Consistently imploring the distance runners to get tougher and work harder. I witnessed many challenges to them to do as many sit-ups and push-ups as he could. He always said it with a smile on his face and I could tell he wanted to get the very best out of his athletes.
- "Experienced and Accomplished" – during various times when I was in Coach's office, I would look around and notice many photographs and meet programs from Olympic and/or international track and field competitions. I realized that Coach was someone who had coached and witnessed the very best to compete in this sport.
- "Ladies Man" – he could always turn on the charm. Anyone who knew him knows this.
- "Encouraging" – during a time in my second year in the program when I had some minor injuries and my competitiveness was lacking, Coach was always there to give me a gentle nudge, even leaving a note on my locker telling me, "Don't Give Up." That made a pretty big impression on me. He cared enough to encourage me, someone who was the very best in high school, but very mediocre at this level of collegiate competition, to improve.
- "Positive" – I remember at the Big Ten Meet in Illinois in 1990, we competed very hard but ended up somewhere in the middle at the end of the first day. I finished ninth in the Long Jump, just missing out on earning a point, but Coach recognized that I was close to contributing to the team total, only shy by an inch or two.

"Observations after Graduating"

- "Serial Supporter" – Coach continued (and continues) to be an avid supporter of the team and all U of M Athletics. It's impressive that, whether it's the Griak Invitational CC event, Snotty Nose Tough Golf Event, personally mailing out information about the meet results, or just talking about the program with Coach; he's Maroon and Gold through and through.

- "Reverence" – after graduating, when I've talked to people about my time at the track and field program and bring up Coach Griak, they all recognize his name and have a fondness and respect for Coach.
- "Nice Guy" – coming back as an alum, Coach is always welcoming and interested in how you and your family are doing after your years wearing the "M".
- "Still Coach" – he says even now, he is still running the kids through stretching drills, sit-up and push-up challenges in his neighborhood. They are very lucky. ☺

Thanks Coach!
Mike Rogalski (aka – "Rogo"), 1987-1990

David Sharp

Coach Griak: *Sharpie has had a tough life. He had little athletic talent but gave everything he had. He is one of the toughest Gopher athletes I have ever encountered. He works as a finish line judge at our track meets and does the job very well.*

Coach Griak truly cared about his athletes. I remember a few instances in my life of his concern. The first was in my freshman year. It was early September. School wouldn't start until the end of the month but cross country practices had started in August. One weekend I had gone to a freshman camp. On Saturday night of that weekend my mother had succumbed to cancer. She had been in the hospital for six months. When I returned from camp I found this out. Her funeral mass was the next day (Monday). I missed practice that day. When I returned to practice on Tuesday I went to Coach and apologized for missing practice and explained about my mother's death. During our run, Coach managed to get a card and get all the guys to sign it. To this day I don't know how he got a card so quickly. I always appreciated it. I never forgot that act of kindness.

The second instance was my last season of cross country. Things were going rather rough for me personally at the time. I had lost my job. I was having to survive on what I had been able to save and going to other homes two or three times a week for a meal. I had lost weight from having to cut back on food to make the money last as long as possible. I know he was aware of my situation and he gave what moral support he could. This meant a lot. {Teammate Dave Casale said that all the members of the team wanted to make the traveling team; however, they knew that David Sharp also wanted to make the team because he knew that he would be able to eat on the road trips.}

Coach always made sure that we remembered that our education was most important. He would remind us that there was no pro track. He also always remembered us after we graduated. He would go out of his way to send cards at Christmas time. It would have a short message and a thank you.

I will always appreciate how he gave me an opportunity to be a member of his cross country and track teams and represent the University of Minnesota. I don't know what coach made of me when he saw me for the first time. Here was this kid from Minneapolis Roosevelt who practiced in cutoff shorts and worn shirts. I didn't have a lot of natural speed but I had endurance and mental toughness and I tried hard to get better. What speed I did have was what I had earned through hard work. I was only a walk on but I did make it into the top seven in cross country two of my four years on the team. Through the years I haven't always been able to give back in a monetary fashion; but I have tried to give back in other ways like being an official at the cross country and track meets.

David Sharp
University of Minnesota Track and CC

Coach and David Sharp

Chuck & Penny Swanum

Coach Griak: *Chuck was a Gopher football player. He and his wife are devoted fans and supporters of our program. They live in Hackensack, Minnesota. Chuck went to Minneapolis Washburn High School. We coached together at St. Louis Park.*

Roy Griak had already established himself as one of the top high school track and field coaches in Minnesota when I arrived at St. Louis Park High School as a first year teacher in 1957. Having been a member of the track team at the University of Minnesota in the early 1950's, I watched the young men he had coached from Nicollet to Mankato and at St. Louis Park consistently perform at a high level at track meets throughout the state.

In 1958 I applied for an assistant track coach position in St. Louis Park. It was my good fortune to be selected for the position, and thus, began my education in the art of coaching young athletes. Roy never lectured me on how best to work with sprinters to improve their start or how to motivate individuals to perform their very best. Instead, he would quietly tell me what worked for him or suggest options to consider.

Coach Griak welcomed any young man who wanted to become part of the track team. He devoted as much time coaching a kid with limited ability as he did with the many state champions who were on his teams. Roy kept meticulous records on each athlete in his program. There were times when an athlete would be disappointed in his performance and Roy could check back in his records and show the young man how much he had improved over the last year or two. He encouraged him to work hard and assured him that future performances would improve. Roy was and continues to be a positive motivator and confidence builder.

It was no surprise that Roy was hired as the head coach of Track and Field and Cross Country at the University of Minnesota in 1963. He replaced my coach, Jim Kelly, and brought with him his extraordinary talents as coach and mentor to the young men on the team. Roy kept in touch with me over the years. When I became aware of the Roy Griak Scholarship Endowment Fund, my wife and I directed our donations to the Golden Gopher Fund for Roy's endowment.

We have had the good fortune to attend an occasional Gopher football game with Roy. It is a joy to watch as former athletes greet Roy with a hug or a handshake and thank him for being a positive influence in their lives. He has quietly touched the lives of many individuals during his journey through life. We are grateful to have Roy as a friend. *Thank you Roy for 50 years of dedicated service to track and field at the U of M!*

Chuck and Penny Swanum
Assistant coach at St. Louis Park

Bill Thornton

Coach Griak: *Bill coached at St. Olaf for many, many years. There were those who felt that there a great chasm between Division III and Division I athletes. We both knew that both our athletes were great young men and Bill did a super job at St. Olaf. We were great friends but when we would meet we would shake hands and look the other way just to pretend that Division III and Division I were miles apart. Bill's son Paul is a fine coach now for the Gophers.*

In August of 1968, just prior to the Mexico City Olympics, my family and I moved to St. Cloud, Minnesota. I had just left a fairly secure teaching/coaching position at Daniel Webster High School in Tulsa, Oklahoma to fill a two-year sabbatical leave position at St. Cloud State College. Among the coaches I met that academic year was Roy Griak.

In those days there were two divisions for collegiate athletics: the College Division and the University Division. Obviously, in Minnesota there was only one University Division institution and many College Division teams. Even after the three NCAA Divisions were established in 1973 the only Division I program in Cross Country and Track and Field in the state was headed by Coach Roy Griak.

Through the years I have always been extremely appreciative of Coach Griak's sensitivity and willingness to help all of the non-Division I programs in Minnesota. This included hosting competitions and providing a place for some of the local collegians to train. I know of many Division III coaches very grateful for Roy's willingness to allow this to happen.

Early on, Coach Griak's willingness to host indoor meets was greatly appreciated. In the early 1970s there were only a few indoor track and field facilities available for competitions. In those days one of the best facilities was the dirt track in the Minnesota field house and Coach Griak always welcomed all of the College Division athletes in meets like the Northwest Open and others. There is still a very great need to provide an indoor experience for high school track and field. Over the forty years I have known Coach Griak I would guess there have been very few early springs when the University of Minnesota has not hosted an indoor track and field competition for high school athletes. I really think he was very quietly reminding all of us collegiate coaches the high school programs in the state of Minnesota were the "life blood" of collegiate track and field in the state. How appropriate it is to have one of the largest cross country meets in the United States, which includes a great number of high school athletes, named after Roy Griak.

One of my most favorite memories was the day my office phone rang and it was Roy Griak calling to ask me to present him for his induction into the United States Cross Country and Track and Field Coaches Association (USCCTFCA) Hall of Fame. I was humbled and yet extremely honored to be asked to do this and my induction speech centered around Roy Griak's service and contributions to the great sports of Cross Country and Track and Field.

In 2008 I retired from my position at St. Olaf College. Surprisingly, Phil Lundin, the coach who replaced Coach Griak when he retired applied for and was appointed as my replacement. But the story continues; the coach who took over the events Coach Lundin had vacated at the University of Minnesota was our youngest son, Paul. His appointment really allows me to continue hearing those wonderful Roy Griak stories. I know every Sunday afternoon during the season Roy calls one of the three coaches, Steve Plasencia, Lynden Reder, or Paul to find out how the "boys" did at that weekend's meet. For all I know he is still keeping the athlete's performances on 3x5 cards with the information he is gathering from these phone calls.

Roy, congratulations for fifty wonderful years at the University of Minnesota. Your contributions are numerous and very much appreciated. Most importantly, thank you from the numerous Division II and III coaches for your concern and contributions to our programs.

Gratefully submitted by,
Bill Thorton
Coach of Cross Country and Track & Field Emeritus
St. Olaf College
(Father of Paul Thorton)

Ian Torchia

Author's Note: *At Coach's Plymouth home there was a picture of Ian Torchia on the desk near the table where Coach sat to eat his meals and make his many phone calls. He spoke often of his close relationship with Ian and the Torchia family.*

A story about Coach Griak, my role model and friend by by Ian Torchia

I first met Roy in 2007 at the age of eleven at the Roy Griak Invitational when he invited me to ride along in his golf cart to watch my brother (Mike Torchia) run in the collegiate race. I was sandwiched in the front seat between Roy and his brother (Steve) as Coach whipped around the hills of the Les Bolstad Golf Course at 15+ mph. I was struck from the start by the friendliness and warmth of this great man, as well as the enthusiasm an 84-year-old could show as he bellowed encouragement to his beloved Gophers. As we said goodbye, he embraced me like an old friend, not someone he had just met thirty minutes ago, and told me to keep in touch.

And keep in touch we did. Over the next eight years, I saw Roy on his visits to the Mayo Clinic, at his invitational and even when he came to my high school graduation party. My favorite times with Roy were his short but meaningful phone calls. He would call just to "see how I was doing." We would discuss my latest race and he would dispatch some priceless life advice such as, "Tell your Mother you love her," or "Listen more than talk." Whatever ups and downs I felt about my racing performance melted away in the face of his advice on how to be a good person. In the times I would reach out first, I was again struck by the genuine happiness in which he would answer my call. I will sure miss those calls.

Hours before Roy's passing, I sat by his bedside holding his hand and told him, "It's Ian Torchia, remember when we first met and we drove around watching Mike, and you drove the cart so fast we almost tipped over?" I felt his frail hand give mine the tiniest squeeze and I knew inside his failing body that the loving and caring spirit of Coach Griak was alive and well and continues to be up in Heaven.

Thank you for everything, Roy.

Love,
Ian Torchia

Ian Torchia in golf cart between Steve Griak and Coach Griak

Mike Torchia

Coach Griak: *Mike is the epitome of being a student-athlete. He never wasted a minute of time. Mike was a steady athlete and a brilliant student. He is probably the most outstanding student-athlete that the University of Minnesota has ever had. From his freshman year on he had a goal to become a doctor. As a senior he earned the prestigious Wayne Duke Postgraduate Award. Only one male is chosen for the entire Big Ten Conference.*

I ran in my first Big Ten Cross Country Championship during my true freshman year. Our season had gone well and we were hoping to finish as one of the top three teams in the conference. We all knew, however, that it would take each one of us running as well as we possible could, since the competition was guaranteed to be tight at the top of the standings.

Mike Torchia in Gopher sweats with the entire Torchia family: Dr. Mike, Ian, Kelsey, Katy, Mike, Tish & Sarah

The meet was hosted by Indiana and the eight-kilometer course was very hilly, at least to my freshman recollection. It was also an uncommonly hot day for late October. The gun went off, and I felt horrible from the start. The hills and heat in addition to my own nerves and immaturity got the best of me that day – I was feeling bad enough by five-kilometers to inadvertently run into a signpost on the course and I subsequently blacked out about one kilometer later. I came around pretty quickly, but once I realized what had happened, I began to feel awful, because I knew from what my coach was telling me during the race that the team race was shaping up to be a tight one and that every point counted.

Thus it was with a mixture of embarrassment, shame at letting the team down, and frustration at my own inability to perform that I watched helplessly from the side of the course. Although Wisconsin ended up winning the title that day, the Gophers team placed third, a great accomplishment. Most of the Minnesota contingent was rightfully celebrating the results at the finish line.

But it was my mom and Roy who helped me up, put both of their arms around me for support, and walked me back to the team camp. I remember very few words being spoken during that 200-meter walk back to camp that felt much longer. Yet sometimes words get in the way of the actual communication. It was as if Roy became a part of my family that day, because his actions spoke volumes to a young, immature and impressionable freshman. Without even speaking, he communicated to me that day that he cared about my welfare, my development, and me as a person no matter what I did or did not accomplish. Roy took the time to be with me at my worst even when he could have been celebrating with the rest of the team at their best. That summed up my experience with Roy – someone who understood that it was the development of the person, not the athlete, that mattered most. Roy proved this again and again over the ensuing five years I was on the team. But nothing quite illustrated his character to me more so than on that hot October day as a freshman.

John Trolander

Coach Griak: *John was one of Oscar Yngve's athletes at Minneapolis Roosevelt. A distance runner, John was quiet, intelligent and had a great attitude. He was a teacher and coach in Owatonna.*

I love to run, but I'm not very fast. Yet, I was able to compete and be part of track and cross country at the U. I learned that I was able to accomplish an amazing amount of work in training. Coach Griak was always helpful and encouraging to me. Even though I was some distance behind the fast guys on the team, coach recognized my success. It was so meaningful to me when I was told that I was a good, hard worker. I felt so good when he recognized and praised me for running a personal best. At the same time, when I was admonished (and I deserved it), I realized I could be better and expectations were higher. The coach, the team, the sport all had a crucial formative impact on me. I am fortunate to have them in my life.

Coach Griak—The Early Years

Lindsay Nielsen

Coach Roy Griak was born in Butte Montana on October 5th, 1923, eldest of the four children born to parents Milan and Mildred Griak.

Coach Griak's mother, Mildred (Milica) Hinic, was born on March 14, 1903 and was the daughter of Anka and Milovan Hinic. She was born in the village of Valluznica in the region of Urkovine in Yugoslavia. During a phone interview in July of 2017 she said that she was from Serbia but also used the name Yugoslavia which is Serbo-Croatian for "the Kingdom of South Slavs." Technically, Bosnia, Croatia, Herzegovina, Serbia and Slovenia united in July of 1917 to become the Kingdom of Serbs, Croats and Slovenes and did not officially become Yugoslavia until 1929.

She was fifteen years old when she sailed to the United States on the Queen Mary. She was the youngest of a big family and by nine years of age was responsible for all the family's cooking. She had five sisters and two brothers. One of her brothers was a lawyer. The other was a General in the Yugoslavian air force. He was executed by the Germans during World War I. Mildred's father reportedly told her that she should have a better life than what was possible for her in Serbia, and scraped together enough money to enable Mildred to travel to the United States to marry a man she'd never seen before. After crossing the Atlantic Ocean, Mildred went from Ellis Island in the harbor of New York City to Butte, Montana. Coach Griak said his mother was assured there would be someone at the train station to meet her but no one came and she was left standing outside a drugstore, fifteen years old, alone and afraid, speaking no English, with just a few coins in her hand and no idea of what to do next. Her husband-to-be was in the hospital, having broken his leg in the copper mine where he worked. An unrelated man, who also spoke Serbian, saw her standing alone at the station and helped her by putting her up at the Young Women's Christian Association (YWCA). This was a story told often by Coach during conversations about his mother, and every time, it was as if he were there himself, almost feeling what his mother must have felt as a young girl.

Mother and son

Coach's father, Milan Grijak, was born on July 7, 1893 in Otocac, which is now in the Lika region of Croatia. He was the son of Ella and Rade Grijak. In recent years (1992-1995) this area was devastated in the Bosnia Herzegovian wars. Milan arrived in the United States on September 20, 1922. As a young man, Milan was inducted into the United States Army and served as a private in Company B, 14th Regiment of the 19th Division. He was a cook, based in the Aleutian Islands in the years shortly following World War I. After his discharge he "sent away" for a bride. Milan worked in a copper mine in Butte Montana.

Coach's sister Kay was born in Butte, Montana in 1926. His brother Steve was born in 1928 and his younger sister Dolly was born in 1930. Both Steve and Dolly were born in Duluth, Minnesota where the Grijak's moved after jobs opened there.

In most conversations about his parents, Coach focused on his mother. "I don't know much about my dad. He was a handsome man. He was an alcoholic. He was a harsh man. I have many more hard memories of him than good ones. The way he lived caused a lot of problems for my mother and for us kids. Macho guy, he had that mentality, that's the way it was. He lost one of his legs in the sawmill. Tough thing. He was unkind to Mom. Mom always worried about him, about him being an amputee. I felt bad for him too working in the garden with his wooden leg. He got drunk and beat on my mother when he felt like it. I got involved trying to protect her a couple times when I was a young boy. He should have thanked his lucky stars that he had my mother." Coach's father was hospitalized in his thirties, and died of tuberculosis on May 1, 1940 at the age of 46. "I really didn't like him for a long time, even after

Grijak family in the late 1930s: Kay, Steve, Roy, Milan, Dolly and Mildred

his death, because he had been so nasty to her. After about 40 or so years, I forgave him, but it took a really long time."

As an amputee athlete, I worked with Coach for years before he told me his dad had also been an amputee. It was my impression that Coach had tightly compartmentalized his memories of his father. Maybe this was the way he could forgive him, by separating him away from his mother and his siblings, even in his memories.

One of the first ways I met coach was in his role of son. At our first workout, Coach told me it was his mother's birthday, "I still think of her every day and I miss her." His memories of his mother and her wise teachings were an overt part of all our training sessions.

When Coach talked about his mom, it was often with a wistful tone, "My mother was an attractive lady. She didn't have any health issues, but it was a significant burden to raise four kids basically by herself. She was smart, a great homemaker, had a tough life, brought up four children with no income and no help. We were always 'on relief' and we kids looked like all the other kids on relief. We all wore the same kind of shoes. That was especially hard on my sisters, but my mom made Kay and Dolly clothes. I always thought they dressed so nice."

Coach and his Mother in 1994

Stories of his mom were often intertwined with food. "We ate well because of her. Legumes, vegetables we grew, mostly potatoes, and sauerkraut. My mother canned everything: peaches, pears, pickles. She was such a great cook that she could have started her own gourmet kitchen. She made the best chicken noodle soup, potica, which is a walnut bread, and strudels, both cheese and apple. My favorite, and anyone else lucky enough to have some, was my mother's amazing apple strudel!"

These stories came alongside the tales of clearing rocks to prepare the garden to grow the vegetables his mother canned, and stories of all the other work the garden required. "Even when I was in 9th and 10th grade, my mom could outwork me. There were three large gardens to care for where we grew the food that would sustain the family through the winter. The growing season was followed by all the canning of what was harvested. The soil in Duluth had a clay base so clearing it of rocks and digging deep enough to plant was very difficult. My mother got up at 4:00 a.m., made dough for bread, and let it rise, and then we would go to the gardens. At 7:00 a.m., mom would go back to the house and bake the bread. I wouldn't want to stay in the garden but one of us had to do it because the other kids were too young to help. She'd come back an hour and a half later, carrying a jar of strawberry jam, the warm fresh bread, and a quart of milk. We'd sit there and eat the whole dang thing."

"We kids came home from school for lunch. Vegetable soup was the big thing. Really, the soup was the only thing. I hated it after a while. She rented the upstairs to a family named Clark. My brother and I had one room and the Clark's had the rest. I remember Mrs. Clark and mom laughing at me one day when I was in third grade, because I was sitting under the table at lunch. I just didn't want to eat that dang soup again. But it was eat it or go hungry. Best was when she went to the grocery store and was able to buy one Bismarck, which she cut into four pieces. Then the negotiations started between the kids about who were going to get the best jelly parts."

"She was the Mom, but she also had to be the man of family. Fortunately, she didn't have any kids that gave her problems, but maybe that was because she was so kind and gentle. She scolded but never spanked. Dad had a strap that came down to a point, hanging up on the wall, always handy when he was around, but my Mom never hit."

The stress of worrying about where the next meal was coming from took its toll, and as Coach explained, showed up in his mother's "mental outlook" as she got older. There were times his mother got despondent and became severely depressed. Sometimes she was hospitalized, though there weren't very effective treatments for depression back then. "The most challenging time with my mom was when she was ill and I was in the eighth grade. Her mental makeup, and bad sinuses landed her in the hospital, which left me home with my three siblings. That was tough. I kept worrying about what the hell we were going to do without her. She went to the hospital multiple times. She ultimately had electroshock therapy, which I think helped."

"My mom was the salt of the earth. She died on January 2, 1996 at 92, just ran out of gas, like we all do. She was in a nursing home when she died. I have always regretted that I didn't take her back to the old country. My brother and I should have done that. There are always the should-haves, could-haves, the 'we can go next year, next year, next year,' but the years go by and then we couldn't do it for health reasons. My brother and I talked about that a lot. She would have loved going with us. One of the few regrets I have. It would have been wonderful for her. There's a lesson there, whatever it takes, do it, and do it now. Time is always running out."

"Work can be so encompassing. But my mother always told me, "If you have something to do, do it today. Tomorrow will take care of itself. Take the first step, malo po malo" (Little by little). "I have tried to live by this, whatever it is. With fundraising: send twenty letters today, you don't hear back from them and then one day you do. I got seven checks yesterday, some of those people I'd never heard from before. Everybody has a reason why they do what they do, and when they do it. You need to never give up."

"My mother had some old country ideas that were really good. She told us time and time again that at the beginning of a project or hardship, things are often difficult, but those first scoops of soil might be the most important work you do for the project. Getting to the starting line, you're tired, but start anyway." And then as Coach always did, he tied the lesson into something personal for me. "Like when you raced the Ironman Triathlon, Lindsay, you had already swum, had already ridden your dang bike all those miles, you probably thought, Geez I'm tired, but you took those first steps of the marathon. Then you just kept on stepping. In life, anytime you can get over those first steps, maybe you can continue."

"As my mother and us kids got older, she became more financially self-sufficient. She rented a room in the Greyhound Bus Depot and start-

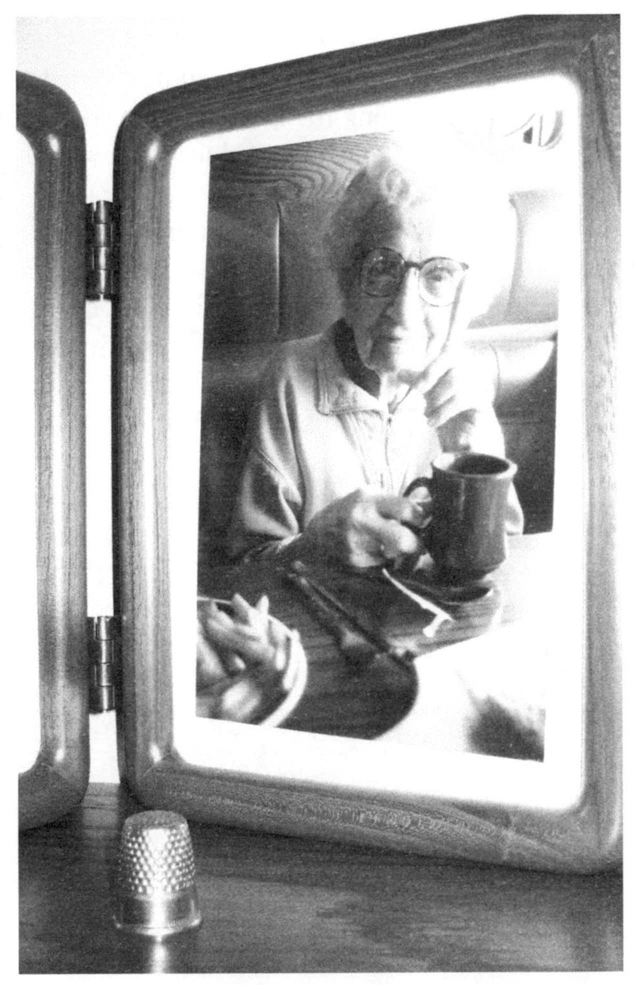

Mildred and her thimble - Coach said this thimble, a reminder of his Mother, was his most cherished possession

ed her own business as a seamstress. She tailored clothes, did a great job and didn't charge much. When word got out that she was pretty doggone good, people lined up for her services. Business got so good she had to rent a bigger room. She became a true businesswoman, and transformed her life completely. She made wedding gowns and formals. She saved, and the first time she spent money on herself, she proudly bought herself a mink coat and hat. After I moved to the cities, she'd come for a visit and I'd pick her up at the Greyhound bus station. Here was this lady getting off the bus in downtown Minneapolis wearing a mink coat and hat. She didn't look like she belonged on that dang bus. That hat and coat were her prized possessions. She sewed until she was eighty. She was one tough bird. She could read Serbian, along with English. She taught English, became an interpreter, President of the Ladies Circle and really a matriarch of the community.

Mildred wearing her mink coat in 1979

Everybody realized what a sharp person she was: loving and caring. My mother meant the world to me and I will love her forever. She absolutely is one of my heroes. She earned her high school diploma the same year I graduated from the University of Minnesota"

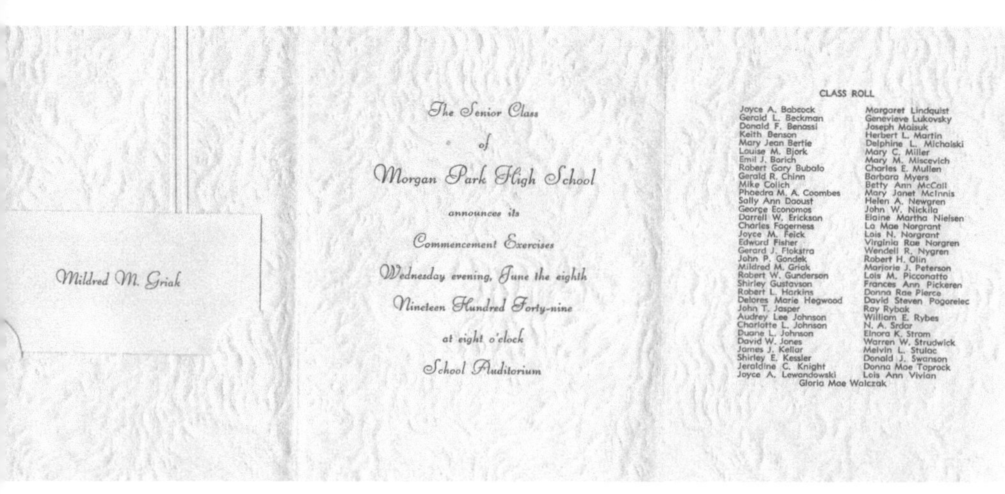

Mildred M. Griak

The Senior Class
of
Morgan Park High School
announces its
Commencement Exercises
Wednesday evening, June the eighth
Nineteen Hundred Forty-nine
at eight o'clock
School Auditorium

CLASS ROLL

Joyce A. Babcock
Gerald L. Beckman
Donald F. Benassi
Keith Benson
Mary Jean Bertie
Louise M. Bjork
Emil J. Borich
Robert Gary Bubalo
Gerald R. Chinn
Mike Colich
Phaedra M. A. Coombes
Sally Ann Daoust
George Economos
Darrell W. Erickson
Charles Fagerness
Joyce M. Feick
Edward Fisher
Gerard J. Flokstra
John P. Gondek
Mildred M. Griak
Robert W. Gunderson
Shirley Gustavson
Robert L. Harkins
Delores Marie Hegwood
John T. Jasper
Audrey Lee Johnson
Charlotte L. Johnson
Duane L. Johnson
David W. Jones
James J. Kellar
Shirley E. Kessler
Jeraldine C. Knight
Joyce A. Lewandowski
Margaret Lindquist
Genevieve Lukovsky
Joseph Maisuk
Herbert L. Martin
Delphine L. Michalski
Mary C. Miller
Mary M. Miscevich
Charles E. Mullen
Barbara Myers
Betty Ann McCall
Mary Janet McInnis
Helen A. Newgren
John W. Nickila
Elaine Martha Nielsen
La Mae Norgrant
Lois N. Norgrant
Virginia Rae Norgren
Wendell R. Nygren
Robert H. Olin
Marjorie J. Peterson
Lois M. Picconatto
Frances Ann Pickeren
Donna Rae Pierce
David Steven Pogorelec
Ray Rybak
William E. Rybes
N. A. Srdar
Elnora K. Strom
Warren W. Strudwick
Melvin L. Stulac
Donald J. Swanson
Donna Mae Toprock
Lois Ann Vivian
Gloria Mae Walczak

1949 Morgan Park High School graduation announcement for Mildred Griak

In reviewing Coach Griak's life, his work, his love for and service to other people, it is clear how much he was driven by his early experiences. While some people respond to a difficult early family life by repeating the worst patterns, Coach Griak repeated the best: hard work, service, study, empathy and integrity.

Wife and Kay

Coach Griak met and married Rose-Mary Brandon in 1950. He described her as a good athlete and a beautiful artist. She was "well educated" and when he got hired at Nicollet, they also hired Rose-Mary, so they were able to work together. Their son Seth was born in 1958 and Jason followed in 1960. Coach and Rose-Mary were divorced in the mid-1970s. Over the years he talked about wishing he had been able to spend more time with the boys when they were young. He worked long hours trying to be the best coach he could be, which reduced the time he spent with his family. Coach lived the work ethic and style he learned from his mother. "I had already learned how to coach from "those dang rocks." In talking with his sons though, I didn't get the impression they resented their father's work.

Coach met his partner, Kay Richardson in 1988 at a prom party. As Kay described, "It was a fabulous party!" Neither Kay nor Roy had gone to their high school proms. Kay had just gotten back to Minnesota from Arizona after the death of her husband. Her sister invited her to a Sports Challenge Benefit. Roy asked her to dance and according to Kay, Coach was a wonderful dancer!" apparently taught by his sister when he was young. Coach and Kay were together until his passing.

Kay told story after story about how connected Coach was to the community. Everywhere they went, restaurants, walks, travel, they saw people who knew Coach. The prevailing message was "I am what I am because of you, and you were like a second father to me." Coach treated everyone the same. He was kind and attentive no matter the person's status. Kay shared Coach with all of us and when recounting these stories after his death, she expressed respect, love and awe for who Coach was and how he conducted his life. They made a good pair.

Jason, Rose-Mary and Seth

Coach Griak's Service Record and Memories of WWII Era

Don Timm

Author's Note: Material in this section came directly from informal interviews with Coach Griak over a period of several years and from his service diary to which I was given access at the insistence of his son, Jason.

Coach was in his social studies class at Morgan Park High School in Duluth when he learned from his teacher, Mrs. Jenny Schwar, the details of the Japanese attack on Pearl Harbor and the ensuing declaration of war announced by President Franklin Roosevelt. It was Monday, December 8, 1941, just six months before his high school graduation in the spring of 1942. Not surprisingly, Coach was senior class president. When he spoke of his high school graduation, Coach recalled that his mother had bought him a suit for the graduation and baccalaureate service. It was the first suit he had ever owned. Commenting on the elaborate open house celebrations of today's high school seniors, Coach said that after the baccalaureate service, he walked alone in the dark from Morgan Park

1942 Morgan Park High School class picture –Roy Grijak is in the front row third from the left

High School to his home in Gary - New Duluth. The Grijaks, as the name was spelled at that time, lived at 1514 101st Ave. West in Gary. He proudly wore his new suit but there was no gala celebration following the ceremony at the high school.

Coach said that he was not aware of all the international politics at that time but he soon came to realize that the war would change his life forever. Many of his friends and acquaintances enlisted or were drafted. He recalled a tremendous contemporary athlete from Duluth Denfeld named Wally Smith who was a great high school running back. Smith led the nation by scoring twenty-three touchdowns in an eight game schedule during his senior year in 1942. Although he scored only one touchdown in the game on September 26, 1942 against Morgan Park, it was the only score as Denfeld defeated the Wildcats 6-0. University of Minnesota Coach, Bernie Bierman, called Smith the best recruit he had ever seen. He was invited to try out for the Gophers but instead enlisted in the Marines. He won a Purple Heart and the Presidential Citation for Bravery for his actions on November 19, 1943 at the Battle of Tarawa in the South Pacific. Tarawa is in the Gilbert Islands and was a strategic step in the United States tactic of "island hopping" across the Pacific toward the main Japanese islands. Although Coach Griak didn't know it at the time he would soon be involved in the fighting in the Pacific. Wally Smith was wounded in the hand and shoulder. He underwent nine surgeries before returning to Duluth in 1945. That fall he tried out with the Gophers but because of his injuries he was unable to securely carry the ball and, although he stayed at the University until graduating in 1948, he was unable to resume his football career.

Coach listed several of his boyhood friends from Duluth who had also gone to war. George Balach became a lieutenant in the 99th Army Infantry and survived the Battle of the Bulge but sadly drowned in a Minnesota lake when he returned home. George's brother, Joe Balach, was an Army Air Force B-26 "marauder" pilot who served in the Mediterranean and in Europe. He flew fifty-seven missions in support of the D-Day (June 6, 1944) invasion of Normandy, the Allied attempt to take the bridge at Arnhem (Netherlands) and the Battle of the Bulge. Another friend, Eli Bubalo, was killed in action in Europe. A high school opponent and acquaintance, George "Pecky" Smilanich was a member of the Buhl High School Minnesota State Championship basketball teams of 1941 when Buhl defeated Red Wing 31-29 in the state title game and 1942 when Buhl defeated Marshall 30-29. Less than a year after that 1942 game he was driving a tank with George S. Patton's Second Armored Division in North Africa. Smilanich became a decorated tank commander who earned a Bronze Star for climbing into a burning tank to save his tank commander's life. He served in Sicily, Italy, the landing at Omaha Beach, the hedgerow fighting in France and in the Battle of the Bulge. After the war, Smilanich became the basketball coach at Buhl. Later, he and another acquaintance of Coach Griak's, Milan Knezovich, coached track and field at Hibbing High School for many years.

Knezovich was 6'4" tall and had been a star center on the Hibbing High School basketball team. He was the captain of the Hibbing Bluejackets in 1948 and 1949. Knezovich had also placed fourth in the discus at the Minnesota State Meet in 1949 behind 1949 and 1950 winner Dave Herbold of Anoka, who would go on to become a football, track and wrestling athlete for the Gophers shortly after Coach's graduation. The man who had coached Smilanich at Buhl and Knezovich at Hibbing was Coach Mario Retica. Retica coached the Bluejackets from 1945-1958. He was the Minnesota basketball Coach of the Year in 1953 as Coach Griak was starting his career at St. Louis Park. At St. Louis Park, Coach Griak would assist another Minnesota basketball coach of the year when Lloyd Holm won the honor in 1962. Coach Retica had replaced Walter McMillan who was the coach at Hibbing when Roy Griak played at Morgan Park.

St. George's Serbian Orthodox Church

Knezovich would also coach Hibbing in basketball from 1966-1974. In getting back to Coach's war experience I must explain that to ask Coach a question about an acquaintance, an event or a town will often evoke a flood of other information. Coach never forgot that the original question had been about his military experience but, in his mind, these names and events were all part of that story. These are Coach's stories and memories in his words.

Another boyhood friend, George Olbin, who had been an altar boy with Coach at St. George Serbian Orthodox Church, served in the Army Air Corps. The church is located on the corner of Gary and 104th Ave. in Gary - New Duluth. The church was dedicated in 1923, the year of Coach's birth. Classmate Al Andreiko, the Minnesota state champion pole vaulter in 1942 when he vaulted 12' 1/2" for Duluth Morgan Park at Memorial Stadium, became a bombardier during the war.

The track and field team was well represented among the class officers in the Morgan Park senior class of 1942 with Coach as President and Al Andreiko as Vice President. Coach said that Andreiko was a gifted athlete in every sport. Larry Ross, a classmate of Coach Griak at Morgan Park, served in the Navy. Coach recalled another boyhood friend who was so impressed by Charles Lindberg's solo flight across the Atlantic in 1927, that he began to build model airplanes of his own. His first planes were powered by rubber bands but eventually he began to build planes that

Above: church marker in Serbian. Below: church marker in English.

1942 Senior Class officers at Morgan Park High School – Vice President Al Andreiko and President Roy Grijak

were powered by gasoline engines. Coach remembered that he envied his friend, Meek Gladney Stalling, because he could build the best model planes in Duluth. That friend and model airplane builder would go on to become an airplane mechanic with the famous Tuskegee airmen during World War II. Many years later, Coach Griak had a picture in his Bierman office of himself with former Gopher quarterback and later coach of the 2007 Super Bowl winning Indianapolis Colts, Tony Dungy, whose father had also been a Tuskegee airman. The United States Army Air Corps had established a training facility for black pilots at Tuskegee, Alabama in 1940. Up to that time black aviators had not been allowed to fly in the military. Black servicemen were not fully integrated into the armed forces until 1946. Gladney Stalling passed away in 1998. Just nine years after his death the Tuskegee Airmen were awarded the Congressional Medal of Honor for their service during WW II. Coach remained in contact with Gladney's brother, Charles Stalling. When Coach's brother, Steve, passed away in 2014, Coach introduced me to Charles at Steve's funeral. Coach recalled in February of 2015 that the Stalling family lived next to a Serbian family named Chetko in Gary. Gladney Stalling was not involved in athletics but his brother, Charles was an excellent football player. Charles Stalling was a member of the Morgan Park High School football team that defeated most of the larger Duluth schools in 1942 even though they had only about fifteen athletes on the team.

Another Morgan Park athlete who became an excellent football player and who also fared well in track and field against the larger schools was the son of Charlie Jasper, the mailman in Coach's neighborhood. That athlete, Chuck Jasper, placed fifth in the pole vault at the 1949 Minnesota State Track and Field Meet when he was just an eighth grader. He won a

Coach in his Bierman Building office with grandson Vincent – the picture directly over his left shoulder is of Tony Dungy

state championship in the pole vault in 1950, placed second in 1951, tied for second in 1952 and won again in 1953. Coach remembered that Charlie, the mailman, was usually "snockered" during the entire Christmas season each year (which was much longer due to the lengthy Serbian Christmas) because everyone would invite him in for a drink while he was delivering his mail. I met George Petrich, Coach's brother-in-law on July 25th, 2015, the day that Coach was buried in the Oneota Cemetery in Duluth. He had been married to Coach's sister, Kay, until her death in 1996. Kay died the same year that Coach retired from active coaching. George confirmed that Charlie Jasper was invited into nearly every home as he delivered the Christmas mail and that he would have been on their "shit list" if he had refused the holiday cheer they offered him. When talking about the Stalling brothers, Coach recalled that they, and the Chetko family, lived near a large field that was used by the neighborhood kids for their sporting events. Coach also recalled that the Chetko family would be visited each summer by their granddaughter from Kenny, Minnesota which is near Buhl on the Iron Range. Coach was sweet on the granddaughter whose name was Daisy Boskovich. Daisy eventually married a man who became a highly decorated WW II fighter pilot. There, you see Coach had not forgotten the war! The reader may be wondering why this account of Coach Griak's military career has taken such a circuitous route to get to Coach's military participation but in listening to Coach, one name or one story will generally trigger his memory about several other names or events and I have tried to stay faithful to the story as it was related to me.

George Petrich and his daughter Patti

At the time of his high school graduation Coach Griak was deferred from the draft because he was the sole support of his family. His brother Steve and sisters Kay and Dolly were all younger than Coach. That deferment lasted only seven or eight months before the rule was changed. After his graduation, Coach got a job in the steel mill in Duluth.

He often worked throughout the night and returned home in the morning. Coach usually worked a twelve-hour shift from midnight to noon. He did this from October of 1943 until early January of 1944. Coach cut steel billets and "pickled" them in acid before they were sent to the lab. After coming home from the

The Duluth steel mill

war Coach said that he was lucky to be able to return to a summer job at the steel mill while he was in college. While in college, he worked in the open hearth measuring the temperature of the steel with a pyrometer before the steel was sent on to the ladle. Another summer job at the steel mill Coach did while he was at the University of Minnesota Duluth (UMD) was to inspect the red hot steel in the rolling mill and record any fissures in the steel. He knew what it was to work hard and to carry a lunch pail. Years later, Coach often would tell his athletes, "Your books are your lunch pail. Study hard so that you can have your choice of occupations rather than just taking what was available or necessary."

When Coach's deferment was lifted he was drafted into the Army. He had tried to enlist in the Navy but they were not taking anyone at that time. He received his induction papers on January 27, 1944 and was required to travel to Fort Snelling in the Twin Cities to take his physical examination. Being in excellent health, he passed. He returned to Duluth and the steel mill while awaiting his orders. Coach remembered that his mother cried when she learned that he would be inducted into the Army. On February 20th, Coach visited his father's grave in the Oneota Cemetery in Duluth. Three days later he received his final induction papers and was ordered to report to the YMCA in West Duluth on March 7th. He worked his last day at the steel plant on March 4th and spent the next few days saying goodbye to his friends and family. On March 8, 1944 he was sworn into the United States Army with the new title of Private Roy Grijak. He received his uniform the next day and spent much of his first week in the Army scrubbing floors and doing K.P. (kitchen patrol) at Fort Snelling in the Twin Cities. He was allowed a brief return trip home and was able to celebrate his mother's birthday with her before returning to Minneapolis and then being shipped out.

Coach was sent from Ft. Snelling to Camp Roberts (California) for basic training in the infantry. Upon reaching the West Coast, Coach was able to see the Golden Gate Bridge. He would see it again early in 1946 as his troop ship sailed home from Japan to San Francisco. Camp Roberts is located near San Jose, California and was named after Corporal Harold W. Roberts, a 19-year old tank driver who lost his life in northeastern France in WW I. Corporal Robert's tank had fallen into a shell crater that was filled with rainwater. As the tank rapidly filled with water Roberts drowned but not before he had pushed his gunner out to safety. He was posthumously awarded the Medal of Honor. Coach Grijak was one of the 436,000 infantry and field artillery troops to go through an intense 17-week training cycle at Fort Roberts. Demolition of the WW II barracks that once housed Roy Grijak began in 2012. While at Camp Roberts he attended church in San Luis Obispo.

Once in the Army, Coach hoped to be placed in the Army Air Corps but instead he was put into the infantry. Most of his friends were already in the service and Coach was with people he did not know and who were not necessarily the same age. Coach said that he was in great shape. He was nineteen years old and had been a talented high school athlete. Basic training was easy for him. He said that he had no prior knowledge about guns but that he was able to quickly learn to clean and care for his gun. What he remembered about basic training was forced marches, close order drill, shooting practice, obstacle courses, throwing grenades and crawling under barbed wire. In late March of 1944 he and the other recruits were sent through tear gas and chlorine chambers. He confided in his diary, "This type of warfare would not be any fun." He studied the manual of arms and spent long days in the field and nights in a tent. He also remembered lectures and frequent barracks inspections and more kitchen patrol. When Coach mentioned close order drill it reminded him of one of the first people he met in basic training, a young man from Oregon who was, "Perhaps the clumsiest kid I ever met." He said that the young man was constantly stepping on his heels in close order drill. Coach joked that he also learned how to make a perfectly taut bed but that he would not use that skill while he was sleeping on the ground or in foxholes in the jungles of numerous islands in the South Pacific during the war. Speaking of sleeping, Coach recalled that during basic training there was a soldier named Kastecki who could rattle the curtains with his snoring. Kastecki was from Hayti, Missouri which is located in Pemiscot County in the very southeastern part of the state. Coach remembers asking him how big Hayti was and Kastecki said, "If you enter the town and said Hayti you would be out of the town before completing the name." Coach then said that he never saw Kastecki after basic training but that he hoped that he had made it home. Apparently Coach's genuine concern for people was an attribute long before he demonstrated those caring qualities with his students and athletes. Coach's mother, Milica (Mildred), had instilled a love for people and an appreciation for life in all of her children at an early age and Coach retained those qualities throughout his life. Among the more useful things Coach learned in basic training, and during his years in the service, were teamwork, learning how to take orders, always looking out for your buddy and the need to, "Keep your head down."

On April 12, 1944 Coach was transferred to the 91st Infantry. This was a rifle company and he realized that he would soon be headed for the front lines. Within days he had been made squad leader. By April 22nd he had been classified as an expert marksman. He and the other three expert marksmen were elevated to acting corporal status. Coach wrote in the April 27th entry of his diary that he had become very good at firing at moving targets but, "The only thing I'm learning is to kill and that's not pleasant." He also practiced firing a bazooka and a grenade launcher. He wrote in his diary, "Sure hope I don't break when the real test comes." On May 8, 1944 he closed his entry for that day with the prayer, "Please God, let's have a quick end to the war." Although, he didn't know it at the time, it would be exactly a year later that the war in Europe would end. The fighting in the Pacific, where he would soon be stationed, would go on even longer. On May 10th, Coach earned an expert marksman classification on the Browning automatic rifle. He was also learning how to use a bayonet, machine gun and a mortar. He practiced climbing a cargo net and ran the obstacle course with a full field pack. He and his fellow soldiers practiced sleeping on the bare ground. Coach wrote in his diary at this time, "I certainly know how to take care of myself when I get across, but I'll need God's help more than anything."

On May 19, 1944 he got his acting sergeant stripes. Coach had been in basic training less than three months when he learned of the June 6, 1944 D-Day landing on the coast of France. A week later he wrote in his diary, "It's no fun crawling on your stomach over gravel and barbed wire with live ammunition being fired above your head." He continued, "Yes, the Army life is great...and I am a liar!" After 26 1/2 hours without rest he wrote on June 27, 1944, "This is what you call a dog's life." He knew that he would soon be heading overseas but also that he would first have a furlough home. Coach had spent seventeen weeks of intense training at Fort Roberts. He left California by train on July 20th and arrived home in Duluth on July 24th. He spent eleven days visiting his mother, brother, sisters and his friends.

Kay, Steve and Dolly - Coach's siblings

His mother was not happy that he had been drafted; her brother Radomir had been in the Yugoslavian Air Force and had been killed by the communists.

Uncle Radomir

It was from this relative that Coach Griak got his given first name, Radomir. Radomir Grijak would eventually become Roy Griak. Coach's mother was disappointed that Coach was in the Army but she knew he had no other choice. He wrote of his departure from Duluth on August 4,

Radomir Grijak with his flight crew

1944, "This is the saddest day of my life." After completing his furlough, Coach was sent to Fort Ord, near Salinas, California. Fort Ord was named for Major General Edward Ord, a Civil War General in the Union Army. Ford Ord was located on Monterey Bay in California. It was closed in 1994 and much of the land went to California State University at Monterey and to the University of California at Santa Cruz. There was more training at Fort Ord. He learned how to get off a landing craft and what to do when drifting on a raft. He tasted his first "K" rations and said that they were much better than the "C" rations. Coach practiced

Coach and his Mother on the steps of their home in Gary – New Duluth

with the Thompson machine gun. He received training in land mines, booby traps, mortars and anti-tank grenades. There were more drills and inspections. He remembered a lecture on what to say if captured by the enemy. He was to give only his name, rank and serial number. On September 22, 1944 he got his Government Issue (G.I) haircut. Coach wrote, "Yes sir, I look like something the cat dragged in." He also took out power of attorney papers for his mother, "So that everything I may have in my name is hers."

From Fort Ord Coach Griak and hundreds of other young men took the train to Oakland and then a ferry to San Francisco. From San Francisco they shipped out on a troop carrier. Coach remembered that the ship left from pier number fifteen on September 25th and sailed under the Golden Gate Bridge. In his diary entry of September 27th he asked, "I wonder when I will be coming back." Coach didn't know it at the time but it would be seventeen months and one week before he would again sail under the Golden Gate on his return to the United States.

The troop ship heading for the South Pacific was just a converted freighter. Coach said that he had never been at sea before and got seasick almost immediately. On October 5 Coach "celebrated" his 21st birthday doing kitchen patrol and slicing 750 loaves of bread. Four days later the ship sailed between Malaita and Guadalcanal in the Solomon Islands. Twenty months earlier Guadalcanal had been the site of a 6-month battle ending on February 9, 1943 that was the first Allied offensive against the Empire of Japan. The Japanese expansion in the South Pacific had been slowed in the spring and summer of 1942 which was about the time that Coach was graduating from Morgan Park High School.

The Battle of the Coral Sea in May of 1942 had kept Australia and part of New Guinea from falling into the hands of the Japanese and the Battle of Midway in June of 1942 had begun to turn the tide of the war against Japan. What followed was the start of a program of "island hopping" as American forces shelled, attacked and cleared a strategic island and then the Corps of Engineers and the Seabees built an airstrip there that would be used to begin the attack on the next strategic island on the way to Japan itself. In this way, large numbers of Japanese were bypassed and eventually cut off from reinforcements and supplies as the Allies got closer and closer to the place where they could bomb Japan itself. Although he may not have been aware of it, Coach Griak, as a combat infantry soldier in the United States Army, would be a part of that "island hopping."

Coach said that none of the soldiers knew where they were going and that they were at sea for more than two weeks. His diary entry for October 13th stated, "We got off the troop ship after nineteen days at sea." He told me, "When you are in the army your life is not your own. You have no say on where you are going to end up. You are just a checker in a game of checkers. You are just a number." Coach said that he learned how to go with the flow because in the Army he was never asked for his opinion or what he would like to do. As we talked in his Plymouth home in the winter of 2014, Coach Griak demonstrated that he had been just a number by reciting his: 37 588 725. He served in the United States Army 24th Division, 21st Regiment, Company E.

Coach didn't know it at the time because it was in the dark of night but the troop ship

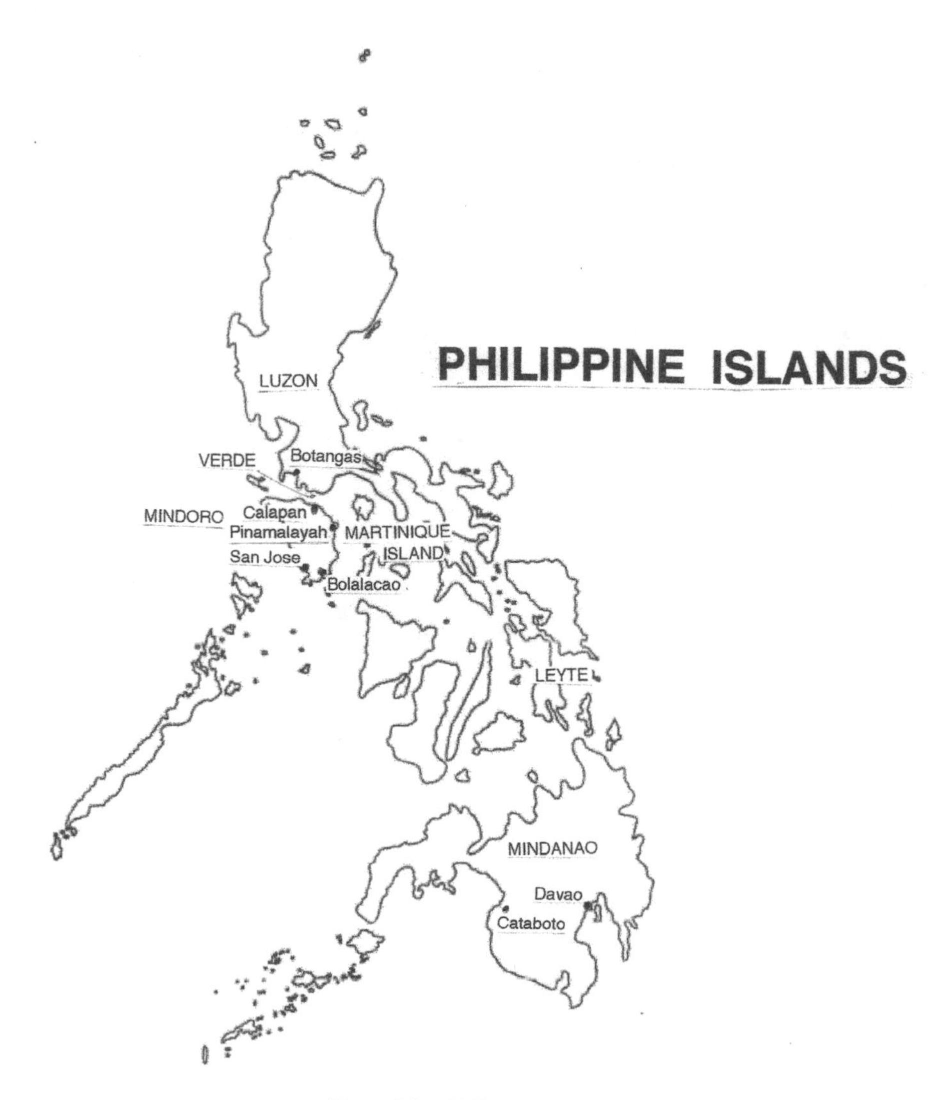

Map of the Philippine Islands

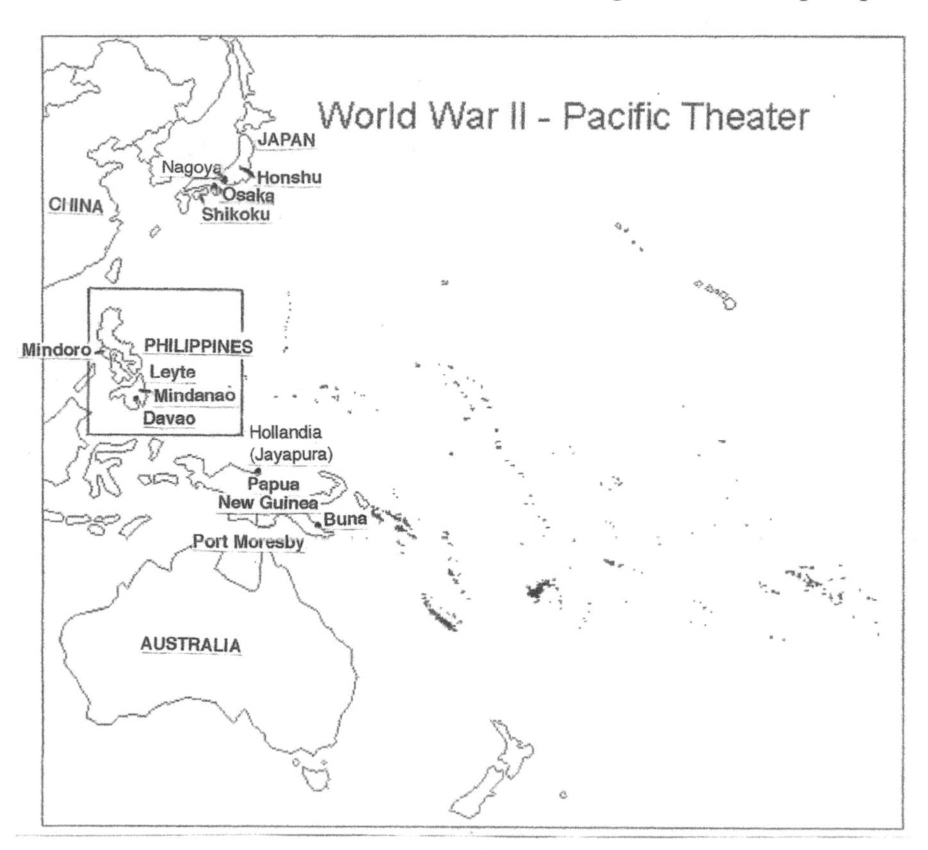

Map of the Pacific Theater of World War II

had landed in New Guinea. The troops had received no training for the jungle conditions they encountered on New Guinea. The Japanese started shelling the soldiers as soon as they landed. Coach had been sent there as part of a replacement unit for the 24th Division (the Pineapple Division). Soldiers were sent to different areas depending on where the need was the greatest. Coach said that he lost contact with most of the men he had come to know from basic training. He was sent to Buna, New Guinea and was directed to bivouac in that area. Buna is located on the north coast near the eastern tip of New Guinea. It is directly across the Owen Stanley range from Port Moresby. Buna is located at approximately 9 degrees south latitude and 148 degrees east longitude; a long way from home and the 47 degrees north and 92 degrees west coordinates of Duluth, Minnesota. Coach said that Buna was, “A tough, tough place.”

In April of 2015 while asking Coach for clarification of the sequence of his wartime stops in the South Pacific, he modified his assessment of Buna to, “Buna was a hellhole.” It rained nearly all the time and it was nearly impossible to stay dry. The native grasses and vegetation grew very fast and some of the grasses were taller than the men. The kunai grass grew to a height of 6’ 6” and had broad leaves that were so sharp that they could cut a soldier walking through them. Coach said that he planted beans by his tent and in a week they were knee high. On New Guinea the water table was so high that whenever the soldiers dug into the ground it filled with water. There were more soldiers lost to malaria, dengue fever and yellow jaundice than to enemy bullets. Dysentery was a persistent problem. He recalled that on New Guinea he encountered all sorts of exotic birds. On Oct. 15, 1944 he had written in his diary, “Tough to sleep with millions of birds chirping at 4:45 a.m.” There were also animals as well as snakes and insects. Mosquitoes and ants were major problems. According to Coach Griak, “Mosquitoes were constant companions.”

Although in basic training he had been instructed on how to make a taut bed, Coach said that initially we slept on the ground inside a tent to protect us from the rain and we used mosquito netting to fend off the mosquitos. He said that he would have written home about the terrible conditions but he knew that the censors would not have let his letter go through. A month after turning twenty-one, his company marched three hours and then dug foxholes into the ground. He wrote in his diary, “I spent the most miserable night of my life in a hole with bugs, dirt and muck.”

On November 17, 1944, Coach and the 24th Division left Buna and sailed toward Hollandia, the provincial capital of Papua New Guinea. The Indonesian name of the city is Jayapura; the Dutch had occupied Hollandia in colonial times. After anchoring at Hollandia for a day, “We left with a few ships as escorts and headed for the Philippine Islands.” Coach remembered having a Thanksgiving dinner of turkey and a cookie for desert while on the troop ship.

The next stop for Coach Griak was Leyte in the Philippine Islands. The island of Leyte stretched 110 miles from north to south and was only forty miles wide at its widest point. The Philippine island of Luzon lay to the north of Leyte and Mindanao was across the Surigao Strait to the south. Leyte was heavily forested and mountainous. General Douglas MacArthur was able to announce on Oct. 20, 1944 that, “I have returned.” General MacArthur had thus fulfilled his famous promise to the Filipino people that, “I shall return.” Coach’s 6th Army, X Corps, 24th Division was soon involved in the fighting on Leyte. Under very strong air support his troop ship arrived at Leyte on November 25, 1944. The soldiers waited all day to disembark as Japanese planes came over and made getting off the ship difficult. Under the cover of darkness the unloading began but Coach did not disembark until 2:30 a.m. Once he had hit the shore he was taken to the 274th Replacement Company. He said that they were about thirty miles from the front and that he could hear big guns. On November 26th, 1944 he wrote, "From the looks of things, I will be up front in short order." When Japanese paratroopers landed just eighteen miles from our camp a heavy raid was expected.

Coach wrote, "I stood out in the rain for three hours awaiting orders; mosquitos almost carried me away." On December 6 he endured an air raid where he said that the shells were falling thick and fast and that on one occasion, "I had really kissed the ground." The next night, exactly three years after the Japanese had attacked Pearl Harbor he wrote that he, "Slept with my pants on, gun by my side, trench knife and ammo at hand." Night alerts and frequent air raids were common in the next days and on December 11th Coach wrote in his diary, "I wonder how long it will be before I get home. Please God, make it soon." Coach told me that he had no thoughts of fame or glory and that all the time he was in the South Pacific he did not feel that he was there so much to serve his country as to do his duty and get home to his family.

Coach remembers getting on a truck and being taken to his division. When he got off the truck he was in an area where the landscape was scarred and barren. Few trees were untouched and there was evidence of heavy artillery shelling. The veteran soldiers there were dug into foxholes and he was told to find one and get into it. There were empty foxholes because of the high casualty rate (those soldiers who were killed, wounded, missing or who had been evacuated because they were sick with malaria). This was Coach's first experience with front line action. He recalled thinking that he, and other young men like him, were just starting to shave and now they were being asked to grow up real fast. They were being asked to think as adults when most of them did not have that degree of maturity. I think that Coach was probably ahead of most of the young men in that situation because of the responsibilities he had in his family after the death of his father in 1940. Today military doctors and psychologists are more in tune with "shell shock" and "battle fatigue." They have even determined new classifications for the soldiers who suffer breakdowns during or after combat (post-traumatic stress disorder). Coach remembers someone in his unit screaming and the medics grabbing a Mexican-American soldier named Cadingo and taking him off the front lines. Coach said that he never saw Cadingo again.

At night while on the front lines the soldiers were ordered to count off, "1 - 2 - 3." Every third hour a soldier would have to pull guard duty and stay alert for any movement that might be an attack by the Japanese. Coach said that during his first night on the front line when it got dark the Japanese started shooting and that "all hell broke loose." He said that it was pitch dark and that he could not see his hand in front of his face. Coach said that the Japanese were yelling "Banzai, Banzai" and that he was really scared. The word "banzai" is a traditional Japanese exclamation meaning "ten thousand years of long life." It often accompanied a desperate military charge.

Coach had a carbine rifle and also grenades strapped to the harness of his uniform. He said that he remembered thinking that his basic training had not prepared him for anything like this. He had asked himself, "What the hell am I doing here?" Coach did lob several grenades and said that he was ready to shoot anything that would have come at him. After that first night things got easier, or as easy as being on the front lines ever could, but he said he would always remember that scary first night. He recalled that it was the most scared he had ever been in his whole life.

Coach's unit moved from one area to the next on Leyte. He said that his unit would often march at night. Contrary to the Army Basic Field Manual (page 29) which stated that, "In all phases of administration, training, and operation make every effort to keep your men informed. Nothing irritates American soldiers so much as to be left in the dark regarding the reason for things," Coach said that in his experiences during World War II, the soldiers were never told much about the overall plans. The soldiers didn't see the big picture of what was happening in the war. They were familiar only with their sector, their foxhole, their immediate needs, their next objective. Someone else was making all the decisions. The soldiers didn't realize the intricacies of the war effort: the procurement of weapons and ammunition, boots, ponchos, potable drinking water, food, medical staff, gasoline, etc. Coach said that there were soldiers assigned to every possible aspect of keeping the army functioning.

Just before Christmas in 1944, the division was moved further north to the island of Mindoro and the Army placed the soldier's duffle bags in storage. This meant that Coach did not have access to his diary until February 18, 1945 when the bags were returned. During this time Coach told me that he kept two things in his helmet: toilet paper and a few pages of American Red Cross stationery. Whenever he had the chance to write, he continued his diary in a tiny script to conserve space on the paper. Those pages were later inserted in his diary and have survived to this day. The diary and those insertions are in the possession of Coach's sons, Seth and Jason.

On the southwestern tip of Mindoro, is the city of San Jose. Coach said that this was a city with houses made of wood rather than straw and that there was a church, a sugar mill and a hospital. There was also an American Red Cross facility where he was able to obtain essentials like shaving cream, soap, shaving blades, a toothbrush and more stationery. To reinforce another company threatened by large numbers of Japanese soldiers in the area, Coach's company was moved about fifty miles to the east to Bolalacao. There was constant rain and so many mosquitos that Coach wrote on January 9, 1945, "I have so many mosquito bites that my mouth is swollen" and "I'd give $10 for a new mosquito net." He also lamented, "If we don't get malaria no one will." Between January 13th and January 21st Coach was part of a group that marched north from Bolalacao to Pinamalayah on the northeast coast of Mindoro. His foxhole buddy was Joe Payne. Coach recalled that they would wake up each morning soaked to skin and that, "Being wet, cold, hungry and waiting for the Japanese was no fun."

On January 21st, Coach's entry on his Red Cross stationery was, "The Japanese are supposed to be on our left flank - I did more praying last night than I ever did in my life." The next day a captured Japanese supply dump yielded smokes, cards, powdered fish, toilet paper, pencils and paper. The booty was divided up but Coach gave his cigarettes to men who smoked. On January 23rd Coach's company marched about twenty miles to the city of Calapan. It is on the northern coast of Mindoro. Much of Calapan had been destroyed by the Japanese just a few days earlier.

Coach noted that a beautiful school was still smoldering. He said that he saw the sun for the first time in ten days. Much of the equipment at Calapan had been made in the United States. This included a burned out 1939 Buick. After being on the march for several weeks, Coach wrote on January 26th, "On the one day we could have rested we had an inspection." By early February, Coach's company was the only one left in Calapan and he and a number of his buddies moved into a vacant schoolhouse.

Only a short time earlier, Coach had been in school himself as a student at Morgan Park High School. He recalled that he had slept on a cot in the schoolhouse in Calapan and that this was the first time he had not slept on the ground for a month.

The company had also found a kitchen in a barracks they occupied and they were able to make warm meals. This was also a great change from the usual diet of C rations. Coach said that the C rations always came in an olive green can and often consisted of canned ham and cheese or what he called "Australian bully beef." The diet for the soldiers was monotonous and seldom involved anything fresh. The eggs were powdered eggs. The breakfasts often consisted of pancakes. The meals certainly didn't compare with his memories of the hot, homemade bread with jam that his mother had made and even his mother's vegetable soup that he had not liked as a boy would have been a feast. He said that there was usually coffee but that he did not drink coffee. The Hershey Chocolate Company had created the D ration which was a bitter tasting version of a chocolate bar. There was also a waxy supplement called the Tropical Bar that could withstand the heat in the South Pacific. The taste of these bars was bad enough that they were often given away to locals, especially the children. Coach said that beer and cigarettes were rationed but that he gave his allowance of these to others in his unit because he neither smoked nor drank.

Coach and Joe Payne with Filipino civilians

Although the soldiers had no real knowledge of what lay in store for them rumors were rampant. Coach said that his machine gun section was sure that they were headed back to Pinamalayah and then would be part of an invasion of the island of Martinique, ten miles to the east of Mindoro. This rumor, like many others, turned out to be false.

Shortly after Coach's company recovered their duffle bags in late February of 1945, Coach started training in a mortar section. He commented that it was easier than firing a machine gun. Soon he was classified as 1st Gunner Grijak. Coach said on March 2, 1945 he left Calapan and landed on Verde Island. Verde Island lays between Mindoro and the major island of Luzon. Expecting Japanese resistance, Coach said that his company had marched inland only a few minutes when they got word that the Japanese guns on Verde had already been knocked out. Instead of engaging in a fight, Coach and the other soldiers waited for a boat to return them to Calapan. The company then left by ship to return to San Jose on March 6, 1945. In the two months since he had last been in San Jose, Coach said that it had now swelled with great amounts of American planes and equipment. On March 7th, which marked the completion of his first year in the Army, Coach received a letter from his mother informing him that one of his friends, Eli Bubalo had been killed in France.

The following picture was taken in March of 1945 at San Jose on Mindoro. Coach Griak is the tall soldier without a cap standing in the back. The soldier kneeling on the left in the front is Joe Breiderhoff. Breiderhoff was Coach's good friend and had been in the war for almost three years. He was a veteran soldier who had taught Coach many of

Seven American soldiers on Mindoro in March 1945. Coach is standing in the center of the back row.

the skills necessary for surviving at the front. As Coach related this to me I was reminded of Paul Baumer, the narrator of Erich Maria Remarque's *All Quiet on the Western Front,* and how he was instructed by the veteran soldier, Katczinsky. Coach described Breiderhoff as a real daredevil who was just crazy about collecting souvenirs. Breiderhoff once disappeared for several days because he was exploring a local village. When he returned, he came back with an American soldier who had been in the Philippines since WW I and had married a Filipino woman. Breiderhoff took the man to division headquarters and tried to help him collect back pay for all the years he had been in the Philippines. Breiderhoff and the other veterans had told young Roy Griak that one thing a soldier never should do was to get out of his foxhole at night. At 6:00 a.m. one morning Beriderhoff left his foxhole for an unknown reason (probably to relieve himself) and was shot and killed by one of his own men. Nearly three quarters of a century later, it still perplexed Coach that some soldiers were wounded or killed and others survived unscathed. He recalled only one time, during an artillery bombardment, that he was keenly aware of being imminently close to death. When the first artillery shells landed, Coach hit the dirt. A piece of red-hot shrapnel hit a coconut tree just above his head. Coach watched as the shrapnel turned from red hot to black as it cooled.

Coach said that he knew very few men really well when he was in the service but that Joe Payne was the one to whom he was the closest. Coach said that Joe Payne was about

Foxhole buddies – Grijak and Payne on the island of Mindoro

the same age, had a similar personality and that they both had the same interest in sports. Coach said that he and Joe had lots to talk about. They were partners in a machine gun and mortar section and became fast friends.

Coach and Joe Payne with mortar

Joe was from Okemah, a small central Oklahoma town seventy-two miles east of Oklahoma City. Okemah is the county seat of Okfuskee County and was also the birthplace of folk music legend Woody Guthrie who had been born there on July 14, 1912. After the war, Coach went to Oklahoma to visit Joe and Joe's family. Joe's father managed the cemetery in Okemah. Upon meeting the elder Mr. Payne, Coach and Joe were put to work digging graves on a day that Coach said was so hot, "Popcorn would have popped on the ears of the corn." Joe's brother Jack later became the color commentator for the football team at the University of Oklahoma. Coach and Joe Payne remained good friends for many years after the war.

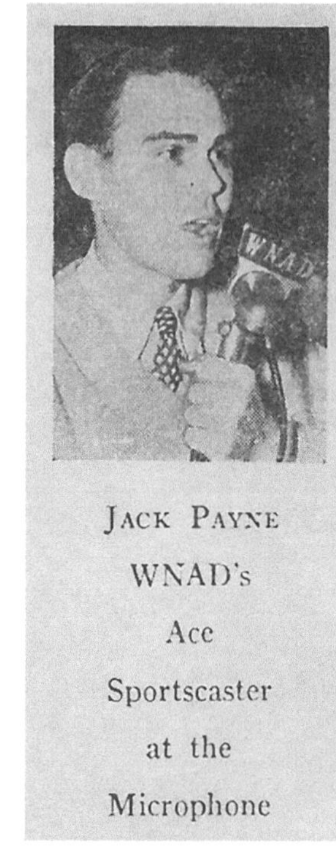

Jack Payne - WNAD's Ace Sportscaster

In 2012, Coach Griak made a special trip to Arlington National Cemetery to visit the grave of Joe Payne and to pay his respects to his long-time friend. Coach had planned another trip to Arlington for May 16th of 2015. He was to be part of a Freedom Flight, a program where the United States government honors WW II veterans with a no-cost flight to Washington, D.C. to visit the WW II Memorial and other historic sights. His trip was cancelled because of the fall and resultant injuries he sustained in April. He was to have been accompanied in his travels by one of his athletes, former Gopher shot putter, Tom Barnes. Tom had put the shot 56' 8 1/4" in 1965.

On March 9, 1945 Coach received the Christmas card his mother had sent him nearly three months earlier. Coach regularly wrote letters home to his mother, his brother and sisters, his girl-friend, Elaine Larson, and other friends, teachers and acquaintances. Much of his Army pay was sent home to his mother. He wrote letters nearly every day and received many letters in return. As we talked about this correspondence nearly seventy years later I was reminded of a book I had in my library. In February of 2014 I loaned Coach a book called Up Front. It had been written in 1945 by Bill Mauldin and chronicled the lives of his GI cartoon characters, Willie and Joe. I had forgotten about the book until

Post WW II Picture of Joe Payne on left and Coach

Coach mentioned it again in late April of 2014. He said he enjoyed the book more than any he had ever read about the war. Where most books he had read described the WW II battles, Mauldin's book describes the everyday life of the American foot soldier in World War II. Coach said that Mauldin's cartoons brought back many memories of his life as a young soldier in the Pacific.

A cartoon about GIs walking in the mud alongside a road and being splattered by an officer's jeep racing by was followed by the same soldiers catching up to the jeep stuck in the mud and them now being asked to push it out of the mud. Coach said that he could just see that happening. When Mauldin pictured Willie thanking Joe for saving his life and giving him his most prized possession, a pair of dry socks, Coach said that dry socks were indeed cherished. There were few comforts and soldiers learned to live without the things they had seen as necessities when they were civilians. Coach said that it always seemed to be raining in New Guinea and the Philippines and that trench foot and jungle rot were common. He said that his feet were never dry. He recalled that during the rain he would often hunch down in his fox hole while sitting on his helmet with his poncho used as a poor tent over his head.

While sitting at the dining room table of his Plymouth home during the very wet Minnesota April of 2014, Coach looked out at his soggy back yard and said, "Imagine being told to dig a fox hole in that ground and then climbing into it for the night." He added, "But when you are nineteen or twenty years old you can do things that you can't when you are ninety." When Coach told about Mauldin's characters, Willie and Joe, saying that another of the most cherished things in a soldier's life was mail from home he related a story about getting mail in the Pacific.

Coach said that many soldiers never got any mail and that most soldiers went weeks or months without hearing from home. Mail delivery was very irregular and letters from home might take weeks or even months to reach their destination. However, Coach Griak told of a time when one day he got seventy-five letters! The next day he got fifty-eight letters. He was the envy of the entire unit. Coach went on to say that the letters were from a Duluth Central girl he had met during his senior year at Morgan Park. She had been a junior at the time they met at a Fourth of July picnic. Her name was Elaine Larson and she wrote him a letter nearly every day when he was in the army. She would seal every letter she sent to Coach with a lipstick kiss on the back of the envelope. The letters were pretty tame and Coach shared the news from the states with the men who didn't get mail, or at least not the volume of mail Coach Griak received! Coach said that the scented lipstick on the envelopes had also survived the long journey from Duluth and was another highlight with all the men. That's how much the mail, or any contact with the United States, meant to the men overseas. Coach said that Elaine had given him a statue of the Virgin Mary on an old shoe-lace. He said that he didn't know what had happened to it but it was important to me then and he wished that he still had it. The letters and gifts from home helped him get through the hardships of the war.

While Coach was in the South Pacific the Larson family would invite Coach's sister, Dolly, to visit them just because she reminded them of Coach. Coach said that Miss Larson was interested in marrying him when he returned from the war but that he declined because he wanted to continue his education. Once he came home, he realized how much he had changed. He said that, "He now saw the world as big and wide and open, with so much to see and so much to do. Elaine was a gorgeous woman but she wanted to get married and I wanted to go to school. I wanted to leave Duluth and to become a teacher. She was a strong Catholic and I was not. For her, everything had to be Catholic. This wasn't true for me. I don't care what you are; it doesn't make any difference to me. I kept track of her over the years. She died in Washington a few years ago. She had been really important to me. I hope she was happy."

The stacks of letters Coach received while serving the United States Army in the South Pacific during the war was rivaled by the mail coming his way daily at the Golden Living Center in Wayzata in May of 2015 as he convalesced following a bad fall he had in April. Another book that Coach enjoyed a great deal was the Armed Forces Edition of *Your Kids and Mine* by Joe E. Brown. The book contained stories of the servicemen Joe E. Brown had met when he was entertaining the troops for the United Service Organization (USO) in both the European and Pacific theaters during WW II.

Coach and his fellow soldiers were given amphibious training and attended lectures on land mines, chemical warfare and gas determination. On April 7, 1945 Coach wrote "We were told that our bags had to be ready by 8:00 p.m. tonight - something is up."He was correct in his assumption as evidenced by his diary entries from April 9th - June 27th again being on folded Red Cross stationary instead of in his regular diary, which was temporarily not in his possession as it was stowed in his duffle bag. Coach wrote on April 14, 1945 that he felt terrible, both because he was seasick again and because he had learned that Franklin Roosevelt had died. On April 18th, the ship hit the island of Mindanao at the town of Cataboto on the southwest coast. Coach was placed in a machine gun detachment. His group was guarding the beach. He remembered standing on the beach, looking out at the vast Philippine Sea, and thinking, "I am a very long way from home." Coach said that even though he was part of a large group of men who were in the "same boat" as he was that he had a very lonely feeling. Coach said that on his mind constantly was not patriotism and the flag but getting back home to his family, and especially his mother. Like Coach, most of the American soldiers were very young. A soldier needed to be in the army three years before he could rotate out and be sent home. That seemed like an eternity. From the coast, Coach and the American soldiers moved inland pushing the Japanese back. They were moving toward Davao, the capital of Mindanao, in the southeastern part of the island.

Coach was selected to be with a small group of soldiers that were sent to capture a Japanese held radio tower. The Americans were in an army gunboat on the Mindanao River. The Filipino people call this river the Rio Grande de Mindanao. It is the largest river on the island. The river has its source in the highlands of central Mindanao. It has many tributaries and flows roughly 232 miles southward and then to the west reaching Illana Bay on the Moro Gulf of the Mindanao Sea on the western coast of the island. Coach said that he saw several things he had never seen before. He saw houses built on stilts. He also saw crocodiles on the banks of the river. Knowing that they had just seen crocodiles, Coach and the other American soldiers waded ashore and went to a path that led up to the radio tower they were supposed to capture. They did not encounter any gunfire.

Eventually they saw three heads looking over the bank on the path ahead. They slowly and stealthily approached the people and saw that they were not moving. The heads were those of three Japanese soldiers and had been severed at the neck. Suddenly, the Americans were surrounded by natives coming out of the jungle. The Japanese had been killed by Moro tribesmen. The Moro are indigenous to Mindanao and had not been subdued either by the Spanish or later by the United States in the Spanish-American War. They still had not been brought under control by the U.S. or any government at the time of WW II. The Moro are Islamic. They were friendly to the American troops and had left the Japanese heads as a signal that the Japanese were not welcome. One of the Moro tribesmen spoke fluent English. Coach remembers that some of the Americans traded rations of meat and cheese to the Moro for daggers and flags.

Unlike many of his comrades, Coach was not captivated by souvenirs but I know that he had at least one, a framed Japanese banner, in the living room of his home. It had the red circle of the "rising sun" in the middle and Japanese writing that Coach said he would like to have had translated but never did. After trading with the Moro the next day the Moro were back and they were very upset because some of the rations had contained tins of ham. The Americans had to return their souvenirs because the Moro were Muslim and were not supposed to eat ham.

Once while on maneuvers Coach's unit entered a field and the Japanese surprised them once they were on the far side of a clearing. The Americans quickly retreated. Coach Griak turned and ran so fast that he passed up the chow truck that was going back down the road. He felt that this may have been the fastest he had ever run in his life. Coach said that his only thought was to save his rear end. He explained that in war there are no heroes. You are either lucky and survive or you are unlucky and are wounded or killed. He felt there were few heroes and that most of the men he was with were just trying to stay alive in the jungles of New Guinea or the Philippines. He felt fortunate to have survived the war and felt bad for those who did not.

The diary entries between April 9th and June 27th, 1945 were sporadic partially because Coach did not have his diary and was writing on Red Cross stationery that he kept in his helmet and partially because he was engaged in heavy fighting and could not write every day. On April 29th he wrote that he was moving forward toward the city of Davao and that Mindanao was, "The hottest place I have ever been in." A week later he was writing from a fox hole during an air attack. On May 14th Coach wrote, "A lot has happened since I last wrote. Some of the boys are gone but not forgotten. Joe Payne got nicked in the arm." Joe Payne had become Coach's closest wartime friend and his foxhole buddy. He had sustained a shoulder wound on what seemed to be a calm, sunny day when Joe was just sitting in his foxhole. Payne had been hit by what Coach Griak called a "knee mortar."

A week later he wrote, "Got back from the front yesterday. It feels like heaven to walk around or sit in the sun without worrying about the Japanese. Heard from Al Andrieko; he expects to be home soon - lucky stiff. Fifteen of our boys went home on furlough - we got more replacements the other day." On June 10, 1945 Coach wrote, "Fired close to fifty rounds of ammunition yesterday - the going was a bit rough." Eight days later he was happy to see his friend again as he wrote, "Joe Payne came back to the company again. He still has shrapnel in his arm." He had rejoined the unit after only partially recovering from a mortar wound.

On June 20th Coach's entry, still on Red Cross stationery, was "Got back from the front yesterday after sixty-three days without a rest. It was a happy day for the 21st Infantry. No more diving into holes for a while anyway. I slept on a cot; lot different than sleeping in a hole." On Sunday June 24th, 1945 Coach attended a memorial service for the boys who died in this campaign. He sent his mother $100 from his pay. After the long stint in the field Coach recovered his duffle bag and was able to resume writing in his diary. At the end of June, 1945 he was asked if he would like to break in as a

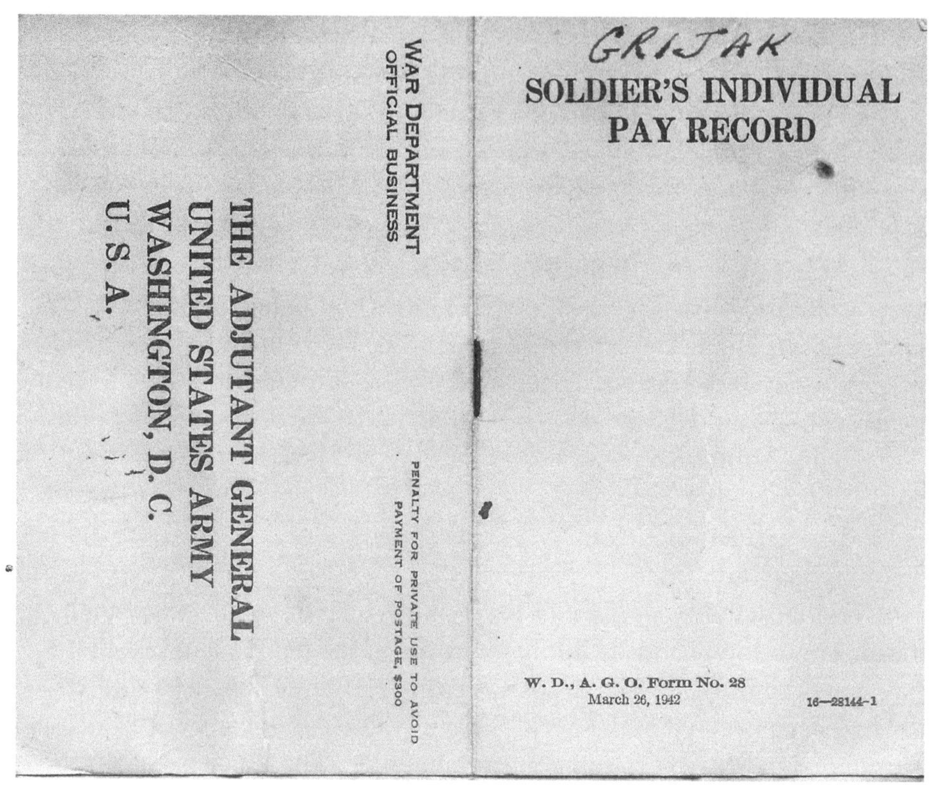

GRIJAK

SOLDIER'S INDIVIDUAL PAY RECORD

W. D., A. G. O. Form No. 28
March 26, 1942
16—28144-1

WAR DEPARTMENT
OFFICIAL BUSINESS

PENALTY FOR PRIVATE USE TO AVOID
PAYMENT OF POSTAGE, $300

THE ADJUTANT GENERAL
UNITED STATES ARMY
WASHINGTON, D. C.
U. S. A.

Soldier's Individual Pay Record – Grijak

personnel clerk. He wrote, "I am going to miss the boys but it's a good break. I hope that I can make good." He began practicing his typing by candlelight and was able to sleep in a tent for the first time since he left San Jose on Mindoro. He also got up early to do more practice with his typing. He wrote in his diary, "I'll never have another opportunity like this - ever. Be good to me typewriter."

Coach continued to study his clerk assignments and on July 3rd was permanently placed in personnel as a clerk. Something he said he never dreamed of was that he got a cot and electric lights inside his tent! On July 14th he wrote, "The Japanese had got through last night and did some damage. One officer was killed and fifteen men were wounded." Coach was still pulling guard duty in addition to typing orders for

Name GRIJAK, ROY
Army serial No. 37 588 725
Grade PVT.
Years of service 0
(On date of opening this book)
Insurance, amount and class N $10000 00
Insurance premium, monthly $ 6.50
Allotments, amount and class F $ 22 00
Compulsory allotments, amount and class $ Nothing.
Pay reservation, class A $ Nothing.
Technician grade Nothing.
Additional pay for Nothing.
Person to be notified in case of emergency:
MILDRED GRIJAK
(Name)
MOTHER
(Relationship; if friend, so state)
1514 101 AVE W.
(Number and street or rural route; if none, so state)
DULUTH, MINN.
(City, town, or post office) (State or country)
Date of opening this book 6 JUL 44
x Roy Griak
(Signature of enlisted man. Name, grade, and arm or service only. Do *not* enter organization)
Witness to signature by officer preparing book:
(Signature—Name, grade, and arm or service only. Do *not* enter organization)
(2)

CHANGES AFFECTING PAY STATUS

CASUAL DATA

Date reported or picked up. (Do *not* enter organization)	Name, grade, and arm or service only of personnel officer or commanding officer

16—28144-1
(3)

Inside of Pay Record

transfers, rosters for Purple Hearts and Good Conduct Medals and doing the payroll. Two weeks later Coach and everyone else spent the rest of the night on guard duty after Japanese grenades exploded in their camp and killed seven of the men. At the end of July Coach reported that he had been given real fresh apples for breakfast.

Coach had good memories of one of his officers, Captain Kilgo. He said that he was a good commander but that he had been killed in the Philippines. He also remembered a Sergeant Froglee who was a bully and was not liked by his men. Nearly seventy years after the war he remembered a soldier named Massingale who looked up from his foxhole one morning and saw someone standing above him. It was Massingale who accidentally shot and killed Joe Breiderhoff. He also recalled a red-haired 1st Lieutenant and recent West Point graduate who joined their 24th Division, then called the Victory Division. The officer was twenty-three or twenty-four years old and had just arrived on Mindanao in the Philippines after the 24th Division had captured an air strip. He arrived one day and the next morning after the air strip had been shelled by the Japanese it was discovered that he had been killed. Coach said that when word of his death reached the men in the division (did you hear the lieutenant was killed?) it did not really startle them. Coach and the men were steeled to the reality of lives ending and he said that they did not allow themselves to "feel" the emotions they would normally have felt in peacetime.

Coach said that he was fortunate to be in a replacement division that was usually involved in a mopping up action rather than being in the first wave of attack on a military objective. He related that there was fighting and that men were killed but he said that in other areas and actions many had it worse. Coach recalled that during the war, "I didn't get a scratch" and that he felt very bad about those young men who were involved in the initial attacks and who lost their lives before they really had a chance to discover who they were.

Coach said that he was happy to have survived the war and that many who didn't just happened to be in the wrong place at the wrong time. He also expressed relief that the war ended without American soldiers storming the beaches of the main Japanese islands because he knew that he would have been in the first wave of the assault.

Coach in fatigues squatting on a Philippine road

Coach recalled helping to guard an airstrip that had been captured from the Japanese. The Japanese were determined to retake it. He noticed a new recruit to E Company who had been assigned a foxhole close to his. Coach knew that it was the recruit's first day in combat and that he appeared to be as scared as Coach had been during his first front line duty. Coach Griak befriended him and tried to calm him down by asking him where he was from. Bob Lundgren was from Minnesota and had attended Minneapolis Edison High School. Coach said that he knew someone in Duluth who had talked about a couple of very good Edison football players. Coach asked Bob Lundgren if he knew these people. Coach found out that he did and that Lundgren's father owned a jewelry store on Nicollet Avenue in Minneapolis. This simple act of compassion for a scared Minnesota soldier resulted in a lifelong friendship. As we were talking (Jan. 4, 2014), Coach said, "I think I will give Bob a call today." I have often wondered just how many people Coach contacted each day. He went on to say that he and Bob Lundgren, who he called "Red," had kept in contact for the seventy years since they met in the South Pacific.

The news from the war traveled fast. Coach's diary entry for August 9, 1945 reported that the Russians had declared war against Japan and that atomic bombs had been dropped on Japan. On August 11th, Coach's diary entry was, "While writing home I heard loud shouting in the camp area. I found out that the Japanese were willing to surrender." Two days later he reported, "The Japanese are still holding out, for what purpose no one knows." It was Tuesday August 14th, 1945 that Coach wrote "This will be a day I will never forget. The news came over the radio that Japan had surrendered and the war is over." Between this tentative surrender and the September 2, 1945 official surrender or Victory in Japan Day (V-J Day), Coach wrote that he and the other men in his camp saw the stage show "Oklahoma" and that "It sure was good to see a real American girl." On September 5th Coach wrote that censorship of letters had been lifted and "That was something to cheer about."

A week later Coach visited the American cemetery and saw Joe Breiderhoff's grave. In his clerk's duties, Coach spent much of his time figuring out how many points each man had as of V-J Day. This total would determine how soon they would be sent home. Coach wrote on September 14th, I now have 39 points. Like many others, Coach would not be going home but would be sent to Japan as occupation forces. He wrote on September 18, 1945, "More of the boys have left for the States today: Duck, Herting, Sands, Dishman, Tilley, Lasky, Thor and Almo. Sure will miss Duck and Sands. I only hope they continue to send them home this fast for the next six months - that means I may get home this coming summer."

Coach Griak became part of the American occupation forces in Japan after the atomic bombs had brought an end to the war in August of 1945. Still in uniform, he celebrated his twenty-second birthday on October 5th and six days later he climbed his first cargo net since basic training as he boarded a landing barge that would take him from Mindanao to Japan. After enduring twelve days at sea and more seasickness, he arrived in a convoy of twenty-six ships on the island of Honshu on October 22, 1945. Knowing that his time in the Army now had an end to it and beginning to plan for his future, Coach wrote on October 18th, "I'd like to go to school more than anything but if I spent four years in school I'd be an old man. I doubt that any girl will wait that long to get married. Little Roy has a lot on his mind."

Coach landed on Honshu just ten weeks after Hiroshima had been hit with a uranium bomb on August 6, 1945. Hiroshima is on Honshu. Nagasaki, on the island of Kyushu, had been hit with a plutonium bomb on August 9, 1945. Coach was then sent to division headquarters on the island of Shikoku. Shikoku was located slightly to the east of Honshu and Kyushu but on a latitude that would place it between those islands. He reported that Japan had a typical Minnesota climate. He wrote, "It was cold but nevertheless it had the Philippines beat."

On October 3, 1945, Coach wrote that he had a real hot water shower and a meal that contained fresh meat and real butter. He recalled how difficult it was for the Japanese people at the end of the war. He remembers them being just petrified with fear of the Americans. The Japanese were assigned to labor details and would do as they were told but would not say anything.

Coach was in the occupation forces for several months. He was in charge of an office of company clerks and eventually was in charge of rationed items like cigarettes, beer and flour. He laughingly said, "I probably could have become a millionaire." As I listened, I thought to myself that the honesty and trust that were hallmarks of Coach's character were already there in 1945 and that he was placed in this position of responsibility because it was known that he could be trusted to do his job without thoughts of advancing himself financially. From a November 3rd diary entry, I learned that the Japanese flag that was framed and hung in the living room of Coach's Plymouth home, he had acquired in a trade for five cigarettes.

Coach said that in Japan everything was in a state of flux with people coming and going all the time. It was a very busy time but that everyone wanted to get home as soon as possible. He remembers a big feast for the servicemen at Thanksgiving in 1945. There was turkey, dressing, cranberries and all of the fixings. However, one part of the meal that was not eaten was the pumpkin pie. Coach explained that with all the servicemen in Japan the facilities were rather primitive. The toilet facilities involved soldiers going up steps to a walkway and then using gravity to fill big barrels placed at ground level. The local farmers used the contents of these barrels to fertilize their pumpkin patch. Coach said that the pumpkin pie both looked like and tasted like the contents of the barrels, although he used more colorful language in his description. This reminded me of a story I once read about Harry Truman, who was President of the United States at the end of World War Two. President Truman had described one politician's efforts as, "A pile of manure." Bess Truman had been chastised by a group who felt that her husband's language was too coarse for a man in his position. Bess Truman replied, "It's taken me twenty-five years to get Harry to use the word manure!" The day after the Thanksgiving feast, Coach received a letter from his mother informing him

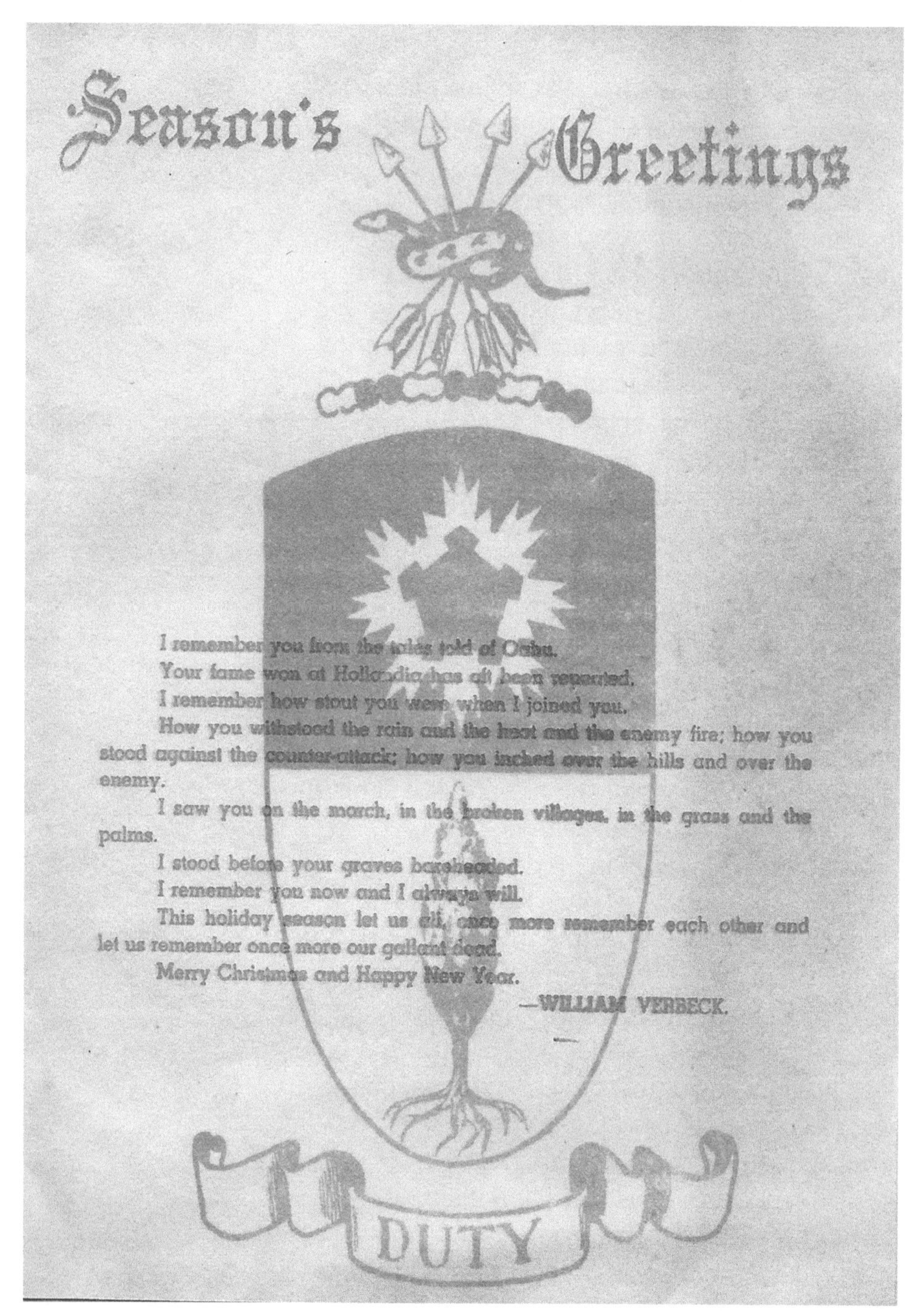

that her brother's family had been tortured in Europe. As the Christmas of 1945 approached, Coach prepared travel papers for those with fifty-five points and pondered, "I wonder when they will get to forty points."

One of the men being sent home at this time was his good friend Joe Payne. On the last day of 1945, Coach wrote, "Everyone seems to be getting out of the Army but yours truly." Like Coach, those who remained in the service received a Christmas card from their Colonel, William J. Verbeck. It contained the following words:

I remember you from the tales told of Oahu.
Your fame won at Hollandia has oft been repeated.
I remember how stout you were when I joined you.
How you withstood the rain and the heat and the enemy fire; how you stood against the counter-attack; how you inched over the hills and over the enemy.
I saw you on the march, in the broken villages, in the grass and the palms.
I stood before your graves bareheaded.
I remember you now and I always will.
This holiday season let us all once more remember each other and let us remember once more our gallant dead.
Merry Christmas and Happy New Year.

Colonel William J. Verbeck

Other Christmases

Was it Oahu or Australia? Was it Leyte or Mindoro—Colubian, Barugo, Jaro, Tunga, Tuk-Tuk, Carigara, San Jose, Calipan? Strange names, and names that burn in the brain leaving an unhealed scar dark with bitter memory, but Christmas names—all of them.

Christmas is a day of joyful reverence. God willing, you will spend it again this year within the circle of those whom you love most. Certainly there is no substitute for this. It is what you prayed for during those weary days of mud and sweat and death.

Can you deny, however, that the memories of other Christmases arise to plague you with thoughts of men, fine men and comrades-in-arms, living and dead, who are absent from your sacred family circle? With them you shared hopes and fears, victories and reverses. Even your family cannot completely fill this void.

You marched with one of the elite Divisions of the War. Although your part may seem obscure, you were in the company of giants like Moon, Mower, and Diamond. Nothing can banish the satisfaction of deeds well-done and a task accomplished. Although you cannot gather around you the men of other Christmases, cherish their memories so that they will be silent guests around this year's Christmas fireside.

How apt are the words that Shakespeare puts into the mouth of the English King, Henry V, on the eve of Agincourt fought on St. Crispin's Feast Day in 1415:

"We few, we happy few, we band of brothers;
For he to-day that sheds his blood with me
Shall be my brother; be he ne'er so vile,
This day shall gentle his condition:
And gentlemen now in England now a-bed
Shall think themselves accursed they were not here,
And hold their manhoods cheap whiles any speaks
That fought with us upon Saint Cripspin's Day."

My regards,

William J. Verbeck
Colonel, Infantry

Coach said that some men lost their common sense and decency while in occupied Japan. There was a lot of drinking and carousing. He had seen this earlier in the Philippines where some of the soldiers and some of the civilians were making a drink called "tuba" out of fermented coconut milk. Coach said that some of the soldiers were so drunk that they could not even crawl out of their tents. He could not understand people who exercised no control. He felt that the Army did not do a good job of educating the GI's about how to handle the end of the war and their reentry to civilian life. On Christmas Eve of 1945 Coach was promoted to Sergeant. He said that it was in the works for him to be promoted to Sergeant Major but that, before the promotion came through, he was discharged from the service.

On Friday January 11, 1946 Coach wrote, "Found out today that as head of Mom's household I get credit for Steve and Dolly. I now have sixty-four points, well over the quota of fifty. I will soon be going home. I am supposed to board a train Tuesday morning. I could leave tomorrow (Saturday) but the lieutenant wants me to help train my understudy, Chappy." Bob "Red" Lundgren, one of Coach's wartime buddies, said at the luncheon following Coach's funeral on July 22, 2015, that he was the one who had informed Coach of the new Army regulation that a soldier could get twenty-five points toward discharge if he was the head of his mother's household.

Unfortunately for Coach, he was sick and his trip home was delayed. He was sent to the hospital instead of home. His temperature reached one hundred-four degrees and he was thought to have either yellow jaundice or malaria.

He was stationed in Osaka on the island of Honshu when he was discharged. On January 16th after arguing with a doctor for fifteen minutes he was given the consent to go home. The next day he quickly said goodbye to those he knew, changed his yen into American dollars, gave his understudy $10 to send his sea-bag home, and boarded a train for Nagoya.

Like so many servicemen, Coach had hoped to be "home alive in '45." This timetable had not been realized but he was home early in 1946. He left Honshu on January 20th in 1946 on board the USS Jean Lafitte and sailed back to San Francisco from the Japanese city of Nagoya. That morning he wrote, "Oh happy day. I'm so thankful I made the boat without getting sick. I was afraid I wouldn't." Being at sea again meant more seasickness. Coach wasn't sure if it was yellow jaundice, malaria or just being seasick but he just lay in his bed afraid to move for the first few days of his voyage home. On January 24th he wrote, "Hereafter, I won't even step into a rowboat."

Golden Gate Bridge

Two days later the ship crossed the International Date Line and Coach said that he celebrated two January 26ths. He recalled that going in the other direction he was partially cheated out of his twenty-first birthday on October 5, 1944. As he began to feel better Coach spent most of his time lying awake and thinking of home. The last entry in the diary he had kept throughout his time in the service was dated Friday, February 1, 1946. He wrote that day, "Should be in Frisco sometime Sunday." Coach said that "Sailing under the Golden Gate Bridge and returning to the United States was like entering paradise."

Army Welcome Home - San Francisco Port of Embarkation Brochure

He said that he would never forget that he landed at pier thirty-one in San Francisco Bay and that being back in the United States was a tremendous feeling. He arrived in the United States on February 3, 1946. "The only thing that kept me going was that I'd eventually get to see my family, and particularly my mother."

Coach returned to the U.S. still suffering from bouts of malaria and the effects of yellow jaundice. He was on a 75% disability for several months after being discharged from the service. The malaria sapped his strength and produced very high fevers. He was treated with quinine. During the war the malaria was treated with quinine which Coach remembered came in a white pill and halazone which came in a yellow pill. Coach recalled that nearly everyone in the South Pacific had problems with malaria, yellow jaundice, jungle rot and trench foot.

The jungle rot and trench foot were treated with sunshine when it was available and clean, dry socks when they were available. Both of these necessities were usually in short supply. He returned to Duluth and was able to start college at Duluth State Teacher's College (UMD) under the Serviceman's Readjustment Act (GI Bill). Coach was very thankful for the GI Bill because he knew that his family did not have the money to send him to college. The United States soldiers who had served as "doughboys" in the WW I era, like Coach's father (Milan), had been promised a bonus at the end of the war but the payment of that bonus was delayed and led to several protests during the Depression in the early 1930s from the "Bonus Army." Thousands of veterans marched, or rode the rails, to protest in Washington. They camped at Anacostia Flats, a short distance from the White House. Many had their families with them. The camp was eventually burned and Bonus Army driven out of the nation's capital by soldiers active under the command of Douglas MacArthur, Dwight D. Eisenhower and George S. Patton. Several people lost their lives. Late in 1943, President Franklin Roosevelt (FDR), perhaps with the memory of the Bonus Army in mind and certainly with the prompting of his wife, Eleanor, asked Congress to pass the GI Bill. It was announced to the American public on June 22, 1944 after passing the Senate by a vote of 50-0 and the House of Representatives by a vote of 387-0. FDR's Vice President, Harry Truman, became President in April of 1945 upon the death of Roosevelt. He had been a doughboy in WW I and he also wanted to make sure that the veterans of WW II were treated better. The GI Bill allowed many veterans, including Coach and both my father and father-in-law to continue their education after their service in the war. According to historian, Doris Kearns Goodwin, in her book *No Ordinary Time*, "In the late forties, veterans would constitute almost fifty percent of the male students in all institutions of higher learning."

Coach repeated his earlier statement that he didn't feel there were any heroes in war. Most soldiers did what they were supposed to do in the setting of wartime and sometimes they did heroic things just by reacting without thinking the deed through beforehand. Mostly he feels that he was one of a large group of young men who were just trying to make it to the next minute and the next day. "We were just trying to survive." He felt that most of the men with whom he served would rather have been someplace else but were willing to do what their government asked. World War II for Coach Griak covered much of the 3-year span from his high school graduation in 1942 to his discharge from the service early in 1946 after the end of the war. Coach used the GI Bill to attend first UMD and then the University of Minnesota Twin Cities. He recalled the contrast between the peach faced freshmen and men like himself who were only a few years older but seemingly much older because they had been aged by their experiences in the war. When Coach told me about his Army diary that he wrote in whenever he had the chance to document his experiences and reflections he said that he still had the diary but that he had not read it. He said that someday he might get a magnifying glass and try to read what he had written in the jungles of the South Pacific when he was a very young man. I don't think that Coach ever did read his wartime diary. Other than recalling his service to our country for this book, Coach did not dwell on the past. Though proud of his service to our country and proud of his fellow soldiers, Coach preferred to live in the present and to look to the future. While trying to respect the privacy of his wartime thoughts I told Coach that firsthand accounts like his are priceless and should be passed on to the next generations. He said that he would give his diary to his sons, Seth and Jason.

In recent years I had the privilege of spending a great deal of time with Coach Griak. From listening to his account of the war, hearing him talk about his war buddies, knowing that he had gone to visit the families or the graves of people with whom he served, I know that the war has never been far from his mind. On September 26th 2013, those who he coached and worked with honored him for his fifty years of service at the University of Minnesota. It was wonderful to honor him for such long service. However, two days later at the Griak Invitational Cross Country Meet, I witnessed Coach giving honor to an organization he has belonged to even longer than he has been affiliated with the University of Minnesota. It was early in the day that Saturday as the meet was about to start with the Division III college races.

Coach and Don Timm in golf cart

My high school team would compete later that day and the bus carrying my runners would not leave the school until 12:30 so I had driven to the University Golf Course to watch some of my former runners compete in the college and university races. I had the privilege of being asked by Coach Griak to ride with him in his golf cart. To ride with Coach was an honor but a frightening experience; he knew that to get from point A to point B in the fastest time meant that the brakes on the cart were seldom, if ever, applied.

As we were out on the course it began to rain. We were on that part of the course which is parallel to Cleveland Avenue when we heard the public address announcer say that they would now play the national anthem. Although I was the only witness to this, Coach Griak stopped the cart. With effort he got out of the cart. He took off his hat and stood in the rain with his hand over his heart until the anthem had ended. As we got back into the cart to return to the starting line in time to catch the gun for the first race of the day I realized that I had just seen a quiet demonstration that although Coach has been at the University for fifty years he has been a patriot even longer.

On the Friday before Memorial Day in 2014 Coach called me and talked for about twenty minutes. This alone was very unusual as Coach's calls, through frequent, were almost invariably short in duration. I know that his calls, sometimes only a hello and how are you doing, were made to a long list of his acquaintances each day.

No matter how many people Coach called he had a way of making each person feel like they were the focal point of his day. On that day in late May of 2014 Coach wanted to talk at length about how our country could be better. Memorial Day was initially known as Decoration Day and was at first a commemoration of those soldiers who had given their lives in the Civil War. After WW I, the red poppy became a symbol honoring our nation's fallen soldiers. May 26, 2014 was Coach Griak's

Coach in uniform – squatting

90th Memorial Day. He said that he wanted to talk about this anniversary.

Coach said that on Memorial Day he would be reflecting about our country and about the men with whom he had served during WW II. He said that he would be thinking about his friends, those who returned from the war, those who did not, and those who returned but have since passed away. He was also deeply affected by a later war (or police action) in Vietnam that claimed the lives of Army Staff Sergeant Mike Elwell and Marine Captain Bart Uplinger who were both Gopher runners killed in February of 1968 during the Tet Offensive. The athletic field in Fairfax, Minnesota is named in honor of Mike Elwell who was killed near Hue when he was only 23. Bart Uplinger was killed in a helicopter accident in Thua Thien Province at the age of 25. Both are listed on the Vietnam Veteran's Memorial Wall in Washington. Bart was a sprinter on Coach Griak's first Minnesota track team.

The war also severely wounded John Valentine. Mike Elwell and John were integral members of his 1964 Gopher Big Ten Championship cross country team. Coach said that many people today, especially the young, have little knowledge of the sacrifices made by the people of his generation. To have lived through the Great Depression and then to have been called into the service of the United States Army as a young man during World War II were forces that had shaped his life. Tom Brokaw correctly entitled his book about

Coach in uniform – seated

those who served in World War II *The Greatest Generation*. Coach said that he would favor a universal draft of all citizens of the United States aged eighteen to twenty-six. He said this would include women as well as men and those with physical handicaps as well as those in perfect physical condition. The service would range from two to six years. Coach felt that everyone should render service to their country so that they would appreciate it more. He said that for some the service might be at a desk job or other noncombatant duty but that all should serve.

Coach expressed that, although he would not like to see the United States endure another depression or war that those two events gave him a greater love for his country and appreciation for what it meant to live in the United States. To those who served in the war, like Coach Griak, the end of the war and the return to civilian life, home, family, friends and work was a long sought-after privilege.

Snotty-Nose Tough

A Collection of Roy Griak Tributes

Larry Berkner

Coach Griak: *A tough, tough kid. He was from Ely, Minnesota. Larry was very devoted to whatever he did. Larry could run in intense pain and not give up. Larry was an excellent Gopher steeplechaser.*

In April 1980 the track team was competing at a meet in windy Wichita, Kansas. I was running the 5000 meters, not my usual event. Halfway through the race I had fallen 20 yards behind the lead pack. When I passed Coach Griak, he said in a gruff and stern voice, "Larry, get back up with those others!" Within a half lap I had caught up with the leaders, mostly out of fear of displeasing Coach. I won that race. I would not have won it without Coach's timely words. Everyone who spent time around Coach knows that he deeply loves and enjoys people. But we respect him just as much for not being a softy. He knew when to put his arm around someone, and when to put his foot in their backside. That balance helped Coach bring the best out of many athletes.

Larry Berkner
Gopher CC, T&F, 1975-80

Dave Casale

Coach Griak: *A Coon Rapids athlete who ran cross country and track at Minnesota. Dave is a true friend of the program: an athlete who never forgets.*

I had the privilege of being coached by Coach Griak in cross country and track from the fall of 1982 through the spring of 1987. Being around Coach during those years, you knew you were around someone special. It seemed everything he did or said was to motivate, teach, or show you the way it ought to be done. He always was meticulous, whether running a track meet, having an itinerary for an away meet, or in how we did our calisthenics in the hallway after a long run.

One thing I learned from being around Coach, or that he ingrained into me is that being tough is a quality more important than anything. All of his athletes were told about being "snotty-nosed tough." It seemed no matter how fast I ran a race, he would say "my Grandma in slippery shoes could run faster." Even the Gatorade type drink Coach provided after practice made you tough because it was Gator Urine, not Gatorade.

During a cross country workout, Coach, during one of his countless motivational speeches, described the toughness of one of my teammates. I still think about this often. This runner didn't have the most efficient stride, or a big kick. Coach said that if there was ever a race where you ran uphill for 10 miles, were then hit on the head with a 2x4 40 times, and then ran uphill another 10 miles, he'd win the race every time, but considering the talent on the team, he had no business making our top 7. Now, as a high school track coach myself, I tell that story to my team usually once each season. I save it for a time when the runners need to refocus on being tough. A few years back I had a runner who gave it all he had, but wasn't the most gifted athlete. For graduation, I gave him a 2x4 with the word "perseverance" written on it. That for me was something I passed on from Coach to one of my runners. That young man earned that piece of wood.

Looking back at the time I ran on Coach's team, I don't think I realized then that he was in his mid-60's, a time when many are considering retiring. He led by example, putting in long hours, was always there, and had the energy of someone much younger. Even now (written in 2013) as Coach is in his late 80's, he is still contributing to the track and cross country programs and works out every day.

Coach has shown us all, no matter your level of success as an athlete, you gotta be snotty-nosed tough!

Thanks Coach!

Dave Casale
U of M athlete 1982-87

Dave Casale

Dave Chatelaine

Coach Griak: Dave is an outstanding coach at Owatonna High School. He has great enthusiasm for what he does. He ran CC and track at Minnesota.

"Snotty nose tough." This is one quote that will stay in my mind for the rest of my life. I heard this message many times during my four years on the Cross Country and Track teams (1976-80) at the University of Minnesota. Coach Griak used messages, stories, and sayings similar to this to keep us motivated to do our best in practices and competitions. These messages also helped us get through those tough courses at the U of M and the challenges we faced in our daily lives.

I began my running career in 8th grade and worked hard to improve my abilities as a distance runner. By the time I was a junior I was experiencing great success. It was exciting to receive letters in the mail from various colleges and universities recruiting me to be a part of their Cross Country and Track programs. Growing up in the Twin Cities and being close to the University of Minnesota, I became familiar with the campus and the athletic programs. I thought it would be great if I could have the opportunity to compete on a Minnesota Golden Gopher team. The day came when I received a letter in the mail from Coach Griak with a golden M embossed on the envelope. Boy, was I excited! Later on Coach Griak took me out to lunch and explained the program to me. I decided to attend the University of Minnesota and be on the Cross Country and Track teams. It was one of the toughest things I have ever done, competing at the NCAA division I level.

During my four-year-career, I was able to earn a few letters but also had some struggles with sickness and injuries along the way. Coach Griak was always there to provide encouragement. He taught us the value of hard work and discipline and how to treat others with respect. I remember my first road trip with the Cross Country team to Des Moines for a meet against Drake. When we arrived at the hotel in Des Moines, the coach from Drake was there to greet us. He and Coach Griak got together later that evening for some socializing. I was impressed to see this camaraderie with the opposing coach. Later I learned that Coach Griak was a friend with many other coaches and I try to follow this example in my own coaching today.

Some other memories I have about Coach Griak are that he tried to keep in good physical condition. He wasn't able to run with us but he liked to do sit-ups with us. I think he enjoyed watching us suffer from mosquito bites when we did our sit-ups at the end of those pre-season workouts down at the lakes. He would always tell us the mosquitoes we were swatting were nothing compared to what he dealt with during his military days in the Philippines. I remember a picture of him in the Minneapolis Tribune running stadium stairs when he was 80.

Four years of college goes fast. I could write a book about all of the experiences and memories I have from that time. Some of the most important memories I have are of how certain adults and fellow students prepared me for the future. During that time, we mature into young adults who are ready to go into the world and try to make an impact through the use of our gifts and talents. Coach Griak was one of those people who along with our professors, parents, and other adults helped us prepare for our future. Coach Griak along with my high school coach influenced me to choose my profession as a teacher and coach. They both were and are great role models for me. I have been teaching and coaching junior high and high school students for over 30 years. I usually see Coach Griak at a couple of meets during the year. He always takes time to talk to me and ask about my family. He has even telephoned me the night before my Cross Country teams have competed in the state meet to wish them good luck. The kids on my team and I really appreciate this.

Coach Griak is definitely a legend and has had a profound impact on the sports of Cross Country and Track and Field in the state of Minnesota and also the USA. He has been and still is a mentor and role model to many and has helped develop the character of many young men throughout his career. It is always a pleasure to visit with former "M" men who are fellow coaches and know we all have the common bond of a University of Minnesota Cross Country and Track experience. I thank Coach Griak for all of the opportunities and coaching he provided me during my time at the University of Minnesota. I was blessed to have had a great coach and a Minnesota CC and Track experience.

Dave Chatelaine, 1980
1979 Cross Country co-captain
(1976-1980 U of M runner)

Chuck Grover

Coach Griak: Chuck played basketball for me at St. Louis Park. He was a tall, skinny kid, a real hustler and a good worker. Chuck became a prominent police official.

Coach Griak,

I graduated from St. Louis Park in 1963. We have talked at several class reunions and also this year when I participated in the basketball game that you attended for the 1962 class reunion. You certainly are not aware of my complete story when it comes to athletics, but you had a profound influence on my success both in athletics and in my personal life. You taught me to believe in my abilities.

As a young boy, I lived in a large neighborhood where we played basketball all the time as many boys had a goal to play for St. Louis Park due to the legacy of the teams in the 1950's. Most of my friends never had their dreams come true, but two who you will recognize did – Whitey Fundingsland and Jerry Orback. Unfortunately for me, my junior high years were filled with several serious health problems, and I never was able to go out for the seventh and eighth grade teams. When I was finally healthy enough, I did try out and made the Central Junior High ninth grade team, but never played a second of any game.

When my tenth grade year came around, I remember questioning myself as to whether I should even try out. The "B" squad would consist of players from two junior high teams with my chances of making such a team very slim. I did try out; however, and for some reason you saw something in my limited abilities, and I made the team. I even was given the opportunity to play a fair share of minutes on an excellent team. You taught us the fundamentals of basketball that year better than at any level that I would play in. You provided me with the incentive to believe that I could play basketball at Park, my childhood dream, if I was willing to put out 110% effort.

In eleventh grade, I certainly did not have the skills to make what was going to be a State High School Championship team, but I did start on a Lake Conference championship "B" squad team, and you provided me the opportunity to play and to improve my skills while many of my classmates on the varsity did not have that opportunity. To make a very long story short, I made the "A" squad in 1963, played in the game that beat undefeated Robbinsdale, and I pretty much started the rest of the year. I went on to play college ball at St. Olaf and in my senior year was co-captain, all conference and led the league in scoring. After graduating, I spent three years teaching and coaching basketball and baseball in high school.

Finally, I remember the St. Louis Park Echo – May 1963 paper, because I still have it, that said – "How Do You Replace An Inspiration." As you well know, coaching is not all about athletics, it is also about teaching kids personal traits that will inspire them in their future careers. The mental toughness that you taught me was a lesson well served in my chosen career in law enforcement, the last sixteen years as Chief of Police in the suburbs of Kansas City. I cannot thank you enough for all that you have given me as my success was built upon a foundation that you helped provide.

Chuck Grover (St. Louis Park basketball 1962-1963)

Chris Harder

Coach Griak: Chris is a young man who got everything out of his ability. He was an excellent distance runner. Chris is a student of the sport who, as a coach is as sharp and intelligent as there is in the state. Chris Harder knows every track and field and basketball athlete in the state of Minnesota.

High School

Coach Griak separated himself in the recruiting process almost instantly by demonstrating how much he cared about me as a person. Some days he would call and just ask how my folks were and how basketball was going. That was it. My senior year of track didn't go as planned. My times weren't as fast as my junior year. My places were not as good as my junior year. To make it worse, I really wanted to go to the University of Minnesota, but was embarrassed I wasn't running as well. After placing 5th in the state the previous spring and qualifying in three events, I was pretty concerned I wouldn't even qualify. The night before the Region 3200, Coach Griak called. The conversation was short, but it has stuck with me my whole life. He said, "Chris, I don't care if you run five minutes for the mile in the Regional, I still want you to run for the University of Minnesota." Those calming and confident words had a profound effect on me. Things did go better the next two weeks.

College

The lessons learned in college go a long way in my coaching profession. One that sticks out for me was my senior year in cross country. At the early season

Purdue Invitational, I ended up in the ambulance at the course. After we got back to Minneapolis, it was recommended that I take a week off, something I didn't want to do but Coach insisted. Even though I competed on the varsity for three seasons, I was not distinguished enough to think that my position in the line-up was locked. Coach dispatched graduate assistant Chris Kanes to work out with me on the hard days as I attempted to regain my perceived lost fitness. Not only was it my last season, but we were hosting the Big 10 meet. I didn't run another race during the regular season, but I was ready to run the week before the conference meet to make the team. Coach pulled me aside and said, "You aren't going to Iowa State this weekend. We want you in the line-up at the Big 10's. You don't have to prove anything to me, I know you are ready." That lesson stuck with me through my high school coaching career. If your eyes tell you that your athlete is ready, show the confidence in him. Your eyes are proof enough.

Coaching

The usual suspects attended the annual MSHSCA clinic held at a local hotel, with some outstanding presentations by local and national coaches. Coach Griak attended, mostly to see old friends than anything else. After one session in particular, where the clinician went into great detail about the cell, Coach surmised for the rest of us what was most important in coaching. "Max V02 this, Lactate Threshold that, if the athlete doesn't' know you care about them, they don't care what you know."

Family

Coach gave my son William (5 at the time) a small pair of spikes. The shoes were still too large for Will, but he was bound and determined to wear them for Halloween at school (he went as a cross country runner). Coach is so respected in our family that Will didn't care that he slipped all over the place. "I got these from Coach Griak," he would say with a smile a mile wide.

Recent

On a summer run, I mentioned to a few of our team members that we could use a cross country shed at Rosemount and it would make a good Eagle Scout project. Ryan Codon heard those words, but he was already an Eagle Scout. He decided that having the Eagle Award didn't prevent him from doing another worthy project. Ryan contacted Coach Griak for some advice. Every year, our team competes in the Roy Griak Invitational at Les Bolstad Golf Course. Only the top 10 team members can compete and we wear our green uniforms for the occasion. Each year I talk about Coach Griak, tell them stories about being "snotty nose tough," and his "grandma in slippery tennis shoes." Ryan figured Coach Griak could provide some suggestions about the shed. Coach Griak did respond enthusiastically. His advice to personalize the shed hit home for Ryan. He told Ryan the shed should be more than just to house equipment and what not, the shed needed to reflect the team and the values of the team. The shed project fundraising came in well above projections.

Chris Harder
CC 1986-1990
T & F 1988-1991

Steve Hoag

Coach Griak: Steve was from Anoka High School and later was a tremendous Gopher distance runner. He was a little dynamo; an outstanding, tough, resilient runner. He remains a good friend.

I always enjoyed seeing Coach Griak in the field house during indoor season. The whole team was confined to a smaller area, and he would visit with each group. He was always in a very good mood… except one day: We were running a one-mile time trial, and of course the baseball players were batting balls against the net, as usual. One player especially took some joy in trying to hit the ball hard into the net just when runners were coming by. When the

Coach's 50th Year at Minnesota Celebration in 2013: (L-R) Tom Heinonen, Norris Peterson, Steve Hoag and Garret Tomczak

mile time trial guys were about 5 meters from this guy, he whacked a line drive right into the net. The net came about 2-3 feet into the first lane and hit the runner leading the mile. It put a big bruise on his shoulder, and he had to drop out. He was in a lot of pain, but the rest of the guys continued. Coach saw all of this happen and raced into the baseball area inside the netting. He picked the guy up about a foot off the ground and just tore into him. I had never seen Coach so mad, and the baseball player was in abject fear for his life, I think. There was dead silence for what seemed like five minutes. We had no more problems with the baseball team the rest of the season!

I knew that I wanted to be a Gopher when I heard that they had won the 1964 Big Ten Cross Country title. I was still at Anoka High School at the time. I fondly remember summer practices at Lake Calhoun. I remember the kool-aid Coach would make for us after practice. {by the time I ran, Coach called it "swamp juice" - either Coach really served Steve Hoag's group kool-aid or he had changed the recipe by the time I arrived.}

Thanks Coach for making me a Big Ten Champion and an All-American at 10,000-meters.

Steve Hoag (U of M runner - 1965-1967)

{Sadly, Steve passed away on September 15, 2017 at the age of 70.}

Chris and Suzanne Morris

Coach Griak: Although they live in Australia, they remain very loyal to Minnesota. Chris was a 440-yard runner for me at St. Louis Park and also at Minnesota.

Roy really did have a talent. It is hard to piece together in words just what that was. He would say something simple like "hard work" or "stay focused" or "practice hard," but it is far more complex, otherwise there would have been thousands of Griaks around. Lombardi had it; that intuitive knowledge of when to push, pull, scream, be kind, become granddad, etc. People who have it often do not know because it just seems so obvious to them.

I have managed to keep in touch with him every year since 1962 at St. Louis Park. My wife and I have lived in Australia (Melbourne) since 1967 but fond memories are as vivid here of the man as they are in Minnesota. Below are a few words you can add with the others. I hope they will be as memorable as the man.

Roy was a champion long before he created champions around him. He became an icon back in 1962 without ever knowing it. He has long been a quality man but also a man of many qualities… and it is an honor to call him an old friend.

The coach and the man are inseparable; intensely determined but with a smile that could be felt across a crowded room. There should be a bronze statue made of him showing the smile and the optimism that can shine on others for years to come.

Roy's job at the U of M was cemented while at St. Louis Park High, a school never regarded highly in sports. In 1962, St. Louis Park won Minnesota State Championships in track and field, cross country and basketball in one year. The unique ability of Roy Griak was the magic ingredient. It never happened before and will never happen again. I was on the track team back then and watched this amazing man make very average kids capable of achieving something far greater than their natural ability. In historical terms, he is up there with the great coaches, great teachers and the greatest motivators. Cheers.

Chris Morris
Melbourne, Australia
St. Louis Park track athlete 1962

Dave Wegner

Coach Griak: David was from Duluth and had run for John Swain. Running for Duluth Central, he was second to St. Louis Park's John Valentine in the state mile in 1963. Four of the top five finishers in that race were members of the Gopher's Big Ten Championship CC team in 1964 as Tom Heinonen of Robbinsdale and Bob Weigel of Minneapolis Southwest were fourth and fifth. David was second in the Big Ten Outdoor 2 Mile in 1965 when the Gophers took the top three places (Norris Peterson, David and Tom Heinonen). David is a great friend and fan of the program.

I was part of Coach's original recruiting class of 1963 joining him from Duluth. I never trained so hard before but in time it paid off because he knew how to get the most out of his boys. I remember being so tired because of training that I overslept or was often late getting to practices. At one point he presented me with a wind up alarm clock he brought from home to assist my training regimen. That solved my problem, mostly. My point here is if something was in the way, Coach cared, took interest and did what he could to help you get beyond it.

He was affectionately known as "Uncle Roy" during my tenure with him. I think Stan Gaffin came up with the name. Also, I recall Coach telling me in one of my frequent visits to his office, "Wegner, you have more ability in one leg than I have in two. Now do something with it." I was often disappointed in myself, but never with the Coach. And lastly, my girlfriend from Duluth was visiting during CC season one time and he let her ride on the team bus to Lake Nokomis so she could be a part of our team race scene there. She thought that was cool.

In time, we won the Big Ten CC championship in 1964 and a few individual races over the next few years, but the championship was probably the highlight for me. Coincidentally, if I recall correctly on this his 50th coaching anniversary, the last time that was done by the U CC team was back in 1914, representing another 50-year milestone event in this man's career as well. {It had indeed been 50 years between the Gopher's CC titles of 1914 and 1964 but the Gophers did win their most recent Big Ten title in 1969}{Coach had Big Ten CC Championship rings from 1964 and 1969 Dave but the one he wore was the one from your 1964 team!}

Once he was your friend, Coach was always your friend. For many years after I left the U to finish my studies at UMD and graduate school at Wisconsin State, Coach would often visit Duluth to see his mother (Coach grew up in Morgan Park, a suburb of Duluth) to put screens/storm windows on her house and things like that. As though he didn't have enough to do during these visits, he would often drop in out of the blue and visit with my folks. I could tell they sure appreciated that as they were telling me about it.

I met up with the Coach 2 years ago in Duluth at a banquet in his honor during one of my frequent return visits there. I was delighted when asked to join him at his table. It was a pleasure to see and talk with him again. I would like to send him my best. Truly a great man and it is my wish that this letter finds him healthy and happy as well.

Sincerely,
David Wegner, U of M athlete, member of the 1964 Big 10 champion CC team

Coach Griak's Schooling and Introduction to Athletics

Don Timm

Roy Griak probably saw more cross country and track and field meets than anyone on the planet; however, the first races he recalled were races against his mother. If he was out playing and his mother came to look for him he would say, "I'll race you home Mom." She would always win. She was a very good athlete. He also ran six to seven blocks home from Stowe Junior High School for lunch each day and then ran back to school after eating with his mother. Coach said that the meal was often vegetable soup which he admitted he hated. He said that he really had to hustle to get home and back to school so that he was not late for class. Coach would later say that his mother was his mentor and that she is the one who taught him his strong work ethic and an attitude of hanging in there when things were difficult. In addition to this persistence, she also instilled in Coach a passion and enthusiasm for whatever task he encountered and an appreciation for what he had rather than jealousy for those things he did not have.

Since there was no organized track at Coach's junior high school, his races home from school to have lunch with his mother became his opportunity to develop his conditioning for running. Coach also remembers that he and his friend, Fred Bell, would always compete. "I'll race you to the next telephone pole, or I'll race you to the corner." When he recalled his childhood friend, Coach's memory was "jogged" and he said, "When I returned home from the war I bought a new Oldsmobile. I was very protective of it and to make sure it wasn't dented, I parked it in the middle of the baseball diamond. Somehow, Fred Bell managed to hit my car and dent the fender." Coach also remembered playing tackle football with the boys in his neighborhood. They played in a farmer's potato field after the potatoes had been harvested. Coach said that there was one boy, Ray Deblack, who was older, bigger, and although rather chunky, a very good athlete. Coach remembered frequently grabbing Deblack around the ankles and then being dragged the length of the potato field because he could not bring him down. Coach also remembered that Ray Deblack's father owned the dry goods store in Gary - New Duluth. The store sold mainly clothing and men's furnishings but Coach recalled that the store was also where his family would go to redeem coupons for shoes provided for those families on local relief. Coach Griak said that Mr. Deblack would take their coupon and then give them new shoes but that they were always last year's models or those he had difficulty selling to his regular customers. The orange coats that Coach and his brother and sisters wore also easily identified them as recipients of welfare. It is likely that the compassion Coach showed for others, and especially those who were in need, came from his early understanding of what it was like to be poor. His ethic of appreciating and never wasting what he had filtered down to his athletes at the University. When we were given running shoes, usually once a year, it was always with the reminder, "these are not for campus wear."

Dolly, Mildred, Steve, Coach and Kay in the mid-1930s

The hills of Duluth were the playground for the kids of Gary - New Duluth. Coach and his brother, Steve, who was four years younger, would roam the area picking berries and having a great time.

He related this to me on October 26, 2014, just days after Steve had passed away. Coach said that he missed his brother a great deal and that he continued to exercise each day for 20 minutes partly because he knew that Steve would have loved to enjoy life and health longer.

Coach and Steve as young men

He related how Steve always loved to draw and that he had become a renowned artist and creator of advertising commercials. Coach said that once he moved to the Twin Cities he, Steve and Gopher athlete, Don Prielipp had lived together for several years. Steve had a job with Consolidated Freight working from 4 -12 each day while attending the Walker Art School. Steve was also a veteran. He had been drafted into the army and had served in Korea. When talking to Coach Griak, I became accustomed to my questions, whether they were about Coach's athletic career, service to our country, his early life or his coaching, leading to side stories about the names or events he recalled. Coach's mind was a rich warehouse of over 91 years of memories and the stories were always fascinating but difficult to be restricted to just one area of his life. I am relating them as they came to Coach's mind.

When he was a young boy, one of the big sports attractions in Coach's hometown of Gary-New Duluth, about ten miles west of downtown Duluth, was town baseball. On Sunday afternoons, most of the population of Gary attended the games of the Gary AC (Gary Athletic Club). Even Coach's mother, who knew nothing about baseball, would go to the games. The fans were dressed in their best clothes. The competition would usually be against local communities like Sturgeon Lake, South Superior, Cloquet or Moose Lake, but Coach recalled watching the traveling team known as The House of David play a game against the Gary AC. He remembered the House of David players because they all had long beards. He also recalled that most of the teams dressed in grey flannel uniforms but that the Cloquet team, sponsored by Phillips 66, showed up in black uniforms with orange lettering. He thought they looked really strange. The baseball games were the big event of the week for everyone in town and after the games the players would pass a hat and collect dimes and quarters from their fans. Coach said that a foul ball hit into the stands could be returned for a nickel. The balls were in short supply and were precious. Concerning the neighborhood games he played, he remembered that he and his buddies would never throw away a baseball that was losing its cover. Instead they would wax a piece of string and resew the cover onto the ball. Growing up in the 1930s during the Great Depression, athletic supplies for youngsters were not readily available and were often glued, nailed, screwed or taped together to make do. Coach said that they used baseball bats that were held together with tape or screws and hockey pucks that were sometimes made out of wood. Coach observed that in recent years he saw so many ball fields and playground areas that were underused by youngsters. "Kids don't play as much today as we did when I was a boy. Today kids don't build things, they just buy them. They spend too much time in front of the TV or with their computers and electronic gadgets and too little time in physical activity." Unless there is an organized practice or game, fields are often empty during much of the day. He said that he and his buddies would have climbed the fences to get into such fields to play. Coach also lamented that, in his mind, physical education today has been deemphasized in the schools.. Many of today's youth are overweight or out of shape and yet they receive little or no physical training in the schools and little encouragement to be physically fit. Coach felt that our schools should make physical education a regular subject in the curriculum for the youth instead of waiting until the kids are so out of shape that they can't get out of a chair. He also believed that instead of schools charging parents to have their children participate in sports, the sports and activities should be free. Coach was in favor of anything that would increase exercise and participation for every boy or girl no matter how great their level of talent. He said that it was unfortunate that in the big high schools today only a small number of the students have the opportunity to be a member of the school's teams and to learn the lessons that come from competition and working hard to achieve goals.

As a youth, Roy Griak developed a deep interest in baseball. Living in northern Minnesota in the 1930s meant that major league baseball was geographically distant. The closest major league teams were the Cubs and White Sox of Chicago and the Cardinals and Browns of St. Louis. While watching baseball in person may have been limited to the Gary AC, newspaper and radio allowed Coach to follow what became his favorite major league team, the Detroit Tigers. When I ran for Coach Griak I was not aware of the depth of his knowledge about pre-World War II baseball. Coach and I shared an interest in current baseball but a fascination with the baseball of yesteryear. Like many men, Coach rued the fact that his mother threw out his boyhood baseball card collection. This happened while he was overseas in the army. However, he could still remember the cards he had and could still discuss the players from the Tigers of the 1930s. Listening to him talk about Charlie Gehringer (his favorite player), Hank Greenberg, Mickey Cochrane, Schoolboy Rowe, Tommy Bridges, Goose Goslin, Rudy York, Birdie Tebbetts, Bobo Newsom, Pinky Higgins, Freddy Hutchinson, Dizzy Trout and others, I sensed that this was a part of his life that he still cherished.

He recalled how the players of the 1930s and 1940s were such colorful characters and how much they loved the game. One name that used to always cause Coach to chuckle was that of Hall of Fame outfielder "Heinie" Manush. Perhaps it was the name "Heinie" which was also the name of the Griak family dog when I ran for Coach in the late 1960s and early 1970s. According to Coach's younger son, Jason, the dog was officially named Heinrich of Oxford and that Coach detested the dog. Heine once ate an entire pot roast dinner that was cooking in a crock pot in the kitchen. The dog would also torment Coach by frequently bolting from the house if the door was opened causing Coach to have to track it down. A portion of Coach's excellent physical condition in the 1970s may be attributed to the time he spent chasing after Heinie.

Heinie with Coach, Jason and Seth in 1973

Coach and I agreed that there was something captivating, less mercenary, and maybe more pure about the players of that time. I think that we both liked to remember it that way rather than have the experts diminish that feeling by informing us that the lack of media scrutiny about the personal lives of the ballplayers of that era gave the public an unrealistic perception of them.

Coach enjoyed borrowing biographies about the players from his youth: Hank Greenberg, Bob Feller, Dizzy Dean, Satchell Paige and Lou Brissie were some that he liked. He was also very interested in the ballplayers of the old Negro Leagues. He speculated about what they may have accomplished if they had been allowed to play in the "white" major leagues while their skills were at their peak. One book that Coach really loved was *The Soul of Baseball: A Road Trip Through Buck O'Neill's America* by Joe Posnanski. Perhaps it was because he, like Buck O'Neill, took every opportunity to look at the bright side of life and to find good in every situation. After his "retirement" from active coaching, Coach Griak became a voracious reader. He had always been a reader but in the last years of his life his scope widened beyond athletic journals, physiology, training programs, athletic technique and diet. He told me that so much of his life had been focused on the mechanics of the shot or the high jump, the best way for a sprinter to come out of the blocks or the many types of training methods for distance runners that he wanted to branch out and learn more about other areas. History was certainly one of Coach's favorite topics and he loved to read and discuss books about the events of the 19th and 20th centuries.

While at Stowe Junior High School and later at Morgan Park High School, Coach Griak's teachers had a big impact on his life. He remembered his English teacher, Mrs. Craig, who would buy pencil boxes and give them to her students as rewards. Another teacher would tell her students about her travels and also buy clothes for the students who were most in need. Over three-quarters of a century later, Coach Griak remembered those teachers as people "who cared." Those teachers would be proud to know that Coach Griak continued the tradition of caring for student athletes and that he multiplied many times over the love for others that they had displayed when he was their student.

Roy Grijak #5 on the Stowe Junior High School basketball team

Perhaps the man who had the greatest impact on young Roy Griak was Glen Card, his physical education teacher and basketball coach. He was also in charge of the 7th-9th grade softball teams that played in an organized city league. Coach Griak remembered that Glenn Card showed a real interest in the kids in his classes and on his teams. He would take money out of his own pocket and give the team members tokens to ride to their games in West Duluth and then give them each an extra nickel for a candy bar. Coach remembered that Mr. Card would post the batting averages and fielding averages for his athletes after each game. He said that the athletes would all gather around the bulletin board to read the results of their latest game. According to Coach Griak, "Glenn Card became my mentor and was really a good guy." Glenn Card later became the principal at Stowe Junior High School. I can remember that 35 years later (in the late 1960s) my college coach (Coach Griak) would post the splits for each of our miles after every 5 mile cross country race. I was one of the runners who could not wait to see and analyze what was posted on the bulletin board each week.

Although his family lived in Gary - New Duluth, Roy Griak went to Morgan Park High School. Morgan Park had been a planned community built by United States Steel to serve the Duluth Steel Works. The company town was named for the founder of United States Steel, J. P.

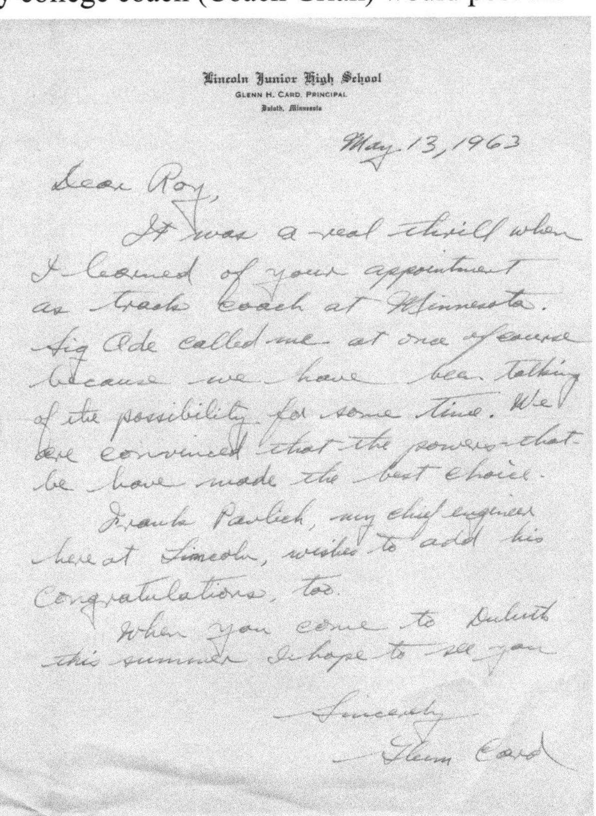

Lincoln Junior High School
GLENN H. CARD, PRINCIPAL
Duluth, Minnesota

May 13, 1963

Dear Roy,

It was a real thrill when I learned of your appointment as track coach at Minnesota. Sig Ode called me at once of course because we have been talking of the possibility for some time. We are convinced that the powers-that-be have made the best choice.

Frank Pavlich, my chief engineer here at Lincoln, wishes to add his congratulations, too.

When you come to Duluth this summer I hope to see you

Sincerely
Glenn Card

Letter from Lincoln Junior High School Principal Glen Card when Coach took the Gopher job in 1963

Morgan Park High School building in 2015

Morgan. Morgan Park High School was 2 miles north of Gary with Duluth itself further north and east. This was where the young people from Gary traveled for their schooling. Although it is no longer in operation as a high school today, the building still stands. Although the Morgan Park Wildcats no longer field a track team there is still a black all-weather track on the athletic grounds behind the building. Coach would have loved to run on such a good track when he was a student there in the early 1940s. When Coach was a student there, Morgan Park did not have a school baseball team in the spring. In order to participate in a sport the boys had to choose between golf and track. He was interested in all types of sporting events as evidenced by the picture of him on horseback. Although he sits in the saddle like a natural, I doubt that this was taken during a Morgan Park polo match!

The track behind Morgan Park High School in 2015

There were no teams for girls in that era. At that time, my mother was one of the best athletes at Roosevelt High School in Minneapolis and yet she did not get the opportunity to compete on a team. Her high school Swedish teacher, Oscar Yngve, was also the cross country and track and field coach for the "Teddies" from 1924-1966. Coach Griak said that he remembered coaching his St. Louis Park Orioles against Ingve's Roosevelt Teddies in the 1950s and that Yngve was a very good coach and friend.

Roy Grijak on horseback

The Duluth high schools had tremendous athletes at the time that Coach participated and, after World War II, they resumed their strong showing in the Minnesota State Track and Field meets. Coach talked at length about some of these great Duluth area athletes and teams and was extremely proud of how the northern athletes could compete with the very best in the state. When Coach graduated in 1942, his Morgan Park track team tied Duluth Central for 7th in the state; in 1946 Duluth Central was 5th; in 1947 Duluth Denfeld was 5th; in 1948 Denfeld was 2nd and Morgan Park was tied for 10th; in 1949 Denfeld was the state champion; in 1950 Denfeld was 4th and in 1952 Morgan Park was 7th.

One of Coach's classmates and good friends at Morgan Park was Larry Ross. Unlike Coach, he did not participate in track and field but went out for the golf team. He was a good golfer at Morgan Park but later became an All-American hockey goalie for the Minnesota Gophers. Larry Ross went on to coach the International Falls Broncos to six state hockey titles and an incredible 58 game winning streak from 1964-1966. Ross was named to the U.S. Hockey Hall of Fame in 1988 and after his death in 1995 was inducted into the University of Minnesota "M Club" Hall of Fame. There his name was united with his Morgan Park classmate, Roy Griak.

Although he competed in the years right after the end of WW II and would serve the United States in the Korean Conflict, Coach Griak said that one of the greatest athletes to come from Duluth was Central's Norman Kragseth. Kragseth won 23 varsity letters in 7 sports: track and field (he won the city discus championship in 1948 and 1949), football (all-state first team), basketball, baseball, tennis, skiing (many state titles) and golf. Kragseth went on to earn football and basketball letters at Northwestern and to also play on the Wildcat golf team. After serving on a destroyer in the Korean Conflict, he returned to Northwestern and played for Coach Lou Sabin in football. Kragseth became a teacher and also a noted National Football League official. To ask Coach Griak to comment on his athletic career often resulted in hearing him expound on other great athletes he knew or had competed against. His unselfish attitude and reluctance to boast remained an integral part of his character as coach of the St. Louis Park Orioles and the Minnesota Gophers. He never talked about his accomplishments and what he had done for his athletes. It was always what his athletes had done for him and what they had added to his life.

While in high school Coach remembered that he spent a great deal of time with his studies and that he always had at least one job outside

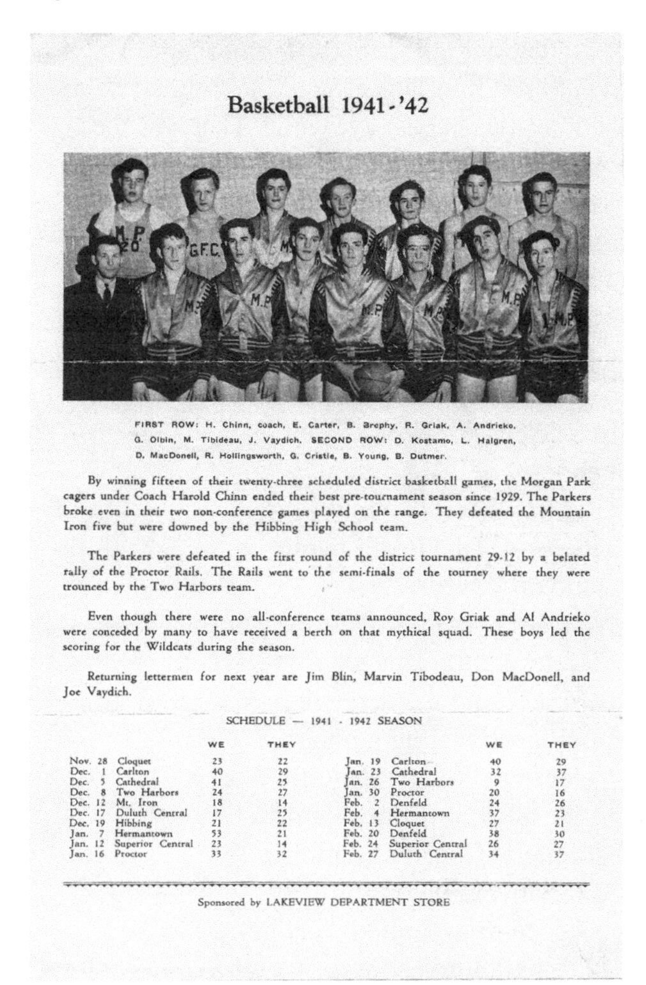

Basketball 1941-'42

FIRST ROW: H. Chinn, coach, E. Carter, B. Brephy, R. Griak, A. Andrieko, G. Olbin, M. Tibideau, J. Vaydich. SECOND ROW: D. Kostamo, L. Halgren, D. MacDonell, R. Hollingsworth, G. Cristie, B. Young, B. Dutmer.

By winning fifteen of their twenty-three scheduled district basketball games, the Morgan Park cagers under Coach Harold Chinn ended their best pre-tournament season since 1929. The Parkers broke even in their two non-conference games played on the range. They defeated the Mountain Iron five but were downed by the Hibbing High School team.

The Parkers were defeated in the first round of the district tournament 29-12 by a belated rally of the Proctor Rails. The Rails went to the semi-finals of the tourney where they were trounced by the Two Harbors team.

Even though there were no all-conference teams announced, Roy Griak and Al Andrieko were conceded by many to have received a berth on that mythical squad. These boys led the scoring for the Wildcats during the season.

Returning lettermen for next year are Jim Blin, Marvin Tibodeau, Don MacDonell, and Joe Vaydich.

SCHEDULE — 1941 - 1942 SEASON

		WE	THEY			WE	THEY
Nov. 28	Cloquet	23	22	Jan. 19	Carlton	40	29
Dec. 1	Carlton	40	29	Jan. 23	Cathedral	32	37
Dec. 5	Cathedral	41	25	Jan. 26	Two Harbors	9	17
Dec. 8	Two Harbors	24	27	Jan. 30	Proctor	20	16
Dec. 12	Mt. Iron	18	14	Feb. 2	Denfeld	24	26
Dec. 17	Duluth Central	17	25	Feb. 4	Hermantown	37	23
Dec. 19	Hibbing	21	22	Feb. 13	Cloquet	27	21
Jan. 7	Hermantown	53	21	Feb. 20	Denfeld	38	30
Jan. 12	Superior Central	23	14	Feb. 24	Superior Central	26	27
Jan. 16	Proctor	33	32	Feb. 27	Duluth Central	34	37

Sponsored by LAKEVIEW DEPARTMENT STORE

Marvin Tibedeau and Coach on the Morgan Park Basketball Team - 1942 Wildcat yearbook

of school. Concerning his participation in athletics, Coach said that his true love was basketball and that he had played on a good team. He recalled that he was a member of a good-sized track team at Morgan Park. He had gone out for track as a sophomore. His mother did not want him to play football but he did run with the football team to stay in shape. They would run four laps around the football field and he always beat everyone. That was the true start of his running. The first year that he participated, he recalled being timed in the 880-yard run with a boy named Marvin Tibedeau. Marvin made it as far as one lap, announced that he was a quarter miler, and stopped. In a discussion with Coach in February of 2015, over a year after first hearing about Marvin Tibedeau, Tibedeau's name came up again.

Coach recalled that Tibedeau once finished a 440-yard race and then crawled from lane one into a pool of water in a ditch on the infield of the track at Cloquet and just laid there. Coach told him, "Marvin, get up or you'll get sick." Marvin replied, "I'll be all right." Sure enough, Marvin was sick the next day. Coach said that Marvin's parents were in their late 60s and that Marvin had all the toys he could have wanted. He said that Marvin was a popular kid partly because of his toy collection. Coach and many of his friends had few toys, if any. He recalled that as a little boy he had one toy, a duck on a string.

Coach related that Marvin Tibedeau grew to be about 6'3" tall and, although he wanted to be a good athlete, he had little success other than in basketball. Coach remembered that Marvin was a good kid and that he later worked as a brick layer for the Civilian Conservation Corps (CCC). The Lester Park area and many of the bridges around Duluth had been CCC projects. Marvin became so good at bricklaying that he made it his career. Tibedeau even built a beautiful home for his family out of bricks he had saved from his work over the years. The 880-yard race against this future bricklayer was Coach's introduction to track and field. He remembered having run that first 880 in about two minutes and twenty seconds. Although Coach Griak later could analyze and discuss the technique needed in every track and field event and could discuss the training philosophies of most coaches and champion athletes in the world, he began his own high school training by religiously following a single workout he found in a magazine. He

Morgan Park Track & Field Team - 1942 yearbook

Track

FIRST ROW: R. Anderson, B. Strand, J. Blazvic, G. Potter, E. Effinger, R. Hadean. SECOND ROW: G. Marjala, J. Paquette, R. Griak, L. Gerard, G. Johnson, E. Gacominie, N. Smith. THIRD ROW: H. Chinn, coach, B. Dutmer, B. McCoy, B. Olmen, A. Steblac, G. Petrich, N. Radich, D. Kastamo, S. Manardt. FOURTH ROW: J. Lindquist, R. Smoots, G. Olbin, B. Olson, M. Tibodeau, M. Coombs, A. Andrieko.

Morgan Park High School was fortunate in having one of the best track teams in the state this year. Led by the state's top pole vaulter, Al Andrieko, and one of the state's ace half-milers, Roy Griak, the team was able to pick up quite a few points every meet they entered. Andrieko took first in the pole-vault at the Carleton Relays held in Northfield. Griak took second in the 880-yard run at this meet. Morgan Park is very proud to be represented by such fine athletes as Roy and Al.

Due respect must be given to Coach Harold Chinn for his splendid work in the handling of the athletes.

Sponsored by MORGAN PARK BARBER SHOP

repeated this same workout every day throughout high school. His coach at Morgan Park, Harold Chinn, was both the football and track and field coach.

Coach Chinn allowed Roy Griak to make his own workouts. Coach Griak said that Mr. Chinn had very limited eyesight and literally could not see the scoreboard from the bench on the football field. Although Mr. Chinn has undoubtedly gone to that great locker room in the sky long ago, Coach Griak was reluctant to say anything negative about his coach. Another teammate at Morgan Park was Al Andrieko. Coach said that Andrieko was an exceptional athlete who won the state pole vault championship in 1942 even though he was self-coached. Andrieko was the first in a line of very successful Morgan Park pole vaulters that included Minnesota state champions Ed Westerhaus (1948) and Chuck Jasper (1950 & 1953) plus Jerry Chinn who placed second to Jasper in the 1949 Duluth City Championship. Coach Griak was not sure if this Chinn was related to his old coach. Coach remembered that this was at a time when the poles were bamboo and the landing pit was sand or eventually foam rubber in burlap bags. Coach related a story about an away meet where Coach Chinn had strapped Andrieko's bamboo pole to the hood and then over the top of his car and then to rear bumper. When the Morgan Park team arrived at the meet, the pole had a permanent bend in it.

Like Coach Griak, Al Andreiko later served the United States in WW II. He was a navigator on a bomber in the European theater of the war. In addition to being a champion high school vaulter, Al Andrieko was also a great basketball player. Coach Griak didn't mention it but so was he according to the 1942 Morgan Park yearbook. When asked about his high school basketball, Coach talked about games from more than seventy years ago as if they had just taken place. He said that his Morgan Park team had lost two games to Two Harbors in the 1941-1942 season. He said that Two Harbors was coached by Cy Magnusson and that Magnusson was an excellent coach. Coach rattled off the names of four of the five starters for Two Harbors (Hamilton, Kernan, Hastings and Nelson) like he had just played them the week before. He was upset that he could not recall the name of the fifth starter. Coach stated that "Punky" Kernan later played basketball for coach Ossie Cowles at the University of Minnesota. He remembered that Two Harbors had beaten Morgan Park narrowly at Morgan Park (27-24) and then quite handily in the game at Two Harbors (17-9). Three-quarters of a century after the games had been played Coach recalled how Two Harbors had used the pick-and-roll play to beat his team.

The Morgan Park Wildcats were 15-8 for the season but were defeated in the first round of the 1942 district tournament by the Proctor Rails. Coach and Al Andrieko led the team in scoring throughout the season. He was disappointed that some of the Morgan Park players lacked discipline and that his team was not coached very well. Although Coach Griak did not boast he said, "I could have done a better job of coaching that team." Anyone who knew Coach Griak would agree with that assessment. Coach loved basketball almost as much as he loved cross country and track and field. Later in life, while at

Above: Roy Grijak alone #35

Below: Roy Griak (far right) with four other Morgan Park Wildcats and the ball boy

St. Louis Park, he was an assistant coach on the Orioles 1962 Minnesota State Championship basketball team. Several years ago, when the Gopher men's basketball team was having trouble inbounding the ball, Coach designed a play for the coach that was used by his friend and fellow Gopher coach, Tubby Smith.

Duluth City Track & Field Results - 1942

1942 Duluth City Championship at Public School Stadium, Duluth, Friday, May 15, 1942

Wet track & blustery winds.

Teams: Central 89 ½, Denfeld 62, Morgan Park 33 ½.

100
1 Chet Thomas, Denfeld 10.6
2 Mel Johnson, Central
3 Stu Johnson, Denfeld
4 Beaudette, Central
5 Glen Johnson, Morgan Park

220
1 George Erickson, Central 24.4
2 Mel Johnson, Central
3 Chet Thomas, Denfeld
4 Eno Giacomini, Morgan Park
5 Stu Johnson, Denfeld

440
1 Eno Giacomini, Morgan Park 55.9
2 George Erickson, Central
3 N. Smith, Morgan Park
4 George Molberg, Central
5 Rudy Doering, Denfeld

880
1 Roy Griak, Morgan Park 2:08.0
2 Laird Gogins, Central
3 Bob Viergutz, Denfeld
4 Paul Lund, Central
5 Dick Johnson, Denfeld

Mile (new event)
1 Lyle Gerard, Morgan Park 4:56.6 **
2 Dave Meismer, Denfeld
3 Bud Lequier, Central
4 Severs, Morgan Park
5 Gordon Soltau, Central

High Hurdles
1 Calvin Main, Central 17.3
2 George Lewis, Central
3 Ben Taylor, Denfeld
4 Clayton Smith, Morgan Park
5 Dick Claveau, Denfeld

200 Yd. Low Hurdles
1 George Lewis, Central 24.5 **
2 Art Johnson, Denfeld
3 Calvin Main, Central
4 Ben Taylor, Denfeld
5 Clayton Smith, Morgan Park

Notes: Central was coached by John Swain.

880 Relay
1 Central (Erickson, M. Johnson, Lewis, Ringsred) 1:39.5
dq Denfeld
dq Morgan Park

Shot Put
1 Mel Johnson, Central 42-4 ½
2 Milt Treb, Denfeld
2 Dick Lundquist, Denfeld
4 Stu Johnson, Denfeld
5 Coopin Johnson, Central

Discus Throw
1 Mel Johnson, Central 121-5
2 Elgin Anderson, Denfeld
3 Coopin Johnson, Central
4 Steve Miletich, Denfeld
5 Gelineau, Central

Broad Jump
1 Calvin Main, Central 19-9 ½
2 Wally Smith, Denfeld 19-1
3 Milt Bailey, Denfeld
4 Tom Boyd, Central
5 Chet Thomas, Denfeld 18-2

High Jump
1 Ben Taylor, Denfeld 5-6
1 Tom Boyd, Central 5-6
1 Elgin Anderson, Denfeld 5-6
4 Calvin Main, Central
4 James Lindquist, Morgan Park
4 Floyd Kotlarek, Central

Pole Vault
1 Al Andrieko, Morgan Park 10-11 ¼
2 Laird Gogins, Central
3 Ed Dieryck, Denfeld
4 Turnquist, Denfeld
4 George Olbin, Morgan Park

* Ties Meet Record
** New Meet Record

Coach also remembered that when he was a high school senior he played basketball against a sophomore from Superior Central High School named Harry "Bud" Grant. Bud Grant would later play three sports for the Gophers: football, basketball and baseball. As a professional athlete he played for the Minneapolis Lakers on two of their world championship basketball teams. Grant also played for the Philadelphia Eagles of the National Football League and the Winnipeg Blue Bombers of the Canadian Football League. He would later coach the Blue Bombers for ten seasons and the Minnesota Vikings for eighteen years.

Many years after competing against Bud Grant, Coach recruited another Superior Central athlete for his track and field program at the University of Minnesota. That athlete, Tim Heikkila, became the first Gopher high jumper to clear 7'. He did this in an outdoor dual meet against Michigan State at Memorial Stadium in 1969. Tim would eventually jump 7' 2" in 1971. Coach recalled that Tim Heikkila was such a terrific athlete that he once won the high jump, the long jump and the high hurdles in a dual meet against Purdue. Purdue coach, Dave Rankin, asked Coach, "Where did you get that kid?" Tim's best long jump was set in 1970 at 23' 8". Not bad for a high jumper! Coach Griak talked wistfully about how the times have changed and that now "We don't have dual meets anymore." He remembered the excellent dual and triangular meet competitions with Iowa, Michigan State and Wisconsin and said that, "Now we mainly just send individuals to big meets and there isn't the same feeling of being a team."

Coach Griak did not run cross country in high school as Morgan Park did not start their cross country program until 1943. The first Minnesota State Cross Country Championships were also held in 1943, one year after Roy Griak had graduated from Morgan Park. The first state champion was Laird Goodman from Duluth Central. The meet was held in south Minneapolis at Lake Nokomis and the distance was 1.5 miles. Coach said that the state cross country meet was held at Lake Nokomis for many years before moving to the University Golf Course, then to Alexandria and most recently to St. Olaf.

Coach placed second in the Duluth City Championship 880-yard run during his junior year at Morgan Park. He claimed the city 880-yard title in his senior year (1942) by running 2:08.0 on a wet track and on a day with blustery winds. Although he had been very successful, he felt that he was still a fairly inexperienced runner (see results on previous page).

Part of Roy Griak's education as a runner, and future coach, came in the Minnesota State Track Meet of 1942. He ran against the state champion, Ralph Ferrin of Minneapolis North, in the 880-yard dash. Ferrin won the race with a time of 1:57.9, a state meet record that would stand until Marty Benson of Minnetonka broke it in 1963. Benson set the new record at 1:55.7. Marty Benson had just turned 18 when he broke the state record and like Coach Griak, he would serve in the military. Marty Benson was a Marine Corps pilot killed in Quang Duc Province in South Vietnam on February 26, 1970 at the age of 24. He is buried at Fort Snelling. In Benson's 1963 state meet race, a St. Louis Park athlete, Bob Wagner, also was under the old record when he ran 1:56.5. Another of Coach Griak's St. Louis Park athletes, Arthur "Archie" Patterson had come very close to breaking Ferrin's record when he won the state 880-yard run in 1:58.0 in 1958. Patterson defeated Ray Miller of Minneapolis Edison. Miller was the state cross country champion and would later run on Coach Griak's first Gopher track team in 1963. In the 1942 race Coach Griak finished 5th in the state with a time of 2:03. Coach told me that he had placed second to Ferrin in the state meet. The mystery was cleared up by noted high school track and field expert, Jeff Renlund. Jeff, who ran for Coach at Minnesota in the late 1980s revealed that there were actually two heats of the 880-yard run in the 1942 state meet and that the times were then combined. Coach had finished second to Ferrin in his heat but the combined results placed Coach fifth. Coach recalled that during the 1942 state meet race he noticed that the Minneapolis North Coach, Lou Barnett, was reading Ferrin his split times every 220 yards. Coach remembered thinking during the race, "Hey, that's a pretty good idea." Coach had already set the Morgan Park Wildcats school record at 2:01.1, a record that still held when the high school closed on June 10, 1982. At that time, Coach was given the record board with his name next to the 880-yard record. For safe keeping he gave it to the coach at the University of Minnesota Duluth (UMD). Coach did not know if UMD still has it. Up to the time of its closing, students marched in protest and community members fought to keep the Morgan Park High School open. However, it merged the next year with Duluth Denfeld and the Morgan Park building became a junior high and later a middle school.

Morgan Park Varsity Letter won by Coach

Coach Griak recalled that when he was in high school the major track and field power in the northern part of Minnesota was Duluth Central. Central was coached by John Swain from 1927-1956. He had come from Indiana and coached the Greyhounds in both basketball and track and field. One of the larger cross country meets in Minnesota is still named in honor of John Swain. It is the Swain Invitational in Duluth. Duluth Central had very good track teams in the 1940s and they set the high school Drake Relays record for the 4 X 880 relay by running just over 8:00. Coach Griak recalled that they had an anchorman named Ingersoll, a red-haired kid who would regularly beat him in the 880. Coach Griak remembered that because of the climate in Duluth, "We were lucky to get three or four weeks of training in the spring before the state meet." The Doc Savage Relays and the Carleton Relays were the two big meets in the spring. The Doc Savage relays were named after the long-time track coach at Hibbing. The meet will celebrate its 62nd year in 2018. Not surprisingly, Garry Bjorklund of Proctor High School, who would later star for Coach Griak at the University of Minnesota, still holds records in this meet. In interviews in December of 2014 and again in early April of 2015, Orv Bies said that he coached at Hibbing High School from 1949-1963 (head coach 1956-1963) and that he remembered that when his team ran in the Lewis Relays in Eveleth in the late 1950s, Coach Griak still held a track record there in the 4 X 880 from his days at Morgan Park. According to Bies, the track at Eveleth was almost square in shape. Orv recalled that the track at Hibbing was a beautiful track but that it measured only 352 yards. The mining industry had discovered iron ore beneath the town of Hibbing and had literally moved the town two miles to the south in 1918 so that the ground under the town could be mined. To try to pacify the residents for being uprooted, a beautiful high school was erected in 1923. It cost four million dollars at the time and Coach Griak remembered it as a palace. Unfortunately, the track was 88 yards short of a quarter-mile. Ironically, Orv Bies would succeed Coach Griak as the track and field coach at St. Louis Park in 1963 and the track at Park measured 341 yards. Coach Bies told me early in 2015 that he had coached many great high school athletes and had led three teams to state championships but that his teams had never competed in home meets on a legal track! Orv Bies coached the Hibbing Bluejackets to top three finishes in the Minnesota State Track and Field Meet: in 1959 (tied for second), 1960 (third) and 1961 (1st place). Coach Bies' first St. Louis Park team placed third in the state in the last state meet held at Memorial Stadium on the University of Minnesota campus (1964) and then had state championship Oriole teams in track and field in 1965 and 1966 at Macalester College in St. Paul.

Coach Griak remembered running the 880 against a kid from Bemidji in the Doc Savage Meet. He was frustrated that he did not recall the runner's name but can be forgiven because this was over seven decades ago and during that time Coach had witnessed thousands of other races. Coach came off the last curve and led into the straightaway. He tightened up, fell down and was passed by the Bemidji runner. Coach vowed that he would never lose to that runner again. He ran hills and worked very hard to earn the success that he had in high school. "The Carleton Relays were bigger than the state meet and you had to be pretty good to run in them." Coach ran in them each year. He remembered that one year at the Carlton Relays, he roomed with vaulter, Al Andreiko and a shot putter named Hanson. The room where they stayed had floors that were so uneven that the shot rolled all the way across the floor and banged into the wall on the other side of the room. During Coach's years as a Morgan Park athlete, many of the powerful track schools, other than the Duluth schools, were located in the southern part of the state: Minneapolis North, Minneapolis Washburn, Minneapolis Southwest, Minneapolis Central, Minneapolis South, St. Paul Central and Rochester. No matter how large the student population, all the schools in Minnesota competed in just one class.

Coach remembered that when he was in high school many of the top collegiate track teams, other than Southern California, were eastern schools like Yale, Fordham and New York University. Upon graduation from Morgan Park in 1942, Roy Griak's plans to continue his education and athletic career were altered by WW II. A Michigan State graduate, who lived near Coach and worked in the cement plant, knew of

LAWRENCE GRANDCHAMP "Larry"
If inches were snowflakes, he'd be a blizzard.
Hi-Y Club 2-3-4
Hi-Y Cabinet 3-4
Service Orchestra 4
Band 3-4

ROY GRIAK "Flash"
We shall always look up at him and say "He was a Man."
Hi-Y Club 4
Track 2-3-4
Basketball 2-3-4

"Happy landings"
Good luck and

Morgan Park High School graduation picture of Roy "Flash" Griak
1942 Wildcat yearbook

Coach's running talent and wrote a letter to the coach at Michigan State encouraging him to recruit young Griak. Nothing came of this though as Coach would instead spend several years in the service of his country.

Coach's Collegiate Athletic Career

After the war, Coach returned to Duluth and attended Duluth Teacher's College (now called UMD) in 1946-47 and 1947-48. He participated in two seasons each of basketball and track. He remembered playing basketball games at the Duluth Armory. Coach said that his UMD team once beat the Harlem Globe Trotters and that this was really fun although he was quick to add that it may have been their second or third team. The *Duluth News-Tribune* of February 14, 1948 wrote that he was the high point man in a game played between the Bulldogs of Duluth and Northland College in Ashland, Wisconsin. The paper stated that, "Guard Griak packed the punch for UMD with four field goals and five free throws." Eleven days later the *UMD Statesman* wrote that UMD had earned second place in the conference by edging the Moorhead Dragons 53-50 largely on the playmaking efforts of Jim McIntyire and Roy Griak. Articles like these were common in the 1948 season. Coach remembered that in 1946 his freshmen classmates differed greatly from the usual first year collegians. Some were 17 year-old kids just out of high school. Some, like Coach, were in their early twenties after coming home from the Pacific or European theaters of the war to start their collegiate education. Some of his classmates were really old-timers who had started their college education and then had served in the war and now were returning to the classroom. Coach Griak used the GI Bill of Rights (Servicemen's Readjustment Act) to pay for his schooling. When Coach transferred to the University of Minnesota (Twin Cities) in 1948 he did not play varsity basketball for the Gophers but he did play intramural basketball in the winter of 1950-1951 while he was in graduate school after completing his athletic eligibility and undergraduate degree. The games were held in Cooke Hall. One of the players on his team was Warren Beson, who had played football for the Gophers, and who later was the football and baseball coach at Edina

Roy Griak - 1942

Coach and his UMD basketball team - He is wearing #18

High School for many years. Beson's Edina football teams had a record of 35-3-2 and his baseball teams were 72-12. He left Edina to become the football coach and athletic director at Carleton College in Northfield in 1956.

Coach's University of Minnesota Duluth Varsity Letter

In the spring Coach Griak left the hard court and ran track for the Bulldogs. He loved basketball but also loved running and was unhappy that he was on a weak track and field team at UMD. Individually, his work ethic and competitiveness made him very successful as a middle-distance runner. A *Duluth News-Tribune* headline stated that, "Griak Breaks 1/2-Mile Mark" and reported in the article that he had done this by, "speeding to a brilliant 2:00.7 in the Hibbing Invitational Relays of 1948." The article also mentioned that he was named the outstanding performer at the meet and that he already was the holder of the Minnesota College Conference half-mile record. Coach remembered winning the conference 880-yard title and setting the conference record of 1:58 for UMD on the Mankato track in 1946. The *UMD Statesman* article of January 11, 1949 reported that the Duluth Bulldog's tremendous Morgan Park athlete, who was both a starter on the basketball team and the conference half-mile champion had transferred to the Twin Cities branch of the University of Minnesota. The article urged its readers to, "Watch for Roy Griak's name in the University of Minnesota track and cross country stories from now on."

Gopher Athlete

Don Timm

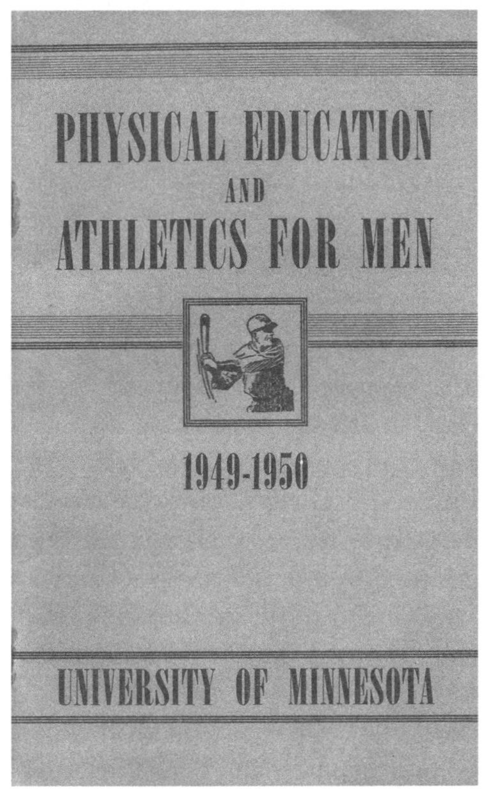

University of Minnesota Physical Education Bulletin 1949-1950

Coach Griak had transferred to the University of Minnesota (Twin Cities) late in 1948. There he studied physical education and also lettered in both cross country and track and field. He earned his Bachelor of Science degree in education in 1949 and a Master's in Education degree in 1950. Coach recalled that his first cross country race as a Gopher was against Drake University at Lake Nokomis. He said that he had no experience in cross country but was able to finish third in the race. He remembered that he was dead tired and was leaning against a tree after the race. He said to Coach Kelly, "I hope to heck I get a letter for this."

Coach recalled that the best runner on the Minnesota team was Dick Kilty and that, "I never could keep up with him." Coach said that he usually tried to run with Gopher teammates Kilty and Bill Schimmel. Bill Schimmel had run for Oscar Ingve while in high school at Minneapolis Roosevelt. When recalling Dick Kilty, Coach said in 2014 that they were the same age and that Kilty lives in Stillwater and still looks good today. Assessing his own running talent, Coach said that he was probably a better cross country runner than half miler. He said that, "In 1948 we ran a cross country meet in Brookings, South Dakota and had dual meets against Iowa and Wisconsin."

U of M letter certificate and bobblehead

2 Miler Kilty Ready For Iowa State Test

Dick Kilty, two miler, will be ready for his first real test tomorrow.

He has been slowed by injuries all season, but appears ready for a winning effort against Iowa State. He will be one of the 30-man squad which leaves today at 12:30 p.m. by bus for its first outdoor dual meet of the season.

Kilty first tried to get back into action in the Drake relays but pulled up with leg pains after holding an early lead.

But he appears to have recovered from the pains completely now. He ran a mile and one half with teammate Roy Grijak on Wednesday and the two of them turned in times under seven minutes.

Three other tracksters, injured at the Drake events, will compete tomorrow. They are hurdlers Lee Hofacre and Jim Nielson and pole vaulter Harry Cooper.

Tom Mason will get his first test of the season at 220 yards against the Cyclones. Up to now Mason has been performing at 100 yards and has turned in a 9.6 mark for the century.

Dick Kilty
Ready to Go

1949 *Minnesota Daily* - Coach is mentioned in the story leading up to the May 7, 1949 meet with Iowa State

Teammate Bill Schimmel at the Flordia Relays - 1949

The best cross country runner in the conference was Don Gehrmann of Wisconsin. He won the Big Nine Conference Championship held at the University of Chicago in 1948 by completing the four-mile course in 20:31.4 to lead his team to the title. The Gophers placed fifth in the meet. Coach remembered that the cross country meet was started on the track and that he placed 20th in the Big Nine that year. The Conference became known as the Big Ten in 1950 when Michigan State was admitted. Teammate Dick Kilty, who placed 6th, was the first Gopher runner. Coach was the third Gopher finisher, placing just behind teammate Bill Schimmel who finished 19th. Tom Good and his brother Roy were the other Gopher scorers, placing 23rd and 29th as the Gophers totaled 93 points (opposing runners from incomplete teams did not count in the total). Coach said that the Good brothers both became doctors. It was at the University of Chicago in 1942, the year that Coach graduated from Morgan Park High School, that scientists working at a laboratory beneath the stadium at Amos Alonzo Stagg Field first split the atom creating a sustained nuclear chain reaction. That scientific achievement would eventually lead to the Manhattan Project and the atomic bombs that ended WW II. Had it not been for the atomic bombs causing Japan to surrender Coach thought that he would certainly have been part of the invasion forces on the main islands of Japan.

Minnesota did not compete in the conference cross country meet between 1933 and 1947 and did not make its first appearance in the

1949 U of M Track & Field Team – Back Row (L-R): Paul Neff, Charles Lindekugel, Byrl Thompson, Roy Grijak, Jim Nielsen, Scott Nelson (manager); Middle Row (L-R): Don Prielipp, Jim Maska, Fred Brass, Tom Mason, Ron Sass, Coach Jim Kelly; Front Row (L-R): Clark Rice, Roy Good, Bob Comer, Lee Hofacre, James Peterson, Bill Schimmel

***1948 NCAA Championship Team:** Top – Scott Nelson, manager, Tom Mason, Paul Neff, Dick Kilty, Jim Kelly, head coach. Center – Roy Good, Fred Brass, William Ewing, Lee Hofacre, Robert Comer. Bottom – Clark Rice, Lloyd LaMois, Fortune Gordien, Charles Lindekugel, James Nielson.*

national meet until 1964 when Minnesota placed 15th. The Michigan State Spartans won the NCAA meet in 1948. For some reason, Michigan State did not join the conference until 1950. Coach related a funny story about his days as a Gopher cross country runner although it was not funny at the time. In recent years Coach Griak was perhaps the most recognizable face on the University of Minnesota campus but that has not always been the case. The 1948 Gophers had run a meet at the University of Minnesota Golf Course (renamed the Les Bolstad Golf Course in 1983) on a Saturday morning. When the meet was over, Coach Kelly asked one of his runners, Roy Griak, to carry the finish chute stakes and banners back to Cooke Hall. When Coach arrived at the entrance to Cooke Hall it was blocked off because of the football game that day. Coach explained to the guard at the gate that he was returning equipment from the cross country meet but the guard would not let him through. Coach said he asked the guard, "What do you think I am carrying all this gear for? Do you think it is a trick to sneak into the game?" Coach said that he had to wait for about thirty minutes before someone came and vouched for him that he was a Gopher athlete. Amazingly, in his first year of coaching at the University in 1963, he had the same experience when he attempted to get into Memorial Stadium on a football Saturday after a cross country meet at the University of Minnesota Golf Course. Again, Coach Griak was trying to put away his cross country equipment and a stadium guard blocked him from getting into the stadium.

Coach Griak recalled that there were only about 16 guys on the Gopher track team in 1949 (see image on previous page). The coach was Jim Kelly. Coach Kelly did not have any assistants so he coached all the events; however, his areas of expertise was probably the shot put and the discus. Coach Kelly's 1948 team had won the national track and field championship held at Memorial Stadium in Minneapolis. Ironically, his 1948 team had earlier placed fourth in the Big Nine.

Roy Griak transferred from Duluth and joined the team the next year but knew many of the athletes from the national championship team. Fortune Gordien, who had won Minnesota State High School Meet titles in the discus in 1940 and 1941 and was also first in the shot put in 1941 for Minneapolis Roosevelt, had thrown 164' 6 1/2" to win the discus in the national meet and he had also placed second in the shot with a put of 52' 7 3/8". Gordien went on to win the bronze medal in the discus at the London Olympic Games of 1948 and would earn a silver medal in the event at Melbourne in 1956. He set a world discus record that would stand for six years when he threw 194' 6" in 1953.

Lloyd LaMois

Just prior to Gordien's years at Minnesota, and while Coach Griak was serving in the United States Army in the South Pacific, Coach Kelly had another discus thrower, Bob Fitch, who also had held the world record. Fitch had been on Bernie Bierman's 1940 and 1941 national championship football teams and, after a three-year absence when he was in the Coast Guard during WW II, he returned to play football in 1945 and also to throw the discus again. He had not competed in track and field for four years when he threw 180' 2 3/4" in 1945 to set the world record. Fitch and Gordien, with the help of Coach Jim Kelly, developed a new technique which is now the universal throwing style in the discus. They called it, "The Minnesota Whip." Although Fitch had been born in Iowa, when he was ten, ironically, **his family had moved to St. Louis Park, Minnesota. Two decades later Coach Griak would establish St. Louis Park High School as a major power in Minnesota cross country and track & field. Bob Fitch coached football briefly and golf for almost four decades at the University of Indiana. Years later, Coach remembered that Bob Fitch was in charge of** the Iowa City golf course used by the University of Iowa for their cross country meets (Finkbine Golf Course). Coach said that Fitch would not let the Gophers, his alma mater, practice on the course before their meet with the Hawkeyes.

Asking Coach Griak a question about a meet, an athlete or a year often prompted interesting sidelights from his remarkable memory. Getting back to the 1948 NCAA championship track and field team and the Gopher athletes who placed in the nationals, Coach recalled that Harry Cooper had placed third in the pole vault at 13' 10." Lloyd Lamois won the triple jump with a distance of 45' 10" even though he had never competed in the triple jump until the national meet. LaMois also placed sixth in the long jump with a leap of 23' 8." Dick Kilty placed third in the 10,000 meter run with a time of 33:04.5. Roy Good earned a fifth place finish in the steeplechase with a time of 10:11.9. Chuck Lindekugel placed sixth in the hammer. The Gophers scored 46 points to defeat Southern California by nearly five points. Southern California had won twelve national titles between 1926 and 1943 under Coach Dean Cromwell. Illinois, led by Coach Leo Johnson had won national titles in 1944, 1946 and 1947. Navy had won the title under Coach E. J. Thomson in 1945 while Coach Griak was still stationed in the South Pacific.

During his time as a Gopher athlete, Coach Griak said, "Without a doubt, the dominant track and field power in the nation was the University of Southern California." After the big Gopher win in 1948, Southern California would reel off seven straight titles between 1949 and 1955, led by coaches Jess Hill and Jess Mortensen. Mortensen also led the Trojans to national titles in 1958 and 1961 before turning the reins over to Vern Wolfe who would add seven more national titles for a total of twenty-six for USC.

Coach's friend, Elwin "Ducky" Drake won a national title at the

Minnesota Gopher Indoor Track & Field Results - 1949

Minnesota Trackmen Win 72-31

Minnesota's track team made its first home appearance since winning the NCAA last summer a good one Saturday afternoon by swamping Iowa State 72 to 31 in the Field House.

Harry Cooper paced the Gophers, taking first place in the pole vault and the broad jump.

Fortune Gordien broke his own Field House shot put record of 52 feet 6 inches when he tossed the ball 54 feet ⅛ inch. This was short of Gordien's record throw of 54 feet 2¼ at the 1947 NCAA.

Things went about as expected in all events with the exception of the two mile, where the Gopher's Dick Kilty was upset by Ames' Gene Shaver.

Iowa State won only one other event, the high jump.

Cooper took only one leap in the broad jump but his effort of 22 feet 3½ inches was good enough to win.

SHOT PUT—Won by Gordien, Minnesota; second, Thompson, Minnesota; third, Doran, Iowa State. Distance: 54 ft. ⅛ inch. A new Field House record.

60-YARD DASH—Won by Rice, Minnesota; second, Mason, Minnesota; third, Bean, Iowa State. Time—:06.3.

POLE VAULT—Won by Cooper, Minnesota; second, Koprucki, Iowa State. (No third place). Height: 13 ft., 6 in.

440-YARD DASH—Won by Comer, Minnesota; second, Wright, Iowa State; third, Barkley, Iowa State. Time: :51.9.

HIGH JUMP—Won by D. Smith, Iowa State; second, Sass, Minnesota, Miska, Minnesota, Verner, Iowa State, Guth, Iowa State, tied. Height: 6 ft. 1½.

MILE RUN—Won by Shimmel, Minnesota; second, Roy Good, Minnesota; third, Baty, Iowa State. Time: 4:31.

70-YARD HIGH HURDLES—Won by Brass, Minnesota; second, Nielsen, Minnesota; third, Wolf, Iowa State. Time: :08.7.

TWO-MILE RUN—Won by Shaver, Iowa State; second, Kilty, Minnesota; third, Ericson, Iowa State. Time: 9:50.4.

880-YARD DASH—Won by Grijak, Minnesota; second, Stevens, Iowa State; third, Barnes, Minnesota. Time: 2:01.7.

70-YARD LOW HURDLES—Won by Brass, Minnesota; second, Nielsen, Minnesota; third, Steinbach, Iowa State. Time: :08.2.

RUNNING BROAD JUMP—Won by Cooper, Minnesota; second, Navratil, Iowa State; third, Rapp, Minnesota. Distance: 22 ft., 3½ in.

MILE RELAY—Won by Minnesota (Comer, Hofacre, Anderson, Prielipp); second, Iowa State. Time: 3:32.1.

Feb. 5, 1949
Minn. 72-Iowa State 31

Gopher fans had to settle for second best.

POLE VAULT—Won by Bennett (W); second, Cooper (M); third, McCormick (W). Height—13 feet, 6 inches.

SHOT PUT—Won by Gordien (M); second, Thompson (M); third, Albright (W). Distance—51 feet, 6⅝ inches.

HIGH JUMP—Won by Sullivan (W); second, Gill (W); third, Miske (M) and Marsh (W), tied. Height—6 feet, 1¾ inches.

BROAD JUMP—Won by Cooper (M); second, LaMois (M) and George Kailas (W) tied. Distance—22 feet, 3 inches.

ONE MILE RUN—Won by Gehrmann (W); second, Schimmel (M); third, Manske (W). Time—4:16.7.

60 YARD DASH—Won by Rice (M); second, Mason (M); third, Reid (W). Time—:06.2 (ties Field House record set by George Franck in 1941).

440 YARD DASH—Won by Mansfield (W); second, Hofacre (M); third, Whipple (W). Time—:50.3.

70-YARD HIGH HURDLES—Won by Gill (W); second, Brass (M); third, Nielson (M). Time—:08.6 (ties Field House mark set by Bob Wright in 1947).

TWO MILE RUN—Won by Urquhart (W); second, Kilty (M); third, Kloser (W). Time—9:33.

HALF MILE RUN—Won by Gehrmann (W); second, Grijak (M); third, Goldin (W). Time—1:56.6 (breaks Field House mark of 1:57.5 set by Mal Whitfield, Ohio State, in 1947).

70-YARD LOW HURDLES—Won by Brass (M); second, Nielson (M); third, Gill (W). Time—:08.2.

MILE RELAY—Won by Wisconsin (Myers, Mansfield, Gehrmann, Whipple). Time—3:25.1.

Feb. 19, 1949
Wisconsin-Minn.

Gopher Track Team Rolls Over Cats

EVANSTON, ILL. — (AP) — Minnesota's NCAA track champions scored heavily in the distance events Saturday to defeat Northwestern, 69-45. The Gophers won seven of the 12 events and tied in the high jump.

Bill Schimmel of Minnesota was the only double winner. He captured the half mile and mile runs.

Northwestern's Rose Bowl football hero, Ed Tunnicliff, upset Minnesota's Clark Rice in the 60-yard dash. Another surprise occurred in the shot put when the Gophers' Olympic discus man, Fortune Gordien, placed second to teammate Byrl Thompson.

One-mile run: 1—Schimmel, Minnesota; 2—Good, Minnesota; 3—Woodley. Time..4:37.

60-yard dash: 1—Tunnicliff, Northwestern; 2—Rice, Minnesota; 3—Holland, Northwestern. Time—:06.3.

440-yard run: 1—Hofacre, Minnesota; 2—Latta, Northwestern; 3 — Neff, Minnesota. Time—:52.6.

Shot-put: 1—Thompson, Minnesota; 2—Gordien, Minnesota; 3—Orlich, Northwestern. Distance—52 feet, 4 inches.

70-yard high hurdles: 1—Kickert, Northwestern; 2—Nielson, Minnesota; 3 — Brass, Minnesota. Time—:08.7.

Two-mile run: 1—Kilty, Minnesota; 2—Lucking, Northwestern; 3—Woodley, Minnesota. Time—9:55.2.

Pole-vault: 1—Cooper, Minnesota; 2—Lundgren, Northwestern; 3 — Drangsholt, Northwestern. Height—13 feet 10¼ inches.

Half-mile run: 1—Schimmel, Minnesota; 2—Grijak, Minnesota; 3—Angner, Northwestern. Time—2:02.1.

70-yard low hurdles: 1—Brass, Minnesota; 2—Kickert, Northwestern; 3—Nielson, Minnesota. Time—:08.2.

Broad jump: 1—Holland, Northwestern; 2—Lamois, Minnesota; 3—Cooper, Minnesota. Distance—23 feet 5¼ inches.

High jump: 1—Dunn, Northwestern, and Miska, Minnesota (tied); 3—Gordien, Minnesota. Height—6 feet 3 inches.

One-mile relay: 1—Northwestern (Holland, Whitney, Tunnicliff, Latta); 2—Minnesota. Time—3:31.2.

Feb. 26, 1949
Minn. 69-Northwestern 45

AWAY
Jan. 29 .... Nebraska
Feb. 12 .... Illinois
Feb. 26 .... Northwestern
Mar. 4-5.....Conference Meet at Champaign
Mar. 19 .... Chicago Relays
Mar. 26 .... Florida Relays

GYMNASTICS
HOME
Sat., Feb. 12.......... Michigan State
Sat., Feb. 12.......... State H.S. Meet
Sat., Feb. 26......Northwest Gymnastic Meet
Tickets: Gen. Adm. $.40, Children $.25
On sale at gate only
AWAY
Feb. 5........Illinois, Wisconsin at Madison
Feb. 19 .... Chicago
Feb. 21 .... Nebraska
Mar. 23 .... Illinois
Mar. 26.. ....Conference Meet at Michigan
April 2....Open meet at University of Illinois
Navy Pier, Chicago
April 9.......... University of Colorado
April 16.......... N.C.A.A. Meet
at University of California

1949 Football Schedule
HOME GAMES
Saturday, Sept. 24 .... Washington
Saturday, Oct. 8 .... Northwestern
Saturday, Oct. 29 .... Purdue
Saturday, Nov. 5 .... Iowa
Saturday, Nov. 19 .... Wisconsin
Prices to be established
AWAY
Saturday, Oct. 1 ....Nebraska—Lincoln
Saturday, Oct. 15 ....Ohio State—Columbus
Saturday, Oct. 22 .....Michigan—Ann Arbor
Saturday, Nov. 12 ....Pittsburgh—Pittsburgh
Mail orders open on all games August 1, 1949
No orders accepted prior to this date
Form 21D—14M—481129

UNIVERSITY OF MINNESOTA
DEPARTMENT OF ATHLETICS
1949 Winter Sports Schedule

BASKETBALL
Preliminary 6:25 p.m. Varsity 8:00 p.m.
Saturday, Dec. 4...West. Ill. St. College
Monday, Dec. 20.......... Navy
Wednesday, Dec. 22...St Mary's (Calif.)
Saturday, Jan. 1......Colgate University
Saturday, Jan. 8.......... Michigan
Monday, Jan. 10.......... Wisconsin
Saturday, Jan. 22.......... Indiana
Monday, Jan. 31.......... Northwestern
Saturday, Feb. 12.......... Iowa
Saturday, Feb. 26.......... Purdue
Tickets: Reserved $1.50, Gen. Adm. $1.00
On sale Monday preceding each game
AWAY
December 6 .... Nebraska
December 18 .... De Paul
December 29-30 .... Drake University
January 15 .... Purdue
January 17 .... Iowa
January 29 .... Illinois
February 5 .... Ohio
February 19 .... Michigan
February 21 .... Michigan State
March 5 .... Wisconsin
HIGH SCHOOL EVENTS—BASKETBALL
February 21........Minneapolis High Schools
March 4.......... Twin City Championship
March 9-10-11.......... District 18 Playoff
March 17-18.......... Region 5 Playoff
March 24-25-26 State High School Tournament

Three 1949 indoor meet results: Feb. 5th; Feb. 19th; Feb.26th
(1949-1950 Gopher Winter Sports Schedule)

HOCKEY
Home Games 8:15 p.m.
Tues., Dec. 28—Yale.......... Arena—Mpls.
Wed., Dec. 29—Yale....Auditorium—St. Paul
Box and Rinkside $1.75, Side Reserved $1.25,
Stud.-Fac. $.75 Res., Gen. Adm. $.75
Thurs., Jan. 6—Winnipeg Can..Arena—Mpls.
Fri., Jan. 7—Winnipeg Can.....Arena—Mpls.
Fri., Jan. 14—Michigan Tech...Arena—Mpls.
Sat., Jan. 15—Michigan Tech..Aud.—St. Paul
Fri., Jan. 28—No. Dakota......Arena—Mpls.
Sat., Jan. 29—No. Dakota....Aud.—St. Paul
Fri., Feb. 4—California........Arena—Mpls.
Sat., Feb. 5—California......Aud.—St. Paul
Fri., Feb. 18—Michigan........Arena—Mpls.
Sat., Feb. 19—Michigan.......... Rochester
Tickets: Box and Rinkside $1.00,
Gen. Adm. $.75
Box and Rinkside on sale week of game
AWAY
Jan. 21 and 22.......... North Dakota
Feb. 11 and 12.......... Michigan Tech
Feb. 25 and 26.......... Michigan
Mar. 4 and 5.......... Colorado College

SWIMMING
HOME MEETS
Sat., Jan. 29.......... Purdue, 7:30 p.m.
Sat., Feb. 5.......... Northwestern, 7:30 p.m.
Mon., Feb. 7.......... Indiana, 7:30 p.m.
Sat., Feb. 26.......... Iowa, 2:00 p.m.
Fri., and Sat., Mar. 4 and 5..State H.S. Meet
Tickets: Gen. Adm. $.40, Children $.25
On sale at gate only
AWAY
Feb. 12 .... Iowa State College
Feb. 14 .... Nebraska
Feb. 21 .... Michigan
Mar. 4 .... Wisconsin
Mar. 10-11-12 .... Conference Meet—Purdue
Mar. 24-25-26.......... N.C.A.A. Meet
North Carolina University

BOXING
Home—8:15 p.m.—Field House
Sat., Jan. 29.......... All-University Finals
Sat., Mar. 5.......... Michigan State
Sat., Mar. 12.......... Miami
Sat., April 2.......... De Paul
Tickets: Ringside $1.25, Reserved $.75,
Gen. Adm. $.60
Ringside on sale Cooke Hall week of match
AWAY
Sat., Feb. 5.......... Washington State
Sat., Feb. 19.......... Syracuse
Sat., Feb. 26.......... John Carroll
Fri., Mar. 25.......... Wisconsin

WRESTLING
HOME
Sat., Jan. 8.......... Carleton
Sat., Jan. 22.......... Iowa State College
Sat., Feb. 5.......... Illinois—3:00 p.m.
Sat., Feb. 19.......Kansas State—3:00 p.m.
Fri. and Sat., Feb. 25-26....State H.S. Meet
Sat., Feb. 26....Iowa State Teachers College
Tickets: Gen. Adm. $.40, Children $.25
AWAY
Jan. 14.......... Colorado State College
Jan. 15......Colorado University—2:00 p.m.
Jan. 15.......Denver University—8:00 p.m.
Jan. 17 .... Nebraska
Jan. 29.......... Ohio State—2:00 p.m.
Jan. 29.......... Purdue—8:00 p.m.
Feb. 12 .... Wisconsin
Feb. 22 .... Carleton
Mar. 4-5.......... Conference Meet—Iowa
Mar. 25-26 .... N.C.A.A.—Iowa T.C.

TRACK
HOME
Sat., Feb. 5.......... Iowa State—1:30 p.m.
Sat., Feb. 19.......... Wisconsin—1:30 p.m.
Tickets: $.25 on sale at gate only

Coach Kelly-1, Grijak-2, Hofacre-3, Rice-4, Comer-5, Neff-6, Lindekugel-7 and LaMois-8 at the Florida Relays

University of California Los Angeles (UCLA) in 1956. He was succeeded as UCLA Bruin coach by another of Coach Griak's very good coaching friends, Coach Jim Bush. Coach Bush won five national titles for UCLA and eventually moved across town to coach the University of Southern California (USC) in 1991. The top national place he achieved at USC was third in 1982. Other members of the 1948 team that Coach recalled were: Lee Hofacre in the intermediate hurdles, his good friend, high hurdler and sprinter Jim Nielsen, sprinter Clark Rice, distance runner Tom Good, who was the brother of Roy Good, and weightman, Leo Nomellini. Coach said that the word on the track team was that Nomellini had been recruited out of a university frat house to throw the shot the day of the national meet. Nomellini was an All-American football player at Minnesota in 1948 and 1949 and later became a member of the Pro Football Hall of Fame. He played fourteen years for the San Francisco 49ers. He also was a professional wrestler and eight-time tag team world champion. He wrestled under the name Leo "the Lion" Nomellini.

Roy Grijak in white t-shirt at the 1949 Florida Relays

Coach with teammate Fred Brass at the 1949 Florida Relays– Coach is on the left in the Gopher singlet

Coach said that Dick Kilty, who placed 11th in the NCAA in cross country in 1949, and Fred Watson, who won Big Ten individual cross country titles in 1913-1915, were probably Minnesota's premier distance runners until the appearance of Norris Peterson, Tom Heinonen, Steve Hoag and Garry Bjorklund. When I ran in the last track meets held at Memorial Stadium in 1969, I did not realize that it had been

Coach holding the 1949 Florida Relays 4 X 880 relay trophy

Coaches Roy Griak and Al Buehler - 1972 Munich Olympic Games

the site of NCAA national meets in 1938, 1940, 1946, 1948 and 1950. In the 1938 meet at Memorial Stadium the NCAA meet mile record of 4:08.3 was set by USC's, Louis Zamperini, the subject of the recent book *Unbroken, a WW II Story of Survival, Resilience and Redemption.* The mile record of 4:08.3 was still the Memorial Stadium record 30 years later when Coach Griak's Gophers won the Big Ten Meet Conference Track and Field Meet there in 1968. Memorial Stadium was true to its name, it held a lot of memories for those who competed there.

Coach Griak recalled that when he was a student athlete at the University of Minnesota, the track and cross country programs were not considered a priority. Although the track team had won the national title in 1948, Coach felt that it was more a team of individuals rather than a true team. As his "M" Cards (next page) from 1948 and 1949 show, Coach was still known as Roy Grijak. Coach competed mainly in the 880 during the 1949 track season. He recalled competing in late March of 1949 at the Florida Relays in Gainesville, Florida. At the Florida Relays on March 26, 1949, Coach ran the third leg as the Gophers won the 4 X 880 relay in a Florida Relays record time of 7:55.3. The other Gopher runners in that relay were Paul Neff, Bob Anderson and Bill Schimmel. In that third leg, Coach "duked" it out against a Maryland Terrapin runner named Al Buehler. Al Buehler would become the long-time coach in cross country and track and field at Duke University in Durham, North Carolina and he and Coach Griak would become very good friends or as Al Buehler said, "Roy Griak is my coaching brother." They were United States Olympic coaches on the 1972 (Munich) and 1984 (Los Angeles) teams. Teammate Jim Nielsen, a hurdler on the 1949 Gopher team, said that he saw "Bugsy" Grijak nipping mineral oil before his race at the Florida Relays." I don't recall Coach suggesting that for his runners when I was on the team.

Coach running at the 1949 Drake Relays

On April 29, 1949 he ran the third leg of the two-mile relay for the Gophers in Des Moines, Iowa at the Drake Relays. In the first of three 1949 news articles on an earlier page, the Gopher success at the Florida Relays is summarized; however, the circled paragraph in the article titled, "Trackmen Eye Spring

Coach's best times for the spring of 1949 in his handwriting

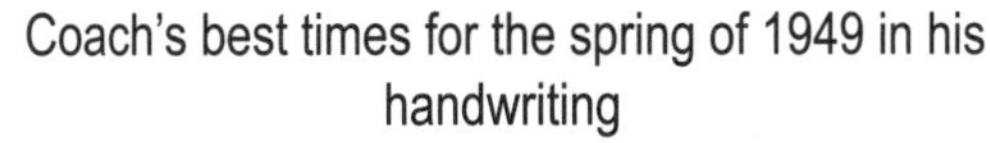

Mile & Half - 7:04.8 May 4th, 49
660 — 1:23.6 April 15, 49
Half mile — 1:58.8 April 30, 49
220 — 23.3 April 26, 49
Mile — 4:28 May 7, 49
3/4 mile - 3.14.[illegible] May 11, 49

1949 University of Minnesota
Outdoor Track & Field Results

Trackmen Eye Spring Season

The Minnesota track team now turns to the spring season and the defense of its NCAA championship after closing out its winter season with some record-breaking individual performances.

Harry Cooper led the team through the winter season and climaxed his pole vaulting with a leap of 14 feet, 8 inches in the Chicago relays. The jump was only good enough for a tie for first place against the nation's best vaulters. But it did set a new Gopher mark for both indoor and outdoor polevaulting.

Weightman Byrl Thompson followed Cooper's amazing effort with performances in last week's Florida relays that earned him the Kearney-Rayburn trophy as the meet's outstanding athlete.

Thompson cracked teammate Fortune Gordien's meet discus mark with a toss over 169 feet and went on to edge Gordien's shot mark also. This was sophomore Thompson's first appearance in the Relays but it marked the end for Gordien, who finished his eligibility with the indoor season.

The Gopher two-mile relay team also broke a Florida relay mark when it raced the distance in 7:55.3. Roy Good, Paul Neff, Roy Grijak and Dick Kilty did the baton-passing.

Seventeen trackmen make up the present traveling squad which will again be powerful in the weight events with Thompson, Leo Nomellini and Charles Lindekugel.

Florida Relays
Mar. 26, 1949

Trackmen Qualify 13

EVANSTON—(Special)—Minnesota qualified 13 men here yesterday for today's 49th Big Nine outdoor track and field meet finals.

The Gopher trackmen shared the top spot in yesterday's preliminaries with Indiana who also qualified 13 for the finals. The Gophers and Hoosiers are being tagged as the teams to beat today.

If the Gophers, last year's NCAA champs, do turn the trick it will be their first outdoor crown in history.

Qualifying for Minnesota were Jim Nielson and Fred Brass in the 120 yard high hurdles; Byrl Thompson in the shot put and discus; Don Prielipp in the 880; Tom Mason in the 220; Bob Comer in the 440; Clark Rice and Mason in the 100 and Lee Hofacre, Brass and Nielsen in the 220 low hurdles.

In addition to these men, Minnesota will send two milers Dick Kilty and Roy Good out today along with milers Roy Griak and Bill Schimel, pole vaulter Harry Cooper, and the mile relay team. These men sat out yesterday as qualifying heats were by-missed in their events.

Biggest surprise of the day for the Gophers was the failure of Thompson to take a first in the discus preliminaries. Thompson came in with a toss of 159 feet, 11¼ inches. Bill Miller of Ohio State flipped the metal 167 feet, four inches for first place.

Lee Hofacre led the hurdle qualifiers with a first heat mark of 27.7 in the 220 yard event.

Other team results found defending champion Ohio State placing eight men, followed by Purdue with seven, Michigan and Illinois six each; Wisconsin five, Northwestern four and Iowa one.

* * *

Dual Meet
May 14, 1949

Minn. 100 1/3
Iowa 31 2/3

Gopher Track Team Winner

MINNEAPOLIS —(AP)— Winning first place in 13 of the 14 events, Minnesota's track team rolled up 100 1-3 points to defeat Iowa yesterday. The Iowans got 31 2-3 points.

The Gophers took all places good for points in four events—the 220-yard low hurdles, the broad jump, the discus throw and the 440-yard dash.

The only Iowan to finish first was Jennett who took the pole vault with a jump of 12 feet, 10 inches.

100-yard dash—1, Rice (M); 2, Hofacre (M); 3, Johnson (I). Time—:10.2.
220-yard dash—1, Comer (M); 2, Simpson (I); 3, Sangster (I). Time :22.5.
440-yard dash—1, Comer (M); 2, Prielipp (M); 3, Neff (M). Time :49.5.
880-yard run—1, Good (M); 2, Brown (I); 3, Copeland (I). Time—1:57.5.
Mile run—1, Schimmel (M); 2, Grijak (M); 3, Bye (I). Time—4:24.2.
Two-mile run—1, Kilty (M); 2, Tupper (I); 3, Collins (I). Time—9:52.7.
120-yard high hurdles—1, Brass (M); 2, Nielsen (M); 3, Merkel (I). Time—:14.8.
220-yard low hurdles—1, Hofacre (M); 2, Brass (M); 3, Nielsen (M). Time—:24.1.
High jump—1, Miska (M); 2, Wilson (I), Metler (I) and Sass (M), tied. Height—6 feet.
Running broad jump—1, Rapp (M); 2, Sass (M); 3, Peterson (M). Distance—21 feet, 6 inches.
Pole vault—1, Jennett (I); 2, Peterson (M); 3, Wilson (I). Height—12 feet, 10 inches.
Shot put—1, Thompson (M); 2, Turner (I); 3, Lindekugel (M). Distance—51 feet, 2⅝ inches.
Discus throw—1, Thompson (M); 2, Lindekugel (M); 3, Hodgins (M). Distance 165 feet, 9½ inches.
Mile relay—1, Minnesota (Anderson, Comer, Prielipp, Neff). 2, Iowa (Sangster, McDonald, Copeland, Brown.) Time—3:24.6.

Lee Hofacre
Sets 220 Hurdle Pace

Gopher Qualifiers
Big Nine Meet
May 20-21, 1949

1949 Gopher Outdoor Track & Field meet results

Season," incorrectly credits Dick Kilty rather than Bob Anderson as a member of the winning two-mile relay. Also listed are the results for the Gopher dual meet with Iowa on May 14, 1949 and an article about the Gopher qualifiers for the Big Nine Conference Meet held in Evanston, Illinois on May 20-21. Coach did not place in the Big Nine Indoor Meet in Champaign, Illinois where the Gophers finished 5th with 21 points. In the spring the Gophers won the Big Nine Meet with 49 points but Coach did not place in the 880. The 1949 team was well balanced and took the conference title even though they had only two first place finishers. Fred Brass (see photo on an earlier page) and teammate Dick Nielsen took one-two in the 120 high hurdles and Lee Hofacre and Fred Brass took one-two in the 220-low hurdles with Nielsen fifth. Clark Rice and Tom Mason took two-four in the 100-yard dash; Mason placed second in the 220-yard dash; Bob Comer was third in the 440-yard dash; Dick Kilty placed fifth in the two-mile; Harry Cooper tied for third in the pole vault; Byrl Thompson took second in both the shot and the discus and the mile relay placed third. After the first place Gophers, Ohio State had 37 points, Wisconsin had 36, Illinois had 35 and Indiana had 34.

Coach recalled that there was a dirt track around the basketball floor in Williams Arena but that they could never work out or race on it if there was a basketball game scheduled that day. He said that they did run some dual meets there against Iowa and Wisconsin. He recalled that on the west end of the arena, "We ran under the bleachers." Outdoors, Coach usually competed in the 880 and also ran on the 4 X 880- relay team. His best times for the 880 were in the range of 1:55-1:56. The

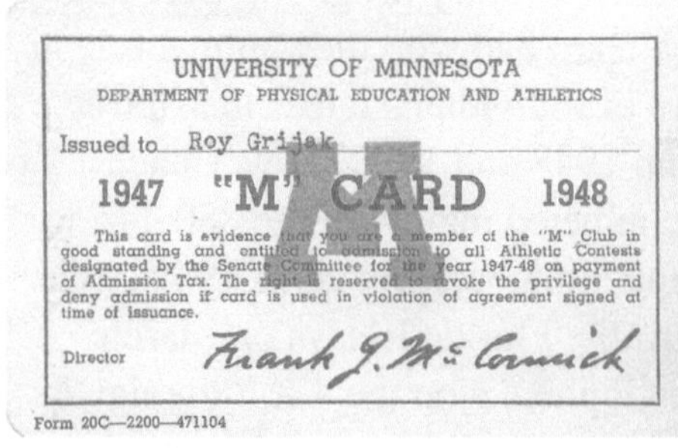

UNIVERSITY OF MINNESOTA
DEPARTMENT OF PHYSICAL EDUCATION AND ATHLETICS

Issued to Roy Grijak

1947 "M" CARD 1948

This card is evidence that you are a member of the "M" Club in good standing and entitled to admission to all Athletic Contests designated by the Senate Committee for the year 1947-48 on payment of Admission Tax. The right is reserved to revoke the privilege and deny admission if card is used in violation of agreement signed at time of issuance.

Director Frank G. McCormick

Form 20C—2200—471104

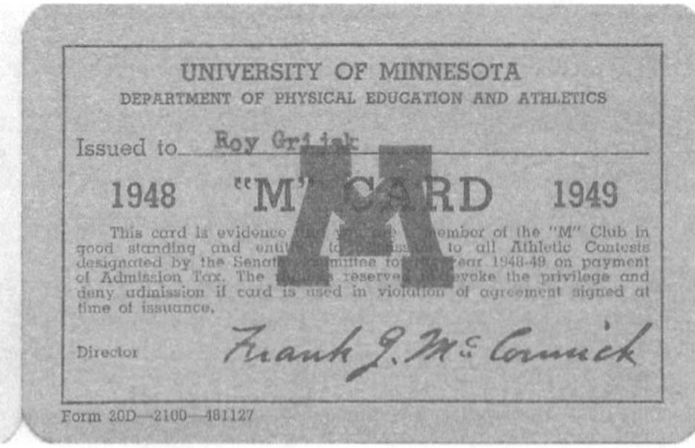

UNIVERSITY OF MINNESOTA
DEPARTMENT OF PHYSICAL EDUCATION AND ATHLETICS

Issued to Roy Grijak

1948 "M" CARD 1949

This card is evidence that you are a member of the "M" Club in good standing and entitled to admission to all Athletic Contests designated by the Senate Committee for the year 1948-49 on payment of Admission Tax. The right is reserved to revoke the privilege and deny admission if card is used in violation of agreement signed at time of issuance.

Director Frank G. McCormick

Form 20D—2100—481127

Roy Grijak's "M" Cards

THE REGENTS AND FACULTIES
OF THE
UNIVERSITY OF MINNESOTA
ANNOUNCE THE
JUNE COMMENCEMENT EXERCISES
SATURDAY EVENING, JUNE THE TENTH
NINETEEN HUNDRED AND FIFTY
AT EIGHT O'CLOCK

MEMORIAL STADIUM — MINNEAPOLIS CAMPUS

1950 U of M Commencement Announcement results

Gophers placed 6th in the Big Ten Indoor Meet in 1950 and tied for second outdoors. As mentioned earlier, with the addition of Michigan State, the Conference was now known as the Big Ten. Coach did not earn a place in the 880 in either meet. He graduated from the University of Minnesota on June 10, 1950. It was also in 1950 that Coach married Rose-Mary Brandon of Grand Rapids, Minnesota.

Coach Griak recalled that the track in Gainesville, Florida for the Florida Relays was, as he put it, "Square." This was similar to the track Orv Bies mentioned where Coach held part of the two-mile relay record at the Lewis Relays in Eveleth, Minnesota. Coach said that there were very long straights and very tight, abrupt curves. As he talked about this oddly shaped track, Coach recalled some of the other strange layouts he had witnessed in his years as an athlete and as a coach. He remembers running in Evanston, Illinois at Northwestern University. The track was in a building with drab, concrete walls. The ceiling was so low (roughly 8') that they did not allow the shot to be thrown and that the high jump and long jump were very precarious and frightening events. On one side of the track, "We ran through a galvanized tunnel so that it felt like we were running in a tin can." At the University of Nebraska in Lincoln, Nebraska the track was literally a figure eight. It was also built on stilts. There was a danger that the lead runners would run into slower runners at the intersection. Coach said that, of all the tracks he had seen, this was the strangest. The indoor tracks at Michigan State and at Purdue each had portions where the runners ran below the spectators on one straight. I can remember that it was still that way at Michigan State's Jenison Field House when I competed there for the Gophers thirty years later. The runners were not visible to the fans for much of each lap. However, Coach said that he also witnessed some very strange high school tracks during his high school and collegiate coaching career.

As the head coach of a Big Ten university, scouting and recruiting student-athletes led him to countless high school track venues. One of the strangest tracks he ever saw was at Askov, Minnesota, the home of future Gopher runner Adrian Deggerstrom (1972). It was a grass track. The discus circle was about four feet above the sector so that the athletes got extra distance on their throws. The pole vault was set up so that the vaulter had to run across the tennis court and then plant the pole at the end of the court and just before a steep drop off. Coach said that the vaulters were vaulting six or seven feet but that they had about a fourteen foot drop to the pit. The vaulters then had to march up a hill to get back to the runway for their next vault.

Seeking Employment

Don Timm

After graduating from the University of Minnesota, Coach Griak said that he literally wrote hundreds of letters seeking employment. I wonder what all those schools thought later when they realized what a wonderful teacher, coach and humanitarian they had turned down. In 1949-1950 Coach worked for the Minneapolis Park Board as a playground director. He also worked at Mount Sinai Hospital in Golden Valley as a recreational director. He was supposed to teach swimming lessons but admits that he was not a very good swimmer. Once while he was rowing a boat where he and a pretty girl were the only occupants, the girl asked, "What would you do if I jumped in the lake?" Coach said that he told her, "I am not a very good swimmer so you would probably drown." After that he felt that he would have to find another job. Finally, the Superintendent of Schools at Nicollet, Minnesota, Al Salmela, hired Coach for the 1950-1951 school year. Al Salmela would later become the Deputy Superintendent of Anoka-Hennepin District #11 Schools.

Coach Griak said that at Nicollet he taught Geography, History and Physical Education and coached six-man football, basketball and baseball, all for $2,300 that first year. He said that he lived in Mankato because if he had rented a room in Nicollet he would have lost money that year. Coach remembers that, for the first football game of his high school coaching career, Nicollet played Henderson, Minnesota. He had come up with all sorts of trick plays including what he called a "spinner play," and was expecting to defeat Henderson handily. The Henderson team was coached by an older man who appeared to be behind the times as far as modern football. Coach recalled that nothing went right for Nicollet and Henderson won the game 48-0. Coach said that, "It was a good lesson."

The best athlete on the Nicollet team was Eddie Grunst and he broke his collarbone the first day of practice. Coach Griak apparently did not have enough to do because he said that he also started a cross country team at Nicollet that first year. The team practiced after football practice was over each day. He said that the first meet was against New Ulm and that his team was shut out but that at least the program had been started. In the spring, Coach did the same thing after baseball practice was over by starting a track and field program at Nicollet. He said that he had only seven or eight boys on the team that year but that at least he initiated the program. Coach was not paid for coaching the cross country and track and field teams. Although he may not have thought it at the time, Coach Griak said that it was a good experience to start at the bottom. After the football season ended he asked Superintendent Salmela how much money he would be allowed for equipment for the next year. He was told that he would be allowed to buy one football helmet. Coach said that after that experience, "Everything else was a plus."

When I ran for him at Minnesota years later I wondered how Coach could stand in the middle of the track with three or four stop watches and time multiple workouts for sprinters, middle distance and distance runners all at the same time and run a quality program without having any paid assistants. Perhaps it was his experiences at Nicollet, where he had literally run the program on a shoestring that allowed him to do so much with so little as a Big Ten coach. In 1951-1952 Coach moved on to Lincoln Junior High School in Mankato, Minnesota where, in addition to his classes he coached the 8th grade basketball team. He also started their cross country program. After working one year at Nicollet and one year at Mankato

Coach's next teaching and coaching position began in 1952 in St. Louis Park, Minnesota where he taught in the junior high and coached at the high school for the next eleven years.

St. Louis Park High School

Coach said that his good friend, Eugene "Lefty" Wright, had run track for him as a senior at St. Louis Park in 1953 and then had come back

Lefty and Coach with Oriole athletes – (L-R): Lefty Wright, Bruce Fischer, Bob Howe, Phil Homme, Bob Wagner, Gerry Brouwer, Mike Gillham, Archie Patterson, John Valentine, Coach Griak

to teach history at Park from 1958-1993. Lefty became an assistant to Coach Griak in the track and field program in 1958. Together they tried to make order on their track at St. Louis Park High School. The track was 341 yards around. To run a 440 the runner would have to complete a lap and then repeat an extended straight away to the finish line. Races with multiple laps necessitated different finish lines and relays and relay exchange zones required the wisdom of Solomon to calculate.

Coach Griak said that he and Lefty had measured all the zones for an 8 X 220-yard relay for a triangular meet they held each year between Park, Ed Hendrickson's Edina and Al Halley's Minneapolis Southwest teams. He remembered that they had used every color imaginable to designate the many different exchange zones. After the race, Southwest coach, Al Halley, came up to Coach Griak and wanted to know why some of his runners had run their 220s in 19 seconds and others had run theirs in 35 seconds. Coach Griak's good friend, Edina coach Ed Hendrickson, just laughed as Coach told coach Haley, "Don't worry about it Al." Halley was a legendary coach who had led Southwest to thirteen state titles in cross country and had also led the Indians to state track and field titles in 1946, 1955 and 1956. When Southwest High School changed their school nickname to Lakers in 1987, they were one of the first schools in the country to make this politically correct move. Coach said that he enjoyed the competitions between these top teams in the state and the friendly rivalry with his coaching friends. Al Halley coached at Minneapolis Southwest High School from 1940-1971.

One of Coach Halley's individual state champions at Southwest was Peter Aurness, who won the 120-yard high hurdles in both 1943 and 1944 while Coach Griak was in the Army. A story told about Peter Aurness when he was posthumously inducted into the Southwest Hall of Fame in 2015 was that Coach Halley had once told him that he would have to make a choice between track and being in the school band. When Aurness told Coach Halley that his choice would be the band, Halley had responded, "We'll work something out." Aurness later changed his name to Peter Graves and starred in the TV program, "Mission Impossible." Peter's brother, James Arness (he kept the name but changed the spelling), starred as Matt Dillon in the TV series "Gunsmoke." Coach Griak commented about his friend, "Al Halley did things that no other coaches were doing at that time, like two a day workouts, long runs and summer workouts. He was very enthusiastic and I learned a great deal from him." Evidence that the respect between Coach and Al Halley was mutual is found in the letter below which was written by Coach Halley after St. Louis Park won the Minnesota State Track and Field championship in 1958. Coach also spoke fondly of the competitions between his St. Louis Park teams and those coached by

Minneapolis Public Schools
SOUTHWEST HIGH SCHOOL
3510 West 47th Street Minneapolis 10, Minnesota

ROBERT H. CLASSON, *Principal*

June 12, 1958

Mr. Roy Griak,
Track Coach
High School
St. Louis Park,
Minnesota.

Dear Roy:

Congratulations to you and Bill Torp on winning the State Track Championship.

After experiencing several disappointments, it is a great feeling of satisfaction to know that hard work really does pay off. I know of no two men or a group of boys more deserving.

Please congratulate your boys for me. They are a fine group and deserve all the honors coming their way. May they always be champions.

Sincerely,

Al Halley

Al Halley

Letter from Al Halley

Bob Hoisington and his assistant, Earl Bowman, at Minneapolis Central. Bob Hoisington's track and field teams at Central won state championships in 1959, 1960 and 1964 and, after succeeding Al Halley at Minneapolis Southwest, his cross country teams won state titles in 1971, 1972, 1973 and 1980. Earl Bowman was Coach Hoisington's lone assistant at Minneapolis Central and was an excellent sprint coach. Both Hoisington and Bowman would continue in track and field after their coaching days as top-notch officials. Coach Griak recalled that Bob Hoisington was a very productive coach who always developed good athletes. He said that when his Park teams

Bob Hoisington

competed against Minneapolis Central, "You better be ready to compete. They would do anything to win a meet and I respected them for that."

Coach said that one year Central defeated Park but that the next time his Park team was able to defeat Central even though Central seemingly ran one athlete, Blaine Chattum, in almost every race. Coach laughingly recalled that since Chattum ran so many times there seemed to be numerous delays of the meet so that Chattum could get more rest. Coach Hoisington said of Coach Griak, "He was devoted to young people and knew how to get the best out of them." Coach Griak also had great admiration for John Swain who coached basketball and track and field at Duluth Central. He said that Coach Swain always had excellent distance runners even though they had nothing but concrete pavement around the school for their training runs. One of Swain's runners, Bart Bontems, would later run for Jim Kelley at the University of Minnesota. Bontems placed 13th in the Big Ten Cross Country Meet in 1958 and 17th in 1959.

In his speech honoring Coach upon his 50th year at the University of Minnesota in 2013, Lefty Wright said that in the locker room at St. Louis Park they had a motto on the wall that read, "The difficult we do now; the impossible takes a little longer." Another saying in the locker room at Park was, "No one ever drowned in sweat." When Coach arrived at St. Louis Park in 1952, the school did not have a cross country program and it did not have a track. With a limited budget, a makeshift track, and very little equipment, Coach Griak's St. Louis Park Orioles won the Minnesota state championship in cross country in 1955.

Park Runners Best In Minnesota

STATE CHAMPIONS: Here is the state championship cross country team of St. Louis Park high school hich won the state meet Friday at Lake Nokomis in Minneapolis. Posing with the trophy (first state ophy ever won by a Park athletic team) are back row, from left: Lloyd Holm, athletic director; Bob Oas, enny Carlson, Charley Berg, Dave Quade and Coach Roy Grijak. Front: Rod Lazorik, Jim Kumpula nd Art Patterson. Details on sports page. (STAFOTO)

Win First State Title In History

(See Photo Page One)

Proving themselves the best high school cross country team in Minnesota, the Park high Orioles have won the state title . . . first athletic championship won by any Park team.

Coach Roy Grijak's young runners—none of whom are seniors—stamped themselves champions Friday in the annual cross country meet at Lake Nokomis in Minneapolis.

Led by junior Dave Quade, the Orioles overpowered a field of 9[illegible] runners from all parts of the state to bring home the previously unknown "blue ribbon bacon."

The mile and eight-tenths race was run on a wind-swept course around the lake with rain and strong winds lashing the competitors.

Park's five-man team finished first with 07 points to smother their foes like the Golden Gophers did the following day to Southern California.

Quade finished fourth, sophomore Rod Lazorik was ninth; sophomore Bob Oas was 19;ht sophomore Art Patterson came in right behind in the 20th spot and Charlie Berg, a freshman, was 34th. Behind young Berg came the other 64 harriers.

Individual winner was Wayne Sullwold of Minneapolis Southwest. Jerry Larson of Minneapolis Central was second, Andy Olsen of St. James third and Norman Gill of Duluth Central fifth behind Park's Quade.

The state high school association had decided just prior to the race to allow only five men from each team to enter instead of the originally planned seven.

Standing by as alternates for the champions were Denny Carlson, a junior, and Jim Kumpula, freshman. Both were vital men in the victorious season culminating with their school's first state trophy.

The Oriole team was honored Monday with a pep fest by classmates.

Here is how the top teams finished in the spectacular race: St. Louis Park 87; Grand Rapids, 144; Minneapolis Roosevelt 160; Duluth Central 194; Moorhead 195; Minneapolis Southwest 210; Alexander Ramsey 248; St. Paul Central 243; St. James 247; St. Paul Murray 276 and Thief River Falls 295.

Right: 1955 News Article: Park Runners best in Minnesota (unknown paper)

Coach Griak's St. Louis Park Runners who finished in the top 25 in the Minnesota State Cross Country Meet

Buddy Edelen (5th)	1953
Duane Cedarblade (23rd)	1953
Peter Tinker (21st)	1954
David Quade (4th)	1955
Rod Lazorik (9th)	1955
Art Patterson (19th)	1955
Bob Oas (20th)	1955
Rod Lazorik (14th)	1956
Art Patterson (18th)	1956
Bob Oas (23rd)	1956
Art Patterson (2nd)	1957
Rod Lazorik (4th)	1957
Bruce Mortenson (6th)	1960
Chuck Patterson (25th)	1960
Bruce Mortenson (2nd)	1961
John Valentine (4th)	1961
Tom Langen (20th)	1961
Howie Winer (24th)	1961
John Valentine (2nd)	1962
Bob Wagner (8th)	1962
Bob Neumer (16th)	1962
Keith Brudevold (25th)	1962

Between 1953 and 1963 Coach Griak had 22 Oriole runners place in the top 25 spots in the Minnesota State Meet. During that span, his Park cross country teams won another state title in 1961 and had great success in large invitational meets and in their conference, section and region.

Top State Meet CC Finishes for Coach Griak's St. Louis Park Teams

St. Louis Park won the 1955 and 1961 MInnesota State Meets

1953	174 points	6th	
1954	187 points	6th	
1955	**87 points**	**1st**	**MINNESOTA STATE CHAMPIONS**
1956	154 points	3rd	
1957	142 points	3rd	
1960	139 points	5th	
1961	**63 points**	**1st**	**MINNESOTA STATE CHAMPIONS**
1962	65 points	2nd	

Lake Conference CC Championships won by Coach Griak at St. Louis Park
1955, 1961, 1962

District 18 CC Championships won By Coach Griak at St. Louis Park
1955, 1957, 1960, 1961

Region CC Championships won by Coach Griak at St. Louis Park
1955, 1958, 1961

Swain Invitational Class A Champions (Duluth) 1961

Coach said that in his quest for challenging practice areas, "We got chased off Meadowbrook Golf Course so many times!" This was confirmed by former Oriole and Gopher runner, Bob Wagner. Coach's Orioles

Minnesota State Track & Field Meet results for St. Louis Park: 1958, 1962, 1963

1958 MINNESOTA STATE TRACK AND FIELD CHAMPIONS

Event	Athlete	Result
220 Yard Dash	- Jim Kumpula	- Champion (22.7)
880 Yard Run	- Art Patterson	- Champion (1:58.0)
Mile Run	- Rod Lazorik	- 3rd Place
880 Yard Relay	- Bill Kaufman	- 2nd Place
	- Ed Gale	
	- Doug Lowry	
	- Jim Kumpula	
Mile Relay	- Lynn Mattis	- Champion (3:28.1)
	- Bill Kaufman	New State Record
	- Ed Gale	
	- Art Patterson	

Roy Griak - Head Coach   Bill Torp - Assistant Coach

1962 MINNESOTA STATE TRACK AND FIELD CHAMPIONS

Event	Athlete	Result
440 Yard Dash	- Mike Gillham	- Champion (49.1) New State Record
880 Yard Run	- Wally Hlavac	- 5th Place
Mile Run	- Bruce Mortenson	- Champion (4:22.2)
180 Low Hurdles	- Gerry Brouwer	- 2nd Place
Mile Relay	- Tom Langen	- Champion (3:25.8)
	- Chris Morris	
	- Gary Smith	
	- Bruce Mortenson	

Roy Griak - Head Coach   R. Eugene Wright - Assistant Coach
Jack Willhite - Assistant Coach

1963 MINNESOTA STATE TRACK AND FIELD CHAMPIONS

Event	Athlete	Result
100 Yard Dash	- Mike Gillham	- 2nd Place
220 Yard Dash	- Mike Gillham	- Champion (22.5)
440 Yard Dash	- Mike Gillham	- Champion (49.3)
880 Yard Run	- Bob Wagner	- 2nd Place
Mile Run	- John Valentine	- Champion (4:20.7)
120 High Hurdles	- Tom Fisher	- 2nd Place
180 Low Hurdles	- Gerry Brouwer	- Champion (19.6) New State Record
Mile Relay	- Gerry Brouwer	- Champion (3:27.0)
	Phill Homme	New State Record
	Bruce Fisher	
	John Valentine	

Roy Griak - Head Coach   R. Eugene Wright - Assistant Coach
Charles Swanum - Assistant Coach
Jack Willhite - Assistant Coach

would win the state titles in track & field in 1958, 1962 and 1963.

Under his leadership, St. Louis Park also won numerous conference, section and regional track and field titles.

Coach Griak's St. Louis Park Lake Conference, District and Region Championships

Lake Conference T & F Championships won by Coach Griak at St. Louis Park
1959, 1960, 1962, 1963

District 18 T & F Championships won by Coach Griak at St. Louis Park
1959, 1960, 1961, 1962, 1963

Region T & F Championships won by Coach Griak at St. Louis Park
1960, 1961, 1963

1958 State Champion 4 X 440 Relay team: Ed Gale, Lynn Mattis, Coach Griak, Archie Patterson, Bill Kaufman

Between 1954 and 1963 he coached nine St. Louis Park athletes to first place finishes in the state track and field meet. He also had three relay teams that won a state title. Those relay teams were all in the 4 X 440 and occurred in each of St. Louis Park's three state championship years.

Coach recalled an incident that occurred one year during the St. Louis Park Invitational. The Park Relays was a big meet involving some of the track powers in the state like Hibbing, Minneapolis Southwest, Edina, St. Louis Park and Northfield. Coach had included an 8 X 220 relay. As described earlier, any long relay was a bit of a circus because of the odd length of the St. Louis Park track. Coach remembers that his team was leading as Gerry Brouwer took the baton to run the seventh leg of the race. He was to hand off to anchor man, Mike Gillham. However, Gillham was not at the exchange zone when Brouwer arrived. He was leaning against a fence by the side of the track and talking to a girl. Brouwer ran an extra 220-yards and then went back and grabbed Gillham by the neck and kicked him in the rear. Both Brouwer and Gillham would recover from this incident to claim first place finishes in the Minnesota State Track and Field Meet. Mike Gillham won the 440-yard dash in 1962 and the 220-yard dash in

1963. In 1963, Gerry Brouwer won the 180-yard low hurdles and also was a member of the first place 440-yard Oriole relay team. Both Gillam and Brouwer would later earn track letters for Coach Griak at the University of Minnesota.

St. Louis Park Athletes who placed in the top 5 spots in the Minnesota State Track and Field Meet for Coach Griak

1954 Don Brown (880 yards **1st**)
1954 Leonard "Buddy" Edelen (Mile 3rd)
1955 Peter Tinker (880 yards 2nd)
1957 Art Patterson (880 yards 2nd)
1957 Roger Plantikow (High Jump 5th)
1958 Art Patterson (880 yards **1st**)
1958 Jim Kumpula (220 yards **1st**)
1958 Rod Lazorik (Mile 3rd)
1959 Jim Kumpula (220 yards 4th)
1959 Doug Lowry (440 yards 5th)
1961 Mike Gillham (220 yards 5th)
1961 Chuck Patterson (880 yards 3rd)
1961 Bruce Mortenson (Mile **1st**)
1961 Andy Boe (High Jump 2nd)
1962 Mike Gillham (440 yards **1st**)
1962 Bruce Mortenson (Mile **1st**)
1962 Chuck Patterson (880 yards 2nd)
1962 Wally Hlavac (880 yards 5th)
1962 Gerry Brouwer (180 Low Hurdles 2nd)
1962 John Valentine (Mile 2nd)
1963 Mike Gillham (100 yard dash 2nd)
1963 Mike Gillham (220 yard dash **1st**)
1963 Bob Wagner (880 yard run 2nd)
1963 John Valentine (Mile **1st**)
1963 Gerry Brouwer, Bruce Fischer, Phil Homme, John Valentine (440 yard relay **1st**)
1963 Bruce Fischer (120 yard High Hurdles 2nd)
1963 Gerry Brouwer (180 yard Low Hurdles **1st**)

The tremendous success of Coach Griak's St. Louis Park athletes was not the result of luck. It was the product of the high expectations he had for his teams and for each team member. These expectations were coupled with his demand for hard work, determination, team work and a positive attitude. The dedication he demanded was explained in the Oriole handout he gave to his athletes when they came out for the team and the athletes quickly realized that they would be held to these requirements: (The *St. Louis Park Cross Country and Track & Field Handout* is available in Appendix at the end of this book.)

When comparing today's litigious society with the era when he began his career, Coach related several examples of how his actions in the 1950s may have led to trouble if done today. He told the story that involved the first day of cross country practice one year at St. Louis Park. Every boy had to have a physical exam before he could compete and the team doctor, Doctor Smith, charged only fifty cents for these physicals. When Coach asked if everyone had been given their physical exam, one little seventh grader replied that he had not. Coach reflected that today he would have been fired or sued for doing this but he grabbed the startled boy by the testicles and told him to cough. Coach said that he did not charge the boy fifty cents either but told him that he had passed the physical. Another incident which today may have led a teacher to be disciplined or even lose his job involved Coach pulling up the pants of a St. Louis Park student who was wearing them too low. Years later the former student told Coach that he still remembered the incident.

A story that today may have resulted in both Coach and the St. Louis Park principal losing their jobs involved a young man in Coach's Physical Education class who had tried to skip out of taking a shower after class. At that time students were required to shower before heading to their next class. The young man had fled the school and was hiding under a car in the teacher's parking lot. He was apprehended and brought back to Mr. Griak. Coach turned on all the showers in the locker room and tossed the fully clothed student into the showers. He then took him, dripping wet, to the principal's office. Coach told the principal what had happened and left the young man sitting in a puddle of water that was forming below his chair in the principal's office. Coach said that as he left to go back to his class he heard "thwack, thwack, thwack" as the student not only suffered the indignity of being in soaking wet clothes but was also physically punished by the principal. Coach said that the student probably got more punishment from his parents when he got home that day. Today the parents, and a lynch mob, would have been looking for the principal and Mr. Griak. Also a taboo today was the time that Coach picked up and dusted off a seventh grade girl who had fallen in the hurdles. Years later the woman told Coach that she remembered his act of kindness and that he had made her feel better after she had tripped.

40th Reunion of St. Louis Park's First Minnesota State Track & Field Championship - 1998 - (L-R): T. Kiernan, T. Rutledge, A. Patterson, K. Cherry, Coach Griak, B. Oas, R. Lazorik, F. Hamel

Coach said about his 1958 state championship team, "There were some wonderful families who were 'the glue' that helped us create a strong program at Park." Note in the quotation that Coach did not refer to the success of his teams as "My" success! He spoke specifically of the families of Bob Oas, Jim Kumpula and Rod Lazorik. Coach remembered that it was after the season in 1958 that one of his runners, Howie Winer, "Broke my ribs in a touch football game." Coach recalled that Rod Lazorik's father was the head baker at the Cafe de Napoli in downtown Minneapolis. I wonder if this was the reason Gopher cross country teams in the late 1960s held their banquets there. On July 5, 2015, just four days before he passed away, I reminded Coach of those meals at the Cafe de Napoli and that he had told us then that some of the same waitresses had been there since his days as a student at the University of Minnesota. He laughed and said that it was probably true.

St. Louis Park Oriole runners won the Minnesota State mile run every year from 1961-1965. Each of those years resulted in a faster winning time. Bruce "Weebie" Mortenson began the streak with a 4:26.1 victory in 1961. In 1962 he bettered his time in winning to 4:22.2 with teammate John Valentine placing second in 4:23.9. Valentine became the state champ in 1963 with a time of 4:20.7. Bob Wagner won state titles in both 1964 and 1965 with times of 4:18.9 and 4:15.1. Almost all of the top milers in the state in the 1962 (Valentine - 2nd and Mike Elwell of Fairfax - 3rd) and 1963 races (Valentine - 1st, Dave Wegner of Duluth Central - 2nd, Tom Heinonen of Robbinsdale - 4th, and Bob Weigel of Southwest - 5th) became Gophers and ran on the varsity for their new, and in Valentine's case, old coach on Minnesota's 1964 Big Ten Championship Cross Country team. The 1964-1969 top finishers in the state mile, Bob Wagner (1st - 1964 and 1st - 1965), Dick Aften of Osseo (3rd - 1964), Pat Kelly of St. Paul Monroe (3rd - 1965 and 2nd - 1966), Garry Bjorklund of Proctor (3rd - 1966, 1st - 1967, 1st - 1968 and 1st - 1969), Ben Grokett of Roosevelt (4th -1966 and 2nd - 1967), Greg Nelson of Minneapolis Washburn (3rd - 1967 and 4th 1968), Mike Hanley of Anoka (5th - 1967 and 2nd - 1968) later helped to form the nucleus of the strong Gopher cross country teams of the mid-1960s to the early-1970s.

The 1965 and 1966 state 880-yard champion, and one-time state record holder at 1:51.7, Tim Turnbull of Hopkins, also ran varsity cross country at Minnesota in that period.

After completing my eligibility at Minnesota, I did my student teaching at Park in 1972 and was in the same history office with Mr. Eugene "Lefty" Wright. He was as accomplished as a teacher as he was as a coach and track and field official. When Coach Griak left St. Louis Park High School for the University of Minnesota after the spring of 1963 he continued his friendship with Lefty Wright and worked with him in the Olympic Festival, the International Special Olympics and the Race for the Cure. Lefty remained a well-known official for cross country and track and field until his death in 2015. One of Coach's other assistants at St. Louis Park was Bill Torp. Bill Torp had attended Minneapolis North High School and had won the Minnesota State Cross Country Championship in 1947. At that time, the race was just 1.8 miles in length and was run at Lake Nokomis. In State Track and Field Meet competition, Torp had placed third in the mile in 1947 as his North team scored 21 points but were edged by Minneapolis Washburn with 22 and Worthington with 21 1/2. In 1948, the year that the Gophers won the NCAA Track and Field title and the year before Coach Griak transferred to the Twin Cities campus, Bill Torp had placed second in the state mile and had helped Minneapolis North to the team title. Another St. Louis Park assistant coach was Jack Willhite.

Coach Willhite was also the wrestling coach at Park. As he recalled this, Coach Griak chuckled and said that Coach Willhite would pace from one open door in the gymnasium to another but that he was too nervous to watch his wrestlers during a match. "He would peek in one door and then another." Coach said that one of the funniest things he ever saw at St. Louis Park was a match between two of the top ranked heavyweight wrestlers in the state. One was from St. Louis Park and the other was from Hopkins. The mother of the Park wrestler felt that the official on the mat was not being fair to her son. She came out of the stands and hit the official with her purse. The purse came open and coins, lipstick and the rest of the contents of the purse flew all over the mat. The audience was laughing and applauding. It was probably the funniest thing that Coach Willhite never saw too or that he only partially witnessed as he was undoubtedly pacing the hall outside the gym. Coach Griak said that Jack Willlhite was, "A good man but quite a character."

Thinking of Jack Willhite caused Coach to recall another funny story about his friend that occurred in one of his first years coaching the Gophers. At Memorial Stadium there were eight lanes of cinders. The track was considered one of the best in the country. However, in heavy rains the track could become flooded. There was a concrete trough outside of lane eight. In a heavy rain, water would pour down the aisles from the bleachers and hit the trough, causing water to gush into lane eight. Coach recalled that at the Pan American Games Trials held at Memorial Stadium in 1967 there were torrential rains that caused the entire track to become a moat around the infield. Luckily, all the running events had been completed and all that remained was the pole vault. There was an all-weather runway for the vault. Coach recalled that the rain had stopped and that the conditions were perfect but that the track was under water. As he told about this meet he chuckled when he recalled that most of the fans had left but that several of his former coaching buddies from St. Louis Park and their wives had stayed to watch the meet to its conclusion. The bleachers were still very wet so the wives, seated in front of Coach and their husbands, had put newspapers down on the bleachers before they sat down.

Coach laughed again as he recalled that at the end of the meet the wives had stood up and one of the husbands, Jack Willhite, told his wife, "You have newsprint on your seat." Coach laughed even louder when he related that that the woman had said, "Oh, honey, what does it say?" Coach laughed even harder when he said that his friend had replied, "Gopher Tales. "

Coach Griak and the teaching and coaching staff at St. Louis Park not only were good teachers and coaches but they had a great deal of fun at their jobs. Coach Griak was a practical joker who said that, "I really looked forward to going to work every day." Always conscious of the safety of the students at St. Louis Park, he once alerted his friend and fellow physical education teacher, Cliff Bohmbach, that there was a fire drill at the school and then waved at Bohmbach and Bohmbach's class from an upper story window as they stood outside in the rain, the only class to participate in the "fire drill." Cliff Bohmbach was wearing a new blue suit. In the video he made for Coach's 50th year at the University celebration in 2013, Cliff said that he and Coach had been friends for 55 years but that he still had not forgiven Coach for sending him and his class out into the rain. Coach told me that he had once placed a dead bat on a string and then hung it in the classroom closet of a young female teacher at Park. He said in his mind he could still hear the terrified scream and the clatter of her high heels as she fled the classroom and ran down the hallway of the school. One of his favorite stories from his days at Park concerned the Christmas gifts presented to the coaching staff by Stu Grosfield, the sales representative for Champion Sports. In the 1950s there were no sports for the girls and there were no women coaches at Park. Champion placed a package containing a tie in the mailbox of each coach. Coach Griak opened his and, realizing that the packages were all the same, guessed that they were identical ties. Coach was able to get to the mailbox of football coach, Dwaine Hoberg, before the intended recipient of the tie came to claim it. Coach took it home and steamed open the package. He took out the Champion purchased tie and substituted a tie he had purchased shortly after World War II at the haberdashery in the Hotel Duluth. The package was then sealed and brought back to school. It was placed in Hoberg's mailbox. The next day Coach Hoberg was wearing his "new" tie. Coach Griak asked him why his tie was different but Dwaine Hoberg did not realize that all of the other coaches were, by now, aware of the story and that he was the butt of the joke. In the 1960s, when Coach Hoberg was coaching football at Moorhead State University, Coach Griak and Hoberg both attended a banquet and Coach Griak explained the story to him. Waiting a decade to lower the boom on someone is a long time but Coach was a patient man. Of course the story about the tie prompted another story. Coach Griak had also bought a fancy sport coat at the Hotel Duluth

Cliff Bohmbach

Coach wearing the jacket in 2015

haberdashery at the same time that he bought the tie. Coach had the coat for a long time and it eventually became worn and out of style.

Although he was a very sharp dresser, the apparel in his coaching wardrobe was usually worn and out of style. This was a trademark of Coach Griak for as long as I knew him. The coaching jacket I remember him wearing when I competed for him in the late 1960s and early 1970s was one given to him by baseball coach, Dick Siebert. Coach Griak displayed the coat for the audience at the celebration honoring his 50th year at the University in 2013. At that time Coach said that he had had the coat for over 50 years. He joked that he had painted in the jacket, planted flowers in the jacket and coached in the jacket. He said that sometimes his neighbors would see him in this tattered old jacket and, feeling sorry for him, would often come and help him with his work. In 2013, he said of the jacket, "It is my trophy; it reminds me of my first salary at the University which was a hell of a lot more than I get right now." The fancy sport coat Coach had purchased after WW II was eventually given away by his wife, Rose-Mary. She felt sorry for a young man and thought that she could both help a kid who was obviously poor and also get rid of a coat she thought best removed from Coach's closet. However, the poor young man decided to alter his financial situation with a five-finger-discount transaction at a local store. This placed him on the wrong side of the authorities. The young man was wearing Coach's former coat during this transaction and Coach's name was still in the jacket. For a time, Coach Griak was implicated in the crime.

Dwaine Hoberg, the St. Louis Park football coach in the late 1950s, had played football for Bernie Bierman at the University of Minnesota from 1947-1949. Like Coach, he had served the United States during World War II, although he had served in the Navy. In addition to later being the head coach of the Moorhead State University football team, he eventually was elected to the Moorhead City Council. He was then elected in 1971 as mayor of Moorhead. After three terms as mayor he was elected to the State Legislature and served in that capacity until shortly before his death in 1984. While working with Coach Griak at St. Louis Park, he once teamed with Coach on the giving end of a practical joke. Coach Griak said that St. Louis Park High School had hired some of the teachers to lay the sod around the new school. It was a dirty two-day project but it enhanced the meager salaries teachers made in the 1950s. The new sod was kept wet by means of a large hose connected to a fire hydrant. The basketball coach and athletic director, Lloyd Holm, was not involved in the dirty work but did come over to see how the workers were doing.

PICTURED HERE are the 1962 state champs. Back row from left to right are Gerry Brouwer, Jim Bloomquist, Larry Soper, Jerry Orbeck and Chuck DeRemer. Second row: Coach Lloyd Holm, Bob Hill, Mark Zanna, Bruce Ackland and Roy Griak, assistant coach. First row: Gary McCulloch, Gary Biewald and John Kappa.

1962 St. Louis Park Minnesota State Basketball Championship team

Lloyd Holm relaxing with no Roy Griak to pester him

Lloyd Holm, like Coach Griak, had left Duluth and made his way to St. Louis Park. Like Hoberg, Holm had been in the United States Navy during World War II. He had then taught and coached at Duluth Denfeld High School. There he won a Minnesota State basketball championship in 1947. This was about the time that Coach was a student at Duluth State Teacher's College. Lloyd Holm had come to St. Louis Park and had won another state basketball title with the Orioles in 1962. Coach Griak was his assistant on that team. In a letter he wrote to Coach In 1962, Morgan Park High School Principal, Sigurd Ode, expressed the pride that the city of Duluth had for three of its native sons. Lloyd Holm's St. Louis Park Orioles were the state basketball champions. Holm had graduated from Duluth Denfeld. Coach Griak was congratulated for his team winning the indoor track championship and another Morgan Park graduate, Larry Ross had coached International Falls to the state title in hockey. At the time that he retired in 1977, Lloyd Holm was the winningest basketball coach in Minnesota history with 531 wins. However, on the day in question, Holm was wearing a nice suit and tie when he approached the day laborers, Hoberg and Griak. Coach said that it was Hoberg's idea to turn the hose on their athletic director turned sod inspector. Coach Holm saw what was about to happen and initiated the type of fast break that would have made him proud of his players on the basketball court. However, he had not taken into consideration the amount of traction provided by a sodden field. Down he went and the hose, or the water pressure it provided, was then used to roll him over and over on the St. Louis Park High School lawn to be but present quagmire. He ended up soaked and muddy.

Morgan Park High School
SIGURD J. ODE, PRINCIPAL
Duluth 8, Minn.

April 9, 1962

Mr. Roy Griak, Track Coach
St. Louis Park High School
St. Louis Park, Minnesota

Dear Roy:

How we enjoyed reading the Sunday Tribune write up on the Championship you garnered over the week end. Yes, it must have been a real thrill for you. What an array of talent you have developed. I am sure that it is a personal accomplishment. Your knowledge of the sport and your dedication to it will pay you dividends as long as you are in it.

I wrote to Lloyd of course after your State Basketball Tournament. I can't get over how sentimental I was about your winning. Having you two as the victorious coaches in the State classic gave it a two-fold thrill for us. Don't think I didn't call Bruce Bennett, the Duluth News Tribune and Herald sports editor, to make mention of you too and that you were a Morgan Park graduate.

We have done well with our alumni this year. Your accomplishments and Larry Ross's State Hockey Championship.

Keep up the good work.

Greetings to your wife.

Sincerely,

Liz

Coach Holm, as the head basketball coach at St. Louis Park, was also on the receiving end of another prank played by his assistant coach, Roy Griak. Both dressed for practice each day in the coaches' locker room. The lockers were not locked. Coach Griak, always eager to help, used ox blood shoe polish on Coach Holm's dress shoes. After many days and many applications of the polish, Coach Holm's shoes had slowly changed color. One night after practice Coach Griak asked Coach Holm, "Lloyd why are your shoes red?" I am not sure if these pranks had anything to do with Dwaine Hoberg and Roy Griak both leaving St. Louis Park for university jobs. I doubt that Coach Griak was on bad terms with the Oriole athletic director, Lloyd Holm, when he took the Minnesota job in 1963 because the May 15, 1963 issue of the St. Louis Park Echo quoted Lloyd Holm as saying, "I can't think of anyone more capable and he'll (Coach Griak) do a tremendous job for track throughout the Upper Midwest." For his decade of teaching and coaching excellence at St. Louis Park, Coach Griak was inducted into the initial class of the St. Louis Park Hall of Fame in 2005.

St. Louis Park Hall of Fame certificate - 2005

The May 29, 1963 issue of the St. Louis Park High School newspaper, *The Echo*, previewed the Orioles' chances in the upcoming Minnesota State Track and Field Meet. The paper also announced that the meet would be Coach Griak's last at Park. The Orioles did win the Minnesota State Meet in 1963. The meet honored long-time Gopher Track and Field coach, Jim Kelly who was retiring after twenty seven years at Minnesota. Coach Griak had announced that he had accepted the positions of Head Cross Country and Head Track and Field coach at the University of Minnesota. The official date that he was hired by the University was July, 1, 1963. In leaving St. Louis Park High School for the U of M, Coach took a pay cut

St. Louis Park Echo – May 29, 1963

from $13,000 to $9,000 a year. For years he remained one of the best but lowest paid coaches in the nation.

Taking over for Coach Griak would be like replacing Charlie Gehringer at second base for the Detroit Tigers or following Willie Mays as center fielder for the Giants. The track and field head coaching job was given to Orv Bies and he was ably assisted by Lefty Wright. Orv Bies coached track and field for five years at St. Louis Park and was then succeeded by Wright. They coached several athletes who would go on to compete for Coach Griak at the University of Minnesota: Arthur Patterson, John Valentine, Bob Wagner, Mike Gillham, Gerry Brouwer, Tom Bracher, Bob Stein, Randy Jones,

Track and Field Records

Minnesota State High School League

Event	Record	Record Holder	High School	Year
100-yd. Dash	9.9 sec.	McClearie, James	Brainerd	1933
		Anderson, Norman	St. James	1954
220-yd. Dash	21.9 sec.	Gehring, Dick	Mpls. Washburn	1942
440-yd. Dash	49.1 sec.	Gillham, Mike	St. Louis Park	1962
Half-Mile Run	1:57.9	Ferrin, Ralph	Mpls. North	1942
120-yd. H. Hurdle	14.5 sec.	Gigler, Byron	Moorhead	1961
200-yd. L. Hurdle	22.2 sec.	Tharp, Ray	Mpls. Washburn	1942
180-yd. L. Hurdle	19.7 sec.	Lynch, Anthony	International Falls	1962
Half Mile Relay	1:30.5	Mpls. Central	Mpls. Central	1962
Pole Vault	13 ft. 2 in.	Dyjak, John	Mpls. Roosevelt	1962
High Jump	6 ft. 2⅝ in.	Patten, James	Bemidji	1957
Broad Jump	23 ft. 4 in.	Jacobs, Carl	Mpls. North	1941
Shot Put	57 ft. 4½ in.	Peterson, Robert	Marshall	1958
Discus	169 ft. 11⅝ in.	Peterson, Robert	Marshall	1958
One-Mile Run	4:19.9	Nelson, Jerry	Faribault	1959
Mile Relay	3:25.6	Edina-Morningside	Edina-Morningside	1961

Note: See current edition of National Federation Track and Field Guide for national high school records.

SCHEDULE OF EVENTS FOR STATE MEET

Finals Saturday

12:00 – Pole Vault
1:00 – Shot Put – (concrete ring)
1:30 – High Jump
2:00 – Discus – (concrete)
2:00 – Broad Jump
2:45 – 120 Yard High Hurdles
2:55 – 100 Yard Dash
3:05 – One Mile Run
3:15 – Half Mile Relay
3:25 – 440 Yard Dash
3:40 – 180 Yard Low Hurdles
3:55 – 880 Yard Run
4:10 – 220 Yard Dash
4:20 – Mile Relay

STATE TEAM CHAMPS
St. Louis Park

Sitting: Tom Langen, Gary Smith, Mike Gillham, Charles Patterson.
Standing: Jack Wilhite, Coach, Gene Wright, Coach, Joe Ptacek, Bruce Fisher, Wallace Hlavac, Chris Morris, Gerald Brouwer, John Valentine, Fent Morton, Bruce Mortenson, Roy Griak, Coach.

1962 Oriole State Champs pictured on 1963 program

1963

41st ANNUAL STATE TRACK MEET

Jim Kelley came to U of M in 1937. He was at U 27 years. He came from U of DePaul. He is a native of Iowa. He had National Championship Team in 1948 – Big Ten Champs in 1949 and was Olympic Coach in 1956.

MINNESOTA STATE TRACK AND FIELD MEET

JUNE 7-8, 1963

PROGRAM DEDICATED TO JIM KELLY

35¢

This program sponsored by
Minnesota State Track Coaches Association.

Jim Kelly honored on 1963 state meet program

Jim Rutz, Al Shapiro, Bob Jones, and Mark Schmidt, to name a few. When asked about the success of Orv Bies' St. Louis Park track and field teams, Coach replied, "I left him quite a bit."Orv Bies remained a close friend of Coach Griak for the rest of Coach's life. Bies left St. Louis Park to coach track and field at St. Olaf for two years and then was with the Minnesota State High School League from 1970 to 1988. His last two years there he was the executive director of the league.

First Years as Gopher Coach

Don Timm

Roy Griak began his coaching career at the University of Minnesota in the summer of 1963. His St. Louis Park team had just won the Minnesota state track and field title during the previous spring. As a former Gopher athlete and a very successful high school coach, he had the credentials to succeed his former coach, Jim Kelly when Kelly retired after coaching the Minnesota cross country and track and field teams from 1936-1963. One of his first memories of representing the University came on a good will tour that summer to northern Minnesota with three other Gopher coaches: basketball coach, John Kundla, baseball coach, Dick Siebert and hockey coach, John Mariucci (see photo next page). At the age of 39, Coach Griak was twelve years younger than Kundla and eight years younger than Siebert and Mariucci. Like Kundla, who had served in the Navy during WW II and Mariucci who had served in the United States Coast Guard, Coach Griak was a World War II veteran. However, Coach Griak recalled that he felt more than a little bit intimidated by his companions as they drove toward their destination, Seppi's, a beautiful lakefront private home with a sauna and basketball court in Virginia, Minnesota. The Seppi family was in the concrete business.

Coach returning to Maroon and Gold

Being from Duluth and having competed in many of the towns on "The Range," Coach was familiar with the area as was John Mariucci who had been born in Eveleth. However, Coach Griak was in his first year of coaching at the University and his coaching career to that point, although excellent, had been entirely at the high school level. As John Mariucci drove, Coach was in the front seat of the car with Siebert and Kundla in the back seat. Coach Griak said he couldn't help but ponder that all three of the other coaches had established themselves with lengthy careers at the professional level as well as many years of collegiate coaching. John Kundla had played basketball for the Gophers in the late 1930s and, after serving in LST units (Landing Ship, Tank) in both the European and Pacific theaters of WW II, had coached one year of basketball at St. Thomas and then had coached the Minneapolis Lakers for eleven years. His Lakers had won five world championships in the six seasons between 1948-49 and 1953-54. He had coached Slater Martin, former Gopher Whitey Skoog, Vern Mikkelsen, Jim Pollard, Howie Schultz, Clyde Lovellette, Bud Grant, George Mikan and the other great Laker players. When the Lakers moved to Los Angeles in 1959, John Kundla stayed in the Twin Cities and coached the Gopher basketball team from 1959-1968. He had already coached many great Gopher players like Ron Johnson from New Prague and Mel Northway from Minneapolis Patrick Henry High School and was currently coaching Lou Hudson from Greensboro, North Carolina, Archie Clark from Ecorse, Michigan and Don Yates from Uniontown, Pennsylvania.

1964 Gopher Athletic Staff – John Kundla is the first person on the left in the 5th row from the bottom; John Mariucci is two people to Kundla's left; Dick Siebert is in the same row but on the far right; Coach Griak is in the back row and 7th from the left. Athletic trainer Lloyd "Snapper" Stein is in the 3rd row from the bottom and is third from the left. Equipment manager Milt Holmgren is in the second row from the bottom and is 8th from the left. Stein and Holmgren are mentioned later in this chapter.

Being a baseball fan during his youth in the 1930s, Roy Griak was very familiar with Dick Siebert. Siebert had an eleven-year major league career and had played with the Brooklyn Dodgers, St. Louis Cardinals and Philadelphia A's as an excellent first baseman. He had been an American League All-Star in 1943. Coach Siebert had begun his collegiate coaching career at Minnesota shortly after his playing days had ended. Now, in 1963, he was almost midway through a 31-year coaching career as the head coach of the Golden Gophers (1948-1978). Coach Siebert would go on to compile a record of 754 wins - 361 losses and six ties and would win twelve Big Ten titles. Coach Griak knew that under Coach Siebert's guidance, and booming voice, the Gophers had won College World

Series Championships in 1956 and 1960. Coach Siebert's Gophers would add a third national title in 1964.

Several of his star players that year were also stars on Coach Kundla's basketball team, Archie Clark, Bill Davis from Richfield High School and Don Yates. Siebert's stellar record would earn him a membership in the College Baseball Hall of Fame. Some of the Gopher baseball All-Americans he coached at Minnesota include: Paul Giel of Winona, Jerry Kindall from St. Paul Washington High School, Jack McCartan from St. Paul Marshall High School, Noel Jenke of Owatonna, Dave Winfield from St. Paul Central High School and Paul Molitor from St. Paul Cretin High School. Perhaps the most intimidating occupant of the Gopher foursome in the car that day though was hockey coach, John Mariucci. Mariucci had played both hockey and football for the Gophers and had been named to the 1940 All-American team in hockey. He went on to play five years for the Chicago Black Hawks of the National Hockey League. He would have had a longer career in the pros had it not been for serving three years in the Coast Guard during WW II. Although not a great goal scorer for the Black Hawks, Mariucci was a hard-nosed defenseman who was among the league leaders in penalty minutes each year.

As Coach Griak related this story to me in July of 2014, he said, "Mariucci was really a tough son-of-a-gun." John Mariucci coached the Gopher hockey teams from 1952-53 to 1965-66 except for the 1955-56 season when he was coaching the United States Olympic team. That team won a silver medal in Cortina d'Ampezzo, Italy. Coach Mariucci's Minnesota Gopher team lost to Rensselaer Polytechnic Institute in a 5-4 overtime game for the national championship in the 1954-55 season. Some of the great Gopher hockey players Mariucci coached include: Jack McCartan, Ken Yackel, Sr. from St. Paul Humbolt High School, John Mayasich from Eveleth High School, Lou Nanne from Sault Ste. Marie, Ontario, Canada and Doug Woog from South St. Paul High School. After leaving the Gophers Mariucci was an assistant general manager for the Minnesota North Stars for twenty years before his death in 1987.

While trying to blend in but feeling dwarfed by these coaching legends, Coach said that the driver, John Mariucci, motioned for him to get a foil pouch of tobacco from the dashboard and to help him fill his pipe. Attempting to be helpful but having no idea about the protocol of caring for tobacco so that it would remain fresh, Coach took the foil pouch and ripped it open. If this situation had ever come up again, Coach would have known that he was to carefully unfold the foil pouch, tenderly remove the tobacco to be used and then carefully fold the foil pouch again. Coach said that Mariucci blew a fuse and uttered some choice words that ended with, "You dumb rookie."

Luckily for Coach Griak, John Mariucci's temper was diverted to a new target when the Gopher coaches reached Virginia, Minnesota. As part of the "good will" stop the Gopher coaches took part in a pickup basketball game in Virginia against some local college and high school coaches. Coach Griak remembers that one of the team captains was former Gopher quarterback (1947-1949), Jim Malosky. Malosky was in his fifth year coaching football at the University of Minnesota Duluth and would, over the next 35 years, become the winningest NCAA Division II football coach in history at the time of his retirement in 1997, with 255 wins. Coach Griak said that the game was played on an outdoor court and that the game became a little rough. He also said that, "John Mariucci was a terrible basketball player. Mariucci would double dribble and travel, often bouncing the ball once and then run with it like a fullback."

Remembering who was driving the car that would carry him home, Coach tried not to laugh. However, this was not easy as Mariucci always wore a suit and tie and this is what he was wearing during the basketball game. Coach Griak said that Mariucci did not teach at the University of Minnesota and thus did not have an office. He had a job at a local paper company and would come to the University only to coach. His suit coat was his office. He carried all the papers he needed with him at all times (workouts, names of prospects, schedules, etc.). At one point in the game, Mariucci broke loose and with several, not necessarily consecutive dribbles, appeared to be going in for a layup. From out of no-where, one of the Virginia high school coaches caught Mariucci as he was in mid-air and according to Coach Griak, "John Mariucci ended up draped over the branch of a nearby birch tree." After extricating himself from the tree, Coach Mariucci approached the Virginia high school coach who had "checked" him off the court and said, "Don't you ever do that again." In a show of Gopher good will, Mariucci then kicked him in the shins. Coach Griak must have felt lucky to have only been subject to a tongue lashing concerning the torn tobacco pouch. He probably felt even luckier when he heard years later that in an ice hockey world championship game in 1977, John Mariucci, the head coach of the United States team, was involved in a confrontation with one of his own players during a game against the Soviet Union. Former Gopher Lou Nanne, whose collegiate coach had been Mariucci was loudly criticized during the game and Nanne and 61-year old John Mariucci became participants in a fist fight that had to be stopped by other players and officials but was resumed after the game!

Listening as Coach Griak related a story often led to an interruption as he recalled another incident about one of the people in the story. This was how the tobacco story expanded into the story about Mariucci's basketball skills and kicking the Virginia coach in the shins. These incidents in turn jogged Coach Griak's memory about other tales concerning the Gopher hockey coach. Coach Griak said that one year in the mid-1960s, he and Mariucci and a number of other Gopher coaches were at a fund-raising event at Breezy Point in Brainerd. Coach recalled coming out a side door from the dining room and hearing an argument on the other side of a hedge. Coach said that he peeked through the hedge in time to see John Mariucci confronting four men and hearing Mariucci say, "All right, which one of you guys is going to be first?" Coach said that Mariucci had apparently challenged all four to a fight.

This story led to one about John Mariucci on the golf course. Coach Griak said that Mariucci was a terrible golfer, as well as being a terrible basketball player, but that he had been a wonderful football player, that he could really skate and that he never shied away from a fight. He was so tough that he would never acknowledge that he might be hurt as he saw this as a sign of weakness. Once, as Mariucci was playing golf at a Gopher fundraiser, he was struck behind the ear by an errant drive hit by a young lady. Even though a huge lump immediately formed behind his ear, Mariucci did not fall down or seek medical help. He refused to rub the injury and continued his round of golf to its conclusion. At the dinner that evening, with Mariucci's injury still very evident, he shrugged off the young lady's attempt to ask if he was all right and implied that the golf course should be reserved for men. Coach Griak said that such behavior today would "get you fired in about two minutes" but there was a different culture then and an acceptance of behaviors that would be questioned or bring litigation today. The ribbing and banter back and forth between some of the coaches on the University staff would not pass the scrutiny of today's sensitivity conscious and litigious generation. As Coach said, "It was a different time."

Practical Jokes Continued at the University

When Coach Griak came to the University of Minnesota in 1963 the coaches shared cramped offices in Cooke Hall. His office was a narrow room that housed his desk and the desks of John Kundla, the basketball coach, Joe Walsh, the tennis coach, and Wally Johnson, the wrestling coach. Coach Griak and Wally Johnson had desks that were facing each other and separated only by a glass partition. Coach and his good friend, Wally Johnson, often played practical jokes on each other or on other staff members. He said that the coaching staff at that time had a real camaraderie and rapport. Wally Johnson added to his meager wrestling salary by selling cars and also selling wrestling mats so it was common for Coach Griak to hear Coach Johnson quoting prices for one of his side jobs. One day he put a handkerchief over the mouthpiece of his phone and called Wally Johnson even though Johnson was just a few feet away. He said that he represented a small consolidated school district that was hoping to purchase a wrestling mat. Coach deliberately dragged out the conversation and asked if it would be possible for all the colors of both schools to be integrated into the mat and also if the initials and logos of both schools could be represented. When Coach Johnson, eager to make a sale, said that he could provide such a mat, Coach Griak began to inquire about the cost per foot and the composition of the mat. Finally, he said, "Johnson, you dumb Swede, this is Griak." Coach said that in a split second, Johnson had him in a Full Nelson.

Joe Walsh was from New York and coaches Johnson and Griak would regularly tease him about his "Neew Yawk" accent. According to Coach Griak, Joe Walsh never cleaned his desk. He had papers, books and tennis equipment spread all over the desk. The desk, and its contents, remained in that condition except for new layers of materials added daily. Coach Griak, with the knowledge of Wally Johnson, burrowed a hole in the papers and planted an old brassiere on the desk. It remained there for days and was eventually discovered by Coach Walsh's wife. As Joe Walsh was attempting to explain this unfortunate find to his wife, Johnson and Griak were laughing their heads off. Coach said that Walsh's response was, "Damn you Griak." Apparently Joe Walsh had forgiven Coach as he would often call him in recent years from his home in Mankato to talk about their time together at Cooke Hall. Johnson and Coach Griak were also responsible for a prank played on baseball coach, Dick Siebert. They traveled to the St. Paul campus and returned with a bucket full of manure. In an elaborate mock ceremony before the coaching staff, they talked of an illustrious award and then presented the half full bucket of manure to Dick Siebert. What Coach Siebert didn't realize until he had started his car that day was that the other half of the bucket full of manure had been spread all over the engine of his car. Dick Siebert, the Chief, was quite a character according to Coach. He said "It was a pretty salty group of coaches at Cooke Hall in those days and you had better keep your back to the wall, I'll tell you."

Coach Griak related a story of how he and two other Cooke Hall staff members had decided to form a car pool to save money. Besides Coach Griak, the trio included a teacher in the Physical Education Department named Jack Alexander and the assistant basketball coach, Dan Spika. Spika worked with John Kundla but eventually would become the head coach of the Eagles of the University of North Texas. On the first day of the car-pooling experiment, Jack Alexander's radiator overheated and everyone was late. With Coach Griak driving the second day, Jack Alexander was still in bed when

Coach pulled up. Eventually, a small boy came out of the house and said that his father wanted them to go on without him. Coach Griak told the boy to tell his dad that, "I drove all the way over here and I am not leaving until your dad comes along with us." Alexander emerged in a few minutes still buttoning his shirt and bleeding from a hasty attempt at shaving. On the third day the trio was late again and Coach said that the car-pooling was over. It had lasted three days.

Reflections on Coaching at Minnesota

Coach Griak said that when he began coaching at Minnesota he was given a very limited budget to fund his program. It reminded him of his days at Nicollet High School. He referred to this as "penny pinching time at the U of M." He said that even in recent years it almost took an act of Congress to appropriate money for Track & Field and Cross Country. In 1963 and 1964 Dean Anderson served as Coach Griak's volunteer assistant coach. Dean Anderson was Coach's first and only assistant those first two years. He is not in the team 1964 picture; the two young men listed as assistant coaches in the picture were former Gopher pole vaulter Chuck Morrow and former Gopher hurdler Dale Lamski. A half century later as we watched the 2015 Big Ten Basketball Tournament championship game between Wisconsin and Michigan State

1964 Gopher Track and Field Team - Front Row (L-R): Bill Stevens, Wayne Triebwasser, Jim Day, Bart Uplinger, Bob Johnson, Ray Miller, Dean Wolbrink, Norris Peterson – Back Row (L-R): Assistant Coach Chuck Morrow, Wayne Thronson, Creighton Flemming, Byron Gigler, Leroy Anderson, Head Coach Roy Griak, Tom Barnes, John Peterson, Wendell Bjorklund, Mike Elwell, Assistant Coach Dale Lamski

from his home in Plymouth, Coach joked about the large contingent of assistant coaches that stood in the huddle at each time out. Coach said to me, "they must have a coach for each player on the team!" When Coach mentioned Dean Anderson, he decided to call him to thank him again for his help so many years ago. The number of letters Coach wrote to his friends and athletes each week and the number of phone calls he made each day would have been enough to keep the U.S. Post Office and the telephone companies solvent if he was their only customer.

In his early days as the head of the University program Coach saw that things needed to be done and would often have them done without seeking official permission or going through the proper channels. The administration was not always sympathetic or even aware of what was needed to run the first class program that Coach Griak wanted and created at Minnesota. As Coach prepared to host the Big Ten Outdoor Track & Field Championships in 1968 (a meet won by his Golden Gophers), he realized that there was no water pit at Memorial Stadium for the 3,000 meter steeplechase event. As a former steeplechase runner, that caused me to wonder how Roy Good had placed 5th in the 1948 NCAA championship in that event which was held at Memorial Stadium! Had the officials allowed the event to be run without a water pit or had there once been a water pit that had been filled in by 1968? Coach gave the orders himself to have the water pit dug inside the curve on the Cooke Hall side of the stadium. This was not far from the ramp leading down to the Gopher locker room and also to Lloyd "Snapper" Stein's training room. Some readers may remember the short ramp from the track that led to a screen door and then another screen door just inside the locker room that led to Snapper Stein's "office." Just down the hallway from the locker room was the equipment room where Gopher athletes could daily find equipment manager, Milt Holmgren, and Snapper as they were playing cribbage at the equipment window. They could be interrupted long enough to have Milt give you clean socks, shirt, towel, jock and shorts and pass them to you across the cribbage board that was drilled into the surface of the equipment window.

Today's athlete might snicker at such facilities but I thought that to change my socks in that locker room was treading on sacred ground. The plush, state of the art locker rooms on the University of Minnesota campus today are very nice but do not evoke thoughts that Fortune Gordien, Bronco Nagurski, Vern Gagne or Roy Griak may once have used one of the lockers. As the excavation for the steeplechase water pit was being done by Virgil Dwinell, the Memorial Stadium groundskeeper, with Coach Griak there acting as site foreman, Coach happened to look up and see Athletic Director, Marsh Ryman, looking over the railing from the front of Cooke Hall. Mr. Ryman said, "Griak, what the hell are you doing?" Coach replied, "building a water pit." Athletic Director Ryman responded, "what the hell is a water pit?" When reminded of this at his home in Plymouth after his 6-week hospital / rehabilitation stay, and shortly before his death on July 9th of 2015, Coach said, "I should have told him I was building a duck blind." Always looking for a positive about everyone, Coach added that Marsh Ryman and his wife never missed a Gopher track meet.

Marsh Ryman

Coach Griak was never one to sit idly by if he felt that his program was not treated as the first class sport he knew it to be. In 1973, he sent then Athletic Director, Paul Giel, an article that had appeared in the Des Moines Register on November 28th, shortly after Coach's Gopher team had improved from a 7th place Big Ten cross country finish to place 19th in the NCAA Meet. This marked the first time since 1970 that the Gophers had been sent to the national meet. The article appears on the next page in its entirety along with Coach's note to Paul Giel and Paul Giel's response.

Coach Griak said that one of the reasons he always liked cross country and track and field was that there were no judgement calls; the stopwatch or the measuring tape determined the outcome of the contest. There were very few times when Coach left a meet with the feeling that the rules of cross country or track and field had not been properly followed. Although Coach did not dwell on the "what ifs," "almosts," and "if onlys," he did remem-

Des Moines Register Page 20
Wed., Nov. 28, 1973

Over the Coffee®

Reward of Virtue

THIS WEEKEND I experienced one of those great moments that serves to convince atheists that there is indeed a God and that he is just.

It was one of those delicious times when retribution follows so close on the heels of outrage that the only plausible explanation is the guiding hand of Divine Providence.

It happened, of all places, in Ann Arbor, Mich., and it involved, of all things, the University of Michigan football team.

In case you weren't tuned in to the Game of The Century (and there's a Game of The Century televised on the average of twice a month) on Saturday, a very good Michigan football team played a tie game with a very good Ohio State football team.

The game was supposed to decide which team went to the Rose Bowl but, being a tie, didn't decide anything. Everybody in Ann Arbor, however, assumed that Michigan would be chosen, if for no other reason than Ohio State went last year and it was Michigan's turn, all things being equal.

The Big 10 athletic directors didn't see it that way. On Sunday, they voted to send Ohio State because they figured Ohio State would have a better chance of winning than Michigan.

Well, I happened to be in Ann Arbor while all of this was going on and you would have thought that the Japanese had bombed Pearl Harbor again.

The people at the university, particularly in the athletic department, treated the vote as an act of treachery unparalelled in human history, with the possible exception of Hitler's invasion of Poland.

THE MICHIGAN coach, Bo Schembechler, was especially moving. He cried real tears as he called the action "a tragic thing for Big 10 football" asked poignantly what he would tell his boys. Touching, very touching.

Laugh, I thought I'd die.

You see, two weeks before the great University of Michigan had not sent its cross-country team to the NCAA finals in California because it cost too much — $1,200 — and they figured their harriers didn't have much chance of winning.

Funny thing about that. Nobody cried tears; not even the cross-country coach. He's got his relationship with his athletic director to think about, after all. Nobody said it was a Big 10 tragedy.

And yet cross-country is one of the most enobling of sports. Sacrifice, hard work, discipline; those are the elements that make the sport. There are no crowds, no cheering, no glamor. You run through the woods all fall and, as a reward, you get a chance to go to the NCAA finals and run through the woods with the best.

So what if you can't win? Competing, that's what amateur athletics are all about, aren't they? Didn't I read that in a brochure somewhere?

That brochure apparently is out of print as far as the new breed college athletic director is concerned, and Michigan's Don Canham is one of those. "If you can't beat 'em, don't play 'em," that's the battle cry these days.

All of which makes Michigan's failure to be voted to the Rose Bowl so delightfully ironic.

YOU SEE, on any moral grounds, Michigan deserved to be the Big 10 representative. Michigan had lost to an inferior Ohio State team last year to lose out on the Rose Bowl bid.

This year they were playing a superior Ohio State team, ranked number one in the nation. Michigan fell behind at the half and looked as though it was going to be run out of the stadium.

But it came back in the second half, exhibiting all of the virtues they tell you football is all about — heart, courage, fortitude. They actually pushed Ohio State around and tied the game; came close to winning it. No wonder they thought they had the Rose Bowl bid wrapped up.

Yet, in retrospect, they should have known better. What do athletic directors care of moral grounds, of rewarding virtue? A majority didn't think Michigan could win on the West Coast so they didn't send it.

The only real difference between the situation of the football team and the cross-country team is that the football team got shafted by strangers. The cross-country team got it from friends.

—*Donald Kaul*

Paul — For your info. R. Griak

Roy — I know your heart is in the right place but it is nice to see the "Haves" get a blast now and then. Boy am I glad I let your team go to the NCAA final. Dave

ber them. Decades or a half century after the outcome of a meet was decided Coach could describe the particulars of certain meets that did not turn out the way they should have ended. Coach Griak was not one to blame any athlete but he was such a competitor that he still rued the outcome of close meets where his Gophers (or St. Louis Park Orioles) ended up on the short end. When I asked Coach about one of his most famous athletes, Leonard "Buddy" Edelen, I could sense that I had hit a nerve. Coach explained how "Buddy" was a trouble maker heading for more trouble when his mother asked Coach if he would put him on his track team. Coach Griak said that Edelen's mother watched him like a hawk but that his father was not a strong disciplinarian. He had turned into a "hell raiser." "Buddy" was unruly and stayed out late. His mother wanted some help for her son and asked if Coach would work with him. Always willing to give every athlete a chance to prove himself, Coach agreed to give Edelen a chance. "Buddy" Edelen was in Coach's description "obese." Buddy was about twenty pounds overweight. In Edelen's biography, A Cold Clear Day, Buddy himself said that his nickname had been "Butterball Bud." However, under Coach's instruction, persistence and guidance, Edelen began to lose weight and to improve by leaps and bounds. Coach saw that he had a desire to excel. He had an internal motivation and a desire to achieve. Eventually, he was beating everyone and was on his way to becoming the best miler in Minnesota. He placed third in the Minnesota State Track and Field Meet in 1954. However, the Edelen family moved to South Dakota just before the next school year. Coach said that he pleaded with the mother to allow "Buddy" to stay so that he could run for St. Louis Park in the state meet of 1955 but she wouldn't listen. "Buddy" Edelen moved to South Dakota and became the South Dakota state champion in cross country and in the mile. He represented Sioux Falls Washington High School. "Buddy" Edelen's training partner and friend, Don Brown, had been Coach Griak's first individual state champion when he won the 880 in 1954. Coach always wished that Edelen had stayed at Park. Edelen returned to Minnesota during his college years and was an All-American in cross

Left: Article from the *Des Moines Register* – Nov. 28, 1973

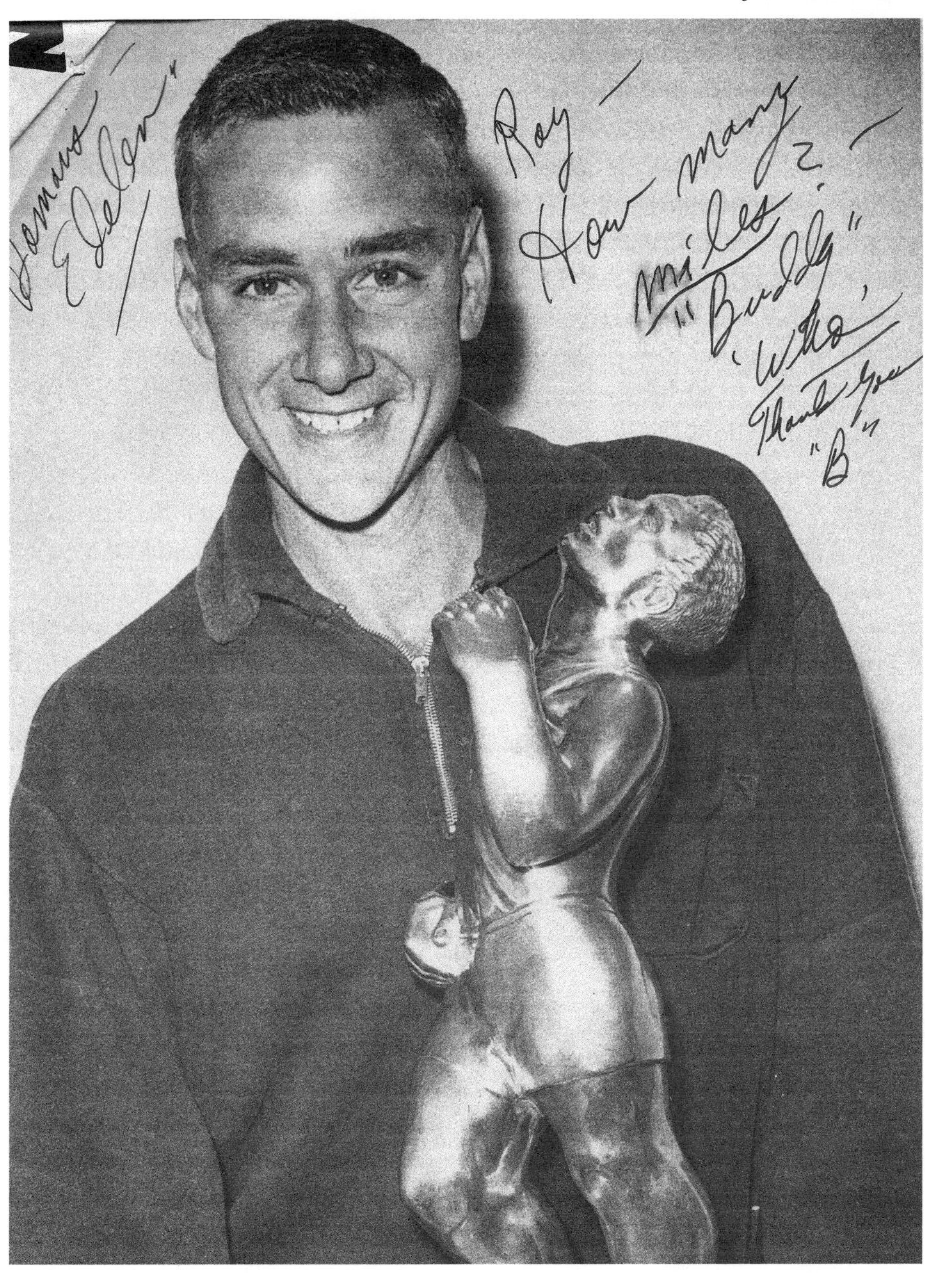

Leonard "Buddy" Edelen's hand written note to Coach

country in both 1956, when he placed 9th in the NCAA and 1957 when he was 4th. He was the Big Ten individual cross country champion in 1957. Buddy Edelen had become a tenacious distance runner. Coach said that Buddy was driven to do well. "A runner can have all the talent in the world but if they don't have a passion for competing success will not happen." Leonard "Buddy" Edelen had that passion and continued to improve. He eventually became the world record holder in the marathon and the first American to break 2 hours 15 minutes for the event. Edelen set the world record in England on June 15, 1963 when he ran 2 hours 14 minutes and 28 seconds. Edelen was the first American to hold the world marathon record since 1925 when Albert Michelsen ran 2:29:01. The only United States runner since "Buddy" Edelen to hold the world record in the marathon was Khalid Khannouchi who ran 2:05:38 in 2002. "Buddy" Edelen also became the first American to break 30 minutes for the 10,000 meter run. Although injured and not in his best shape physically, he placed sixth in the Tokyo Olympics marathon in 1964. Leonard Edelen died in Tulsa, Oklahoma in 1997 at the age of 59. Like so many young people over the years, Buddy Edelen may never have known of his talent and potential had it not been for Coach Griak's encouragement, patience and guidance.

Concerning the 1972 NCAA Cross Country Championship contested in Knoxville, Tennessee, Coach Griak was certain that Garry Bjorklund would have beaten Steve Prefontaine

Coach with a stop watch and a twinkle in his eye

had Garry not been troubled by a bad back that was aggravated by the numerous down-hill portions of the course. Garry led a good portion of the race and finished second in the NCAA Meet. The third place finisher was another Minnesotan. Mike Slack, representing St. Paul Harding High School, had finished third to Garry in the state mile in 1968 and placed second to Garry in 1969 when Garry ran 4:05.1. Mike Slack had run 4:11.6. Unfortunately for Coach Griak and the Gophers, Mike had gone to North Dakota State.

With basketball, football, hockey and so many other sports there were controversial judgements and also some parents who were unhappy that their son was not playing or being treated fairly. Decisions about who made the varsity and who got to compete in a meet were usually clear cut with cross country and track and field. In April of 2014 as we were watching the Penn Relays on his television, Coach watched as an American woman passed the anchor woman of the Jamaican team in the last 20 meters of the 800 meter relay to win the race for the United States. Immediately the two athletes embraced. Coach Griak said that he felt that the congratulations in track and field are more genuine than those "staged" handshaking demonstrations at the end of contests in other sports. He said that having players line up and shake hands "doesn't mean a thing" but that track athletes can be both competitive and real sportsmen (women). Coach also said that, compared to some sports, he always felt that the athletes who competed in cross country or track and field were more likely to stay in school for four years and also were more likely to earn their degree.

Reflecting on the seven Kentucky basketball players (2015) who had almost immediately announced that they would be available for the NBA draft, Coach chuckled and said that Wisconsin Coach, Bo Ryan hit the nail on the head when he referred to this as "rent an athlete." Coach Griak said that he could usually count on his athletes being on the team for four years and that this allowed him to watch them mature not only physically but academically and emotionally. He said that he enjoyed watching them "turn from boys into men." Speaking from his home in Plymouth, Coach told me early in 2015 that "bringing a neophyte athlete toward his (or her) goals created the most lasting memories for him and made coaching fun." "What an athlete's Mom and Dad want is fine but the motivation had to come from within the person himself (herself). An athlete had to want to succeed; they would not do well because of someone else wanting them to do well." In March of 2015 Coach reflected that his profession was very different than a job that had a beginning and an end. He said, "it's not like a math problem, where if worked properly will result in the same answer each time." "Working with young athletes, you are never done." "When you are working with a human mind you are never finished. Teaching is so great because you can follow your athletes while they compete but also later in life."

Thousands of us know that Coach has certainly followed us and our careers and families, long after we concluded our last athletic competitions on his teams. Unlike the mathematics problem that might be worked on for a period of time and then forgotten, the humans are never really forgotten. He then went on to give several examples. He said he would never forget Tom Page often arriving late at Thomas Beach for cross country practice with his Mach I steaming and also that he would never forget the constant smile on Tom's face. He also said that he would never forget the look on future Gopher shot putter Tom Bracher's face when he caught him shooting spitballs in his home room class at St. Louis Park. Coach supervised a 15-minute home room in the St. Louis Park auditorium at the beginning of each school day. He said that when the students left each day there were spitballs all over the auditorium. One day he looked up in time to see Tom Bracher making a "V" with his fingers and shooting a spitball with a rubber band. Bracher was given a paddling in front of the whole class. Coach Griak never let "Mouse," as Bracher was called, forget it. He would never forget what "beautiful" running form St. Louis Park half miler, Archie Patterson had. Coach said that Archie's feet never stayed on the ground for long. He said that he would never forget the Tarzan yell that Dick Aften would give after each victorious cross country race. He would never forget pole vaulter and daredevil Glen Bullick yelling "hey, Coach" from the rafters of the U of M field house. He would never forget the late Colin Anderson, being hit in the face with a pie at the Northwest Open. When asked directly if he was a part of this joke, Coach said, "no, but I knew it was going to happen." Coach said that the instigator was distance runner, Tim Oliver. Coach said he would never forget the wonderful students he was privileged to coach. He was as impressed by their academic excellence as he was by their successes in track and field.

He related that he would always remember a track trip in 1974 where Steve Croy, who still holds the Gopher freshman record of 8:58.4 in the steeplechase, chuckled when he found an error in the medical journal he was reading. Coach recalled that Steve Croy and later, Mike Torchia, never wasted a moment of time as they prepared for their careers in medicine. One of the biggest surprises, or most unexpected things Coach saw in his long tenure at Minnesota was Adam Steele, from Eden Prairie, winning the NCAA 400-meter dash in 2003. At that time Coach was already retired from active coaching but he was still traveling with the team and then, as he did throughout his life, still had a great rapport with all the athletes. Adam beat all the seeded runners in the center lanes while running his race from lane eight. At the time of the Regional Meet he did not have a qualifying time and advanced from that meet to the national meet because of his place in the regionals rather than time. Adam Steele shocked everyone, including Coach Griak, by winning the national meet. Gopher Mitch Potter, from St. Michael-Albertville, was third in the NCAA finals in the 400 meter. To have two kids from Minnesota be at the front of the national meet in the 400 meter race was a pleasant surprise. Coach also said he would never forget Swedish high jumper, Steffan Strand, who set the current Gopher record at 7' 7" in 1998. Coach said that Steffan was very cocky but that he backed up everything he said as evidenced by his NCAA finishes of 2nd indoors and outdoors in 1997, 3rd outdoors in 1998 and 2nd outdoors in 1999. Coach Griak remembers sitting with Coach Phil Lundin on a bank near the high jump area of the track and watching Steffan competing in a big invitational. There were two jumpers who had already cleared 7" 4" and Steffan had missed his first two attempts. On one of the failed attempts Coach Lundin had called out to him, "I think you were a little close to the bar." Steffan turned and replied, "Oh, really?" He then had the bar moved up to 7' 6" and cleared the bar on his first attempt to win the competition.

Coach Lundin told me that Steffan Strand once shrugged off his advice to make an insurance clearance at a lower height and waited until all his competitors were out of the competition before entering the high jump at 7' 1.' After making that clearance on his initial attempt Strand came over to coaches Griak and Lundin and said, "one jump, Big Ten Champion." Coach said that he would never forget how limited David Sharp was in his running ability and yet how determined and tough he was as a competitor. Coach said that he would always remember the courage, positive attitude and unique sense of humor of Carter Holmes. The list of memories collected over his coaching career was endless (and priceless).

Coach said that in track and field he could recall very few times when a meet or a race was decided by something other than the athlete who ran the fastest, jumped the highest or threw the furthest. There were a few exceptions. He recalled that in the Big Ten Indoor Meet in 1968, his Minnesota team was fighting to climb to second place in the team standings as they entered the final event, the mile relay. The Gophers were leading the race going into the final exchange. The anchor leg for the Gophers was run by Richard Simonsen. Simonsen was leading the race and was only 10 yards from the finish line when the Michigan State anchor man, Bill Wehrwein, hit the Minnesota baton with his baton. Richard Simonsen crossed the line first but without a baton. Michigan State was awarded first place. Coach said that even though there was green paint from the Spartan baton on the Minnesota baton, the officials disqualified the Gophers and the Gophers received no points in the event. That meet was run on March 2, 1968 in Michigan. In the winter of 2014 Coach Griak stated that "this was one of the biggest disappointments in all my years of coaching." "It was a complete violation of the rules and it was just not fair."

Coach's disappointment was not so much that his team had been on the wrong side of the decision but that the rules of track and field were not honored. I am sure that if the roles were reversed and he was asked, Coach Griak would have called an infraction on his own team. Coach Griak honored his 1942 senior class motto at Morgan Park High School: "Cheaters Never Win." The meet was won by Wisconsin with 51 points. Michigan was second with 48 1/2 points. The Gophers were third with 33 1/2 and Michigan State was fourth with 25 followed by Indiana, Ohio State, Purdue, Iowa, Illinois and Northwestern. When asked for his memories of this race, Richard Simonsen admitted in an email in 2015 that the bitterness had not faded in the 47 years since the race. He said that he remembers the race vividly. He wrote, "we ran a good team race and it was neck and neck most of the way. Coming off the final turn, I was carrying the baton in my right hand. On my outside the MSU runner (Wehrwein) was carrying the baton in his left hand. As he tried to pass me in the final 20 yards his left arm came down hard on my right hand and the baton was knocked from my hand. I had a fleeting question in my mind - should I stop and pick it up (thereby losing for sure) or continue to the finish. The finish was only 10 yards away and I decided to keep going and crossed the line in first place, but without the baton. We were disqualified despite appeals that the baton had been knocked out of my hand. A fair result would have been to keep the placing order the way we finished (Minn. #1 and MSU #2) although with film documentation, MSU could have been disqualified for encroaching on my lane position. I was my usual grumpy self after losing, and so on the bus on the way home (yes, bus was the order of the day at that time) I was tossing the baton around when I noticed a streak of green paint on our aluminum baton!

There was the evidence that the Spartan runner's baton had hit ours (MSU of course used green, in this case on their wooden baton). It's one of the most bitter memories of my running career as I felt like I had let the team down and I was very disappointed in the Michigan State anchor for not 'fessing up" to what had happened - but I suppose one couldn't expect him to pass up the event championship that they now had in their guilty hands!"Tell us how you really feel about it Richard! He recalled that, although Coach may have been seething inside, "He was both philosophic and magnanimous in accepting this injustice." Over four decades later, Simonsen said that Coach's reaction that day was "A lesson that did not go unnoticed, nor unused, later in my life."

Coach also related a story about an injustice during the fall season. The kingpin for cross country in the Big Ten for many years was Michigan State. However, Minnesota started to challenge that dynasty, winning the conference title in 1964 and having strong teams in the next few years. Always anxious to run against the best, in the cross country season of 1968, Coach scheduled the Gophers to run in a triangular meet in East Lansing against Michigan State and Eastern Michigan. Cross Country meets then were often run quite early in the morning, usually on a Saturday. The dew on the grass in East Lansing made it very difficult for the Gopher runners, who were not familiar with the course, to follow the chalk line that marked the course. There were no meet officials to guide the lead runners. The lead runner for the Gophers, and the entire race, was Steve Hoag of Anoka, Minnesota. Steve had placed third in the Big Ten Meet in 1967 as the Gophers had been second to Indiana. Michigan State had placed 8th in the conference in 1967. In the 1968 triangular meet Hoag had a considerable lead on his teammates and the Spartan and Eagle runners when he approached the finish of the race. Hoag deviated slightly from the chalk line because with the sun shining on the wet grass he could not see it. When asked about this race in early March of 2015, Steve Hoag said that someone in a Michigan State letter jacket pointed for him to go what turned out to be the wrong way.

When he was presented with this account and asked if he thought that anyone would intentionally misdirect a runner Coach Griak replied "Gibbard would do that." The Michigan State coach, Coach Jim Gibbard who coached MSU cross country teams from 1968-1983, disqualified Steve Hoag causing the Gophers to lose the meet. The Michigan State runners acknowledged that Hoag would have easily won the race and that Minnesota should win the meet, however, Coach Gibbard upheld the disqualification. Although I was not a member of the Gopher traveling squad in 1968, and did not know of the disqualification until Coach told me the story in the winter of 2014, it made me feel good that Minnesota defeated Michigan State at the University Golf Course the next fall (October 18, 1969). Coach Griak's Gophers did this without disqualifying any of the MSU runners. I recall picking up a large wood chip in the last 200 yards of the race, having it impaled on my shoe, and not quite being able to catch Kim Hartman, the top Spartan runner, at the finish line. My frustration would have been even greater if Minnesota had not won the meet 28-29. In the Big Ten Conference Meet later that year the gap was expanded to 66 points over the Spartans. In the days leading up to the 1969 Big Ten CC Meet in Bloomington, Indiana, Coach told us to believe that we were ready for our best race of the year. Minnesota placed 4 runners in the top 8 spots in the conference meet to win Coach Griak his second Big Ten cross country title.

It was the same MSU coach, Jim Gibbard, who two years later at East Lansing left one of his top runners at the course and without a ride back to campus because he had not run as well as the coach expected in a meet against the Gophers. That runner was Ken Popejoy, from Glenbard West High School in Chicago. He was one of the best Spartan runners and would break 4:00 for the mile many times during his collegiate career. However, Coach Griak remembers that Coach Gibbard was so mad at Popejoy that day that he berated him in front of his teammates and the Gopher team. Coach Griak was so moved by the way Popejoy was treated that he invited Ken to go out to dinner with the Gopher team before they returned to the Twin Cities. Coach said from that day on, Ken Popejoy was his friend and that Ken "would have transferred to Minnesota if he could have."

Travels and Travails

Don Timm

Injuries

Coach Griak was very thankful that during his lengthy coaching career at Minnesota there were no life and death matters involving any of his athletes. He said he was always concerned that "one of my kids would get hurt." Obviously there were numerous examples of athletes having their seasons shortened or curtailed by pulled muscles, broken bones, sprains, strains, and various illnesses. Perhaps Coach's finest distance runner, Garry Bjorklund, of Twig, Minnesota, had an emergency appendectomy the day after winning the Big Ten Cross Country Championship in 1970. Garry missed the NCAA CC Meet in Williamsburg, Virginia that fall and sat out almost the entire indoor season of 1971 but was able to train for two weeks and still win the Big Ten indoor 2 mile title in Madison, Wisconsin. Garry also injured his foot during the summer leading up to his senior year and was not able to compete at the level that had earned him three consecutive Big Ten Cross Country titles (1969-1971). Another scare for the Gophers was when 1997 indoor Big Ten Champion and three-time All-American pole vaulter, Tye Harvey, was injured while traveling to a meet at the University of Illinois. The Gopher team had flown to Chicago and then rented cars for the trip to Champaign-Urbana. On the outskirts of Chicago one of the cars, driven by another vaulter, was in an accident and Tye Harvey broke his arm. He was unable to compete and instead watched the meet. Harvey still holds five of the top ten vaults in Gopher history and is tied for the top Minnesota indoor vault ever at 18' 2 1/2". One of the most frightening events of Coach's career occurred at a Big Ten Cross Country Championships in 1984. David Duvick from Eden Prairie was one of the varsity seven Gopher runners that year and, along with Paul Gisselquist from Richfield, would co-captain the cross country team in 1985. Near the end of the 1984 race he began to weave and wobble but he refused to give up. Finally, he collapsed. Duvick recalls that he threw up on Coach's leg that day. Coach got the medics immediately and David was packed in ice. David remembers that he was taken to the emergency room at a local hospital but was released the same day. Gopher teammate Dave Casale, from Coon Rapids, recalls that Duvick wasn't the only Gopher runner to be taken to the emergency room that day as Blaise Schweitzer, from Cretin, collapsed at the finish line and also needed medical assistance. Blaise was a good cross country runner and steeplechaser in track who passed away from cancer in 2008.

Another time one of coach's pole vaulters came down in the planting box. He began to turn purple and Coach called for an ambulance from the University Hospital. Thankfully for the vaulter and for Coach, this situation was not as terrible as when Penn State vaulter, Kevin Dare, was fatally injured during the Big Ten Indoor Championships at the Minnesota field house in 2002. Kevin's tragic death on the Saturday portion of the meet caused the Sunday portion of the championship to be cancelled. Coach recalled that distance runner John Myers was severely injured when he fell and gouged his leg on the low shot put wall that used to be just inside of lane one on the track at the field house. The shot used to be thrown on the infield of the track with the circle in the center of the track and the shot being thrown toward the track. The shotput area was on the end of the track near where the University Avenue entrance to the track and the display of Big Ten Champions, All-Americans and records is located today. There was a wall to keep the shot from rolling onto the track. The wall stood about 1 1/2 feet high and arced along the track. For those of you familiar with the old dirt track in the field house, the wall started at the end of the pole vault pit and ended just about where the large, white, thirty second sweep hand clock stood on the west wall of the building. John Myers gashed his leg on the corner of that wall and has a permanent scar as a result. Although it led to no injury, Coach said that he was scared out of his mind when 1973 indoor and 1975 outdoor Big Ten Champion and All-American pole vaulter, Glen Bullick, yelled, "hey, Coach," as he was climbing in the rafters high above the track in the field house. Coach Griak related a story about an injury he personally suffered concerning the water pit at the original Bierman track. Unlike the later track layout, the original Bierman track had a water jump located outside the curve on the south end of the track. Having lugged the heavy hurdles onto the track with fellow steeplechaser Carter Holmes many times and having filled the water pit for practices and meets I was very familiar with the man hole cover located near the water pit. It was covered with Tartan and was very difficult to pry open, lift and then slide to the side in order to get to the valve below that would turn on the water to fill the pit. Coach said that he once had the pry bar slip and he smashed his fingers in an effort to prepare the water pit for a meet. I wonder how many other coaches in the Big Ten did the many varied tasks that Coach Griak faithfully did to prepare the track for a competition. Coach always wanted to make sure that everything was just right if he and the Gophers were hosting a competition. He was the first one there and he would be the last one to leave after the meet and after he had thanked each official and everyone who had worked setting the hurdles, raking the jumping pits, moving the starting blocks, or helping in any way. Coach Griak had always told his runners to go ten yards beyond the finish line in their races. He demonstrated that attitude in conducting a well-run meet.

Taking charge at a Bierman Field track meet

Gopher T & F Athletes from Other Sports

Coach Griak coached many athletes who were recruited by the university to participate in other sports. Joe Lane was recruited by Dick Siebert to pitch for the Gopher baseball team. Joe was from Proctor High School, a school that would later send distance runners Garry Bjorklund, Tim Oliver and most recently, Matt Welch to the university. Joe realized that his future as a baseball pitcher was limited and, with encouragement from Coach, became an excellent shot putter. In 1966, Joe Lane put the shot 58' 0" to tie Bob Henry's 1958 school record. I know that one of my teammates, Jeff Crawford, came to the university to play baseball and, instead, developed into an excellent triple jumper. In 1969, Jeff hopped, stepped and jumped 45' 7", a mark that at that time had been exceeded in Gopher history only by Lloyd LaMois (45' 10"). Rick Upchurch was an excellent football player who also long jumped 24' 6 1/4" in 1974. Coach said that in all his years of coaching, he remembers only one Gopher basketball player who came out for track. That has changed with the second place NCAA high jump finish in 2014 for former Gopher basketball player, Wally Ellenson. The basketball player Coach referred to was long jumper Lou Hudson. Without pausing to look it up, Coach proudly mentioned that Lou Hudson later became mayor of Park City, Utah. "Sweet Lou" Hudson, who passed away in 2014 at the age of 69, also had a 13 year career in the National Basketball Association with the Hawks of St. Louis & Atlanta and the Los Angeles Lakers. He was a 6 time NBA All-Star and scored just shy of 18,000 points in his career.

Coach recalled several Minnesota hockey players who also participated in track and field. Brad Beutow from Mounds View High School, who later coached the Gopher hockey team for 6 winning seasons and also coached at Colorado College, was a very good high jumper, clearing 6' 11 3/4" in 1970. Brad had been a Minnesota state champion in 1968 when he won the event with a leap of 6' 3." Unlike most of the jumpers of today, Buetow and teammate Tim Heikkila used the straddle rather than the Fosbury flop. Gopher hockey player Craig Sarner, from North St. Paul, was also a Gopher hurdler, running 56.4 in the intermediate hurdles in 1968. There have been many Minnesota football players who have also competed for Coach Griak's track and field teams. Brad Buetow's brother, Bart, threw the discus 165' 5" in 1972 to place fourth in the Big Ten Conference Meet. After his days at Minnesota, Bart played football in the National Football League with the New York Giants and the Minnesota Vikings.

"Jumping Jim" Brunzell, a Gopher football player from White Bear Lake High School high jumped an indoor best of 6' 6" in 1969 for the Gophers. He had won the Minnesota State high jump title for White Bear Lake High School in 1967 with a jump of 6'2". Jim later became a professional wrestler. His wrestling partner was Greg Gagne, the son of 4-time Gopher Big Ten champion and 2-time NCAA Gopher wrestling champion Verne Gagne. Jim Brunzell and Greg Gagne, won the AWA World Tag Team Championship in 1977 and then again in 1981. In the 1981 title match, "The High Flyers," as Brunzell and Gagne were called, defeated Adrian Adonis and future Minnesota governor, Jesse "The Body" Ventura. Gopher football star, Hubie Bryant, who like Bart Beutow, would later play in the NFL, was a Big Ten champion in the 60 yard dash in 1967 and in the 220 in 1968. He was a receiver and punt and kickoff specialist with Pittsburgh and New England in the NFL where he used his sprint speed to avoid large tacklers. Hubie Bryant's 220 victory in the 1968 Big Ten Meet was instrumental in helping Coach Griak's Gophers to a one-point victory in the outdoor championships that year at Memorial Stadium. Other Gopher football players who became sprinters for Coach Griak were Chester Cooper, Omar Douglas (1994 Big Ten champ at 55 meters), and Chris Darkins (1996 Big Ten champ at 55 meters).

Coach recalled that before his time at the helm of the track team, the Gopher football team had a great running back who was also a great sprinter. This was George "Sonny" Franck of Davenport, Iowa. Franck won the Big Ten 60-yard dash during the indoor season of 1941 (6.3 seconds) when Coach Griak was a junior in high school. Franck had been co-captain of the Gopher team that year. Coach said that Franck may also have been as good a football player as fellow Gopher, Bruce Smith who won the Heisman Trophy in 1941. Franck had been an All-American and was third in the voting for the Heisman Trophy in 1940 when it was won by Michigan's Tom Harmon. Franck had led the Gophers to an 8-0 record and a national championship in 1940. That year he also won the Big Ten Medal for Scholarship and Athletics. He and Harmon were the starting running backs for the College All-Stars when they played the Chicago Bears in 1941. Franck was chosen as the college MVP for that game.

A reserve running back on that team was UCLA's Jackie Robinson, who would become the first African-American in the twentieth century to integrate baseball's major leagues when he played for the Brooklyn Dodgers in 1947. Like Coach Griak, "Sonny" Franck also served the United States in the military during WW II. He joined the Marines and saw action as an officer on Iwo Jima and later as a fighter pilot on the USS Hornet. It was from that ship earlier in the war (April 18, 1942) that Jimmy Doolittle had launched his bombing raid on Tokyo. Franck played 4 years of professional football with the New York Giants. Coach Griak said that "Sonny" Franck was a dapper dresser; "he wore the loudest clothes possible and looked like one of those exotic birds from South America."

Tom Brown, who won the state shot put title in 1953 for Minneapolis Central and placed tied for second in 1952 and then second in 1954, became an All-American tackle for the Gophers. In 1954 he was defeated by Bob Henry of University High School who placed third in the NCAA Meet in 1957 and 1958 for the Gophers and established the shot record of 58" 0" that would be tied by Joe Lane in 1966. Tom Brown also had placed second in the state discus in 1953 and had been the champion for Minneapolis Central in 1954. Robert Blakely was another football player who became a standout sprinter for the Gophers. He did his sprinting in 1957-1958 which would be after Coach had run for the Gophers and before he became the head of the track and field program in 1963.

Coach Griak said that Bernie Bierman was a sprinter on the track team at Minnesota and that Bierman always used to come to the track meets when Jim Kelly was coaching. Coach recalled that he met the legendary Gopher football coach once when Bierman was waiting for a bus and Coach picked him up in his car and drove him to the campus. Coach Griak gave a lift, literally and figuratively, to untold thousands during his long life.

Stories About Other Coaches He Has Known and International Competitions

Coach Griak has rubbed shoulders with just about every coach in Minnesota, most coaches in the country and many of the top coaches in the world. I remember calling Coach in 2003 to tell him that Arthur Lydiard, the great distance coach from New Zealand, would be speaking at

Armstrong High School near Coach's home in Plymouth. We agreed to go together and planned to get there early because we thought that there would be a crowd. We expected that the meeting would be in the auditorium but were surprised to find that Arthur Lydiard would be speaking in a small classroom. We were even more surprised to find an audience of only about 15 people waiting to hear the famous Kiwi coach. When Lydiard entered the room and looked around he immediately spied Coach Griak and said, "I know you." They had met in the mid-1950s and Coach Griak had made a lasting impression on Arthur Lydiard. Listening to Coach's stories about his coaching friends, like Payton Jordan, who coached the 1968 USA Olympic team in Mexico City and had coached at Stanford for 23 years, or Elvin "Ducky" Drake, who had been the track coach at UCLA from 1947-1964, or Al Buehler, who had coached at Duke just about as long as Coach Griak was coaching at Minnesota added a deeper understanding to a sport and an era I realize I knew only superficially. I had competed several times at UCLA's Drake Stadium but I did not know that it was named for their famous coach. Those of us who competed and knew Coach Griak are hopeful that the new track facility at the University of Minnesota will bear the name of our Coach.

"Ducky" Drake had been the coach for two great UCLA and Olympic decathletes at the same time. They were Rafer Johnson and C. K. Yang. They were teammates at UCLA but in the 1960 Olympic Games in Rome, Johnson represented the United States while Yang represented Taiwan (Nationalist China). In a very close contest Johnson won the gold medal and Yang the silver. In 1968 Rafer Johnson would team up with former NFL football player Rosie Grier to disarm and capture Sirhan Sirhan after he had shot Bobby Kennedy in Los Angeles. According to Coach's memory "Ducky" Drake once had an extra relay member on the track behind some hedges and that the runner took off with a baton when his teammate entered the hedges alongside the track. Coach Drake was succeeded by a man who became one of Coach Griak's very good friends. That was Jim Bush, who would win five NCAA Track and Field titles at UCLA. While doing research for this book, I had the privilege of getting a phone call from Jim Bush. I remember that during the conversation he said, "if I was a young man I would have loved to have had the opportunity to compete for Coach Griak." I told him, "Coach Bush, I was lucky enough to have had that opportunity."

In addition to the great number of athletes Coach helped to prominence at the University of Minnesota he also worked with many of the top athletes in the United States because of his involvement on Olympic and national teams. He made a lasting impression on many not only because of his expertise in track and field but because of the warmth of his character. He is pictured below with three time Olympic Gold Medalist Jackie Joyner-Kersee. She won a silver medal in the heptathlon in Los Angeles in

Jackie Joyner-Kersee with Coach in 1984

1984 and won gold medals in the heptathlon in Seoul in 1988 and Barcelona in 1992. She also won a gold medal in the long jump in 1988 and bronze medals in the long jump in 1992 and in the Atlanta games of 1996.

Also pictured below is Coach with two time Olympic High Jump Bronze Medalist (Munich in 1972 and Montreal in 1976) Dwight Stones. A secret to Coach's popularity was that he treated everyone with respect and that he always

Dwight Stones and Coach

took time to "stop and smell the roses" even if the flowers hat he was appreciating during the Los Angeles Olympiad of 1984 were not roses (see picture on this page).

Smelling the flowers

Coach Griak was a member of the USA Olympic coaching staff in 1972 when the games were in Munich, West Germany. Another member of thc staff was thc Univcrsity of Orcgon coach, Bill Bowcrman. Hc was one of the founders of the Nike shoe company. Coach Bowerman wanted a training shoe for his distance runners that would give them better traction in the often wet conditions they experienced in Oregon. Supposedly, Coach Bowerman concocted a rubber-like substance and poured it into his wife's waffle iron. The product was then trimmed and glued to the bottom of a pair of training shoes. Thus was born the Nike waffle trainer. Coach said that "Bowerman was a crusty guy." Bowerman had told Coach that the "1972 Olympics was the worst experience of his life." Before the competition, the US team had gone to the practice track outside the Olympic stadium for a training session. The German officials did not want to let the US team into the stadium. A big, tall German guard, confronted the American team and told them "it's not your time." Coach Bowerman begged to differ and began to argue. Coach Griak remembers that Bowerman finally said to the German official, "we whipped your ass in WW I, we whipped your ass in WW II and we can do it again." With that the US team entered the practice track for their workout. I asked Steve Savage, who was both a runner at Oregon for Coach Bowerman and a steeplechase runner on the 1972 U.S. Olympic team, if he remembered that story. He said that he didn't but that it sounded like something that Coach Bowerman would say and do. Coach Griak also recalled that in 1972 there were several time trials and pre-Olympic meets for the United States team before they left for Europe. At one of these meets at a college near Boston, Massachusetts Coach Bowerman told some of the American sprinters to turn off their boom box. Coach said that his exact words were, "no more boom box." They were directly below his second floor room and the music was too loud in Bowerman's opinion. When they did not comply with his request he dumped water on their heads. Coach also said that Bill Bowerman's great idea about getting the entire Eugene, Oregon community, young and old, to take up running was copied from Arthur Lydiard, who had done the same thing earlier in New Zealand.

An attack by Arab terrorists on Israeli athletes in Munich put a damper on the spirit of the entire games in 1972. It also resulted in the deaths of 11 Israeli athletes / coaches. The attack began on September 5, 1972 and put the games on hold for two days. Coach Griak recalled that he could see the Israeli headquarters from his room in the United States quarters. The United States team was ordered to stay in their rooms during the standoff between the terrorists and the soldiers who were trying to end the hostage crisis. Coach remembers that he saw one of the terrorists come out onto a balcony in the Israeli quarters and that he had a gun with him. Security was very tight in Munich with a tall fence and barbed wire around the Olympic village. "How they got in there I don't know." Coach Griak said that he also remembered how his coaching friend, Stan Wright was subject to unfair criticism in Munich. Coach Wright was one of the most respected coaches in the United States. He had been the first Black head coach of a United States national team when he led the team against Poland and then the U.S.S.R. in dual meets in Los Angeles in 1966. He had coached at Texas Southern for 26 years and had been the head coach at the school from 1950-1967. There he had coached, Jim Hines, who won the 1968 Olympic Gold Medal in the 100 meter dash in Mexico City. Coach Wright had also coached at Western Illinois from 1967-69 and at the time of the 1972 Olympic Games was the head coach at California State University in Sacramento. He would remain there from 1969-1979 and then would become the Athletic Director at Fairleigh Dickinson College from 1979-1985. Coach Wright had been the sprint coach of the U.S. team in Mexico City in 1968 and had been severely criticized for the actions of two of his athletes. Tommie Smith had won the Gold Medal and John Carlos had won the Bronze Medal in the 200-meter dash. On the victory stand, the two sprinters appeared barefooted to express Black poverty and, during the playing of the National Anthem, had bowed their heads and each had raised a gloved fist in a statement of Black Power. They were both sent home by the United States Olympic Committee. Coach Wright was blamed for allowing his athletes to make such a statement. He said that he could not control the actions of any athlete and that they, like anyone else, were free to act as they chose as long as they were willing to accept the consequences. In Munich, Coach Wright was again the sprint coach for the United States team. This meant that he was in charge of three of the favorites in the 100 meter dash: Eddie Hart, Rey Robinson and Robert Taylor. On August 31,1972 all three advanced from their first-round races to the quarter-finals to be held later that day. They were relaxing in the Olympic village shortly after 4:00 P.M. believing that they would run their quarter-final races that evening when they saw 100 meter races on the television. At first, they thought that this must be a replay of the morning races. However, they soon realized that it was the quarter-final heats. They rushed to the Olympic Stadium but both Hart and Robinson had missed their races. Robert Taylor arrived with just a minute to warm up and he managed to finish second to Valery Borzov in his heat and advance to the final the next day. Taylor was able to win the Silver Medal behind the Soviet (Ukranian) sprinter, Valery Borzov. Coach Wright was berated on national (and maybe international) television by ABC's Howard Cosell for allowing the United States' sprinters to miss their races. Stan Wright took the responsibility, and the brunt of Cosell's venom, because he did not want his athletes to be blamed. Coach Wright had been operating from an outdated schedule. He had asked German officials at the track the day of the race if the schedule was still correct and they had confirmed that it was. Eddie Hart, in particular, stood up for Coach Wright. Hart and Taylor helped the United States to win the Gold medal in the 4 X 100 meter relay.

Coach Griak recalled that he roomed next door to Coach Wright in the Olympic village and that he could hear him sobbing all night long. When I heard this my thoughts were that if Coach Wright needed a friend at that time, the most compassionate friend he could ask for was "right" next door. Stan Wright died at the age of 78 in 1998. His cousin, Larry Ellis, had died just two days earlier. Coach Ellis had been the coach of the 1984 United States Olympic Track and Field team in Los Angeles. Coach Roy Griak was also on the coaching staff of that U.S. team.

Howard Cosell may have had free reign with his remarks against a United States' coach who was virtually defenseless because he did not want any of the blame to fall on his sprinters; however, Howard Cosell was given a lesson in geo-politics that Olympic Games in Munich by the Gold Medal winner in the 100 meter and 200 meter dashes. Howard Cosell, who knew everything and if you didn't believe that you could have just asked him, attempted to interview the Olympic sprint champion. Valery Borzov was from the Ukraine, which was then a part, but a very reluctant part, of the Soviet Union. With an interpreter there, Howard Cosell told Valery Borzov on national television, "Well Mr. Borzov, you have certainly made Russia proud to have won these two races." Without waiting for translation, Valery Borzov replied. "nyet!" There was then an exchange between Borzov and the interpreter before the interpreter turned to Howard Cosell and stated, "Mr. Borzov would like to inform you that he is NOT a Russian." Perhaps Stan Wright could have been allowed to give a critique of Cosell's ignorance of the weak bonds that held the old Union of Soviet Socialist Republic's together. Perhaps he could have related a story that was told to me while I was a student in a class on "Russian" history at the University of Minnesota. Professor Adams told of the peasant from the U. S. S. R. who was unhappy and was told by a soviet official, "the Russian soil is your mother and the Communist Party is your father; what more could you want than to be a child of Russia?" The peasant replied "I would like to be an orphan."

On a lighter note, Coach recalled that at the opening ceremonies in

Munich the East Germans were very stern, somber and straight faced. However, this changed when the teams were all in the stadium and the host country had released hundreds of pigeons. The pigeons circled the field and began crapping on everything and everyone below. Coach remembers that most of the US team, dressed in their red blazers, had white streaks on their coats. The East Germans had been prepared for this event and had taken out newspapers to cover their heads. The East Germans thought that the predicament was very funny and they were laughing at the Americans.

Coach Griak was not able to watch much of the Olympic Games in 1972 because of team meetings and practices for the track team. He said that he did watch a boxing match. He also commented on the controversial finish to the basketball gold medal game between the United States and the Soviet Union. When they lined up for the Olympic gold medal game on September 10, 1972 the United States had won 63 consecutive games and every gold medal in men's basketball from the inception of Olympic basketball at the Berlin Games of 1936 through the Mexico City Games of 1968. They also won in 1972 but were deprived of the gold medal by some Soviet chicanery. After Doug Collins had stolen the ball with 10 seconds remaining, he had been fouled. He made both free throws to give the United States their first lead of the game 50-49. The last few seconds of the game were played 3 times due to a mysterious time out called by the Soviets and due to an "error with the clock" at the scorer's bench. Finally, the desired Soviet result was manufactured (USSR 51 - United States 50). In the last replay of those final seconds, a timekeeper was tardy in starting the clock and this allowed the Soviets to go the length of the floor where Aleksandr Belov bowled over a U.S. player and scored the "winning" basket. Jim Brewer, who had been a Mr. Basketball in the state of Illinois and was then a star for Coach Bill Musselman's Minnesota Gophers was a member of the Olympic team and scored 9 points in that final game. The United States team was coached by Hank Iba. Coach Iba had recently retired from a collegiate career where he had been at Oklahoma A & M (renamed Oklahoma State University in 1957) for 36 years (1934-1970). His teams won NCAA titles in 1945 and 1946. They were the first team to win back to back titles. Oklahoma A & M also was the runner up in 1949 to the next team to claim back to back titles, Adolph Rupp's University of Kentucky team (1948 & 1949). At this time Coach Griak was making the transfer from UMD to the U of M Twin Cities. In the 1972 Olympic Games, Coach Iba and the United States team protested the outcome of the final game and refused to accept the silver medals. The medals are still locked away in a vault in Switzerland and several of the team members have it written in their wills that no family member is ever to accept that silver medal.

As he talked about the opening ceremonies in Munich Coach was reminded of a time when he was a coach for the World University Games in Winnipeg, Manitoba, Canada. He said that before the athletes and coaches were paraded into the stadium they were marshaled at an adjacent stadium and told to wait for the ceremony to begin. Coach said that the wait was long and the grass in that stadium was very high and that the mosquitoes were eating everyone alive. This must have reminded Coach of his time in the service in the South Pacific where the mosquitoes were a constant presence. Less than perfect conditions at major events was something that Coach would encounter again. He recalled that at the Pan American Games in Mexico City in 1975 the stadium was literally falling apart. This stadium had hosted the Olympic Games in 1968 but, after only 7 years, was now crumbling. Coach said that Joe Vigil,

USA Pan-American Games coaches – Joe Vigil is on the far left and Coach is fourth from the left

from Adams State in Alamosa, Colorado, was also on the coaching staff in Mexico City and that they became very close friends.

Vigil's cross country and track teams won a total of 19 national titles in NCAA Division II. His 1995 cross country team won the national meet with a perfect score of 15. One of the highlights of the Pan American Games that Coach and Joe Vigil witnessed was a world record set in the triple jump. On October 15, 1975, Joao Carlos de Oliveira bettered the existing record in the triple jump by 17 3/4 inches when he jumped 58' 8 1/2".

Coach Griak remembered traveling to California with his friend Niilo "Ed" Hendrickson for the 1960 United States Olympic Trials which were held in Palo Alto at Stanford University. Like Coach Griak, Ed Hendrickson had served in the Army in WW II and had later run for the Gophers. Hendrickson had earned Gopher track letters in 1946 and 1947. Ed was from the Iron Range and, after graduating from the University, coached at Embarrass, Minnesota. He started the track and field program at Embarrass and had had great success there. He was nicknamed "the Flying Finn" after the original flying Finn, Paavo Nurmi. Coach Hendrickson's teams at Embarrass were known as "the Flying Finns." Hendrickson later moved south and coached in Edina. In his 29 years at Edina and Edina East high schools he would have three state track and field team titles. Edina won Minnesota State Track and Field titles in 1969, 1970 and 1974. His mile relay teams at Edina won state titles in 1961, 1964, 1965, 1966, 1968 and 1969. He also coached cross country and had an individual state champion, Tom Page, who would be a star on Coach Griak's 1969 Big Ten Championship cross country team.

At the time of their trip west in the summer of 1960, Coach Griak was coaching at St. Louis Park. They did not have a great deal of money for the trip and he and Ed Hendrickson slept in their car as they first drove to Las Vegas and then to San Diego. They stayed in a room at the YMCA in San Diego. Since they had arrived several days early they decided to cross the border to visit Mexico. Coach and Ed went to Tijuana, Mexico. Coach Griak was a little leery of staying in Mexico and drove back to San Diego for another night at the YMCA. Ed Hendrickson decided to spend the night in Tijuana. Coach had two wallets as Ed Hendrickson had given his to him so that it wouldn't be stolen. I recall that as Coach told this story, he laughed and said that Ed would probably still be there if he hadn't gone back to get him as he had no identification or money.

When Coach returned the next day to pick up his friend he found Ed under a sombrero and sleeping in the street. He had been mugged during the night. They were able to get back into the United States and made it to Stanford in time for the meet. Coach remembers that they watched

Don Bragg set the world record in the pole vault on July 2, 1960. Bragg used an aluminum pole to vault 15' 9 1/4". Later that year he would win the gold medal in the vault at the Rome Olympics and then startle the audience by giving a Tarzan yell on the victory stand. The Tarzan yell was also the trademark of Dick Aften when he ran on Coach's teams in the mid to late 1960s. Coach said that Bragg was hoping to become the next Tarzan in the movies but that he failed in that endeavor. Coach and Ed Hendrickson were gone for a week and a half watching the Olympic Trials but survived their trip and enjoyed many years of friendship and friendly rivalry as coaches. Coach Griak said about Ed Hendrickson, "he was a good friend, a real good guy and tremendous coach." They are pictured below with Gary Hanson who had the honor of running for Hendrickson at Edina and Coach Griak at the University of Minnesota. The picture was taken on a visit to Virginia, Minnesota and was taken shortly before Ed Hendrickson's death on January 11, 2010. He was 89 years old. Coach Griak was 87 at the time and although he had not been actively coaching for 14 years he was still active as an administrative assistant for the Gopher cross country and track and field teams.

Coach, Gary Hanson and Ed Hendrickson

While driving Coach to a doctor's appointment in early January of 2015 he told me that he had gotten a call from Gary Weineke, the former coach at the University of Illinois. He chuckled at the memory of being the best man at Gary's wedding. He had arrived late so that they performed the ceremony a second time. I mentioned to Coach that at the Big Ten Track and Field Meet a few years ago at the University of Minnesota I had talked briefly with Coach Weineke. He was in his last year as the Illinois coach and I wanted to wish him well. I introduced myself and said that I had run during the era when he had coached Ken House, Lee Labadie and Rick Gross. He said that he remembered me and then proceeded to tell me a story about Ken House. House was an excellent distance runner and had placed 4th in the 1969 Big Ten CC Meet when the Gophers had placed three runners ahead of him and won the meet at Bloomington, Indiana. He said that Ken House was a very dedicated runner who would often run alone at odd hours of the night. One night at 2:00 A.M. Coach Weineke received a call from the police in Champaign-Urbana informing him that they had House in jail and that he should come there, vouch for him and bail him out. Apparently there had been a robbery near the campus and the police had seen House running down the railroad tracks in the early hours of the morning. They chased and caught him and were not completely convinced that he was an Illinois runner out for a training run. The story reminded Coach Griak of a similar situation involving two of his athletes. The Gopher Track & Field team was scheduled to leave the campus very early one morning for an out of town competition. The campus police, in what was likely a blatant case of racial profiling, stopped two Gopher athletes who were walking down the street toward Cooke Hall and carrying big travel bags on their backs. One of the athletes was sprinter, Francis Ude. Ude had run 100 meters in 10.40 in 1981, a time which still ranks 4th on the all-time Gopher list.

The track and field coach of the Iowa Hawkeyes from 1948 to 1977 was Francis Cretzmeyer. Coach Cretzmeyer had been an excellent trackman for the Hawkeyes in the mid 1930s and, as a hurdler, had been an alternate on the United States team for the 1936 Berlin Olympics. He was quite traditional and had trouble accepting the dress and appearance of modern athletes. Coach Griak recalled that in the early 1970s his Gopher team competed against Iowa and that the Hawkeyes had a miler who was the favorite in the race against Minnesota. The runner had very long hair and Coach Griak said that Coach Cretzmeyer didn't like his style. In the meet, the Iowa miler was soundly defeated by Gopher runner, John Hopko, who, like Tom Heinonen before him, had attended Robbinsdale High School. After the race Coach said that he heard coach Cretzmeyer say to his miler, "not only do you look like shit but you run like shit." Coach Cretzmeyer was succeeded as coach at Iowa by one of his best runners, Ted Wheeler. Wheeler had placed fifth in the NCAA 1,500 meters in 1956 and then had placed second in that race at the 1956 United States Olympic Trials. Wheeler did compete in the Olympic Games in Melbourne, Australia but his 3:50.02 did not advance him to the finals. He had run personal bests of 3:48.0 in the 1,500 meters and 4:04.7 in the mile while at Iowa. Ted Wheeler coached the Iowa Hawkeyes in cross country and track and field from 1978 to 1996. He and Coach Griak left active coaching in the same year. Coach said that he enjoyed his association with Wheeler. As he did with most of his peers, Coach Griak had several good stories about Ted Wheeler. Coach said that a farmer near Des Moines once presented Wheeler with a live pig that would serve as the meal at a pig roast for the Iowa team. Coach Griak said that Wheeler told him that he had driven from the farm through downtown Des Moines with a live and squealing pig tied to the roof of his car. On another occasion, Coach Wheeler had asked a stewardess during a flight, "how long until we get to Cedar Falls." The stewardess replied, "this plane is going to California." Coach Wheeler was succeeded by another great Iowa distance runner. Larry Wieczorek won six Big Ten Championships and was a four time All-American while competing for the Hawkeyes in the 1960s. As a coach he led Iowa to the Big Ten Outdoor Track and Field Championship in 2011 when it was held at Francis Cretzmeyer Stadium in Iowa City. He retired as Iowa coach in 2014. In the video he made for Coach Griak's 50th year at the University celebration, Larry Wieczorek referred to Coach as "one of the most revered coaches in the country and as a coach who loved his athletes and they loved him." Coach Griak chuckled as he recalled Purdue track coach, Dave Rankin. Coach said that he was "such a stickler for detail" that he would bring a tape measure to every meet and measure everything. He would measure the runways for the horizontal jumps; he would measure the depth of the planting box for the pole vault; he would measure the shot ring; he would measure the length of the exchange zones; he would measure anything else that could be measured. Coach Griak said that coach Rankin hated coach Sam Bell of Indiana and that the two of them would argue rules at every Big Ten meeting. Coach Griak said that the Michigan coach, Don Canham, later became Athletic Director for the Wolverines but that in cross country he would only run four runners if he didn't have a strong team. In that way Michigan would not get a team score. In my research for this book, I found that in the two Big Ten Cross Country Championships where I was a member of the Gopher varsity (1969 and 1970), Michigan did not enter a team. When I was competing most of the runners I saw at the front of the conference championship were wearing maroon and gold and I never noticed the absence of Wolverines!

Coach Griak was also very familiar with the coaches of other sports at the University and with other coaches around the Big Ten. He told me a story about the longtime Michigan State basketball coach, George "Jud" Heathcote. Heathcote coached the Spartans from 1976-1999 and won the NCAA title in 1978-1979 with the help of his great player, Ervin "Magic" Johnson. Some of Coach Heathcote's friends had pestered him for basketball tickets and he had given them three tickets for seats right behind the MSU bench. Only two of his friends had shown up but, during the game, they began to ride the referees mercilessly. The referees warned Heathcote and the hecklers and finally had the coach's two friends thrown out of the arena. As they were being led out they pleaded with Jud Heathcote to help them. As Coach told the story he said that the two "friends" had said to Heathcote, "do something Jud; what can we do?" Jud Heathcote replied, "use the other ticket." Coach held season tickets for Gopher basketball for many years (section 106, row 24 and seats 1-4). He remembered one game at Williams' Arena in early February of 1994 when the Northwestern coach, Ricky Birdsong, left the Wildcat bench during the game and came up to sit in the stands with the Gopher fans. He said that Coach Birdsong sat in the aisle one section to his left and just a couple of rows below him and shook hands with the fans and gave a high five to Goldie Gopher. Coach Birdsong was placed on disability when he returned to Evanston and eventually was relieved of his job. Tragically, he was murdered by a white supremacist group on July 2, 1999 in Skokie, Illinois while jogging with his children near his home.

Strange Incidents from a Career in Coaching

Coach Griak recalled there were so many muggings in Detroit that when his teams would go to a meet like the NCAA indoor championship it was not safe to walk the seven blocks from the Cadillac Hotel to Cobo Arena. The coaches and athletes were advised to travel in groups and never to go out the back door of the Cadillac Hotel. I remember hearing that one-time world record holder in the high jump (7' 6" in 1971), Pat Matzdorf, of Wisconsin, had been robbed on the way to Cobo Arena. When coach mentioned Detroit he thought of another strange trip he had to the motor city. He had been invited to speak at a track and field clinic in Guelph, Ontario, Canada. However, there was a plane strike and a railroad strike that prevented him from leaving Detroit. He was in Detroit but he had no money and no food. Coach told how there was a Republican caucus in Detroit and how he had put on a Republican elephant button and then gone from caucus room to caucus room munching on the food provided for the delegates. He said that the clinic in Canada was usually very good but that "the British thought they knew it all."

A high school coach who made a funny impression on Coach Griak was Minneapolis Roosevelt's Freeman McInroy. One of his runners was Ben Grokett who later ran cross country and track for Coach at Minnesota. Ben had placed fourth to Garry Bjorklund's third in the 1966 Minnesota State Track Meet mile with future Gopher, Pat Kelly of St. Paul Monroe improving to second from his 1965 place of third. Ben Grokett finished only .4 seconds behind Garry in the 1966 race but in the 1967 race Ben placed second, again behind Garry, and was only .1 second off Garry's winning time of 4:14.0. Coach Griak was already coaching at the University when he attended a meet at the Burnsville Relays in 1984. Coach McInroy, who had a booming voice, was yelling at some of his Roosevelt athletes to "hurry up" as they got out of a limousine. They had come directly from their high school prom and after their relay race they left the stadium and got back in their limo to return to the prom. Coach said that this was one of the strangest things he had witnessed at a track meet in his entire career.

After the Munich Olympic Games Coach Griak accompanied the United States team to the Soviet Union for a dual meet in Leningrad. The city that is now St. Petersburg was known as Leningrad from 1924 to 1991. Coach related that as he entered the stadium his attention was drawn to a disc sailing seemingly higher and further than he had seen one thrown before. To his surprise, the disc had been thrown by a young woman. After the competition there was

Coach Griak in 1972

a dinner and celebration for the Soviet and U.S. athletes, coaches and officials. Coach Griak said that the woman who had made the great throw earlier in the day came over and asked him to dance. Coach said that she was a huge woman and "she had more hair on her legs than I had on my head." Coach said she picked me up in a bear hug so that "my feet never touched the floor." She waltzed around the room with me. "I was like a feather in her arms." "There was no chance that my shoes would get dirty as they never touched the floor." This was Coach Griak's dance with Faina Melnick, who had won the gold medal in the discus in Munich in 1972. She had broken the Olympic record three times during the finals of the 1972 games and would eventually set eleven world records. Coach Griak had the reputation of being an excellent dancer; however, Faina Melnick never gave him the chance to demonstrate his fancy footwork because his feet never touched the ground!

In another competition in the old Soviet Union Coach Griak roomed with fellow coach, Stan Huntsman of the University of Tennessee. He recalled that Huntsman was approached on the street by a Soviet citizen who wanted to buy his blue jeans. Coach Huntsman asked Coach how he would get back to the hotel if he did indeed sell his pants. He thought about this and decided to keep his pants. The United States team stayed at the Europa Hotel in Moscow. Coach said that, although the hotel was new, the floors were uneven and the plumbing did not work very well. Coach recalled that Stan Huntsman would usually go out each night and talk to reporters. One night he failed to return so Coach Griak went out looking for him. Coach walked across Red Square and finally spotted Huntsman. He had apparently imbibed a great deal of vodka and thought he was talking to an agent of the KGB. Coach tried to escort him back to the hotel but just before they arrived his roommate decided that it was time to relieve himself of some of the liquids he had been drinking. Coach Griak realized that they were on a public street and within sight of a small car that he knew to be a police car. Coach Huntsman said, "I'll just go behind this tree" and then proceeded to do his business behind a tree that was about an inch in diameter. Coach was certain that they would be arrested but apparently the police officers were sleeping in their car. When recalling Stan Huntsman, Coach Griak told a story about a national competition where Tennessee and Minnesota were both involved. One of Coach's runners, former Marine, Gerald Metzler, was very tough but not the most graceful runner in the world. He ran a personal best of 3:43.1 in the 1,500 meters in 1978. Huntsman asked, "Griak, where in the hell did you get that guy?"

One year at the Texas Relays in Austin, Coach Griak was on the rules committee. This was one of many times that he served on the rules committee of a big invitational where Minnesota competed. One of the Texas coaches was also on the committee. That coach had what Coach Griak referred to as a "rendezvous" with a young woman the night before the meet and, afraid that he would be recognized when the rules committee was announced before the entire stadium, he pulled his Texas Relays hat down over his eyes to conceal his identity and pleaded with Coach Griak to "hide me." The mention of the Texas Relays caused Coach to recall a year when the pole vault had not yet been decided when the Gopher team was scheduled to leave for the airport. Glen Bullick, who won Big Ten titles indoors in 1973 and outdoors in 1975 and would have a personal best of 16' 5" (1975) was winning the event and had to be left behind in Austin, Texas. Bullick won the event and then spent the night sleeping in a farmer's field before returning to Minnesota. Coach said that "there are some incidents and some guys I will never forget." In July of 2015, at the visitation the night before Coach Griak's funeral, my wife and I were in a long line and happened to be directly behind Glen Bullick. When he introduced himself, I recalled the story and asked him for his recollections. Glen said that he had indeed been left behind and that he did win the event but that he had actually spent the night in a barn rather than a farmer's field.

Once in Oslo, Norway with the United States team, Coach was getting off a train and ran into the superintendent of schools from his days in Duluth. He said of this incident, "it is a small world." Coach Griak said that in one of his first years as a coach at the University he was asked to participate in a charity golf tournament in Crookston, Minnesota. Coach had never played golf. He said that he bought an old set of clubs and a bag from a teacher at St. Louis Park. The total expenditure amounted to $15. The teacher who sold Coach the clubs was named Del Daly. Daly had been an excellent gymnast and had won the 1941 NCCA title in the flying rings while a student at the University of Minnesota. He served in the United States Navy during World War II and also served in the Korean Conflict. Del Daly taught for 37 years at St. Louis Park and became the head of the physical education department. He was a very organized teacher and, according to Coach, "I learned a great deal from him about being a good teacher." Using his "new" clubs and with a large crowd watching, Coach hit a car in the parking lot with his first drive. His second drive went into a sugar beet field. His third swing was a whiff and by that time everyone was laughing at him. He said that it took him so many hours to play 9 holes that he needed a box lunch before he finished. After this exhibition on the links, Coach Griak subscribed to the Mark Twain adage that "golf is a good walk ruined." Coach Griak loved golf courses, and the hillier the better, but he preferred encouraging his cross country runners on them rather than chasing an elusive golf ball.

Coach remembered traveling to the University of Michigan in Ann Arbor for a meet and having his roommate, the man who coached the Gopher javelin throwers, returning to the room in a state of inebriation after a night on the town with some of the Wolverine coaches. Coach recalled that he had placed his clothes over the radiator to dry and that the Gopher coach stumbled into the room, walked over to Coach's clothes and urinated all over them. In the morning when Coach confronted him with the evidence he refused to believe that he had done it. Coach also remembered a Gopher trainer, in a similar state of intoxication, walking into an empty swimming pool. Strange roommates for Coach Griak who had said that "altogether, I don't think I had a full can of beer in my life." The annual spring trip to Louisiana State University in Baton Rouge produced many stories about athletes and coaches from the North being confronted by the culture of the deep South. Coach related a story about one of his assistant coaches, a volunteer javelin coach named Lenny McLaughlin. Lenny had befriended some of the LSU coaches and was invited to accompany them for a night out at another campus, the University of Louisiana at Lafayette, Louisiana. Lenny's new friends advised him not to let on that he was from the North or to suggest to any rednecks they might encounter that the South had indeed lost the Civil War. They suggested that if the questions about who he was or where he was from became too pointed he should respond with "I brung da truck." That evening at a bar in Lafayette Lenny was approached by a good looking young woman who asked him if he would like to dance. Lenny responded, "I brung da truck."

Coach Griak's Memories of Traveling With Athletes

Traveling with a team of young athletes led to many strange incidents. Although Coach did not want the names of the athletes involved in the following incident made public he said that in his first years at Minnesota, two members of his Gopher track team each took out a life insurance policy on themselves before the Gophers flew to a meet. The two athletes, along with the entire team, were on the same flight but they took the precaution of naming each other as their beneficiary.

Coach Griak said that he once brought a group of hungry track men into a restaurant in Iowa. The restaurant was short staffed and Coach ended up helping the waitress serve his team. When recalling the incident, Coach's comment was "that was a lot of fun." This was not the first time, or the last, that Coach resolved a problem by recognizing a need and then pitching in to accomplish whatever needed to be done.

When the topic of food came up, we both remembered a time when the Gopher team had flown into O'Hare airport in Chicago and had a short layover before catching a flight to the Twin Cities. As usual, the team was starving and was just being served their meals at The Trade Winds Restaurant when Coach Griak appeared and said that our plane was boarding and that we would have to leave our food and run for the gate. I can still see the indecision on shot putter Tom Bracher's face as he pondered whether the food or catching the flight was more important. Many of the athletes on Coach's teams can recall their splits in every race they ever ran or how high or far they jumped or threw at particular meets around the Big Ten but Tom Bracher, who had earlier attended St. Louis Park High School, also remembers the eating establishments! Tom was a gentle giant but I did see him irate once when someone had hidden one of the two foot-long sandwiches from the Red Barn on Oak Street he

Memorial Stadium groundskeeper – Colin Anderson in background

had brought on to the team bus for a road trip. Coach Griak said that on a trip to Purdue Tom Bracher was so caught up in an all you can eat smorgasbord that he hyperventilated and Coach almost had to call for medical assistance. Coach commented in the last year of his life that although "it has been over 45 years since Tom last competed for the Gophers, and well over a half century since I paddled him in junior high school for throwing spitballs, Tom Bracher has faithfully worked as an official in the weight events at nearly every meet in Minnesota for as long as anyone can remember."

Lost luggage was another headache. Steeplechaser, John "Carter" Holmes, from Minneapolis Washburn, was part of a small group that had their bags sent to Pittsburgh instead of Bloomington, Indiana after a stop in Chicago. Carter and three other Gophers were outfitted by the host school with new spikes and Indiana uniforms for our meet with Indiana. I was a part of that group too and I recall Indiana coach, Sam Bell, collecting my spikes immediately after my steeplechase race. Carter said that he represented the University of Minnesota while wearing an Indiana uniform and that he was a "Go-Hoosier" that day!

Thanks to Coach Griak's generosity, Carter Holmes may be the only person in the Twin Cities to have a "fully functional" steeplechase barrier in his south Minneapolis yard. Thoughts of traveling with poles for the vault elicited more memories from Coach Griak. He recalled times when the poles were threaded through the windows of the cockpit of a plane so that they could then be stored in the aisle. I can remember that when the track team would travel by car there were often poles attached by towels to the side of the car and then held in place by windows rolled up almost to the top. Coach said that once when the team traveled by train, the poles had been placed on top of a boxcar, forgotten and were declared lost. They traveled all over the United States for about a month before they were discovered and returned. Larry Berkner, from Ely, Minnesota once inadvertently discarded his return airplane ticket and would probably not have been allowed to get on the flight if Coach had not intervened. As with so many of Coach's stories, the mention of an athlete's name in one context "jogged" Coach's mind with other stories of that athlete.

Coach said that Larry Berkner finished every race doubled over in pain but that he was so tough that he never quit. In 1980 Larry ran a time of 8:42.6 in the steeplechase and this remains the third fastest time for the event in Gopher history. John Shaffer, who was from Pine City, Minnesota vaulted for the Gophers between 1964-1966. He studied engineering at the University but lived over a noisy tavern on campus while a student. John had to work so much during his collegiate days that it took him 7 years to graduate but, as with his pole vaulting, he was persistent. Once at Iowa City, Shaffer received a large gash in his shin when he came down awkwardly on a poorly constructed landing pit. He looked at his injury and then went back to the start and cleared his next vault. Coach remembers him as a tough kid who did not have much speed but had very strong arms and shoulders. He became one of the better vaulters in the Big Ten. Coach remembered that, while the Gophers were guests on the Louisiana State campus during their spring break, Shaffer knocked over a vase at a sorority house. Again, Coach Griak came to the rescue to deal with the damages.

In Coach's first year at Minnesota, as he was making the transition from coaching high school boys to collegiate young men, Coach recalled a dilemma that presented itself on a train trip with his new track and field team. As Coach was walking between the various passenger cars that carried his team he encountered one of his athletes drinking a bottle of beer.

A half century later Coach related that he knew that he had to do something immediately as the team was as new to him as he was to them and he wanted to establish the type of discipline he expected from his Gopher athletes. Coach took $25 out of his wallet and gave it to the young man. He told him that he would be leaving the train at the next stop and that he could find his way back to campus but that he would not be competing with the team in that meet. Reflecting on this years later Coach said that this may not have been the responsible or proper course of action but it did set the tone for his team.

Thinking of athletes who had to be closely watched on trips with the university, Coach recalled many sleepless nights as he waited for his charges to return to their quarters. He was not immune from these headaches even on the U of M campus. Coach related a story about a time when he was interrogated for over an hour by a group he called "the Gestapo" concerning a large carp that had been placed in the bed of a dorm counselor at Pioneer Hall by two of his athletes. Coach said that the incensed counselor and his associates couldn't prove anything and they eventually left his office. However, Coach said that from then on he had to watch Pat Kelly of St. Paul Monroe and Dan Wicks of Watertown, South Dakota all the time.

The annual spring trip to Louisiana State University in Baton Rouge provided a number of funny stories. In the late 1960s and early 1970s the Gopher track and field team stayed in Ruffin G. Pleasant Hall during their spring break on the campus of Louisiana State University. Ruffin G. Pleasant had been the governor of Louisiana from 1916-1920 but "pleasant" was not always the word for Coach's stay as he tried to supervise an entire team away from home and away from their books. Before the late Colin Anderson began to outdistance him in the shot, Dan Wicks used Colin as his personal caddy and had him carry the shots and discs to all the meets. Dan and his friend in practical jokes, Pat Kelly, often made Colin the butt of their jokes. They once wrote Colin a provocative letter from a Louisiana State University resident named "Mike." Mike wrote that she really wanted to meet Colin and gave him the location where she would like to have their meeting. When Colin showed up at the site he was standing in front of the cage of the LSU mascot, a tiger named Mike. In the spring of 1970, the Gopher track team ventured from Baton Rouge to Lafayette, Louisiana for an evening meet hosted by the Ragin' Cajuns of the University of Southwestern Louisiana. The school is now called the University of Louisiana-Lafayette. The Gopher team arrived early after an interminable bus ride through the bayou country of southern Louisiana. We were housed in what appeared to be a dusty former army barracks. The building was so filthy that many of us decided to do some sightseeing on the campus.

As we walked down fraternity row, all of us wearing Minnesota garb, a confederate flag was waved out the window of one frat house. The occupants were chanting at us, "Minnesota, go to hell." One of our hurdlers, Greg Lokken, responded, "we thought this was it!" Greg Lokken had won both the 100 and 200 yard dashes in the 1967 Minnesota State Meet while he was sprinting for Moorhead High School. He needed every bit of his sprint speed to outdistance the frat boys who chased him through the campus. The stadium at USL was so poorly lit that night that another Gopher hurdler, Phil Hanks, could not see the last flight of hurdles in his race.

An incident of which Coach Griak was not aware until 2014 when I related it to him took place in the fall of 1969 as the Gopher cross country team traveled with the football team to Bloomington, Indiana. We were to run against Indiana and Ohio State and the Gopher football team would play the Hoosiers. The motor lodge where our team stayed was on a busy highway and had a large illuminated billboard that read "enjoy the World Series games on our large picture color TV in the Hoosier den." This sign was noted by the CC team as we stretched our legs with a short walk before heading for bed on the eve of our race. Somehow, I found myself in the company of Pat Kelly, Tom Page and Garry Bjorklund and was actually used as a support for Bjorklund as Kelly was for Page so that they could stand on our shoulders and alter the sign. In my memory I can still hear Tom Page laughing his head off as he and BJ were illuminated in front of the sign alongside the busy highway. The next morning as Coach Griak and his seven runners were having a pre-race breakfast in the lodge restaurant, the four runners who had been involved in the evening prank began to intently study the menu as two waitresses exclaimed, "now, who did that?" They were standing by a window looking out on the billboard and were referring to the sign that now read "enjoy the Gopher win." Unfortunately, the Gopher football team did not hold up their end that day but the cross country team defeated Indiana and Ohio State. The scores of the triangular meet that day were: Minnesota (20), Indiana (62) and Ohio State (64). After 47 years, the story was related to Coach. "Hats off to thee."

Philosophy and Reflections on Coaching

Don Timm

Coach Griak's Athletic Family

There was no one more loyal to Gopher athletics than Coach Griak. If an athlete was wearing maroon and gold, Coach pulled for them to succeed. Whether the sport was cross country, track and field, football, baseball, volleyball, basketball, hockey, swimming, gymnastics, golf, soccer or any other Minnesota sport Coach was a fan. He wanted every Gopher athlete to do well and he was for every Gopher coach no matter what the sport. Coach Griak saw the University of Minnesota as his family and every athlete, male or female, was a part of that family. Coach told me that he had a habit for as long as he was at the University of walking down the hallways first of Cooke Hall and later at the Bierman building and wishing the coaches good luck in their next contest. That the other coaches over the years did not always return the favor for Coach's cross country and track and field teams did not stop Coach from continuing to support each team and each coach. Just as he did for his athletes who had struggled and needed a word of encouragement, Coach Griak befriended Gopher coaches who had lost a tough game or who had struggled through a tough season.

With Gopher Womens' CC Team

Coach was not a fair weather friend or one who would jump on the bandwagon calling for the head of a coach whose team had a disappointing season. In 2007, during the first year of former Gopher football coach Tim Brewster's tenure at Minnesota, the local media and many within the University criticized the coach for the 1-11 record of his team. At one of Coach

Brewster's weekly news conferences when the media seemed to be ganging up on the Gopher football coach, Coach Griak interrupted the conference by walking to the front of the room and giving an impassioned speech urging the media to support the program and to be more positive. He talked about how the revenue sports are important to the success of the entire athletic program. Coach feared that the non-revenue sports at every university will be threatened, and perhaps dropped in the next decade. This has happened recently to a number of sports at the University of North Dakota and at St. Cloud State. In the Big Ten Men's Cross Country Championship hosted by the University of Minnesota in 2016, Northwestern and Maryland did not field teams.

Looking cool in his pith helmet and shades

Coach told me in early March of 2015 that he had frequently attended university press conferences and that he often would look around and think to himself, "there in not one guy in here that ever served in a war or lived through the Depression and yet they have so much to say and can be so critical." Having lived through the Great Depression and the Second World War, Coach had a deep appreciation for life and for the opportunities brought by each day. Coach Griak was concerned about student-athletes and Golden Gophers. He never cared about the local professional teams. It was a standing joke between us when I would ask him if he had watched the last Viking game. However, if anyone badmouthed or picked on an athlete, a team or a coach representing the University of Minnesota, Coach would stand up for them just as if someone was picking on a member of his own family. Coach Griak always told his runners, jumpers and throwers to think positive. He demonstrated that positive attitude toward anyone associated with the Gophers for the 52 years he was employed by the University. Coach never forgot the many people who helped at Gopher meets. Those who timed, judged exchange zones, recorded or announced were always thanked for their efforts.

The same was true for those who raked the long jump pit, marshaled the runners, or set the pole vault or high jump bars. Coach Griak was usually the first person to arrive at a meet and the last person to leave because he personally thanked each of his workers. One young lady, Deborah Plumb, initially came to meets because her boyfriend was on the team but she became a loyal fan and, according to Coach "worked at many meets setting hurdles or doing anything that needed to be done."

Directing traffic at the Griak Meet

Although his salary never reflected his real value to his athletes and to the University of Minnesota, his loyalty never wavered. A more lucrative offer from the University of Michigan did not tempt him to leave Minnesota. Coach had a reverence for the University and for those who have shaped its traditions. Rather than relegating the athletes of the early years of the University to the category of "ancient history" Coach went out of his way to befriend and honor the elder statesmen of Gopher lore.

In the late 1960s, I remember Coach frequently going to visit an elderly man named Russell "Bunny" Rathbun at Rathbun's home near Lake Calhoun. While his current Gophers were engaged in an eleven mile run that crisscrossed Lake Calhoun, Lake of the Isles and Lake Harriet, Coach was not idly waiting at Thomas Beach on Lake Calhoun for our return. In addition to visiting the water pump on Lake Harriet to ensure that we would have something to drink (usually a concoction he called "swamp juice") he would often spend time visiting "Bunny." Rathbun had lettered in cross country for the Gophers in 1909 and had become a great supporter of the University.

—1917— —1979—

Russell "Bunny" Rathbun – Golden Gopher and Doughboy

To help foster a respect for the accomplishments and traditions of the past, Coach Griak made sure that Mr. Rathbun was an honored guest at our cross country banquets each fall. This diminutive former runner, who had helped to finance the banquets, was often given the opportunity to speak to the younger Gophers. Coach wanted to show his appreciation to this man, who, over a half-century after completing his athletic eligibility, was still supporting the Gopher runners, not only with his money but with his enthusiasm.

Coach told me in February of 2015 that "Bunny" Rathbun had also been the first male cheerleader at the University and that in 1910 he had been instrumental in creating the uniforms and gymnastic routines for the Gopher cheering

In the office at Bierman

squad. I also found out from Coach that Mr. Rathbun had been a commissioned officer in the United States Army during World War I. As a cheerleader, "Bunny" Rathbun was part of a group that pushed for a new school song. He, and others, thought that "Hail, Minnesota," was "too mournful to warm the feet in the bleachers." A nationwide search was conducted that eventually led to the selection of a song written by Floyd Hutsell, the choir director at the First Methodist Episcopal Church in Minneapolis. It was called Minnesota, Hats Off To Thee and has come to be known as the Minnesota Rouser. The rouser was played by the University of Minnesota Marching Band on September 26th of 2013 at the banquet celebrating Coach Griak's 50th year as an employee at Minnesota.

Minnesota, hats off to thee!
To thy colors true we shall ever be,
Firm and strong, united are we.
Rah, rah, rah, for Ski-U-Mah,
Rah! Rah! Rah! Rah!
Rah for the U of M.

Coach had been on the staff from 1963-1996 as a coach and from 1996-2013 as an administrative assistant. He added two more years of faithful service to the University before his death in 2015. The 2013 celebration was held in the (Dairy Queen) DQ room at the Twin City Federal Football Stadium. Just before the program started, Coach Griak and guests were invited to go from the DQ room to the stands outside and the Gopher marching band not only played the rouser but spelled out GRIAK on the football field as they played.

GRIAK spelled out on the football field

Coach Griak the Technician

Watching a track meet with Coach Griak was an educational experience. Whether it was jumpers, throwers, sprinters or distance runners, Coach's keen eye analyzed their technique. If they were doing it just right Coach would comment on that. If there was a flaw Coach would quietly mention it. In 2014, the two of us were watching an international track meet on television. As the sprinters got into the blocks, coach noticed that one of the athletes had his hips too high. He said, "the hips should always be just slightly higher than the shoulders, that man could be more efficient."

The runner was the Jamaican world record holder, Yusen Bolt. In April of 2015 I showed Coach Griak a book on the history of the Minnesota State High School Track and Field Meet that had been compiled by one of his former runners, Jeff Renlund. I had purchased the book earlier in the day but, seeing that Coach was completely captivated by it, I gave him the copy. We looked at the book together and Coach recalled past state meets and state meet athletes. Many of these athletes had either competed for Coach at St. Louis Park or later at the University.

Coach and Jeff Renlund

For the decade starting in 1953, his St. Louis Park teams were often at or near the front in state competitions and many of the athletes who placed in the state in those years were from his Oriole teams. As I was about to leave, Coach pointed to the athlete pictured on the front of the book. He said, "that young man sprinted for Eveleth." Turning over the cover page, we saw that the picture was from 1956 and the athlete was state champion sprinter Jack Ferrazzi of Eveleth. Coach said about the athlete, who he recognized from his form coming out of the blocks rather than his name, "look at that back leg, he's got it right. The back leg should be straight as an arrow propelling the body forward. Jeff Renlund sure picked a good picture for the cover of his book."

Seeing Coach recognize an athlete by his form rather than his face reminded me of an incident involving one of Coach's favorite baseball players, Yogi Berra. A ballplayer who had had only a "cup of coffee" in the major leaguers once encountered the former Yankee catcher in a hotel elevator. He said, "Yogi, do you remember me?" Yogi looked at him and replied, "no, but we pitched you low and outside." Yogi Berra, like Coach Griak, passed away in 2015.

For me, watching a field event athlete successfully clear a bar or throw an implement at near world record levels is all a mysterious blur. However, Coach would say, "look at her right knee" or "that last step has to be faster" or "he has to open his hips more." I would nod in agreement though Coach's analysis was always beyond me.

Giving sage advice to high jumper Katie Timm

NCAA Rules and the Law

In early January of 2015, shortly after Coach's return from a 12 day stay in the hospital, he talked about the many restrictions placed on coaches so that they would remain in compliance with the NCAA. He admitted that some of the things he had done during his coaching career probably would have been considered illegal. He talked about a young African athlete who had been on his track team for just one year. The young man had never experienced a harsh Minnesota winter before, or even a mild one, and that this was what probably caused him to eventually disappear from the campus and return home. However, during his one winter stay, the young man was completely without the clothing needed to keep him even moderately warm. Coach Griak bought him boots and gloves and the winter gear he needed.

Richard Simonsen, a freshman from Norway in 1964, was new to the country and a long way from home during his first Christmas in the United States. Coach Griak invited Richard to stay with the Griak family. This act of kindness allowed a lonely young man to feel welcome and to enjoy the warmth of a family during a tough time in his life but it would certainly have violated NCAA rules. Richard Simonsen went on to become a renowned dentist and teacher. Until retirement recently he was the Dean of the School of Dentistry at the University of Sharjah in the United Arab Emirates.

Coach admitted that he gave a young shot putter, Chad Goldstein, a ride home during the young man's entire career at Minnesota, not because he was trying to circumvent NCAA restrictions but because they both lived in St. Louis Park and it was a common sense act of kindness. I can remember Coach giving $2 to one of the runners on the cross country team in the late 1960s and telling him to get a haircut. In 1970, I had the

Richard Simonsen and Coach in front of Cooke Hall – 1964

privilege of spending a weekend with Coach in Gary - New Duluth and helping him paint his mother's house. I saw it as an opportunity to work with Coach, to meet his mother, to eat copious amounts of her delicious strudel, and to be accompanied by Coach each evening as he drove alongside me as I ran in Jay Cooke State Park. I would imagine that the $10 he gave me for helping with the painting may have been looked at differently by the NCAA. This was the only time I met Coach's mother but she made a lasting impression on me. I recall eating at least half of a huge pan of apple strudel she had made and when she asked if I would like some more I had declined because I was more than full already. Her response was "oh, you don't like my strudel."

Coach and his Mother – 1993

Coaching Philosophy and Advice to Other Coaches

According to Coach Griak, "coaching is the best occupation in the world." In scores of informal interviews that totaled hundreds of hours in recent years, Coach Griak never mentioned that he was a member of the University of Minnesota "M" Club Hall of Fame, or that he had been inducted into the United States Track & Field Coaches Hall of Fame, or the Drake Relays Hall of Fame, or the St. Louis Park Hall of Fame. He never mentioned until asked about his experiences that he had been on the coaching staff for three different United States Olympic teams (1972, 1980 and 1984). The United States did not compete in Moscow in 1980 but the team was invited to the White House.

President Jimmy Carter and First Lady Rosyln having the privilege of meeting Coach – 1980

He served on the United States Track & Field coaching staff again in 1984 for the Los Angeles games and was able to take his sons Seth and Jason along to share the experience. Coach did not mention that

1980 Olympic sweats – boycotted games

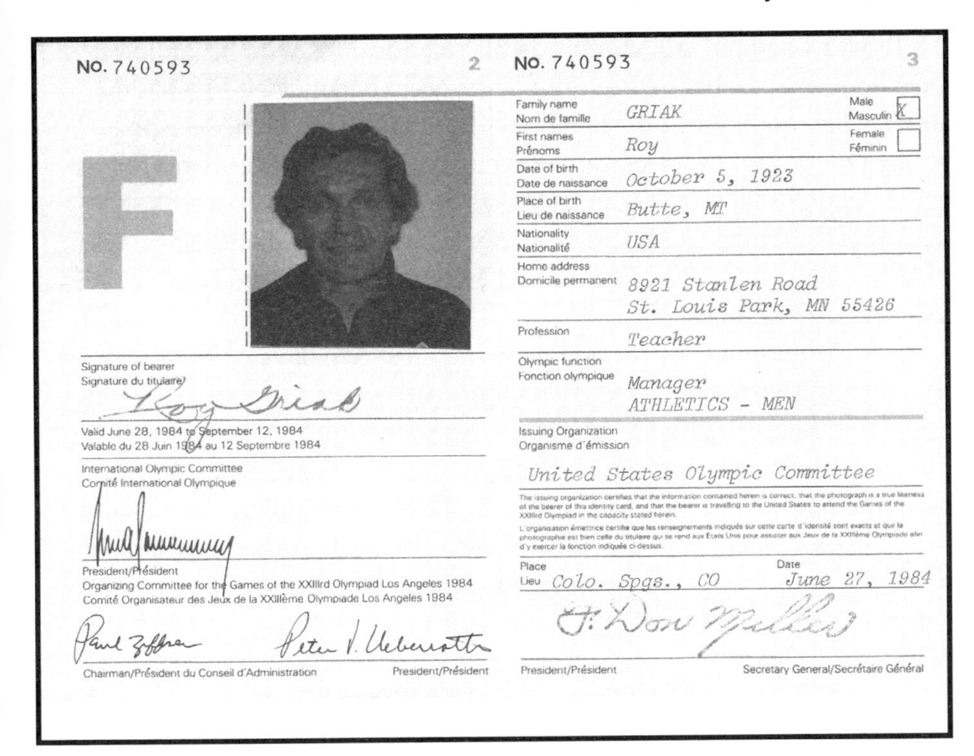

NO. 740593 2

F

Signature of bearer
Signature du titulaire

Valid June 28, 1984 to September 12, 1984
Valable du 28 Juin 1984 au 12 Septembre 1984

International Olympic Committee
Comité International Olympique

President/Président
Organizing Committee for the Games of the XXIIIrd Olympiad Los Angeles 1984
Comité Organisateur des Jeux de la XXIIIème Olympiade Los Angeles 1984

Chairman/Président du Conseil d'Administration
President/Président

NO. 740593 3

Family name / Nom de famille: GRIAK
Male / Masculin: X
First names / Prénoms: Roy
Female / Féminin:
Date of birth / Date de naissance: October 5, 1923
Place of birth / Lieu de naissance: Butte, MT
Nationality / Nationalité: USA
Home address / Domicile permanent: 8921 Stanlen Road
St. Louis Park, MN 55426
Profession: Teacher
Olympic function / Fonction olympique: Manager
ATHLETICS - MEN

Issuing Organization
Organisme d'émission
United States Olympic Committee

The issuing organization certifies that the information contained herein is correct, that the photograph is a true likeness of the bearer of this identity card, and that the bearer is travelling to the United States to attend the Games of the XXIIIrd Olympiad in the capacity stated herein.

L'organisation émettrice certifie que les renseignements indiqués sur cette carte d'identité sont exacts et que la photographie est bien celle du titulaire qui se rend aux États Unis pour assister aux Jeux de la XXIIIème Olympiade afin d'y exercer la fonction indiquée ci-dessus.

Place / Lieu: Colo. Spgs., CO
Date: June 27, 1984

President/Président
Secretary General/Secrétaire Général

1984 Los Angeles Olympic Team identification – Roy Griak

his Olympic experiences were just some of the ten international teams where he had been coach or manager of a United States team. Other than to relate stories about some events he had witnessed in Mexico City, he did not mention that he had been the head coach for the United States team for the Pan American Games held there in 1975. He said nothing about being the head coach for the U. S. team that competed in the World Indoor Championships in Paris in 2000. He did not mention that Mayor R. T. Rybak of Minneapolis had proclaimed September 26, 2013 (the celebration of Coach's 50th year at the University) as Roy Griak Day in the city of Minneapolis, or that Chris Coleman, the Mayor of St. Paul and Governor Mark Dayton had also made special proclamations in his name. He did not mention that he had received commendations in 1990 from Minnesota Governor Rudy Perpich and in 1992 from Minnesota Governor Arne Carlson.

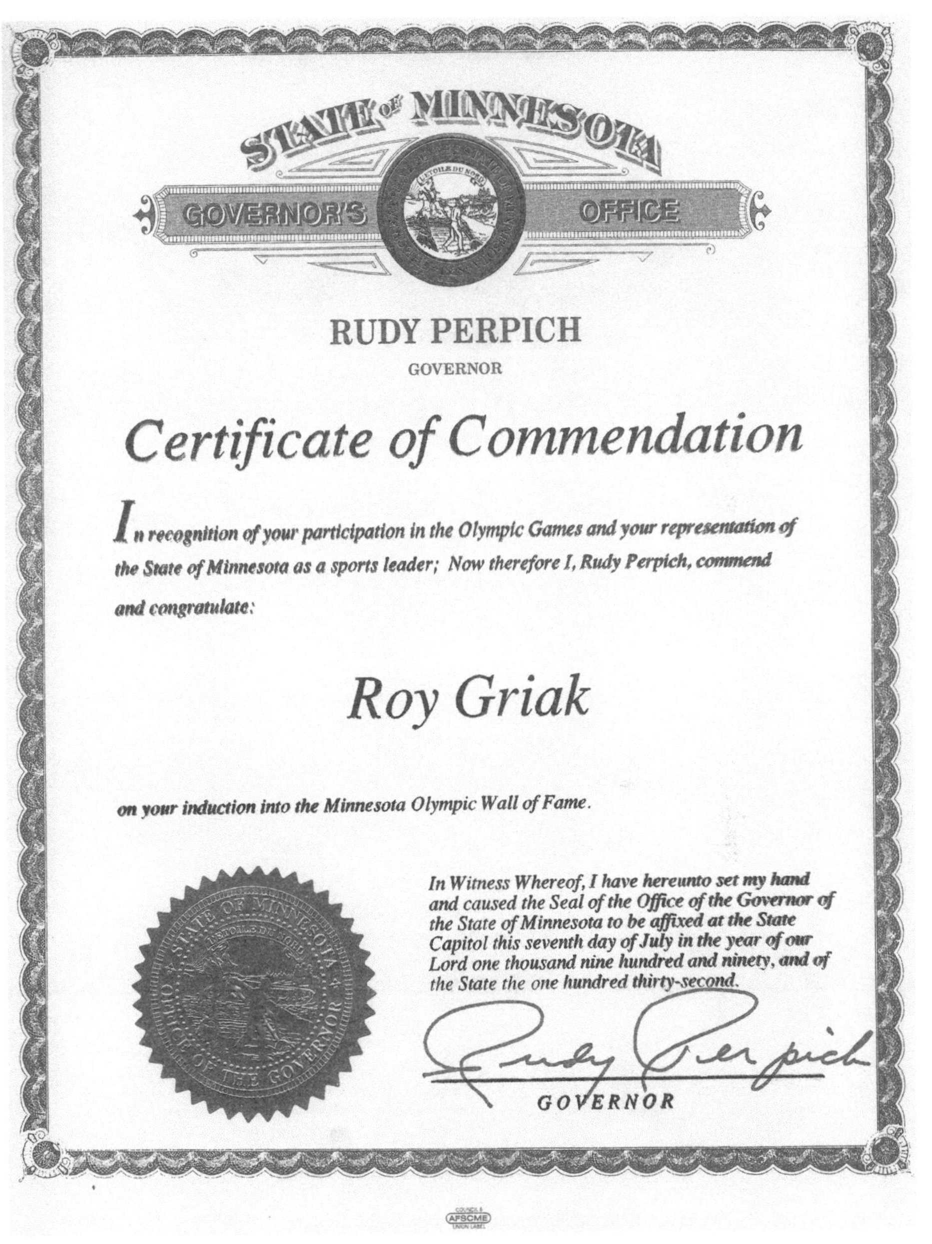

STATE of MINNESOTA
GOVERNOR'S OFFICE

RUDY PERPICH
GOVERNOR

Certificate of Commendation

In recognition of your participation in the Olympic Games and your representation of the State of Minnesota as a sports leader; Now therefore I, Rudy Perpich, commend and congratulate:

Roy Griak

on your induction into the Minnesota Olympic Wall of Fame.

In Witness Whereof, I have hereunto set my hand and caused the Seal of the Office of the Governor of the State of Minnesota to be affixed at the State Capitol this seventh day of July in the year of our Lord one thousand nine hundred and ninety, and of the State the one hundred thirty-second.

GOVERNOR

Commendation from Governor Rudy Perpich

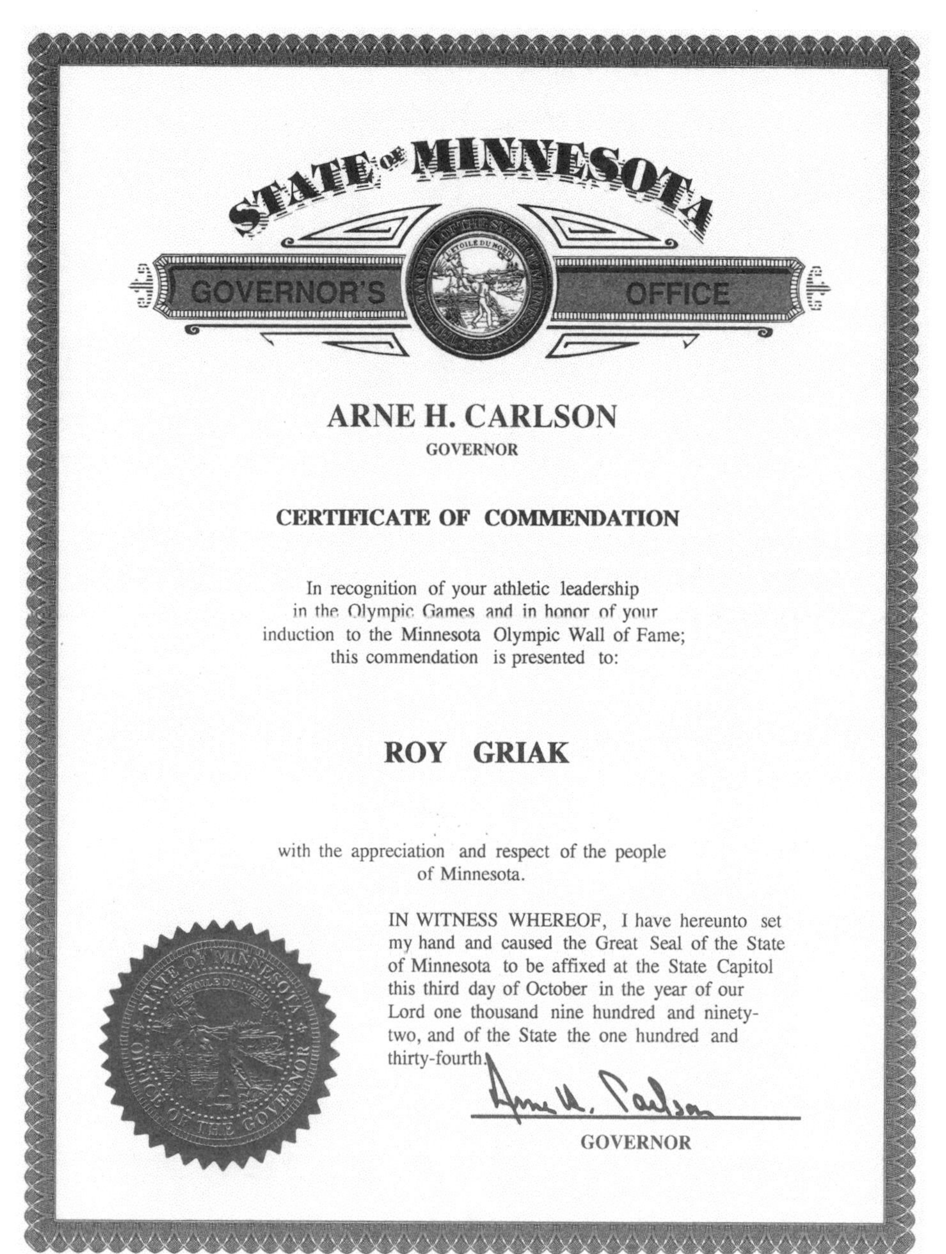

STATE OF MINNESOTA

GOVERNOR'S OFFICE

ARNE H. CARLSON
GOVERNOR

CERTIFICATE OF COMMENDATION

In recognition of your athletic leadership in the Olympic Games and in honor of your induction to the Minnesota Olympic Wall of Fame; this commendation is presented to:

ROY GRIAK

with the appreciation and respect of the people of Minnesota.

IN WITNESS WHEREOF, I have hereunto set my hand and caused the Great Seal of the State of Minnesota to be affixed at the State Capitol this third day of October in the year of our Lord one thousand nine hundred and ninety-two, and of the State the one hundred and thirty-fourth.

Arne H. Carlson
GOVERNOR

Commendation from Governor Arne Carlson

What Coach did talk about was his relationships with his athletes. Questions about what he had done were quickly deflected to what the athletes had done for him. He talked of the privilege of encouraging young people and of watching them develop not only as athletes but as people and productive citizens. He was as proud of Peter Jarosak, his track and field manager in the late 1960s, becoming a doctor as he was of Garry Bjorklund, Ron Backes and Martin Eriksson who were NCAA individual champions.

In a Minnesota Daily article published just two days before the 1970 Big Ten Cross Country Championship Meet in East Lansing, Michigan Coach did not focus his comments on his powerful Gopher team that would defend its conference championship that weekend but on what participation in cross country would do for his young men "in the long run." He explained, "there's just something more to running than trying to beat the other man. The courage and drive that cross country gives a person is what rcally counts. I can't think of onc of my runners who wasn't as much of a success off the track as he was on it. In fact, many of my boys have been more impressive persons than they were runners, because a lot of them weren't able to break records or win dual meets. But I can't see turning these guys away if they really want to run, because I'm certain they'll benefit from it."

Garry Bjorklund, who as a sophomore that year would win his second straight conference title, said in that Daily article in 1970, "I've known Coach Griak since I was in high school, and I don't think I've ever heard him say a bad word about anybody. His whole philosophy is centered around athletes. He's always asking us how we're doing in class, or if we're okay, and if everything is all right at home. That's why whenever he asks us to do something, we do it, because you can't help loving a guy like him, "Coach said that he saw his athletes as human beings first and runners second and that he considered himself more of a teacher than a coach. If he was able to teach his athletes things that would help them for the rest of their lives he said that he would feel he had served a purpose in their lives as well as his. In the November 10, 1970 Minnesota Daily article, Coach stated, "I think that the most important thing I try to teach them (my runners) is to never say 'I'll try.' The logic behind that is that any man who in any endeavor says, "I will' instead of "I'll try' is a lot better off and is hard to beat."

Coach Griak felt that a good coach should keep coaching as long as they possibly could because "the headaches are far outweighed by the benefits." He said that through coaching "you are entering the lives of your athletes through your presence and by the way you handle yourself." He encouraged coaches to "enjoy what you are doing." "The biggest thing in coaching is common sense. There is a point of diminishing returns so a coach has to know when to work an athlete hard and when to back off and when to rest. A good coach will develop a sense for how to bring an athlete to their peak at the championship time of a season."

After his "retirement" from active coaching in 1996, Coach remained on the staff as an administrative assistant to the cross country and track and field teams. He worked with budget, scheduling and special events and also served as a liaison for the teams with the University administration. He continued to raise money for the Roy Griak Endowment Fund. At the 2013 celebration for his 50th year as an employee of the University of Minnesota Coach said that the present Gopher coaching staff was a delight. He said that Steve Plasencia, Lynden Reder and Paul Thornton inspired him and that he would have liked to have coaches like them when he was the head coach of the Gophers. Coach said that they care about people and that they are willing to be there early and stay late to do a good job.

When asked about the relationship between coach and athlete, Coach Griak did not talk about how much he could get out of an athlete in a quest for record performances or how many points that athlete could secure for the team. Instead, Coach talked about rapport, discovery, enthusiasm, love of

Coach and Steve Plasencia

Lynden Reder

Paul Thornton

Coach's 1995 Gopher CC team (L-R): Unidentified runner holding bottle, Paul Michalek, Al Broderius, Tony Riter and Coach

the sport and respect for each other. An incident that exemplifies Coach's respect for the individual was the collapse of his top runner, Steve Hoag, in the last 50 yards of the Big Ten CC championship meet in 1968. In talking with both Steve and Coach Griak, I know that the incident was a bitter pill to swallow for both and one that was not forgotten even decades later. Coach said that to ask Steve to continue when he was obviously in physical trouble would not have been fair. In evaluating the incident in later years Steve said that Coach told him that he could see that Steve was in trouble at 4 miles and that he should have told Steve to back off and run more conservatively. That was hindsight though. Both Steve and Coach were striving for an individual Big Ten championship for Steve. Steve did get that Big Ten championship in 1969 in the indoor 2 mile.

Coach said that through coaching he was helping to create a frame of mind where the coach and the athlete were comrades working together toward a goal. In helping a young athlete discover and develop their physical abilities there was an opportunity to guide them in the other areas of their life. Reaching a point in the coach-athlete relationship where both believe in each other allowed for values to be passed on and to leave

Coach, Garry Bjorklund and Don Timm - 2013

a legacy that may last long beyond the finish line of a race. I remember Coach's adages like "be good to your mother" and "always be a gentleman" and "remember those who have helped you in life" as much as I remember those adages that dealt more with athletics like "it is a privilege to work hard," "you are Minnesota tough" and "you are never tired."

Coach's declining health in the late spring and early summer of 2015 was a source of concern for athletes scattered all over the United States and brought his "boys" closer together. In a phone conversation with Garry Bjorklund late in April of 2015 we discussed our years as Gopher athletes. Garry was perhaps the most noted distance runner to have competed for Coach Griak having won 10 Big Ten individual titles and the 1971 NCAA Six Mile championship. Garry and I agreed that in four years of running for Coach it never entered our minds to question him about a workout or a racing suggestion. We agreed that our years at Minnesota under his guidance were some of the best years of our lives and that he had taught us much more than how to run a race. Garry related a story that I had not heard before. He said that while he was coaching at Colorado State he was approached by the legendary Oregon distance coach, Bill Dellinger. As an athlete, Dellinger had competed at Oregon and had represented the United States in the Olympic Games of 1956 (Melbourne), 1960 (Rome) and 1964 (Tokyo). He had won the bronze medal in the 5,000m run in Tokyo.

Dellinger started his coaching at Oregon in 1969 as a track assistant to Bill Bowerman and as the head cross country coach. He had succeeded Bowerman in 1973 as the Oregon track and field coach and had held that post as well as his cross country position through 1998. Coach Dellinger had arrived at Oregon the same year as Steve Prefontaine and is credited with aiding "Pre" in his very successful career. By the time that Garry Bjorklund met with Bill Dellinger when they were both collegiate coaches, Garry had established a tremendous collegiate record of his own at Minnesota. Garry said that Coach Dellinger had approached him and asked, "do you realize what you and Prefontaine could have done together at Oregon? You two would have been the best ever." Garry responded, "that may have been true Coach Dillinger but then I would not have gotten to know Roy Griak."

Garry said that that Coach Dellinger had no come back for his response and just walked away. Bruce Mortensen ran for Coach Griak at St. Louis Park and then for Bill Bowerman at the University of Oregon. Comparing the styles of his two coaches in Kenny Moore's book, Bowerman and the Men of Oregon, Bruce Mortensen said that Bowerman was not at all like his high school coach, Roy Griak, who "was like a member of the family, looking out for us and keeping us from harm."

Different coaches have different personalities and styles and use different methods to achieve results. Never one to say anything negative about a fellow coach, Coach Griak said, "the stopwatch measures time only but there are so many other factors that determine an athlete's success. Every coach has something that the other guy does not. A coach has to develop their own style and way of working with young athletes." Like, Garry Bjorklund and thousands of others, I am so glad to have been a member of Coach Griak's family.

Coach with a stopwatch

Don Timm, Tom Page, Gene Daly and Garry Bjorklund at Coach's funeral – Mount Olivet Lutheran Church – July 22, 2015 - A sad day but a celebration of how blessed we were to have known him

"You Are Only as Good as Your Last Runner"

A Collection of Roy Griak Tributes

"You Are Only As Good As Your Last Runner"

"Camaraderie and pride."

"Always remember where you came from and who you represent."

Dick Aften

Coach Griak: *Dick was a steeplechaser on the 1968 Big Ten Championship Gopher Track and Field team. He was coached by Jim Deane at Osseo and placed third in the state mile in 1964. He placed 16th, 4th and 2nd in the state cross country meets of 1961, 1962 and 1963. After each Gopher cross country race he would give a Tarzan yell that would scare the apes in Africa.*

I am sorry I missed the ceremony the University gave you. I just viewed the video and I gratefully endorse all the many tributes to your career. I am very proud to have been a small part of your amazing life.

Running for you at the U was a wonderful time of my life. Thank you for bringing me into your program. I remember it as if it was yesterday, running those workouts along the shores of Calhoun and the Mississippi. I cherish those memories running hard and long with the guys. My favorite was when we set out early on frosty mornings to run the three lakes. How cold you must have been waiting for us. Those preseason workouts at dawn and dusk in the Minnesota fall were glorious. Little did I understand how much time and effort you had to put in. You were there helping to make training feel more like fun and play. But for you it was long hours of very serious business. You were so giving of yourself to us young men. Your hand is felt on our shoulders even today. Thank you, Coach.

Since my graduation I am so happy we have kept in touch over some forty-five years. Do you remember when you came to dinner in our little bargain rental in Eugene? You were attending either the NCAA, or the Olympic trials held in Eugene in 1972. Beth and I remember it well. We had had several runners visit us from Minnesota: Tom Stuart, Heino, Wags, Ron Dawes, and Ed Twomey. However other than parents, you were our first adult guest. We were nervous. You were so kind and gracious that we all had a great evening with lots of reminiscing. Our daughter Heather was almost one-year old and no doubt bounced on your knee.

We saw you a few more times at those great meets at Hayward field. Then we moved to Salem for my career in the wine business, and Heino and his new wife moved into that same rental in Eugene. We kept running into you at Eugene meets over the years, but it became less frequent as Beth and I got busy raising a family and working. In the last decade or so, I am thrilled that we have had a number of opportunities to visit again. I think you know how much I value what you did for me, and what you have done for so many young athletes. Wearing the "M" made me proud. It gave me confidence that followed me into my adulthood and successful career.

It delights me that my wife (who I met at the U in '66) has gotten to know you over these years. She refers to you not as "Coach," but that "handsome man who was always teasing her." She echoes all the wonderful things that are deservedly said about you.

Beth and I are so happy that we are able to give back to the program that has made so many young athletes into better people.

Dick Aften, class of '68

Andy Bunge

Coach Griak: *Andy Bunge ran 800-meters for the Gophers. Andy is a very special person; he is so kind and sensitive. He loves people. He has great concern for everyone. He is a beautiful human being. The world would be better off with more people like Andy Bunge. {Andy Bunge was asked to give a eulogy at Coach's funeral on July 22, 2015.}*

Besides having a wonderful relationship with coach Griak a memory that stands out was from the 1976 Kansas Relays. In a steady rain the Minnesota 4 X 800 relay team was to run with Randy Beebe leading off among fifteen other teams on a tear drop start. I was standing on the infield near the steeplechase pit which was full of murky water. There were three false starts to the relay due to runners slipping and falling and pushing and shoving. Randy got so upset, being from Chicago, that he threw his baton and it went skipping across the track and landed in the pit full of water.

Coach saw what had happened and yelled, "Bunge, get the baton," because they were about to start the race again. Being soaked already, I jumped in the pit and, up to my chin in water, had to feel around until I found the baton. I thrust it up out of the pit, raising it above my head to the delight of the crowd. The race finally had a fair start on the fourth try. I don't recall how Minnesota fared in the outcome but it was a memorable start.

My junior year I had classes on the St. Paul campus. We were to have our team picture at Bierman Field in the track bleachers. I completely forgot and arrived on a later campus bus. I saw my teammates sitting in the stands and posing for the camera. I panicked and ran to the locker room to get my uniform on but by the time I got outside the team was disbanding. I was so upset with myself because it was important to me to be in the picture with my teammates. Coach came up to me, knowing that I had missed the photo and feeling bad about it. He put his arm over my shoulder and told me that the team had voted me their captain for the 1977 season. I was shocked at the news never thinking that would be a possibility for me. I had never even thought about it. To this day that honor, of being recognized by my peers, has never been topped. I was humbled and proud to be the sole 1977 track captain.

I was recruited by several college track coaches after participating in four Minnesota State Track Meets. I missed the finals as an 8th grader, was runner up as a 10th grader, and was state champion my junior and senior years in the 880. I never had thoughts of attending college until I was encouraged by others to consider these scholarship offers.

On my campus visit to the University of Minnesota Roy Griak impressed me so much as a man of integrity. On that visit, I stayed with Tim Oliver and John Purves. We attended a Michigan State vs. Minnesota basketball game at Williams Arena and Minnesota won. Later, Coach Griak drove to Preston on a miserable March day. He had to park at the end of our 100-yard driveway and trudge up the icy, slushy, and muddy driveway. My mom had prepared a delicious roast beef dinner and I signed my letter of intent at the dining room table with Coach and my family present. That was a turning point in the direction of my life. It was a great decision for me. Coach Griak was my father when I was away from home and I loved him deeply.

Sincerely,

Andy Bunge

Douglas Laird

Coach Griak: *He was a short, stocky distance runner at St. Louis Park. He became a security officer at the airport.*

Like most stories of how Coach Griak contributed to who we are today, I have some fond memories of my experiences with him at St. Louis Park, 1955 to 1960.

For whatever reason, maybe because I was a skinny kid and thought I could run, I went out for track as an eighth grader in the spring of 1955. Of course the first thing I discovered was that I only thought that I was in shape to run. Not having any great speed, the only choice was the mile. This planted the seed to go out for cross-country in the fall. Having run "the lakes" of Minneapolis over the summer I was certainly in better shape that fall than I'd been the previous spring.

It became clear to me that cross country was "my thing" and even though we'd run, sometimes until we puked, we all made progress. Like any great Coach, Roy had the uncanny ability to know when a kick in the pants was needed or just a pat on the shoulder. Having lost my dad when I was ten, Coach Griak was "the male influence" in my life throughout high school.

Under Coach Griak we won the Minnesota State High School Cross Country Championship and placed well in many invitationals. My teammates selected me as the cross country Captain for two years and this provided me with a confidence that carried through into my later life.

The background gained under the leadership of Coach Griak enabled me to run cross-country at Mankato State University under another great cross country coach, Bud Myers. Just like my days at St. Louis Park, the years at Mankato were fantastic as we traveled the country to take part in meets. It was Coach Myers that influenced many of us to become officers in the United States Marine Corps. Here again, running the infamous "Hill Trail" at Quantico, VA in the Virginia summer heat and humidity, carrying full gear, having done those interval quarter miles on the St. Louis Park High School track, twenty in fact, gave me the strength and guts to know that I wouldn't be the one to fall out.

At the end of the day, I have often thought of my days at St. Louis Park High School and especially Coach Griak and his influence on "his boys." To this day, fifty-eight years from the time I went out for track, I'm still friends with guys that were bonded by our shared experiences on the cross country team under Coach Griak's leadership. What a gift, Coach. We all thank you from the bottom of our hearts.

Douglas Laird

St. Louis Park 1955-1960

Mike Lawless

Coach Griak: *Mike was a Wisconsin private school mile champion. He was a member of the 1969 Gopher Big Ten Champion CC team. Mike is a great guy who was the coach of the women's program at Minnesota when it was first getting started.*

I remember visiting the University as a senior in high school. You told me that the most important thing you could give me was your time. I don't know if it meant that much to me as a seventeen or eighteen-year-old but came to mean so much and it still does.

I remember the rush of putting on my Minnesota uniform for the first time for my first cross country meet, a feeling that stayed with me for the next four years. Because of you and my teammates I was and always will be proud to be a Gopher.

It was an honor, a privilege and a pleasure to compete for you and the University of Minnesota.

Thank you Coach for everything.

Mike Lawless

Gopher CC and Track and Field (1969-1973)

Greg Nelson

Coach Griak: *Greg was an excellent miler and cross country runner for me at the University of Minnesota. Greg is 1968 Olympian, Van's brother.*

Thanks Coach for all that you have done for me. I got to travel and make great friends. I loved being on your team.

Greg Nelson

Gopher miler (4:04) 1968-1971

George Podolsky

Coach Griak: *George was from Minneapolis Southwest. He was a tough little guy who excelled beyond his ability. George was one of Al Halley's boys. He was a member of the 1964 Gopher Big Ten Championship CC team.*

I had the privilege of running under Coach Griak from 1963-1967. During those years, he helped prepare me for many of life's challenges. I owe my work ethic and sense of discipline to the years of training and running. And, I'm still running every day, Coach!

I first met Coach during the high school running seasons at Minneapolis Southwest. He and Al Halley, the SW coach, had a very good relationship which made my freshman year at the U feel like a smooth transition with a continuation of the same high standards.

I guess one of the more memorable workouts I recall would be the torture at the Mississippi sand flats. I still can almost hear Coach's whistle signaling the start of a sprint in the sand and remember praying that the stop whistle would come before I collapsed!

Besides character building, the hard work did pay off as Coach led us to the University of Minnesota's first Big Ten Cross Country Championship in fifty years in 1964! I am reminded of Coach Griak every day I wear that Championship ring!

Thank you for being such a great person and role model, Coach,

George Podolsky

1964 Big 10 CC team

1963-1967

George Podolsky

4X400 Relay Team 2003

Roy,

We want to take this opportunity to express our infinite gratitude for your hard work and service to our program. Though it may seem that your countless hours spent furthering our program go unnoticed, we would like to express just the opposite. We are very grateful for you and your contributions and are giving honor where honor is due. We have recently received recognition for our accomplishments and would like to pass this recognition on to those who are at the root of it all. From the very first day we came to this university, you have helped us develop into the student-athletes we are today.

We would like you to have this picture {the picture hung in the den of Coach Griak's home until 2015} to remember us by because, although others may forget as they pass through this system, we will always remember you and what you have done for us. The confidence you have shown in us, the dedication, knowledge and respect you have given to us, and the friendship we share will be remembered for the rest of our lives. We all still have a lot of time left here in the track program, but the recognition and thanks are long overdue.

From all of us, Thanks a Million and Go Gophers!

Sincerely,

Andy Wohlin

Adam Steele

Mitch Potter

Mikael Jakobsson

(4x400 m relay team, 3:02:33, 2003) (Wohlin, Steele and Potter would be joined by Robb Merritt to run even faster (3:01.80) in 2004)

"Ten Yards Beyond the Finish Line"

A Collection of Roy Griak Tributes

"Run through the finish line in everything you do."

"Give your best effort and the best will come back to you."

Garry Bjorklund

Coach Griak: *Garry was a Proctor Rail who won the NCAA Six Mile in 1971. Garry is one of the greatest athletes we have ever had at Minnesota. Garry was a true team person. I once bought turtle neck sweaters for the top seven on the CC team; Garry would not wear his until I got them for the whole team. He got all the accolades but he never thought he was better than anyone else. BJ had grit (determination, toughness and discipline).*

One of my favorite recollections about Coach Griak occurred at a Northwest Open Indoor Track Meet. I don't remember which year but after cooling down from my race I was leaning against the north wall of the field house watching one of many heats of the two mile. Some people might think running five or six heats of a two mile excessive, but the Northwest Open drew teams from Minnesota, North Dakota, South Dakota and Wisconsin. Roy cared that every track athlete in our region deserved an opportunity to compete.

The north wall of the field house was a great place to hang out because from this vantage point you could observe everything that happened around the track. Typically, Roy was so busy giving instructions to officials or setting hurdles, etc. that he blended into the background and you barely noticed him. But this day was different. Roy was at the finish line jumping up and down and more animated than I had ever seen him. Something or someone really had his full attention.

Eventually I realized the focus of Roy's attention was Gopher teammate, Keith Ottoson. Apparently they had worked out a race plan and Otto was running the race of his life. Every lap you could feel the positive energy between coach and athlete building and building. With one lap to go it was impossible to tell who was more excited, Roy or Otto. As Keith crossed the finish line he and Roy embraced in a victory dance and both had tears of elation in their eyes.

Standing there mesmerized by Otto's performance and Roy's reaction to it, I felt humbled because I couldn't think of anything I had done to bring such joy to a coach. Roy Griak was one of the most respected track coaches in America. He was often a favorite of the United States Olympic Committee to coach or manage US teams that traveled all over the world. He advised Olympic Champions and World Record Holders. Some coaches of his stature didn't have time for the little people and yet, here was Roy Griak performing a world class dance in celebration of what one of his boys had accomplished.

Garry Bjorklund

More than forty years after running for Roy I am so proud to have had the privilege to run for him. Occasionally he calls on the phone to say hello. He fills me in on the latest Gopher news and we reminisce about the good old days. More important, every conversation ends with the same closing. He will say, "BJ, I love you." And, I always say, "Coach, I love you, too." Speaking as one of Roy's boys, we all love him because he is such an example of what a good man should be. Everything he taught us was intended to help us become better athletes and hopefully, better men.

Garry Bjorklund

One of Roy's "Pumpkins"

U of M Track & Cross Country

1969-1974

Ken Cherry

Coach Griak: *Ken ran for me at St. Louis Park. He was a good little athlete and a devoted person who will always proudly remember his track days at Park. Ken is a Vietnam veteran.*

I was a member of the track team at St. Louis Park High School in 1956, 1957 and 1958. In 1958, the team was Minnesota State Champions! When I joined the team in 1956, Coach Griak talked to me about commitment, work ethic and honesty, on and off the track. It wasn't always what he said – sometimes it was what he didn't say! As a team, we were very close and remain so today.

At the time, I didn't realize all that I accomplished in my track career would become a foundation for the rest of my life! The training, discipline, hard work and support Coach Griak shared with me and everyone else, gave us the ability to go out into the world and be successful. I was allowed to believe I could be anything I wanted to be. The payoff was a tour in the USMC – Vietnam Vet, a college degree, a successful business career and a good family.

I now know the meaning of 'play it forward' – I coached young kids in a variety of sports – I had the opportunity to teach at the college level (part-time) – and I too, was making a difference in helping others to chase their dreams – it all started with Coach Roy Griak – I felt privileged to be one of Griak's Boys!

Ken Cherry

St. Louis Park High School

Class of 1958

Steve Eklund

Coach Griak: *Steve was a Gopher 800-meter runner and a good one. He is on the school board in Braham, Minnesota and is also on the board of the State High School League. He is an outstanding individual.*

Congratulations on fifty years at the University of Minnesota. I am honored that I had the opportunity to have had you as a coach and a lifelong friend. You took a chance on a farm kid from Braham and made him into a man. I attended the University from 1970-1974 and was proud to be a track and field co-captain my senior year. My official recruiting visit was a short tour of campus and a burger and glass of milk at the "Big 10" on Washington Avenue.

One spring on our annual trip to Louisiana State University, LSU Coach Joe May let you borrow his car, but forgot to tell you it didn't have any brakes. While driving around beautiful Baton Rouge, you "lightly" rear-ended the same car three times. You were lucky to get away with a "dirty look." Our track meets at LSU were always competitive. I was scheduled to run the 880, and you told me you wanted me to lead the first 440 regardless of the time. I believe you said, "Lead the first lap or walk home." Naïve me, I thought you were serious. I knew I was in big trouble when they yelled the splits, "48-49-50." Needless to say, that was the worst "bear" I ever experienced. The last 100 yards felt like a mile. When I was flat on my back in the infield, you walked over and said, "Say Ek, that was one of the best 'bears' I have ever seen" And you were laughing!

My four years at the University of Minnesota and being part of the track and field team were four of the best years of my life. Your ability to push my teammates and me to our fullest potential is a true gift. Many values and positive attributes that I have today can be traced back to my relationship with you. I will always be in your debt.

Thank you, Coach!

Steve Eklund

Track & Field 1970-1974

Tom Heinonen

Coach Griak: *Tom ran for Marv Wrucke at Robbinsdale High School and later was a member of Minnesota's 1964 Big Ten Championship CC team. He became an outstanding coach in the women's program at the University of Oregon. Tom Heinonen was always ready to compete, no matter what. Tom was a Big Ten 3-Mile champion and All-American 6-miler in 1967.*

Coach, here are some random memories from the 1960's:

In cross country season we ran straightaway 440 yard repeats on the grass east of the river. You stood across the busy street and waved a flag (dropped your hand? Blew a whistle?) when it was time to go again. It was so narrow in one spot that we had to run on the sidewalk for a few steps. Late in the workout, some guys ran on the sidewalk all the way to keep up. The most we ever did was seventeen reps.

In high school, your St. Louis Park guys always beat me…Bruce Mortensen, of course, and John Valentine (twenty straight races, as I recall). John claimed that he sometimes worked out three times a day, including "no breath" 100s on the football field where he occasionally passed out. But in college I got your coaching too, and within a year, I could beat John…frustrating for him and satisfying for me.

I remember coming up to your office in Cooke Hall to just sit and read *Track & Field News*. You'd work, I'd read, and we'd chat a little. That was nice!

In the spring on sunny, warm days, I remember grabbing my sack lunch and climbing to the press box roof at Memorial Stadium in order to suntan. We baked up there, then came down and did our best to do the track workout. Sometimes they were pretty tough!

Did this really happen? We were driving to Des Moines in a car, probably a station wagon, with a bench seat in front. You were driving, I was in the middle, and Bob Wagner was on the right. At some point, Bob reached across me and grabbed the wheel because you had dozed off. True or imagined? I don't know.

At the 1972 Olympic Trials in Eugene, you and I were sitting next to the dormitory, talking about the semifinals of the 1500m which had been run that afternoon. A pretty girl came up to unlock her bike at the rack next to us. I asked her if she knew where room 150 of the geology building was. She said yes, and I asked her if she wanted to go there that evening to watch the 1936 Berlin Olympic movie with me. She said yes again. A year later, we were married.

In 1967, I had just (finally) won a Big Ten title, the first ever three-mile at the championships. A Wisconsin grad student, Jack Daniels, walked up and asked if I would be willing to be in his high-altitude study that summer in Alamosa, Colorado. I'd get two weeks at 7500 feet before going DOWN to 4500 feet for the NCAA Championships in Provo. I asked you, and you gave me permission and blessing to go off with this guy and his group for the last two weeks of my collegiate career. At Provo, I went from tenth to third in the last two miles of the six-mile, my best performance at NCAA's. You let me do it.

Tom Heinonen

I remember Lloyd Stein, the trainer, coming back from a clinic at Illinois, saying that the new recommendation was to use ice, not heat! What a shock that was!

We didn't lift weights (which would make us "muscle bound") but there were pulleys on the walls of the locker room where we occasionally did some work.

The equipment room used to issue a gray tee-shirt, white cotton shorts with elastic in the back, a jockstrap, and those goofy socks without elastic that would just lie on your ankles. We got clean workout clothes every day.

When Jack Trolander would do a workout in that gray tee-shirt, he'd get a little dark spot of sweat right in the middle of his chest, at his sternum. Eventually, it would become a triangle, then as he ran more, it would grow antlers and look like a deer head. If the workout was really hard, or it was really warm, the antlers would smudge and Jack would have a perfect image of Mickey Mouse on his chest. Or maybe I was hallucinating!

Random memories of a great time…a time that you created for us, let us be part of. And, ever since, we've wanted to be like you, and for all these years we've tried to be. Thank you!

Tom Heinonen

(Tommy from Robbinsdale)

U of M athlete

All-American 1967

1964-1967

Lindsay Nielsen

(as related to co-author, Don Timm by Coach Griak)

Coach Griak: *Lindsay is a gem! I volunteered to coach her and we worked together nearly every day. She is a smart, enthusiastic lady and a dear friend. Lindsay has the heart of a lion. She held world records in numerous events and also completed the ironman triathlon.*

Dear Coach,

I came to work with you late in your career in athletics, but early in mine, even though I was already in my forties.

While you were bringing your 1969 team to the Cross Country championships, I was a block away from the University of Minnesota Bierman Athletic Center, at Marshall U-High. I was entering ninth grade, taking my first steps on a new prosthetic leg.

I was always an athletic kid, and played every sport I had access to. I was one of the fastest runners in grade school and I loved adventures and speed, whether on the football field and baseball field, racing bikes, or for that matter, when hopping freight trains.

I was thirteen at the time of the accident, turning fourteen in the hospital. I was there for four months as the surgeons tried unsuccessfully to save my left foot. I was devastated when they finally had to amputate. What I couldn't know then is that I would have been more limited had they managed to save the foot. Life is funny like that. The worst can become the best. At the time, I knew that I needed to be tougher than the situation, or as you say, I needed to be snotty-nose tough, but in 1969, prosthetic legs were heavy and unwieldy, certainly not designed for running and while I acted tough, I sure didn't feel that way.

I tried running on and off through the next decades but always with a significant hitch and resulting injury. I was able to play racquetball without much difficulty but I wanted to run a lot further than across a court. Finally, as I faced my fortieth birthday I gave running one more try. Technology had improved enough that there was a running foot I eventually was able to use and after a particularly successful marathon, was called by a US Paralympics Team coach who asked me to come out to the National Championships and run track. I was 42, had never run track, and had no idea how to proceed.

That was in 1997. One of my business partners gave me the birthday present of a training consultation with you to help me prepare for the track meet that was weeks away. So, a few blocks from the train tracks where my accident had changed up my future, I had the good fortune of meeting you.

I'm sure you had no idea what you were getting into, but after getting to know you, I understand you would have taken me on anyway.

You've been a great coach, a dear friend, and, in a number of ways, a father figure for me. You've given me the best of yourself and asked only that I give the best of myself to the sport in return.

I've come to realize that I'm not an easy person to coach. My parents were in the throes of their alcoholism while I was trying to grow up, so I was sorely under-parented. I didn't go to school until I didn't have to, and often see rules more as the beginning point of negotiation rather than an end onto themselves. I'm stubborn, which is often just a half-step away from stupid, and left to my own, I overdo my training. And, I'd never had a serious coach before you. Somehow I think you'd seen this before, because you found an effective way to work with me anyway.

You were unendingly positive but firm. You've always had confidence in my ability to acclimate to new technology, a new sport, and a completely new training philosophy. When I got my first running "blade", I fell, which isn't unusual. On a sprint blade, the part of the foot that touches the track is just a few inches in diameter. I wasn't used to running on such a small area of contact. You assured me that once I got used to it, I'd wonder how I ever ran on anything else. How did you know to tell me that? I don't think you've worked with other amputees. And of course, you were completely right. I've never run on a different foot since. But everything was so new to me and I felt insecure. Your confidence allowed me to shed that anxiety and focus on getting faster. Working with you helped remind me that "competent authority" is trustworthy so while you worried about the coaching part, I was then allowed the luxury of only worrying about my part.

Folding myself into the starting blocks felt awkward. As I did my version of "exploding" out of the blocks, my forty-plus-year-old body torqued in painful and previously un-experienced ways. I usually left the track with one or more parts of my body in cramps. I was accustomed to being good at things I worked for and carrying myself with a modicum of cool and neither was true for me with track. Some days it took everything I had just to get there but when I felt discouraged, you encouraged. You got me back on task, frequently reminding me that I was just learning, trying to offset my sense of humiliation with the much better option of humility. When I was cocky and full of myself, you laughed and refused to burst my bubble. You never told me I couldn't do something, never questioned my sanity about running marathons or setting my sights on the Ironman Triathlon. You just grinned and told me how great my enthusiasm was.

Spending so much time with athletes half my age was hard on my ego. I understood that like most people wrestling with issues related to aging, I had to get over it and make the best of what I had to work with. I knew enough to recognize that if I was lucky enough to live a long life, I would look back on my forties as part of my youth. You were always so clear about that. I remember you telling me how much you loved your forties and fifties, and how much we need to appreciate wherever we are.

We have had many conversations over the years and I remember all of them. I have always known that you believe in me, that you think the best of me and believed I could achieve whatever endeavors I set my mind to. You believed there was still time if I believed there was still time. There isn't a better mentor for this particular struggle than you, Coach.

You helped me all along the way, to the Paralympics, to marathons, and to the Ironman. I could always count on you to fax me a new training schedule, sometimes an hour after telling you what was next on my race schedule.

Here are just a few things I have learned from you;

- Keep learning. It's never too late to learn and you never know when you or more importantly, someone else, will need the information.

- Never give up. It's okay to change your mind but do it because it's right for you, not because others tell you to or because you lack courage.

- Always be tough, but be kind at the same time, whenever possible, and it's always possible.
- Make time for people, always.
- Give back.
- Keep going and keep doing.
- Use the phone. More. Call people just to say hi. Let them know you are thinking of them.

Coach, I know you understand even though we haven't had this specific conversation, that I needed you, in so many ways I didn't even know, and you have never let me down. I have shared your wisdom and fire with family members, friends, clients, and even with strangers at the gym. I brought my youngest to you for a visit and you became one of his coaches right on the spot. Your legacy is hard to capture in its enormity, but you keep adding to it, just by being you.

Lastly Coach, I know I'm your favorite. But so does everyone else know they are your favorite. That's just one of the gifts you give, every single day. And Coach, that, along with every bit of your coaching, every bit of your wisdom and every bit of your heart is a gift that will keep getting passed along. Forever.

I love you, Linds

Lindsay Nielsen

David Quade

***Coach Griak:** David was a St. Louis Park athlete with good ability. He was a tough kid. David placed 4th in the state cross country meet in 1955. He loved horses and I often had a hard time getting him to practice because he loved horses so much. He now lives in New Mexico and still loves horses.*

Reflecting back – A number of years ago, Mr. Griak called and left a message to call him back. I did so and he mentioned that at the Faribault Relays, fifty some years ago, he told me to stay out of the sun and wait for my events in the locker room. Later, when he could not find me, he asked our then track equipment manager, Marvin Shedlov, if he had seen me. Marvin said, "He had observed me going toward the river with a fishing pole." Mr. Griak stated that he went to the river and "caught" me! He said, "I remember it as if it were yesterday!" Since I had no recall of the event, it was on the tip of my tongue to deny having done that, when it occurred to me, that was something I would do. Fishing is good! Later, I remembered the "event." However, since I won the mile run, I was in my mind partially vindicated. I never thought of Mr. Griak just as a coach, I knew him to be much more complex. I learn something every time we talk. By the way, where is Marvin Shedlov and my fishing pole? And, that locker room I was supposed to wait in was boring and stinky! The river bank was fresh, cool, redolent of pine, lovely, and shady, very shady!

Best wishes,

David Quade / St. Louis Park athlete

Bob Wagner

Coach Griak: *Bob was a very talented runner. He won the Minnesota state mile twice and the state cross country meet twice at St. Louis Park. He came from a difficult home situation and track and field was his way of demonstrating what he was made of. Bob loved to run and still does. He was an excellent miler for the Gophers and a member of the 1968 Championship T & F team. {Bob's wife, Linda, sang at Coach Griak's funeral on July 22, 2015.}*

Dear Roy, "Chief", "Coach", "Mr. Griak"...

We go back a long way, to ninth grade at St. Louis Park. You were my P.E. teacher, a strict one, who didn't play favorites. That wallop you gave me with the big board, when I was talking when I shouldn't have been, was proof of that. Also, on my third day at the junior high school, you did not excuse me from doing the distance run when I forgot my gym clothes, I remember that I was about fifty yards behind Terry Neidlinger, when I realized that everyone was cheering on the "new guy," (me!) wearing long black pants and black leather dress shoes with my white undershirt!

After that introduction to the "Chief," running in Minnesota really started when you stopped me in gym class and asked me to come out for cross country the next season...and you told me to run "a few miles!" I ran about 900 to 1000 miles that summer, because you told me to (or I thought you had told me), mostly around Lake Calhoun. I can't remember seeing another runner the whole summer. That fall cross country season, at the state meet, I placed eighth but was disappointed because I had a lot left at the finish. I just ran without much experience. I was lucky to have Bruce Mortenson and Johnny Valentine to help me along the next few years. I remember that you told me to follow them and "do what they do...when they pass gas, you pass gas!"

I still remember you and Lefty (Wright) yelling and cheering me on to the victory, breaking the twenty-one-year-old 880 record at the Carlton Relays..."Lift your knees, pump your arms!" When I tell other friends and runners, I can hardly get through the story with dry eyes. It was the start of my racing career. And now, more than fifty years later, I'm still at it, even after two open heart surgeries to repair a leaky valve. Without your special help, I could not have accomplished all that I did.

Thank you so much, Roy. We haven't seen each other very often but you will never be forgotten. You and Lefty have been the most influential people in my life. I am appreciative of all that you have done for me and for hundreds or thousands of others. I love you, Coach.

Congratulations on your long, successful career.

Sincerely,

"Wags" (thanks, Roy)

Bob Wagner. (St. Louis Park and U of M runner, 1966-1968)

Bob Wagner, Don Timm and Tom Page at the 2016 Griak Invitational

Minnesota's 1964 Big Ten Championship Cross Country Team

Don Timm

When Coach Griak began his coaching career at Minnesota in 1963, Big Ten Cross Country (Big Nine until 1950) in the twentieth century had been dominated by three teams. Between 1910 and 1950, Wisconsin had won fourteen conference championships and had tied with Indiana in 1946 for another. Why that tie had not been broken through the rules of cross country is a mystery. In addition to the 1946 "tie," Indiana had won eight titles between 1928 and 1942. However, from the time that Coach ran as a Gopher to the time he started his long tenure at the Gopher helm, the kingpin of Big Ten cross country was found in East Lansing at Michigan State University (MSU).

The Spartans were not a member of the conference in 1948 or 1949 when they won NCAA titles in both of those years. They joined the conference in 1950. It was their addition that actually made the conference the Big Ten. As a Gopher runner himself, Coach's twentieth place individual finish in the conference meet in 1948, when he ran 21:54 for four miles, helped the Gophers to fifth place that year. The Gophers would place fourth in 1949. They would duplicate that fourth place finish in 1956 but would get no higher in the conference standing until Coach's first year guiding the program in 1963 when they were third to Michigan State. Coach Griak's 1963 team had a dual meet record of 4-1 and was captained by Jim Day. Wisconsin had won conference titles in 1948, 1949 and 1950 with MSU placing second in 1950. However, starting in 1951 the Spartans won eleven Big Ten titles in the next thirteen years. They also won seven National Collegiate Athletic Association (NCAA) titles between 1948 and 1959. This was the cross country powerhouse that Coach Griak would challenge when he arrived to coach the program at Minnesota.

In 1964, the Gopher cross country team unseated MSU and won Coach's first Big Ten conference title. In dual meets prior to the championship in 1964 the Gophers had earned perfect scores of fifteen in defeating both Drake and Iowa. They had also soundly defeated Iowa State and Nebraska. The only blemish on their season was a 28-27 loss to Michigan State. The Gopher captain in 1964 was Norris Peterson who had been the top Minnesota finisher in the Big Ten Meet in 1963 when he placed fifth. The 1964 conference championship meet was held at the Savoy Golf Course in Champaign-Urbana, Illinois.

As with so many of Coach Griak's athletes, the places, score and detailed account of the race are not as memorable as the day to day association with Coach Griak during their collegiate careers. Some of those memories have been graciously submitted by two of the Gophers who helped Coach earn his first title that day: Norris Peterson and Tom Heinonen. Peterson ran the four-mile course in 20:13 and placed second in the conference meet. Heinonen placed fourth with a time of 20:18. The Gophers placed their top five runners between second and eleventh in the meet and within thirty-seven seconds of each other. Pack running would become a hallmark of Coach Griak's cross country teams. Bob Weigel was eighth in 20:36; Dave Wegner was tenth in 20:46 and John Valentine was eleventh in 20:50. Pushing the second place Michigan State team further back were the Gopher sixth and seventh runners. Mike Elwell, who would later be killed in Vietnam, was fourteenth in 20:59 and Stan Gaffin was seventeenth in 21:18. Minnesota had thirty-five points with the second place Spartans totaling fifty-nine. Wisconsin placed third with ninety-one points followed by Northwestern with ninety-nine, Iowa with one hundred and nine and Indiana with one hundred and seventeen.

Although a half century has passed since the 1964 championship, and some of the memories of that day have faded, Norris Peterson and Tom Heinonen have clear memories of their

1964 Big Ten Champion Minnesota Gopher CC Team. Front Row (L-R): Larry Wittig, Tom Heinonen, Jack Trolander, John Valentine, John Beale, George Podolsky, Bob Weigel Back Row (L-R): Dave Atkinson, John Moon, Dave Wegner, Mike Elwell, Bob Wandberg, Ted Halpern, Norris Peterson, Coach Roy Griak

Coach. They have supplied what they remember of the Big Ten Championship but more importantly what they remember about their relationship with Coach Griak. Norris Peterson won two indoor Big Ten two-mile titles and one outdoor two-mile title. He ran two miles in 8:58.7 in 1965. In addition to his fourth place finish in the 1964 CC championship, Tom Heinonen ran 13:40.5 for three miles to earn All-American status in the outdoor track season of 1967. He would go on to coach the women's program at the University of Oregon from 1976 to 2003. While there he coached one hundred and thirty-four All-Americans, ten Olympians, fourteen NCAA individual champions, was named PAC 10 Coach of the Year eight times and had ten Academic All-Americans. Tom's teams won National CC titles in 1983 and 1987 and the Track and Field title in 1985. After retiring in 2003 he served as mentor for the University of Oregon running club. Tom said that after coaching for almost forty years he has seen so many races and been through so many seasons that his personal memories of the 1964 Big Ten CC Championship race itself have blended with the countless other races he has seen but that his memories of Coach Griak remain strong.

Tom's coaching philosophy of alternating tough and easy days was modeled after how he had been coached by Roy Griak at Minnesota. Likewise, Norris doesn't boast of his individual titles and his second place finish in the CC championship of 1964 but of his relationship with the Coach. Norris said that Coach Griak always kidded him that he had more than a lifetime supply of green towels and grey tee-shirts from the equipment room at Cooke Hall but that actually he had run out of them long before his fiftieth birthday.

Norris recounted that he had the privilege to run for Roy Griak during Coach's first two years at Minnesota. He recalled spring break trips by bus to Tulsa and Albuquerque. He joked that the two-a-day workouts at 5,300 feet in Albuquerque were toned down in later years by a "kinder and gentler" Coach Griak. Coach's top finisher in the 1964 CC title race claims Coach Griak as one of a select few mentors and role models who have had a huge impact on his life and that Coach's influence extended far beyond the athletic field and far into his life and for which he is very thankful.

Tom Heinonen recalled that the Friday afternoon before the Saturday title race in 1964 the Michigan State Spartan runners were throwing a football in the parking lot and generally goofing around with other shenanigans. Norris Peterson and Mike Elwell had said, "Let them do it. The next day we ambushed them and won Coach his first Big Ten title." Tom recalled that Stan Gaffin, who placed seventeenth in the entire conference as the Gophers' seventh man that day was from Wisconsin and that he had to overcome his "outsider" status as a foreigner. Gaffin also bumped George Podolsky, a teammate of Bob "Skip" Weigel at Minneapolis Roosevelt, from the varsity seven for the championship meet.

Tom's memories of the race are vague other than recalling that the Savoy Golf Course was flat as a tabletop. Tom's day-to-day memories of his college Coach and his teammates are much more vivid. He remembers doing intervals on both sides of the River Road and kicking up leaves on the jog recovery. He recalled a smell familiar to any Gopher athlete of the era, the smell of the dirt track in field house which he said was "like a musty garage." In recalling the 220-yard track in the field house, Coach Griak said that there was a mixture of dirt and sawdust used to keep the dust down. Anyone who practiced or competed in the field house during that era can only wonder what the place would have been like if the dust had not been kept "down." Nor can any athlete from that time forget when the big doors on University Avenue would be opened during the winter and runners would literally run through a visible cold bank on the back stretch of the track. Tom Heinonen also recalled the darkness and smell of the tunnel from Cooke Hall to the field house. He remembers getting his gear each day at the equipment window: white cotton shorts with elastic in the back, socks with no elastic, a jock that often chafed and a grey tee-shirt. That is a grey tee-shirt if Norris Peterson hadn't confiscated them all! Tom recalled the rancor between the track and baseball teams as they tried to share the field house with the baseball team inside the net and the track team on the outside. He remembers getting Coach to let us "just run to the Ford Bridge" instead of doing an interval workout on a decent weather day when we were dragging after a tough day.

Tom recalled that he and the other runners discovered a hallway under Memorial Stadium where they could run, but not very far, on an indoor long run. Tom remembers specifically Coach letting the team go for a run or take the day off on November 22, 1963 after hearing that President John F. Kennedy had been shot. Teammates Dave Atkinson, George Podolsky and Tom Stuart all remember running sand workouts on the river flats and dreading the sound of Coach's whistle signifying that the team should all pick up the pace until they heard the whistle again.

The 1964 cross country team placed fifteenth in the NCAA meet in 1964 with 359 points. The race was won by Western Michigan with 86 points. They did finish six points ahead of the sixteenth team, Michigan State! The meet was run in East Lansing, Michigan. The Gopher finishers in the NCAA Meet in 1964 and their team points were: Dave Wegner (49th), Norris Peterson (60th), Tom Heinonen (63rd), Stan Gaffin (92nd), Bob Weigel (95th), John Valentine (96th) and Mike Elwell (135th). The Gophers who competed that day had attended the following high schools: Dave Wegner (Duluth Central); Norris Peterson (Augustana Academy in Canton, South Dakota); Tom Heinonen (Robbinsdale); Stan Gaffin (Polaski in Milwaukee, Wisconsin); Bob Weigel (Minneapolis Southwest); John Valentine (St. Louis Park) and Mike Elwell (Fairfax, Minnesota).

The Gophers also placed third with a total of ninety points in the 1964 United States Track and Field Federation (USTFF) Meet in Chicago. The Gopher places in the meet were: Tom Heinonen (11th), Dave Wegner (14th), Norris Peterson (16th), Bob Weigel (22nd), John

Valentine (27th) and George Podolsky (46th). Coach Griak remembered that at the USTFF Meet, it was a beautiful, sunny day. The course included a narrow bridge over a swift flowing stream and that the runners were in danger of getting shoved off the bridge if they were in a crowd when they crossed it.

Always modest in his assessments, Coach Griak admitted, "We had a pretty good team in 1964." He chuckled when he recalled that in high school, Tom Heinonen from Robbinsdale, could not beat John Valentine from St. Louis Park; however, when they were teammates for Coach at Minnesota, Valentine could not beat Heinonen.

Six Gopher Runners at Memorial Stadium in 1964 – all the USTFF runners except Peterson. (L-R): George Podolsky, Stan Gaffin, Dave Wegner, John Valentine, Skip Weigel and Tom Heinonen

"Your Books Are Your Lunch Pail"

A Collection of Roy Griak Tributes

"Hit the books."

"Be a competitor in the classroom as well as on the athletic field."

"Stay focused."

"Commitment."

Melissa Engstrom

Coach Griak: *Melissa Engstrom is a beautiful young lady but more important she is beautiful on the inside too. Like a good pie, what is on the inside is more important than the crust. Like the pies and strudel my mother made, with Melissa, both the outside and inside are good. God, Mom's strudel was good. {Author's notes: I can personally testify to that.}{Melissa ran for Coon Rapids High School and then for St. Thomas. Coach followed her progress since she was in the seventh grade and was so proud that Melissa won the Minnesota Intercollegiate Athletic Conference (MIAC) 5,000-meter title in her last collegiate race - 2015.}*

My first impression of Coach Griak was before even meeting him, hearing about his big cross country invitational held in his honor every year. I thought that he must be pretty famous and far more superior than some "dweeby" high school team. This was not the case at all. He came to multiple competitions, bearing all the elements to cheer on the Coon Rapids Cardinals. I remember him being there when we won sections and headed to state and also when we lost. He is one of the most genuinely caring people I have ever met. When I had my first college Griak Invitational race, he went out of his way to wish me good luck. It is one of those memories I will never forget. I also ran one of my best races to make the traveling team to Boston that year. He has seen it all and been through so much as a coach and person in general that he holds so many valuable lessons. I will never forget the day a few high school teammates and I spent at his house raking leaves and listening to Coach Griak's stories about running. There was more to those stories than the running aspects. He instilled the importance of family and education, which I have learned, myself, to be key elements in life. His optimism is contagious and five minutes with him inspired me to do and be my best on and off the cross country course or track. He is a special person, inside and out, and makes everyone he talks to feel just as special.

Melissa Engstrom

Coon Rapids High School and St. Thomas

Melissa Engstrom running for St. Thomas

Rick Iverson

Coach Griak: *Rick was our student manager at St. Louis Park. Lefty Wright and I convinced him to come out for cross country and he became a very good runner.*

How High School Cross Country helped Me Pass College Calculus. What???!

Of all my college and medical school courses, calculus was by far the most challenging for me. Although I ended up getting an "A" in the course, I had to work harder for it than any other course I had ever taken. It was very common for me to spend two to three hours each day studying in order to understand that day's assignment. I would mutter repeatedly to myself, "It's not fair! No one should have to work this hard." I complained bitterly at times. Why should I have to spend so much time for one subject that even then I was certain I would never use again. What kept me going was those long hours of preparation for high school cross country. When I didn't think I could go another step, make it up one more hill or run one more fartlek, time and again, Mr. Wright and Mr. Griak's encouragement came back to me. It turns out that the same lesson learned then would carry me through long hours assisting at surgery, waiting to deliver babies and even to keep trying to help a terminal patient in spite of hopeless odds.

My introduction to Mr. Griak was in eighth grade PE. He was the teacher and the class was large. There needed to be strict rules in order to contain the adolescent energy levels that are normal at that age. The penalty for stepping out of line was "the paddle." Teachers then were commonly allowed to use a wooden paddle to punish misbehavior. What my infraction was has long since disappeared from my mind, but it was probably something like talking when I should have been listening. That was the only time I ever gave a teacher a reason to discipline me.

Fast forward to my sophomore year in high school. Lefty Wright was my across-the-street neighbor. He was one of my teachers, and also assistant track and cross country coach. He asked me to be the track team's manager, which involved passing out sweats, uniforms, towels, etc. It also involved collecting them afterwards for laundering, and other miscellaneous chores as directed by the coaches. That fit my obsessive-compulsive nature very well. Even better was the fact that our team was very successful and even won the Minnesota State Track Meet that spring.

Shortly after the track season, Mr. Wright and Mr. Griak came across the street and suggested that I run cross country that coming fall. I was extremely flattered, but to myself I was saying, "What are you thinking? You felt like you were dying running once around the track in junior high! How could you possibly even consider this?" But their encouragement won out. Several of the team members took me under their wings and helped me get through the necessary conditioning program and by the end of the summer I was able to run around Lake of the Isles, Lake Calhoun and Lake Harriet without stopping, a distance of about eleven miles. Just being able to run the workouts gave me tremendous confidence in my abilities. During our first meet in the fall I was able to be in the top fifteen on a team of sixty. Being part of that team was a great experience for me!

After our junior year. Mr. Griak accepted the position of head track and cross country coach at the University of Minnesota, a position he held with great honor and success for thirty-three years. Shortly after my senior year cross country season ended, one Wednesday evening at work I began having abdominal pain. It smoldered on for two days, gradually getting worse until I actually passed out in my second period English class. I was sent home to lie on the couch until my parents took me to our family doctor who sent me to the ER to see a surgeon. He too was puzzled, but after surgery he told my parents that I was very sick and my appendix had ruptured a day or two beforehand. I was to stay in the hospital for almost two weeks instead of the usual two to three days. My surgery was on a Friday evening. I was drugged pretty heavily so I do not remember much of that weekend, but I do remember one thing very clearly. Mr. Griak had come to see me right after returning from the Big Ten Cross Country championship meet. That is something that seems remarkable to me now some forty-nine years later! There is tremendous healing power in care and concern for another. Thank you for caring, Mr. Griak!

Rick Iverson

St. Louis Park

Marty Johnson

Coach Griak: *Marty was an 880-yard runner who was on the Big Ten Championship Track and Field team in 1968. He became an excellent lawyer and has often done work for me. Marty is a true friend and a loyal Gopher.*

My memories of Coach Griak:

In reflection, many vignettes, some good, some bad and some funny and some sad, came to mind. What I have tried to set forth below is what I remember, when I think back over almost forty-five years to my time under Coach.

There are several days in my life that I can remember very vividly. All of us can. Where I was when John F. Kennedy was killed. What I was doing when I heard about the Twin Towers being hit by terrorists. But interestingly enough, one of my clear memories is the night I got the call from Coach Griak. My family lived in Temple Village in Minnetonka in a story-and-a-half. My bedroom was in the lower level. One March evening in 1966, about 7:00 p.m., I was studying in my room, when my mother called down, saying I had a phone call. I yelled back, "Who is it?" She replied, "I don't know." So, up the stairs I trudged. As I picked up the phone, I heard this voice say, "Hi Marty, this is Coach Griak." My mind went blank. In fact, the silence must have lasted several seconds, for the next thing I heard was Coach Griak saying, "Are you still there?" I woke up and said, "Sorry, yes." The rest of the conversation was a blur, but I remember it ending with Coach Griak asking me if I would like to run for the University. Without hesitation I said, "Yes." That was the beginning.

The next four years flew by very quickly. I met and competed with some exceptional individuals. But some memories stick out:

Freshman year, jogging over to a cross-country workout with Stan Gaffin and John Valentine and Stan constantly ribbing Johnny about needing help getting up and over the curbs. Later that year, Roy called me into his office. He had seen my fall freshman grades. All "C's." Angrily he told me that this was unacceptable. As he led me from his office by the ear, he made it clear that I had to get my act together. Next thing I knew he moved my roommate, Pat Kelly in with Tim Turnbull.

I remember running at Iowa City during my sophomore year. It was cold, windy and wet. Doug Cozad was scheduled to run the steeplechase. Well, Doug fell behind a bit or a lot behind, and on his last lap, the field crew must have wanted to get home, because they started to carry off one of the hurdles as Doug approached. Without lowering the hurdle, they made poor Doug jump an additional 8" more than necessary. I laughed all the way to Minneapolis.

I recall several incidents at the U of M field house from my sophomore indoor season. We shared the space with the baseball team. As the baseball players would lean into the draped netting, Richard Simonsen would tee up some more unsuspecting freshman ball player and send him rolling into a ball. I remember John Myers falling against the shot put wall and ripping his thigh, resulting in him being carried off on a stretcher.

At the Big Ten Outdoor Championship during my sophomore year, a journeyman named Richard Landwehr was in the finals of the 660-yard dash. The track was muddy, the air cold and wet. By sheer guts, Richard held off all his competitors to pull the upset of the meet. During the finals of the 4 x 440 in that conference meet, Richard Simonsen took the baton and fought with the Iowa anchorman throughout the gun lap, only to lose at the tape.

In an indoor meet at Illinois during my junior year, Tim Turnbull and I were running second and third behind an Illinois runner. Suddenly, with two laps to go, I heard a "pop" like someone had shot a gun. Suddenly, Tim pulled up into the infield, with a torn Achilles tendon.

At the Drake Relays during my junior year, the Minnesota and Texas 4x440 teams were ranked second and first in the nation. Hubie Bryant was running the third leg and took the baton in first place. As he headed down the back stretch, he held a small but consistent lead. I was standing at the start of the last turn, screaming at the top of my lungs. Suddenly, unbelievably, not fifteen yards away, I saw the baton slowly arch into the air, and roll down into the infield. My heart stopped. The race was over.

Later that year, in a meet at Missouri, the wind was, as I remember it, at hurricane levels out of the west, which made calculating tempo in the wind impossible. As I crossed the 440-yard line at world record pace, I knew I was in trouble. And I was. The bear jumped on my back shortly thereafter and would not get off.

I remember the experience that year of flying to the Florida Relays and rooming with Bob Wagner. We helped Minnesota get third in the Distance Medley behind Yale and Southern Illinois.

Memorial Stadium where the wind was always in your face. In practice, stadium steps – endless stadium steps.

"Griak Roulette" at the University of Minnesota golf course. Wondering when the workout would ever end.

Then there was the rumor of an enterprising hurdler from California, who was awarded a scholarship after sending Coach a newspaper article indicating he had beaten Edwin Moses in the 440-intermediate hurdles only to discover later that Moses had fallen during the race.

Coming to practice at the field house and checking the board to see what we were scheduled to do, only to whine when I saw that we must work the meat grinder – infinite number of 330's, followed by infinite number of 220's and ending with an infinite number of something else, all with a 220 jog recover. There must have been a law against that kind of treatment somewhere.

Sitting and talking to Hubie Bryant as he etched "Smoke" on the side of his shoes, or listening to him rib "Daddy Roy."

The ugly green gray lockers in old Cooke Hall, water always on the floor, the concrete always cold. Trying to figure out how to smuggle those gray-tee shirts out of Cooke Hall without getting caught.

During my senior year senior year Missouri came to Minnesota for a meet. I ran the 660-yard dash and, at 330-yards I was in front. Suddenly, and without warning, Missouri's two runners went around me so fast that they actually startled me. I never saw anything on two legs accelerate that fast. Later, I found out that they were number one and number two on the Jamaican Olympic team in the 440-yard dash.

If I thought about it enough, I am sure I could come up with more mental "snapshots" from my years competing for the University of Minnesota. I remember running a lot of miles, I recall some pain, and some laughter; a few victories and a lot of defeats; some triumphs and some disappointments. But mostly I remember the guys I had the honor and privilege to compete with and alongside and to call my teammates: Warford, Wicks, Landwehr, Bryant, Simonsen, McNee, Ohnstad, Kelly, Twomey, Top, Jones, Stuart, Cozad, Myers, Edmonson, Shea, Eriksson, Turnbull, Hoag, Docktor, and Timm to name a few. Unbelievable athletes.

If my grandchildren were ever to ask me if I was a track star, in all honesty, I would have to say no, but I was on a team of stars. More importantly I would say that I had the privilege of studying and training under one of the finest gentleman I have ever known, Coach Griak. And to this day, whenever anyone asks me if I ran for Coach Griak, as happens from time to time, I look them in the eye, stand a bit taller and stick my chest out a little bit further and respond, yes, I am proud to say I was one of Roy's Boys.

Martin Johnson

U of M Runner, 1965-1968

Tim Oliver

Coach Griak: *Tim ran cross country and was a captain and leader on our Gopher track and field team. He had placed 5th in the state cross country meet in 1971. He became a lawyer and was a major contributor to the Roy Griak endowment fund.*

It is said that the value of a person can be measured by the lives one touches while here on earth. Using this yardstick, it is hard to imagine anyone receiving a higher score than Coach Griak. I think of the countless athletes, students and others that he has touched in a positive way.

For me, I had no idea when I came to the University of Minnesota how profoundly he would influence my life in so many ways. I had lost my father when I was only twelve years old. So while on his track and cross country teams, Roy Griak was not just a coach but a teacher, mentor, and father figure for me. Like all the athletes that competed for him, he instilled in me the characteristics of diligence and hard work, not just in our athletic endeavors, but also in the classroom and all that we pursued.

I still remember like it was yesterday the first time I met Coach. As part of the recruiting process, he had made a trek to the tundra of northern Minnesota to visit me at my home. What I didn't realize was that he was really there to recruit my mother. I am sure he had learned long before that trip that if the mom is convinced, the student athlete will follow. Well, it wasn't many minutes into the visit before my mother became a huge fan. I am sure she knew intuitively that Coach Griak would be the perfect mentor to guide her son.

At the end of the visit he said to me, "Coach Griak would be pleased if you matriculated to the University of Minnesota." It was the first time I had heard anyone speak in the third person, and I had no idea what "matriculate" meant. So once he left, the first thing I did was grab a dictionary and look it up. I remember thinking that college was going to be more difficult than I had anticipated if this was any indication. My mother then shared with me that it had always been her father's dream to have a grandchild compete for the University of Minnesota. At that point there was no question where I wanted to go.

While at the University of Minnesota, I had so many incredible experiences that it is impossible to enumerate them all. To compete on the Big Ten and national level is something very few ever have an opportunity to experience. From taking my first airplane trip to visiting cities and campuses across the country, participating on the track and cross country teams provided experiences I would never have had any other way. I will be forever grateful for those experiences.

Whether world-class athlete or a walk-on with no chance of making the team, Coach gave everyone an opportunity and treated them all with the same dignity and respect. While never a superstar, I have always felt that I reached my potential and became the best I could be as a result of his technical expertise and constant encouragement. He truly has a way of bringing out the best in people.

One of the other things I have admired about Coach is his humble, unselfish willingness to serve the institutions and people around him. He has poured countless hours into the lives of thousands of people and numerous organizations without the slightest expectation or concern for what he would receive. Coach epitomized "servant leadership" long before it was popularized in the boardrooms of America.

While there are many cherished memories of Coach from my time at the University of Minnesota, I wanted to share a couple of them:

One of my fondest memories occurred while on spring break during my senior year. The team had traveled to LSU for training and several track meets. The distance runners completed their workout and I was the last one on the track. Coach Griak was in the infield and asked me to come over and join him. We sat on the grass under a bright warm sun and discussed life. He shared with me his wisdom on the importance of family, caring for one another and making a difference in the lives of others. His words of wisdom shared that day have guided me in making countless life decisions over the past thirty-seven years and I know will continue to guide me in the future.

Another memory I will never forget involved a cross country team trip to Iowa. Like many of the meets in neighboring states, the team was schedule to drive to the meet, taking two station wagons. I was the captain of the team that year and, as was Coach's practice, he drove one of the cars, and I, as the team captain, drove the other car. We started our journey early in the morning. While en route, the two cars got separated from one another. During the time the cars were separated, a couple of my teammates spotted two young ladies hitchhiking along the highway. Motivated by chivalry and compassion, my teammates pressured me to stop and give the young ladies a ride. We stopped, picked them up, and continued on our way. This, of course, was done assuming we had avoided Coach Griak's watchful eye.

Only a few minutes after getting back on the highway with our new passengers, Coach pulled alongside our car. This was well before the invention of cell phones, so there was no way to communicate between the cars but through the use of several hand signals, he made it clear that he did not approve and wanted us to pull over. We immediately did so, and he explained with tough love all the reasons we shouldn't have taken on these passengers. More than a little embarrassed, we let the young ladies out and got back on the road to continue our trip. Five to ten miles down the highway, we were surprised once again to see

Coach pull alongside our car. This time, however, there was no effort to get us to pull over, but rather just waves and smiles coming from his car. As we looked closer, we realized that two of the passengers waving and smiling at us were the very young ladies we had just dropped off! He had waited until we pulled out and headed down the highway and then had the young ladies get into his car. In the end, he had the last laugh and taught us all a good lesson. {Author's note: Either Coach was in the habit of picking up co-ed hitchhikers on trips to the Drake Relays or Iowa City or the memories of his athletes have dimmed over the decades as Steve Holl told this story with him at the wheel and Coach as his passenger and with Terry Thomas, not Tim Oliver driving the other car.}

I could go on and on recounting all of the wonderful times and experiences provided for me and all those that had the pleasure of Coach Griak's mentorship. As I look back over my life, one of my proudest accomplishments is that I was, and still am, one of Roy's Boys.

Coach, thanks again for who you are and what you have done for me.

With the greatest love and respect,

Tim Oliver

U of M athlete

1970-1973

Jeff Renlund

Coach Griak: *Jeff ran for me at the University for a short time. He now coaches at Minnetonka and is an expert on the history of track and field in the state. He has compiled a great book on the Minnesota State High School Track and Field Meet and has recently released a book on the Minnesota State High School Cross Country Meet.*

I came to the University of Minnesota in the fall of 1987 with a passion for running and competing, but unfortunately was academically unfocused. One winter morning during indoor track season, I brought my new leather basketball to the Bierman courts to try it out. I was shooting around for a while, when I noticed Coach coming over to me. I proudly passed him the new ball, knowing he was a former basketball coach. Surprisingly, he began to sternly scold me, as only he could, for wasting my time here at the court instead of being at the library studying and getting my grades up. It was not necessarily what he said, but the way he said it that had a strong influence on me to start seriously thinking about my future. He took my new ball, and I never saw it again, and was too afraid to ever ask for it back. What I got from this lecture was far more valuable than the cost of a basketball.

A few Coach Griak quotes I remember:

"The quicker you remember this the better... Don't think that life is supposed to be fair, because it isn't!"

"Time to get up there and run with the big boys!"

"The hardest thing about the workout is not the actual workout itself, but just stepping out the door and getting started."

I remember him leading by example, working just as hard as anyone on the team in his sixties with his core exercises and medicine balls...him giving us apples after a hard run and sharing a laugh...his genuine concern / caring for our overall well-being, not just running...How he would take me aside from time to time and just talk about how things were going.

Jeff Renlund

Physical Education Teacher

Cross Country / Distance Track Coach

Minnetonka School District

U of M runner, 1987

Sharyl Renlund

***Coach Griak:** Sharyl is the mother of Jeff Renlund who ran at the University for a short time. She is a good supporter of the program. Sharyl was a St. Louis Park student.*

As a high schooler, 'class of '63, I was never really involved in sports, as there were only limited opportunities for girls, other than the Girls' Athletic Association (GAA). However, I was a big fan of the boys' basketball team that Roy coached. I know Roy made a very positive influence on all of them.

My son, Jeff Renlund has grown to respect, love and admire him after running cross country and track at the University of Minnesota.

Jeff has written a book, *The History of Minnesota High School Track and Field*, published in the late 90's. He dedicated it to Roy Griak. Roy's picture is in the forward. Jeff went onto become a teacher and coach for Minnetonka High School as head cross country and distance track coach. Roy has taken time, at Jeff's request, to visit with his boys and inspire them as well.

Over the years, my husband, Doug and I attended many Roy Griak Invitationals at the U of M golf course. We always see Roy out there cheering the high school and college runners on along with Eugene "Lefty" Wright, my old high school history teacher, who lived across the street from me on Utica Avenue when I was growing up.

They both taught Jeff to work hard, especially in academics, to train hard, and do his best! These concepts have certainly helped Jeff become who he is today.

Sincerely,

Sharyl Wilson Renlund

St. Louis Park Class of '63

Bill Twomey

***Coach Griak:** Bill was a quarter-miler for Minnesota and a wonderful person. His father was an outstanding surgeon who died very young. {Author's note: Coach Griak did not say this but Bill and Ed's mother told my parents that Coach Griak was like a second father to her sons}*

In the late 1960s and early 70s while running in the infamous indoor field house at the U of M, I often felt I was an actor recreating the dust bowl days of the 1930s. The black blizzards as the storm clouds of that era were called were artfully reproduced by a certain U of M tractor driver who sometimes chose the most inopportune times to drag the indoor field house baseball diamond.

One day, Coach Griak had us running shin splitting 220s on the lovely indoor dirt track. As sure as the sun comes up, our "Tractor Man" felt that the only time during his twenty-four-hour day to drag the baseball diamond on the inside of the track (with its "superb" netting that of course prevented any batted baseballs from flying through) was during our afternoon practice when the desire for oxygen was at a premium. It was during one of these 220s that I witnessed a side of Coach Griak I had never experienced. I was running at top speed and rounding the curve of the oval track when out of nowhere Tractor Man decided he was finished dragging the baseball field. Without warning, he drove his tractor over the track right in front of me, missing me by only a few feet. When I completed the sprint, I told Coach Griak about my close call with the tractor. Within a split second of my telling him of my near tragic experience, he tore over to Tractor Man and verbally ripped him apart for almost ending my career. The expression, "got my back" was not used in the 70s but if ever there was a time when Coach Griak got my back, it was that day. I had never seen him so mad. I sincerely appreciated his concern for me through his message to Tractor Man that his lack of attentiveness was totally reprehensible.

All of our narratives of Coach Griak have the same universal theme; he cared about us. He cared about us as both students and athletes and had the best interests of all of us at heart. Coach attended my mother's funeral and stood up and said many kind words about her. Thanks Coach for what you have done for my family and for all the other families of track athletes over the last fifty years. You have been a blessing to us and for the University of Minnesota.

Bill Twomey '71

U of M Track, 1969-1971

Big Ten Conference Championship Track and Field Team 1968

Don Timm

Thanks to Steve Hoag, Tom Stuart and Rich Simonsen for their recollections and comments on the meet.

One of the biggest moments in Gopher track and field history happened on a gloomy mid-May weekend in 1968. The occasion was the Big Ten Outdoor Track and Field Championship held at Memorial Stadium on the campus of the University of Minnesota. The weather was ugly, even by Minnesota standards and no one knew what was in store for us. While we were excited to be performing at home, in front of friends, family and fans, we had no idea that we had a chance to win the 1968 title. Michigan and Wisconsin were the overwhelming favorites, with Minnesota and a few other teams considered dark horses. Minnesota had finished third in the 1968 Big Ten Indoor Meet with a well-balanced team but no superstars. What happened during that weekend was an extraordinary sequence of track and field events that led to Minnesota winning its second ever Big Ten Track and Field Championship 50-49-48 over Michigan and Wisconsin! What follows are some of the facts and memories of that remarkable Gopher win:

Before the meet, Coach Griak said, "I'm not sure how much of an advantage the home field will be, but if there is an advantage, we'll need it. I imagine our boys will have a little extra incentive competing here at home." He went on to say that he hoped the Gophers could land somewhere in the first division. "Our winning the title is in the realm of possibility, but our chances are slim." He ticked off a series of ifs that had to materialize if the Gophers were to win their first championship since 1949. Those "ifs" included everyone performing at their best with wins in both the 440 and mile relays, big points from sprinters Hubie Bryant and Rich Simonsen, big points from high jumper Tom Stuart, hurdler John Warford, and some points from Randy Jones, Bob Wagner, Rich Landwehr, Ed Twomey and Steve Hoag. A point here and there from other events would also be needed.

DAY ONE

On a cold, rainy day, nine Gophers qualified for the finals on Saturday. Michigan also qualified nine athletes and Wisconsin had ten. Landwehr, Bryant and Simonsen won their heats. The Gophers got two unexpected and very welcome points from Bruce Hella, who placed fourth in the long jump. Unfortunately, John Warford fell on the last hurdle of the intermediate hurdles and failed to qualify. So, after the first day... some good, some bad for the Gophers but they were right in it. Rich Landwehr said, "We could just win this thing if something gets us charged up." Perhaps he didn't realize at the time just how prophetic his statement was! Landwehr was a transfer from Mankato and was a non-scholarship walk-on athlete who had come to Minnesota to study at its architecture school.

His upset victory in the 660-yard run would get the Gophers the "charge" they needed! Coach Griak said after the first day, "That's more kids than I figured we'd have qualify...but it's what you do on Saturday that counts the most." He would soon find out!

DAY 2 (FINALS)

The weather was just as gloomy as it was the day before. There was a light rain and it was about forty-five degrees. The Gophers got off to a great start with the expected 440-yard relay win (Rich Simonsen, Randy Jones, Pete Shea and Hubie Bryant). Two events later Rich Landwehr pulled off the upset of the day with a gritty .1 second win in the 660. In the mile, Bob Wagner earned three points. Randy Jones got a point in the 440-yard dash. John Warford placed third in the 120-yard high hurdles. Hubie Bryant placed second in the 100-yard dash and later got a big win in the 220! Rich Simonsen also placed in the 220 taking third. Simonsen's third place finish was disputed by Michigan and the final verdict was not made for several days. Ed Twomey placed fifth in the 880-yard run. Steve Hoag took third in the three mile run. Everything was going as planned with only the mile relay left on the track and the mile relay was a strong Gopher event. In that relay, the Gophers built a small lead for anchorman Rich Simonsen; however, Iowa's Mike Mondane ran an incredible forty-six second leg to pass Simonsen in the last ten yards for a Hawkeye win. The Gophers placed second in the mile relay. Rich Simonsen was devastated as it looked like the Gopher chances for victory in the meet were gone. Wisconsin held a one point lead on Minnesota. However, there were some field events that had not yet been included in the scoring. Dan Wicks picked up a welcome point in the shot put; however, the huge event in the field for the Gophers was the high jump. Tom Stuart had an unusual sub-par day but still placed fourth. Teammate Marv Top pulled off a remarkable third place to give the Gophers five big points in the high jump and this was enough to put the Gophers over the "top."

Shortly after the points had been tabulated, Hubie Bryant could be heard yelling, "We won, we won!" It soon became known to the athletes and crowd at Memorial Stadium that the Minnesota Gophers had pulled off a remarkable upset to win the Big Ten title in one of the closest finishes ever. The team scores at the top were Minnesota (50), Michigan (49) and Wisconsin (48). Coach Griak was hoisted on the shoulders of his athletes and promptly thrown into the steeplechase water pit. Although he went in wearing his sweatsuit, jacket and overshoes he didn't mind at all!

On the shoulders of his athletes after Minnesota won the Big Ten Meet

Al Bender, Coach and Hubie Bryant on the way to the water pit

Coach in the water pit after the big win

SOME AFTERTHOUGHTS, FACTS AND TRIVIA ABOUT THE MEET

Minnesota had great balance, scoring in all but five events. Michigan scored in all but seven events and Wisconsin in all but four. The Gophers had two individual champions: Hubie Bryant in the 220-yard dash and Rich Landwehr in the 660-yard run. They also had a win in the 440-yard relay.

An estimated 2,600 fans attended the finals on Saturday. This was a pretty large crowd for a U of M track meet, especially on a cold, rainy day. In huge Memorial Stadium the crowd seemed small but it was very vocal. According to Steve Hoag and Tom Stuart who collaborated on this summary, "it helped being at home, with fan support and familiarity. The weather may have helped somewhat, but most schools in the Big Ten are used to dealing with similar weather. Probably the biggest benefit to being at home was the fact that Coach Griak could enter more athletes than he would have if we had been traveling to another school. His budget would not have allowed him to take athletes who did actually score some points in the meet. This was perhaps the biggest home-field advantage."

In 1968 Coach Griak was forty-five years old and had been coaching at Minnesota for just five years. He had started with a program that had not placed above seventh in the conference outdoor meet since 1960. After a great coaching career at St. Louis Park High School, Coach Griak, in his first six years at the helm, led the Gophers to a Big Ten title in track and field in 1968 and cross country titles in 1964 and 1969.

Hubie Bryant scored a total of nine points with his finishes in the 100 and 220 yard dashes. He also anchored the winning 440-yard relay team and was an important part of the second place mile-relay team. For an athlete who was a Gopher football star, he had a very productive day on the track.

Michigan filed a protest concerning the results of the 220-yard dash. They claimed that Michigan's Sol Espie edged out Minnesota's Rich Simonsen for third place and requested that the film of the 220 finish be reviewed. If the Michigan protest had been successful and the judge's decision reversed it would have given Michigan the team title over the Gophers 50-49. After a few suspenseful days, the Big Ten upheld the judges' ruling with Simonsen third and Espie fourth. It was now official. Minnesota was the champion! On the Gopher campus the celebration was now really on!

The 660-yard run was a pivotal event for the Gophers. It should be noted that the 660 was an event that wasn't even contested in other conferences. It was pretty much just a Big Ten event! Rich Landwehr won this event for the Gophers and earned five huge and unexpected points for the team.

SOME RECOLLECTIONS

When Steve Hoag and Tom Stuart met recently to write this meet summary they recalled that "We were not even thinking about a Big Ten Championship that spring. We had a good team, but we were not in the class of Michigan or Wisconsin. Both of us were looking forward to competing on our home track for the Big Ten Championship. It was always nice to compete in front of friends and family. Winning the Big Ten Meet was not in the realm of possibilities."

Steve Hoag stated that, "Tom, who had won the Big Ten high jump title as a sophomore, had an off day and placed fourth but Marvin Top picked up the slack by coming through with a pivotal third place performance in the event. While Tom was disappointed in his own performance, or at least as disappointed as one can be after jumping 6' 7" and placing fourth in the Big Ten, he was happy for Marv and for the whole Gopher Track and Field team. It was their combined five points that sealed the Gopher win."

"I (Steve Hoag) was entered in the three mile and was seeded fourth. Larry Wieczorik from Iowa was the prohibitive favorite. Jim Dolan of Michigan was also picked to do very well. Bob Gordon of Wisconsin had beaten me recently in Madison. I was nursing a cold and talked to Coach Griak about the possibility of running someone else in my place. Coach convinced me, however, to try it. Since the three mile was one of the last events, I knew that I needed to get third place or better if we were to have a chance to win the meet. It didn't help that one of the favorites was Jim Dolan of... MICHIGAN! The race separated quickly with Wieczorik and Dolan taking off. I followed until about the two mile when I caught up to the two leaders and actually even led for a lap. Both Wieczorik and Dolan took off in the last lap leaving me third. My Gopher teammates were all around the track, encouraging me to beat Gordon from Wisconsin... and I did! I'm really glad that I decided to run after all because we needed those three points! It was also good that Wieczorik beat Dolan or Michigan would have gotten one more point and tied us. Thank you, Larry!"

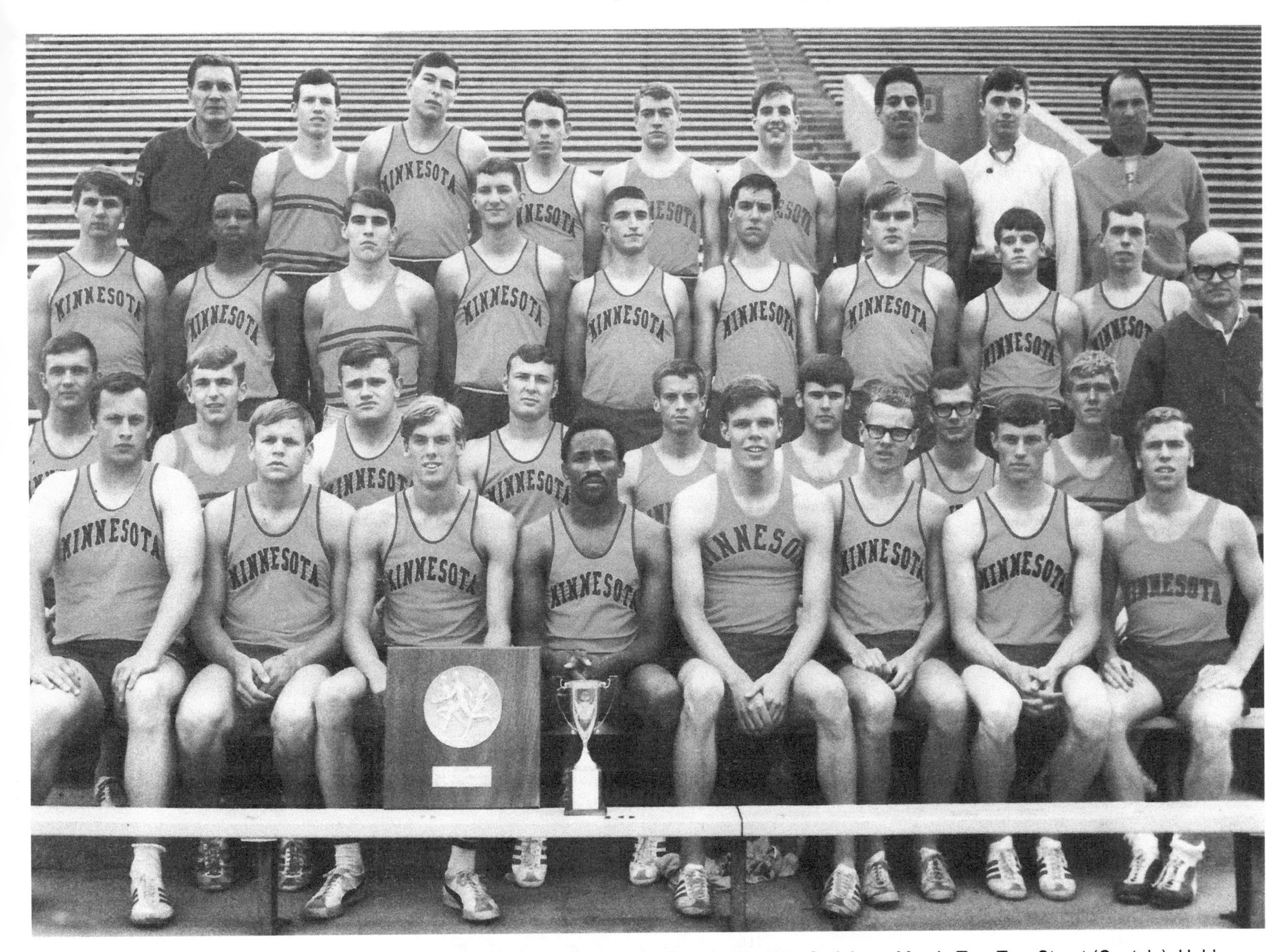

1968 Minnesota Gopher Big Ten Champion Track & Field Team Front Row (L-R): John Creighton, Marvin Top, Tom Stuart (Captain), Hubie Bryant, John Warford, Dick Aften, Dick Landwehr, Charles Tuchfarber Second Row (L-R): Bruce Johnson, Richard Simonsen, Tom Bracher, Dan Wicks, Bob Wagner, Bill McNee, Curtis Dockter, Randy Jones, Coach Dick DeShriver Third Row (L-R): Jim Ohnstad, Jeff Crawford, Pat Kelly, John Myers, Marty Johnson, Doug Cozad, Al Auerbach, Steve Hoag, Ed Twomey Back Row (L-R): Coach Roy Griak, Doug Edmonson, Steve Ericksson, Pete Shea, Tim Turnbull, Bruce Hella, Mike Curtis, Pete Jarosak (manager), Coach Gil Weingarten

Big 10 Conference Championship, Track and Field Team 1968

"The 1968 Big Ten Championship Track and Field team had a fortieth reunion a few years ago and it was very well attended. Team members came from all over the country and we shared wonderful memories of those two days in May of 1968. Just about everyone had a story about how their event played out...if this had happened or if it hadn't happened and so on. The margin for error was so slim; it seemed like destiny had a hand in our winning!"

"Memories can fade after forty-seven years. However, to a band of Gopher track and field men, it seems like yesterday. Our memories can be attributed to Coach Roy Griak and his assistant coaches, Gil Weingarten and Dick DeShriver, and also to those underdog Golden Gophers who came up big on a cold, soggy weekend in May of 1968."

Championship plaque

"Have a Sense of Humor"

A Collection of Roy Griak Tributes

"You can work hard and still have fun doing it."

"I have a 98-year-old grandmother who can run faster than that."

John Bohan

Coach Griak: *As a Gopher, John was a beautiful high jumper; a great technician. A very quiet young man.*

The first time I met Coach was in 1972 at his early evening weekday all-comer meets. It was the first time I saw his uncanny ability to get the impossible instantly organized. With little or no hired help and few volunteers, Coach could simply smile and ask for help, and pull off a credible event with everyone looking forward to the next meet – and their expected meet chores. This ability wasn't limited to simple high school meets. It would happen at Gopher dual meets, home Big Ten meets, and even the Olympic Festival. A few phone calls and coach asking how would you like to help and everything would magically come together.

My first one-on-one meeting with coach was in 1973 when I was deciding where to go to college. This is when I learned how Coach could walk. We must have walked five miles that day with Coach showing me every building, walking in on classes and then completing the tour with ice cream at the West Bank Bridgeman's.

I also remember Coach always used references to one's mother, mom or mamma. Is that how your mom taught you to dress, your mother could do better than that, are those the manners your mom taught you and make sure you take care of your mother.

Some specific memories of my years with Coach:

- Dreading when Coach would say let's go for a run on spring trips to LSU. Coach was a running machine and pride would make sure you kept up with him.
- Coach holding up a 747 at O'Hare airport while team members tracked down Dennis Fee who was getting a haircut.
- Coach many times driving me home at 2:00 a.m. after returning from away meets on the bus.
- The joy of Coach getting me a 4' x 8' piece of rubber so my last two approach steps wouldn't be on the field house dirt.
- The excitement of Coach deciding it was time to get a new pair of jump shoes.
- Coach always making sure to place the four 4' X 8' plywood sheets over the pit every night and then chain and lock them down.
- After Texas Relays, Coach asking me if I knew how much the University of Minnesota spent on each of my three jumps.
- Helping Glen Bullick get his vaulting poles into the plane's cabin and securing them to the aisle chairs (you don't see this anymore)!
- Getting a ½ point my freshman year in the Big Ten outdoor meet.

- Jumping 6'10" in the Big Ten meet my senior year and finishing one place short of scoring.
- Waking up to the LSU tiger every morning while staying in the very austere LSU stadium dorm.
- Working out in the field house and watching out for baseballs that would come through the net.
- Coach always wearing his long maroon jacket with the big Gold M on the back.
- All of the incredible stories told by Coach.
- Coach's regular statement that, "All things being equal, the one who trains the hardest will win."

My four years under Coach were an unbelievable gift.

John Bohan
1973-1976 U of M High Jumper

Tom Bracher

Coach Griak: *Tom was a student at St. Louis Park and later a shot putter at the University. He was a very quiet guy who got the nickname "Mouse." He looked like an angel but he was a real hell raiser. He staged keggers on the river flats while at the U of M. He was mischievous but was so quiet that he wouldn't say poop if he had a mouthful but he was very sneaky. Tom has officiated the weight events for many years and is a great guy.*

I want to mention three stories that stand out over the fifty-three years that I've known Roy Griak.

I met Roy for the first time during the 1960-1961

Tom Bracher and Coach at the fieldhouse

school year at Central Junior High School in St. Louis Park. Roy was my eighth grade gym teacher and he didn't put up with any "horseplay" during the class. If a student misbehaved, the punishment was to proceed to the front of the class and bend over and touch your toes. After doing this, Roy would promptly whack the student in the rear end with the wooden paddle. One day Roy caught me throwing spit balls in class and proceeded to give me the aforementioned punishment. The wooden paddle was the tool of discipline during that period and Roy would drill holes in the paddle so you could "hear it coming."

Another memory I have of Roy was in 1969 when I was a senior at the University of Minnesota. The U of M Track and Field team had just finished the Big Ten Outdoor Championships at Purdue and Roy took the team to an all-you-can-eat buffet at a restaurant in West Lafayette, Indiana. Roy said the bus was all loaded to go home but that it couldn't leave until Bracher finished eating at the buffet.

The final memory comes from one of my early officiating years in 1973. Colin Anderson was a senior that year and was standing on the award stand to receive his first place medal when all of a sudden, someone ran into the field house from the west side with a cream pie, proceeded to run up to the award stand, and throw the pie in Colin's face. The mystery runner quickly tried to exit the field house on the east (University Avenue) side while a stunned Colin remained on the stand. This prank was one of the funniest in Roy's tenure at the U of M and although he never admitted to any participation in the prank, I'm sure he was aware it was going to happen.

Sincerely,

Tom Bracher

U of M Thrower

1966-1969

Keita Cline

***Coach Griak:** He was from Tortola in the British Virgin Islands. Keita was a tremendous triple jumper and one of the best athletes ever at Minnesota in any sport. He was recently inducted into the Minnesota Gopher Sports Hall of Fame. This was long overdue.*

I was sixteen when I came to the University and I was welcomed in the same way as others by Coach Griak and soon became familiar with the term "Gol Dang It!" among others. I have many stories that I hold onto from Coach Griak, but one in particular always comes up among my teammates when we get together.

When I came to the University of Minnesota, I had recently graduated from Gainesville High School in Florida and prior to that had grown up in the British Virgin Islands. I had no exposure to hunting or other outdoorsman sports other than fishing. As I happened to walk into the locker room one day, the guys and Coach were having conversations about "bow hunting." I proceeded to ask what this was. It was explained to me that a bow was a rabbit looking creature with antlers, fast as lightning and thus very elusive. Well, I bought it hook line and sinker, never expecting to see one of these but thought it possible in the age of Ligers and other cross-bred animals.

It was shortly after this conversation on a bus ride to Madison or Iowa I recall, where Coach Griak on occasion would yell back to me as I sat by the window, "Keita, did you see that Bow along the side of the road? You gotta sit by the window and keep an eye out!"

"Nah, Coach, I didn't see it!" I replied.

"Those Gosh Darn things are so quick, I'll let you know if I see another."

This continued until the scheduled stop at a Golden Coral Buffet restaurant where I was made all the wiser by a teammate that had to tell me because his stomach hurt from laughing so much.

I'll never forget it, and I'll always swear up and down that I indeed saw the elusive "BOW."

Keita Cline

Gopher Track and Field

1991-1995

Cynthia and Pete Heaney

Coach Griak: *Track and field officials who have worked the long jump and triple jump for many years. She and Pete make a good team and she always has a smile.*

Getting to know Roy Griak has come through the arena of meet officiating for Pete and me, specifically the Griak Invitational and indoor track and field events at the U of M field house. We were always aware Roy had great enthusiasm for life and quite a sense of humor.

Last February (2012), Pete and I were being honored as USATF "Meet Officials of the Year" along with many other athletes of all ages and accomplishments. Roy Griak was the keynote speaker that evening. All eyes turned in his direction. Right off the bat Roy took everyone by surprise (me included) when he announced, "Cynthia, stand up." I thought to myself "Oh no, what's going on?" Nervously, I stood. With a huge grin on his face, Roy told the attentive audience "I did her hair!" Chuckles erupted throughout the room. Over the years of being acquainted with Roy he has never failed to comment on how nice my hair looked – we do share the same color. Yes, Roy Griak has quite a sense of humor.

Cynthia Heaney

(track worker)

Bob Hoisington

Coach Griak: *Bob is a dear friend and was a tremendous coach, first at Minneapolis Central and then at Minneapolis Southwest. We had some great battles when I was coaching at St. Louis Park. Bob knew how to get the best from his athletes. He devoted his career to athletics both as a coach and then as a long time official. He is a man of integrity and I have complete respect for him and what he has accomplished. {Author's note:* ***:*** *Like Coach Griak, Bob Hoisington was drafted into the United States Army. Mr. Hoisington had such a great mind for mathematics that when the government drafted him, they had him teach mathematical applications at the Aberdeen Proving Grounds. He would later teach mathematics at Minneapolis Central and Minneapolis Southwest.}*

Many people do not know the relationship that Roy and I had way back when we were coaching, he at St. Louis Park and me at Minneapolis Central. We were rival coaches but very solid friends as we worked with our dedicated teenagers in track and field and in cross country. Roy joked that we were "friendly enemas" and a pain in the you know what as we competed for several state championships.

Roy and I touched base many times each month for every year until he passed away in July of 2015. We were more like brothers than friends. He always had a joke or story to tell. Roy had a magnetic personality. He was always humble and never bragged about what he and his athletes accomplished. People always wanted to talk to him, or say hello, whenever we were together socially or at meets. He always made the other person feel more important than himself. He made his athletes feel comfortable and respected as he taught them the skills and proper attitude for each event.

I will hold memories of Roy Griak in my head, mind and soul forever. Life is a blessing and knowing Roy has been a blessing in my life.

Coach Bob Hoisington

Steve Holl

Coach Griak: *He was an average runner at Minnesota but he became a different person in the steeplechase. He became an outstanding athlete. Steve lives in San Diego and he has been a great financial supporter of the University and our program. He raises money to send his local high school team to the Griak Invitational.*

As a walk-on athlete in the fall of 1971 to a top NCAA Division I Cross Country program, it was somewhat overwhelming to be running with upper class team members that had succeeded in winning the Big 10 Championship just two years prior. These guys were finely trained and accomplished at the highest national and world class levels.

I was grateful that Coach Griak had chosen me to make the first road trip of the season to compete in Des Moines against Drake University. There were two maroon U of M station wagons at the Friday morning departure lot to transport the team south. While the cars were loading, Coach walked up to me and asked if I had a valid driver's license. Freshman me, upon responding to the positive, was handed the car keys. What the heck! Having only trained with the team for a month, I immediately changed my demeanor and assumed this responsibility. He had no idea that up to that time I had never driven a car out of Hennepin County!

The real story began on the way back to Minneapolis after the competition. I was driving one car with Coach at shotgun, and I remember Carter Holmes, Garry Bjorklund, and Bill Smith were also in the car. The other car was driven by Terry Thomas and included Greg Nelson, Gene Daly, John Purves, Mike Lawless, and Mike Hanley. About thirty miles north of Des Moines, we approached two cute college co-eds hitch-hiking our way. As we passed, Coach looked back and authoritatively stated that the guys in the following car had better not stop and pick them up. Well, sure enough, that car pulled over and the girls were welcomed in. Coach said, "Gol dang it!" He was fuming and several miles up the road told me to pull over at the highway exit and wait for them to catch up to us. Their car pulled up behind at the side of the road. Terry Thomas walked up to the right front window and adamantly argued that the girls were heading

Steve Holl and his coach at the University Golf Course

to Minneapolis and it was only charitable that they get the ride. Coach was stern in his response with the fact that it was against U of M policy to transport unauthorized personnel in these vehicles. There was a pregnant moment of deliberation before Terry reluctantly returned to the car to deliver the ultimatum. We waited several minutes as the guys in the second car exchanged goodbyes and the girls exited the vehicle. As that car pulled out, the hitchhikers walked by our car on the right shoulder of the road. They playfully stuck out their thumbs to our car. Coach Griak looked over at me and with an impish expression said, "Now pick them up!" I had to oblige and we giggled in our car for the next twenty miles!

Coach Griak is a unique and true champion of Minnesota values. He teaches that the pillars of success come from commitment, focus, preparation, and execution. Oh, and a good running maroon Ford Falcon. Give kids responsibility and vigilantly guide them to grow into productive adults. His leadership and thoughtful communications are forever cherished by the thousands that have had the good fortune to know him.

Steve Holl

Cross Country & Track, 1971-1975

Phil Lundin

***Coach Griak:** Phil was a volunteer coach who became my assistant and then succeeded me when I retired from coaching. He is the current coach at St. Olaf. While at Minnesota he was named United States Track Coaches Association National Coach of the Year in 2003. Phil is a good friend with a great sense of humor.*

Roy and I shared an office for twenty-two years in the Bierman Building (1986-2008). We had a good time together. His jokes and stories were, and still are, legendary.

As the years went by, I went from a full head of hair to being balder than a stone; Roy had all his lower extremity joints replaced. On the night after one of his last surgeries (installation of a new hip), I called Mayo to check up on him. Here was our conversation:

Roy: Hello

Me (Disguising voice): Is this the pecker replacement ward?

Roy: (Without hesitation): No, this is the pecker reduction ward, Philip, you little shit!

Phil Lundin and Coach

I was very lucky to have been able to hang around Roy Griak. He was (and still is) a mentor, friend, and colleague par excellence. If I have offended anyone with this story, I don't care. It is a good one. Fifty plus years in Maroon and Gold, Roy! Hats off to thee…

Phil Lundin

Assistant Coach at U of M with Coach Griak

Head Coach after Griak retired

Coached together (1986-2008); shared same office

Joe Nabbefeld

***Coach Griak:** Joe was a good worker as a Gopher distance runner and a very enjoyable young man. He was a camper and outdoorsman. He and his girlfriend once biked across the country and back.*

Coach Griak had a great mix of leadership, maturity and responsibility on the one hand and a youthfulness and spunk on the other hand. One probably needs both when ushering folk through college, and Coach had all of that.

A story that I would add to the mix is those dinners for the cross country team members at Mama Rosa's in Dinkytown with a fellow named "Bunny" Rathbun. One dinner per year, after the season was over. My memory is that Bunny was a benefactor for the cross country program and Coach set up the dinners for us to connect with Bunny and vice versa.

I also remember how Don Timm, Mike Slack and Garry Bjorklund, who were still all three competing at high levels back then, would show up to run in something with us seemingly at least once each season. I remember a mile race early in one of the outdoor track seasons in which Steve Plasencia hung in there against Mike Slack and Garry Bjorklund right through the kick. That had the right wow factor for the rest of us, it seemed.

Joe Nabbefeld

U of M runner

Seattle

John Purves

***Coach Griak:** John was an outstanding student-athlete at Minnesota with better than average talent. He remains a staunch supporter of the program to this day. He organizes the bike ride portion of the Snotty Nose Tough Golf Tournament / Bike Ride each year.*

{John related a story that had been submitted by two others: Steve Holl and Tim Oliver. His version of the story corroborates the one told by Steve Holl although John states that Coach Griak was driving the other car, not Steve. With Coach's sense of humor, the situation may have occurred multiple times!}

On my first cross country trip with the Gophers, the team took two University of Minnesota cars from Minneapolis to Des Moines to run against Drake University. In Belmont, Iowa, the driver of the car I was in, Terry Thomas, stopped and picked up two young girls. Coach Griak was driving the other car. He saw what Terry had done and waited at the next intersection. Coach waved us over and told Terry that he would have to tell the girls to get out. They did and Coach picked them up in his car.

This was just one example of Coach's "wicked sense of humor."

Thanks for everything Coach,

John Purves

University of Minnesota Miler (mid-1970s)

Dan Roach

***Coach Griak:** Dan was one of Al Halley's boys at Southwest. If you ran for Al Halley, you didn't mess around. Al always got every ounce out of his runners. Dan ran distance for the Gophers.*

Coach Griak had a few favorite sayings that were meant to spur us on to greater effort during tough cross country workouts. One of them I remember best was something he said to me on more than one occasion: "Danny, my grandma could go faster than that wearing slippery tennis shoes!"

Coach was also full of practical words of wisdom and life lessons. One in particular stands out: "Don't smoke, don't chew, and don't go out with girls who do!"

Dan Roach

Class of '85

(U of M runner, 1982-1985)

Jane Rollins

***Coach Griak:** Jane was a student and cheerleader at St. Louis Park. She is a wonderful person who remains a good friend.*

Reflections on Roy Griak

June 3, 2013

I knew Roy Griak as the track and assistant basketball coach at St. Louis Park High School. I wasn't an athlete; I was a cheerleader there from 1958 to 1961 so I saw Mr. Griak from a slightly different perspective.

Mr. Griak's athletes were known as "Roy's Boys" which meant, in part, we girls were to keep our hands off them! They were athletes, according to their coach, not to be distracted from True Purpose by the petty likes of holding hands in the hallway between classes or steaming up a windshield on the shadowy banks of Lake Harriet. To me, there is irony in these admonitions. Because Mr. Griak was (and still is) one of the most consummate flirts I know. He loved the girls of the 1950's and 1960's at Park High, and we loved him back. He was a dashingly good dresser, funny and irreverent, and a huge tease. What's not to like in that?

He made my evening at the 1958 Christmas Ball when he asked me to dance. He gave new direction to the cheerleading squad when he suggested we come out – in uniform – for his team the year they won the Minnesota State Track and Field Championship. Years later when he visited my husband and me over Thanksgiving, I was so nervous about impressing him that I dropped the full bowl of green beans upside down on the carpet. When I scooped them up, plopped them back in the bowl again, and set them on the Thanksgiving table, he complimented me for my resilience. Again, what's not to like? In fact, what's not to love?

Somehow Roy Griak has maintained contact with a multitude of people who love him. I am honored and grateful to be part of the crowd.

Congratulations, Roy, on your fifty years of service, inspiration, devotion, and affection to the University of Minnesota. We love you for it and more!

Jane Johnson Rollins

St. Louis Park High Class of '61

(cheerleader 1958-1961)

Chris Schmid

Coach Griak: *Chris ran at the University after graduating from high school at White Bear Lake. He was a real plugger with a passion for being on the team. A very nice person.*

When I showed up in the fall of 1988, I realized that I had to check my ego at the door. First of all, Coach pronounced my name "Schmyde" instead of Schmid, and that stuck for all four years. And throughout my time there, I was on the wrong end of some of Coach's one-liners, for example: "Your girlfriend weighs two hundred pounds, and that's only with one leg on the scale." And I recall once, he described my hair as looking like a "duck's butt," which in retrospect seems kind of accurate. I told myself that the more he picked on you, the more he liked you. He must have liked me a lot.

In all seriousness, I'll always admire Coach Griak for the way he did his job. Year after year, he dealt with young people who came with a range of backgrounds and personalities. No matter the situation and even in the face of adversity, he demonstrated the utmost in class and professionalism. I recall in 1991, the cross country team had a rash of injuries and there were just five of us running in the last meet of the season. Plus, two feet of snow had fallen in October. But Coach took it all in stride – he was still out there encouraging us as we practiced in November. No one was going to phone it in. Above all, he had the aforementioned great sense of humor, which helped keep things in perspective. Looking back, my experiences on the team were a huge part of my college education.

Chris Schmid in the fall of 1989

I was lucky to be able to witness firsthand a consummate professional like Roy Griak. So Coach, thank you for the opportunity to wear the maroon and gold. It was an honor and a privilege!

Chris Schmid 88-'91

Ken Shannon

Coach Griak: *Ken was an outstanding throws coach at the University of Washington. He and his wife are outstanding people.*

To this day I consider Roy as one of my most cherished friends. This relationship evolved through our involvement as members of the NCAA Rules Committee and many U.S. track and field teams in international competition – most notably the 1984 Olympic Games.

During these times together, I became a witness to Roy Griak's character. His wisdom and wit, his honesty and good ol' homespun philosophy have served as symbols for me to follow over the years. My wife Janet's memory of Roy speaks volumes about him, "He is a very sincere, polite and kind man." His engaging manner will be with me always.

Ken Shannon

Retired University of Washington Track and Field Coach

1968-2000

Bob Stein

***Coach Griak:** Bob was a great football player and a talented discus thrower. He played basketball for me when he was in junior high and later threw the discus for St. Louis Park and then for the Gophers. He was the Minnesota State Meet discus champion in 1965. Bob was a two time All-American in football at Minnesota and played from 1969-1975 as a linebacker in the National Football League. He was a member of the 1969 Kansas City Chiefs Super Bowl Championship team. Bob was the first president and CEO of the Minnesota Timberwolves. Bob is a very talented young man who became a lawyer.*

In the winter of 1961-62 I was in 9th grade at Central Jr. High in St. Louis Park.

Roy was my phy-ed teacher and basketball coach.

As a phy-ed teacher he earned broad respect for his knowledge of many sports, sense of humor and excellent wrist snap with a wooden paddle when the boys got out of control. I can personally attest to his home run swing!

I was an enthusiastic basketball player, but my aggression and effort far surpassed my skill and coordination, and I fouled a lot. One game I was particularly frustrated, everything I attempted led to another mistake and wound up fouling out…in the first half. I was beside myself and stomped back to our bench with smoke steaming out of my ears.

Always the kind, supportive mentor, Roy turned to me as I sat down and said, "What's wrong, Stein, didn't you feel like playing much today?" Coach Griak had his own way of motivating you.

I nearly blew a gasket when I heard that…along with my teammates' howling laughter. Roy still reminds me of my transgression fifty years later. Now THAT'S a caring coach.

I am proud to be his friend and one of "Roy's Boys." I cannot imagine having more respect and affection for a coach than I (and many, many others) have for "Mr. Griak."

Sincerely,

Bob Stein

(Central Jr. High, St. Louis Park, 9th grade basketball and Phy-Ed, All-American football at the U of M, Kansas City Chiefs)

{Author's note: When this tribute arrived in the mail, I commented to Coach that I had received a letter from someone who had said they had once fouled out in the first half of a junior high basketball game. Coach immediately replied, "Oh, that hatchet man, Bob Stein."}

Howard Sundberg

***Coach Griak:** Howie was a California sprinter who ran the 400-meters for the Gophers. He became the superintendent of schools in Lancaster, California. Howie and his wife have sons who are all doctors or lawyers.*

Based on my very informal, non-scientific research, I am convinced that maybe once, or maybe twice, someone steps into your life and puts you on a profoundly different and better path. For me, Coach Griak was that person,

I came from a family that struggled to make ends meet. My Mom and Dad were hardworking, conscientious parents who did all they could to send their five kids in the right direction. At that time, however, they did not appreciate the importance of a college education. That attitude and very tight finances meant a four-year university was out of the question.

Coach Griak changed all that by offering me a track scholarship. His faith in my potential as a student-athlete certainly altered my future. Instead of a life of blue-collar labor, or perhaps one that would have ended in Vietnam, I got the opportunity to follow in his footsteps as a coach and educator, back in my hometown. Thirty-eight years in that wonderful profession, the last six as superintendent of a fairly large school district, allowed me a fulfilling career and a good life. Thanks to Coach, I was also able to bring home a beautiful Minnesota bride who gave me four wonderful sons – all now with college degrees. Coach's influence extends across generations!

Anecdote

Prior to 35W being completed, I had the "fun" of driving a University vehicle on country highways to the Drake Relays. In 1972, after arriving at the Hotel Ft. Des Moines, Coach forcefully pushed open the door to our room and rather loudly exclaimed, "Sundberg!" (It was "Howie" when I wasn't in trouble). "I got a call from the athletic director saying he received a complaint that a University car had driven through Belnap, Iowa at a high rate of speed." Feigning indignation and surprise, I responded, "Coach my car didn't even go through Belnap!" I felt some relief as Coach left the room – I wasn't in trouble and didn't lie. It was Belmond, Iowa.

Howard Sundberg

U of M athlete

1972

Gary Wieneke

***Coach Griak:** Gary was an outstanding coach at the University of Illinois. Gary was a great friend when we coached against each other and he remains a great friend today.*

I met Roy Griak when I joined the Big Ten Conference in 1967. It was apparent very quickly that he was an excellent coach, and a humble, sincere man. As the years passed, we became close friends. In December 1988, he was the Best Man at my wedding. There are conflicting stories concerning his travel to Champaign-Urbana for the wedding, but no matter whose story you hear or believe, he was late, and missed the wedding. He arrived just as people were leaving the church for the reception! Since he missed the ceremony we were joking that he couldn't officially sign the marriage certificate. I said we'd have to do the ceremony over and he asked, "could we?" The minister took us back in the chapel, and in five minutes performed the official part of the ceremony – thanks to Roy, I was married twice in one night! I was pleased that he could be there to share that evening with us.

Roy is a very special person, and deserves the very best in life.

Coach Wieneke

Coach at the University of Illinois

Tim Zbikowski

***Coach Griak:** Tim ran at Armstrong High School. He was an average runner but was very devoted to the program at Minnesota. He continues to participate. He and his wife take care of the meet of miles. He is a very nice fellow.*

I competed on the U of M cross country and track teams starting in 1974 as a walk-on. Unfortunately, my varsity eligibility was limited to one year. I began attending classes at the University in 1970 and did not participate in sports then. After a couple years at school, I dropped out, worked for a while, and returned to school in 1974. By that time, my younger brother Rick was competing on the team and Coach welcomed me aboard.

When my eligibility ended in 1975, Coach was kind enough to allow me to remain on the team through 1977, use the locker room facilities, and compete with the "B" squad. It was truly an enjoyable experience and I continue to value the friendships I formed during that time.

I stayed involved with running beyond my University days, competing in open events and becoming involved in running-based organizations. I've run every "Rocky's Run" on the University Golf Course for the past thirty-one years. As President of the Minnesota Distance Running Association (MDRA), I had the honor of presenting coach Griak the MDRA Distinguished Service Award in 1987. I also prompted adding the U of M indoor all-comer Meet of Miles to the MDRA Grand Prix race series. It was included starting in 1988, and I volunteered to co-direct the meet with Coach. I have continued to do that every year since then. All proceeds from the meet are donated to the U of M track program. In the past twenty-five years, we've raised a total of around $10,000.

I think my positive experience on the U of M track team under Coach Griak helped lead me to a lifelong enjoyment of running and to the contributions I've made to support our sport. The Griak legacy reaches far beyond his record at the University of Minnesota.

It is always interesting working with Coach and often amusing thanks to his great sense of humor. One time, while packing up equipment late in the evening of a Meet of the Miles event, Coach remarked, "I'm so hungry I could eat the rear end of a skunk!" It's hard to forget a comment like that, and even harder to forget a guy named Roy Griak. Thanks, Coach.

Tim Zbikowski,

U of M athlete, 1974-75

1968 NCAA 4th Place Cross Country Team

Don Timm

When the Gopher team journeyed to New York City for the November 25, 1968 National Collegiate Athletic Association championship cross country meet, they were trying to avenge two close and frustrating losses that fall to Michigan State (MSU). In a dual meet in the middle of the season the Spartans had been credited with a 27-29 win that came only because the MSU coach, Jim Gibbard, had disqualified Steve Hoag, the top Gopher runner, when Steve was misdirected by a Spartan letterman near the finish of the race. Hoag had a huge lead and could not see the chalk line as it was obscured by the sun shining on the wet grass. An MSU letterman-spectator pointed down a fairway parallel to the one next to the fairway that led to the finish line. Steve followed that instruction and was disqualified. In the meets leading up to the conference championship the Gophers were 5-1 with the controversial "loss" to MSU being the lone blemish on their record.

In the 1968 Big Ten Championship held in Columbus, Ohio, Michigan State again was the beneficiary of Gopher misfortune. The Spartans won the meet 70-79 over the second place Gophers but that score did not include the number one Minnesota runner. Steve Hoag had finished third in the 1967 conference meet when he ran 24:44 for the five-mile race. He was considered one of the favorites to win the individual title in the 1968 meet. Steve Hoag led the race until the last fifty yards when he collapsed and was unable to finish the race. Instead of counting a single point or a single digit place the Gophers had to count their sixth runner who was thirty-third. Also hampering Minnesota's performance in the Big Ten meet was the side ache that Bob Wagner incurred early in the race. Bob Wagner was a graduate of St. Louis Park High School and had the distinction of having Coach Griak as his coach in both high school and college. He had placed ninth in the meet in 1967 but was thirty-sixth in 1968.

The Gopher scorers in the meet were Tom Page (Edina High School) who placed seventh, Pat Kelly (St. Paul Monroe) who was tenth, Ed Twomey (Benilde) who placed eleventh, Ben Grokett (Minneapolis Roosevelt) who was eighteenth and Curt Docktor (Osseo) who finished thirty-third. Concerning the outcome of the meet, Coach Griak was quoted in the *Minnesota Daily,* "Steve wanted to excel so much that he just pushed himself too hard and used some of his energy too early. It's too bad because he's been running so well all year. It'll take a while to forget this race." Griak said, "I'm sure the kids feel worse than I do. It isn't very often you have such a good chance to win a championship, and then you lose it." Despite the frustrating second place finish, Coach Griak said in 1968, "Even if we didn't win, this was our finest cross country team ever. The kids worked hard and developed as a team."

The team would have another opportunity to prove themselves ten days later in the NCAA Meet. They would also have another opportunity to avenge the bitter losses to Michigan State. Curt Dockter recalled that in the week following the Big Ten Meet Coach Griak had read the team a letter that he had received from John Valentine (member of the 1964 Big Ten Champion Gopher team). John had been severely wounded in Vietnam. This news helped to put our disappointment into perspective.

It was with this background that the 1968 Minnesota Gopher Cross Country team traveled to Van Cortlandt Park in the northwestern part of the Bronx in New York City to compete in the NCAA cross country championship. Steve Hoag recalled that, "The team had flown to New York City on a mission. After a dismal Big Ten Championship, where Minnesota was expected to win, the team was down, but we wanted to prove that we were indeed the best team in the Big Ten." Despite Hoag's collapse, the Gophers still lost the title by only nine points to Michigan State. After some motivational talks by Coach Griak, Hoag remembers that the team couldn't wait to race in the nationals. The seven Gopher runners who represented Minnesota were the same seven who had competed in the Big Ten Meet in Columbus. They were: senior Captain Steve Hoag, seniors Ed Twomey, Bob Wagner and Curt Docktor, junior Pat Kelly and sophomores Tom Page and Ben Grokett.

Steve Hoag recalled that when the Gopher runners were jogging the course to prepare for the race they were impressed by the rugged terrain on the backside of the course. After leaving a flat soccer field area at the start, the course went through a gate and then narrowed to a rocky, rutted trail. The trail went up, gradually at first and then quite steep in places. One hill had been dubbed, Cemetery Hill, and was quite daunting. After the uphill section of the course, the trail went down in a series of switchbacks. Some of the sharpest downhill turns had chicken wire fences along the edge to keep the runners from going off the path! The trail was treacherous in spots even as the Minnesota runners did their pre-race tour of the course and it would prove to be more treacherous in heavy traffic at race pace. Steve Hoag said that, "There was an art to negotiating the sharpest turns and that the chicken wire fence often came into play because of the pushing and shoving during the race." The runners used a narrow, wooden bridge to cross a small creek and then the course leveled again as the runners returned to the soccer field. Two laps of this challenging course comprised the 6-mile race.

As usual, Coach Griak had examined the course and arrived at a strategy for his runners. He stressed the importance of getting out extra fast so that the Gophers would not get caught in the main pack of the field of athletes. In a race of this magnitude, the first twenty to forty runners had fairly good running room and had fairly good vision of where they were and where they were going to plant their next steps. The last twenty to forty runners are behind the pack and also have a fairly good line of vision although they would likely be inhaling dust. That left two hundred runners in the main pack fighting for every inch as they tried to stay upright and also look for opportunities to move up. Coach Griak told his runners that they should establish themselves in contention before they reached the narrow path with many turns on the back of the course because there would be very little room to pass in that section.

Coach also stressed the importance of every second and every place. In an NCAA field of runners, it would not be unusual for five seconds to make a difference of five places in the team scoring. He also told his athletes, "When you get to the starting line if you are not a little scared, you are not ready." Coach Griak's memories of the course and the race had faded very little over the last forty-seven years of his life. He remembered that there was discussion among the coaches concerning the course. Coach said, "In the Big Ten we always designed a course so that there was plenty of distance before a major turn so that the runners would all have a fair chance." Of the course at Van Cortlandt Park Coach commented, "Out East, they didn't care." Coach then related a similar protest at another national meet where Navy Coach Al Cantello had told those who raised objections to his course, "If you don't like it go home." Confirming the old adage, "He swore like a sailor," Cantello's advice to the other coaches contained some additional verbage that has not been repeated here. Wikipedia states about Al Cantello, "He is known for his creative use of the English language."

At the time of this interview with Coach Griak, Al Cantello was still the cross country coach at the Naval Academy. He had won the AAU javelin title in 1959 and 1960, held the world javelin record in 1959 and placed tenth in the Olympic Games javelin in Rome in 1960. Having run at Van Cortlandt Park in 1969, I know that after the start the runners ran only a few hundred yards across a flat field before there was a post where the runners made a ninety degree turn to the left. Coach instructed us to not get trapped on the inside at that turn where we might be forced inside the post or have to wait for the traffic to thin so that we could go around it. Coach Griak said, "This was an unbelievable course; there were rocks, cliffs, steep trails, bridges, hair pin ninety degree turns, and just about anything else you can imagine. With all the shoving and pushing going on in the pack the race was for men only. Van Cortlandt was a tough course, but our kids ran tough." He remembers the morning of the race that the team had a hectic ride to Van Cortlandt because of detours and New York City traffic. He said, "We made it just in time." He also remembers people stealing sweat clothes from the team camps.

Once the race started, Steve Hoag recalls following Coach's instructions and sprinting the first three hundred yards of the race. Because of the quality of the competition he said that he was discouraged that his fast start only placed him in the top fifty in the race. "Coach was absolutely right that there would be little room to pass once we reached the dirt path in the hills." Steve remembers being frustrated and wanting to move up but being unable to pass on the tight turns. Descending the second part of the loop on lap one, Steve passed a few more runners, using the chicken wire fence on the turns to maintain his speed and keep from going over the edge. Not so lucky was Pat Kelly who reported that he was pushed off the path and had to scramble back up a cliff to continue the race. Pat felt that his tumble may have cost him twenty spots in the race. Steve said that as he approached the soccer field to begin the second lap, "I made a conscious effort to really open it up!" He was able to move up about ten spots in the only place on the course where passing was possible before the runners reached the hills again. Hoag remembers that he was starting to tire as the runners entered the trail section on the back of the course. He stated that, "The course seemed tougher the second time around." It must have been tougher for all the runners because Steve said that oddly, he wasn't passed in that stretch of the race. He recalls leading a pack of about twelve runners in a mad dash for the finish line once they descended from the hills and entered the open field. Steve said that only ten seconds separated those dozen runners but that he had held the lead of that pack. Hoag finished the 6-mile race in 30:21. He recalls being pleased to see his teammates also finishing strong. Manhattan College was using a new computer system to score the meet and there were some technical problems.

Few people could watch a race involving twenty-four teams and 233 runners and mentally tabulate his team's finish. However, Coach Griak told his runners that he thought that the Gophers might be in the top five teams. It took a while for the official results to be announced. Steve Hoag said, "We knew that we had done well and that we had given 100%. We were elated to hear that we had placed fourth in the NCAA with 239 points." It was the best finish ever for a Gopher cross country squad. Now, nearly a half-century later, the fourth place finish for the 1968 Gophers remains the highest NCAA finish for a Minnesota CC team. Only Villanova,

1968 NCAA 4th Place Cross Country Team

Minnesota Gopher Cross Country Team. Front Row (L-R): Tom Beltz, Ben Grokett, Mark Schmidt, Curtis Dockter, Steve Hoag, Ed Twomey, Doug Edmonson Back Row (L-R): Assistant Coach Dick DeSchriver, Dog Cozad, Bob Jones, Don Timm, John Myers, Tom Page, Pat Kelly, Bob Wagner, Coach Roy Griak

Stanford and Southern California were ahead of the Gophers in 1968. Michigan State finished in twelfth place forty-eight points behind Minnesota. In an article written by the sports editor of the *Minnesota Daily*, Marshall Tanick, Coach Griak said, "We've waited all year to beat Michigan State, and now we've finally done it. We've really done ourselves proud. It's a nice way to end the season."

The individual places and times for the Minnesota runners were: Steve Hoag 30:21 thirty-fourth (twenty team points - individual runners from schools not fielding a complete team did not count in the team score); Bob Wagner 30:58 67th (forty-first); Ed Twomey 31:04 74th (forty-seventh); Tom Page 31:28 102nd (sixty-fifth); Pat Kelly 31:29 103rd (sixty-sixth); Curt Docktor 32:06 141st (ninety-fourth); Ben Grokett (Did Not Finish). The NCAA individual champion was Mike Ryan of the Air Force Academy who ran 29:16.8. Following the meet, Coach Griak treated his athletes to a fantastic dinner at Mama Leone's in Manhattan and then took them on a brief tour of New York City before the team returned to Minneapolis tired but very satisfied with their NCAA performance.

Revenge losses to Spartans

Thinclads nab 4th in NCAA

Special to the Daily

New York, N.Y. — Minnesota's cross country team and its captain Steve Hoag revenged the two blemishes on their 1968 season record in the National Collegiate Athletic Association championship meet here yesterday.

Crossing the treacherous six-mile Van Cortland Park course in 30:21, Hoag finished 21st in the field of 233 runners from 24 teams and led the Gophers to a tie for fourth-place with Colorado.

Villanova won the meet with 83 points, followed by Stanford with 107, Southern California with 124, and Minnesota and Colorado with 254. San Diego State, Drake, California Tech, Miami of Ohio, and Harvard rounded out the top ten.

MINNESOTA easily outdistanced all other Big Ten teams. The next best performance by a conference team was the 12th-place finish of Michigan State, the squad that won the league championship 10 days ago.

Finishing ahead of the Spartans was particularly sweet for Gopher coach Roy Griak and his seven-man unit. MSU was the only team that defeated the Gophers in the dual meet season and also edged them out for the conference title.

It also was gratifying for Hoag, who had twice experienced supreme frustration against the Spartans. In the dual loss at Michigan State, Hoag was disqualified for missing a turn, and this cost Minnesota the contest. In the conference meet, Hoag collapsed 50 yards short of the finish, and again this helped the Spartans top Minnesota.

"We've waited all year long to beat Michigan State," Griak happily said after the meet, "and now we've finally done it.

"YES, WE really did ourselves proud. It's a nice way to end the season."

It might have been even nicer had not the hazardous course hindered Minnesota runners, as well as other competitors. "This was an unbelievable course," Griak said, "Why, there were rocks, cliffs, steep trails, bridges, hair-pin (90 degree) turns, and just about anything else you can imagine.

"With all of the shoving and pushing going on in the pack, the race was for men only."

One casualty was Pat Kelly, who tumbled on one of the numerous cliffs in the park that runs near a residential district of this metropolis. The spill cost him about 20 positions, but he still managed to finish in 31:37, 70th in the field.

BOB WAGNER'S 30:59 timing gave him 44th place, Ed Twomey finished 50th in 31:05, Tom Page edged Kelly by one second for 69th place, Curtis Docktor finished 99th and didn't score, and Ben Grokett was one of 16 runners who failed to finish the race.

Air Force's Mike Ryan won the race in 29:28, a new course record. Michigan State's Ken Leonowicz finished 16th to edge Hoag for Big Ten honors.

sports in perspective

By MARSHALL TANICK, Daily Sports Editor

Photo by Ted Hammond

Hoag bows out in style

Leads team to 4th in NCAA

Thinclads Nab 4th in NCAA – Hoag Bows Out in Style (Photo by Ted Hammond of the *Minnesota Daily*)

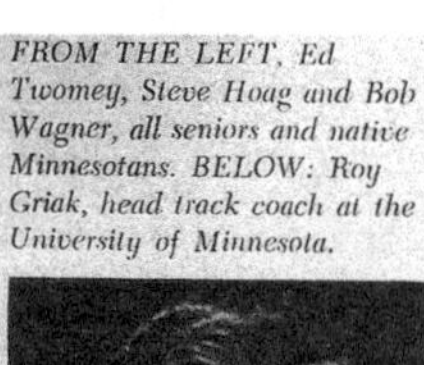

FROM THE LEFT, Ed Twomey, Steve Hoag and Bob Wagner, all seniors and native Minnesotans. BELOW: Roy Griak, head track coach at the University of Minnesota.

Cross Country Shows Good Season

By Gregg S. Wong
Sports Information Office

THE 1968 Minnesota cross country team had the greatest season a Gopher team has ever had—but it may have been one of the strangest, too.

Coach Roy Griak's squad finished the season with a 5-1 dual meet record, a second place in the Big Ten meet and a fourth place in the NCAA meet. Yet the record could have been better had it not been for a couple of unfortunate events—both happening to Captain Steve Hoag.

Hoag, the Gophers' number one runner and an All-American in track last spring, was hit with luck you wouldn't want wished on anyone. In a dual meet at Michigan State last October, he was the apparent individual winner making the Gophers the team victor; but, after finishing the race, it was discovered that the former Anoka high school star had taken a wrong turn. Instead of a Minnesota victory, Michigan State won 27-29 (low score wins).

The Gophers were determined to forget that meet and make up for it in the future competition. Easy wins over Drake and Iowa followed.

Going into the Big Ten meet at Columbus, Ohio, the Gophers were one of the favorites for the championship. More than halfway through the race, Coach Griak "knew Minnesota would win." But, unfortunately, Hoag again was victimized by the unforeseen. About 50 yards from the finish line, Hoag, who was running in third place at the time, collapsed.

"Steve just pushed himself to the limit," Griak said recently. "He wanted to finish the race and win the championship so much that he thoroughly exhausted himself."

Since Hoag did not complete the race, the Gophers lost 37 points and the team championship. Once again they bowed to Michigan State, who won the meet, scoring 70 points to Minnesota's 79.

After finishing second to Michigan State twice within a month, the Gophers were more determined than ever to finish higher than the Spartans in the NCAA meet. The fourth place earned by Minnesota was the highest in history for a Gopher cross country team. And, most of all, Michigan State was well behind Minnesota, finishing twelfth.

"After losing those two meets like we did, it was gratifying to come back and finish higher than State," Griak said. "I was so proud to see the kids come back and run well in the NCAA meet."

Hoag led the Gophers to their fourth-place finish, winding up 34th.

And though it was an unlucky year for Hoag, his performance and leadership was acknowledged by those who mean the most to an athlete—his teammates. For the second straight year, Hoag was the recipient of the Fred Watson Award, which goes to the most valuable runner on the Minnesota cross country team, as chosen by his teammates. Watson, a former Minnesota cross country star, was the first and only individual in Big Ten competition to win the conference title three successive years—in 1913-1915. The award was instituted by Griak in 1967.

Although Griak loses four of his top seven runners through graduation, he looks to next fall with enthusiasm. "Last year's freshman team is the best I've had at Minnesota," Griak said. "And with three top lettermen returning, it should be a very interesting year."

Back will be senior Pat Kelly, St. Paul and juniors Ben Grokett, Minneapolis and Tom Page, Edina. A pair of freshmen, Gene Daly, St. Cloud and Mike Hanley, Anoka, lead the highly- regarded frosh squad. Other top freshmen who may help next year are Carter Holmes and Greg Nelson, Minneapolis; John Hopko, Robbinsdale; Dean Swamspm, North St. Paul, and Terry Thomas, Mounds View. Returning non-lettermen who will aid the 1969 Minnesota harriers are juniors Doug Cozad, Shawnee Mission, Kansas; Doug Edmonson, Richfield, and John Myers, Rochester.

Gone from the team will be Hoag; Curtis Dockter, Osseo; Ed Twomey, Golden Valley and Bob Wagner, St. Louis Park. "We lose four outstanding competitors," Griak said. "They are all winners and their record proves it."

Each of the four lettered three times in cross country. And, in their three years of competition, they participated in only three losing dual meets and finished second twice and third once in the Big Ten meet, not to forget the fourth place earned in the 1968 NCAA meet.

"That's a lot of talent to lose," Griak said, "but I'm not singing the blues yet. With the returning lettermen and another year of experience for the freshmen, we should have a respectable year."

Part of Griak's enthusiasm for the freshmen is the showing that they made in the Central Collegiate Four-Mile Cross Country Meet held in Chicago last November. The Gopher frosh won the team title, with Daly and Hanley leading Minnesota, finishing seventh and eighth, respectively. At the Carleton Open Meet, Hanley was first and Daly second.

Although it's only February, Griak already has sights on next fall. "It should be a five-team race between Minnesota Michigan State, Illinois, Indiana and Ohio State," he said. "But, by next fall, it could change. From looking at the rosters of each team, it appears that these five should be the strongest. But things can happen."

And for the Minnesota cross country team of 1969, the hope is that the "things that can happen" already did in 1968 and what lies ahead is the happening of a Big Ten cross country title.

MINNESOTA'S four "minor" (*"minor" only in the sense of income earned from each sport*) winter sports teams—gymnastics, indoor track, swimming and wrestling—will not be top contenders for any Big Ten or national honors. But on each of the teams are fine individual performers who may finish high in the conference meets.

Dave Stende

GYMNASTICS: Coach Pat Bird starts his first season as head gymnastics coach, taking over for Ralph Piper who was head coach for 38 years. Piper stepped down from his position and is now Bird's assistant.

"We've got some individuals who should place high in the Big Ten meet," Bird says, "but our lack of depth will hurt in dual meets." The Gopher gymnasts are led by Captain Dave Stende, the number one man in the all-around competition—participation in all seven events—and one of the conference's finest in the parallel bars.

Other top performers are juniors Fred Kueffer and Mark Howell and senior Larry Peterson. Kueffer also competes in the all-around and is one of the Big Ten's best on the rings. Howell and Peterson give the gymnasts strength in floor exercise and the long horse (vaulting).

INDOOR TRACK: After winning last spring's Big Ten outdoor track championship, many would rate Coach Roy Griak's Minnesota track team as one of the favorites for the Big Ten indoor title. But according to Griak, this is not so.

"We lost a lot of quality from last spring's champions," he says. "We've got some fine personnel returning, but not enough to make us a strong contender. The key to our season will be the development of the large number of sophomores we have."

The Gophers' strength will be in the running events from 440 yards to two miles. In the 300, 440 and 600, the Gophers' top men will be senior Randy Jones, junior Steve Erikkson and sophomores Mark Finneman and Al Shapiro. In the half mile, senior Captain Ed Twomey, juniors Tim Turnbull and Marty Johnson and sophomore Tom Beltz give Minnesota fine depth. Three of the Big Ten's best—Steve Hoag, Bob Wagner and Ben Grokett—will run the mile and two-mile events. Another feature of the 1969 indoor track squad is the return of three lettermen in the broad jump. Seniors Bruce Johnson and Jim Ohnsad and junior Bruce Hella give the Gophers an excellent one-two-three punch.

Juniors Pete Shea, Allen Auerbach and Mike Curtis and sophomores Greg Lokken and Al Shapiro are vying to give Minnesota the strength in the sprints needed to overcome the loss of Hubie Bryant and Rich Simonsen.

"There's potential in this group of sprinters," Griak says, "but they're unproven Big Ten performers." A pair of sophomores, Phil Hanks and Tom Heikkila, are top choices to replace two prior gopher standouts in the hurdles and high jump.

"I'm usually an optimist," Griak says, "but I'm not quite so sure this year. We've got a long way to go."

(Continued on page 34)

Coach Griak's evaluation of the 1968 cross country season and his comments about the prospects for 1969. Sports Information Office – *Alumni News* – February 1969

"Gol darn it"

A Collection of Roy Griak Tributes

Gary Hanson

Coach Griak: *Gary was an 880-yard runner for the Gophers. He never forgot his old coaches. Gary is a very special person. He is sincere, honest and loves people.*

It was May of 1970, shortly after the bombings in Cambodia and the shootings at Kent State. Many college campuses were filled with tension and unrest – none more so than the University of Wisconsin. Ironically, our Gopher track team was scheduled for a dual meet in Madison during that time. Actually, nearby Memorial High School would be the venue because the campus track and field area had become the holding grounds for the National Guard.

We arrived late Friday afternoon at our Edgewater Hotel accommodations on Lake Mendota. Before he would let us off the bus, Coach gave a brief speech, reminding us of the campus violence and instability. He warned us not to get into trouble, and to always remember that we were representing the University. Realizing that many of us wanted a little exercise after the tiring four-hour ride, he cautioned the runners in particular, "Listen up. When you leave the hotel this afternoon and head up Wisconsin Avenue, if you turn to the right, you'll find yourself in the State Street section of campus where all the craziness is happening. If you turn to the left, you go into a nice residential neighborhood much better for jogging. Gol' Dang it, I don't want anyone going up the hill and turning toward the right!"

Of course the half-dozen or so of us who went out for that "little exercise" ran up the hill, turned to the right and headed directly into the epicenter of the conflict. What we saw looked like a third world revolution and military occupation. There were police barricades, jeeps, trucks and guns. Students were demonstrating and hanging out of windows jeering and taunting the cops and militia. Some young National Guardsmen, who didn't look any older than we were, gestured back in anger. We noticed that the troops became especially anxious and wary at the five or six of us jogging; perhaps in our maroon uniforms we appeared to be a unified, menacing sight. Told by authorities to move on from the standoff on State Street, we eventually heeded Coach's advice and turned back the other way. I won't say that that's the only time we ever disobeyed Coach Griak, but this one stands out in my mind. Yet, what wide-eyed twenty-year-old college student wouldn't have done the same thing?

I've enjoyed my relationship with Coach these many years. I was particularly blessed during a seven-hour roundtrip drive to a Virginia, Minnesota nursing home with him in 2009. We visited one of our favorite people, Ed Hendrickson, his good friend and my high school coach. The conversation, stories, and memories related that day will remain with me forever.

Congratulations Coach Griak on your fifty years at the University of Minnesota! I am honored to have been with you for a small portion of that time.

Class of 1971, U of M runner

Tom Kiernan

Coach Griak: *Tim was an excellent hurdler at St. Louis Park. He is a very loyal person who as a carpenter / contractor has done some work around my house. I have never forgotten him either.*

How do I start to talk about a giant of a man in the world of track and cross country and bring to light the influence he had upon me? Maybe I can start with the junior high memory of him choosing me to show the rest of the gym class the proper form to jump over the hurdles. I went on to use that same form during my years on the track team at St. Louis Park. He encouraged my hidden talent because of something he saw in me. Or maybe he saw a lost kid who needed some structure in his life.

To help me get ready for the coming track season, he "suggested" that I go to the thousand step stairway behind the gym, outside his classroom, and run up and down those steps one hundred times a day. It was the first Stairmaster of the twentieth century. The best part of that whole exercise was the trust he had in me to complete the task and accept my word that I had done so. It was a great feeling to please the COACH. And best of all, I did build those muscles that helped me get over most hurdles in life.

He was like an ex-marine in his discipline, but his approach did not include the yelling and profanity that some coaches used. He was able to take the runner aside and tell him how to improve to help himself and the team. I think the harshest words out of his mouth were, "Gol dang." That, however, did not take away the threat of his wooden paddle which was used on occasion. You wanted to do what the COACH told you. You knew deep down, he was looking out for your best interests.

To that end, he was very protective of "his boys" and the undue influence that outside forces had upon them. He was especially aware of the major threats of beer, hoods with knives and mostly, girls. His approach to winning was capped by St. Louis Park High School's first state titles: Cross Country in 1955 and Track and Field in 1958.

After high school, he was again kind to me and let me practice my craft of carpentry in his basement on Stanlen Road. He praised me for the effort while overlooking craftsmanship which was not the best. He went on to a lifetime career at the U of M and we lost touch somewhat while "his boys" went on to their careers throughout the country. But he never lost interest in what we were doing and how our lives were going. As an example, I was working on campus remodeling a credit union when he showed up to exclaim, that, "He was blinded by the glare off the forehead of the bearded carpenter." Even with a great disguise, I couldn't escape his watchful eye.

With his busy schedule, he would often make time for a bunch of us from the class of '58. When Rod Lazorik from New Mexico, Bob Oas from Florida joined Art Patterson, Bob Erickson, Joe Gosnell, Neil Berthe and me for a poker game or dinner, Mr. Griak would try to spend some time with us catching up on all our lives.

The most amazing part of COACH and his influence on ALL he met, was brought home to me when I attended his "retirement (Yeah – right) party." Every man there was "his boy" and each story they told could be told by all of us. His father-like encouragement, the military discipline, and the concern for the future lives of all these men, young and old, was a legacy beyond compare.

I realized again that night, that with his wit and wisdom, both spoken and by example, I have become a better person for having known "ROY."

Tim Kiernan

St. Louis Park High School

John Kromer

***Coach Griak:** As a Gopher, John was the Big Ten steeplechase champion in 1984. He was a hard working athlete; anyone who places in the Big Ten Meet has to have a passion for what they are doing. John lives in Hudson, Wisconsin.*

I ran for Roy from 1981 to 1984 in cross country and track, and clearly look back on my college years as one of the best times of my life. There were many "Roy-isms" like, "Gol dang it Johnny…my Grandma could run faster than that with slippery tennis shoes!" or the constant lectures to avoid the girls! He was looking out for our best interests. No one can forget the image of Roy barking instructions from his megaphone when he was five feet away from you in the field house!

One of my favorite memories was when Roy would have the team bus stop at the Amana Colonies on the way to Iowa. We would feast on home-cooked food. Well, we had some Nigerians on the team that had never tasted sauerkraut so we encouraged them to try it, and they did not like it. Let's just say I have never seen one of these guys turn green before!

When Roy had a knee replacement surgery recently, I called to ask how he was doing. He said, "Johnny, these guys that say I can play tennis after getting my knees replaced are full of (you know what)! I feel like I'm going to fall down trying to cross Fifteenth Avenue!"

But the biggest influence has probably been how he keeps in touch with his former athletes. He will call and ask how my family is doing and tell me that he loves me, and I love him right back! GO GOPHERS but more importantly, GO ROY!

Coach Griak should be in the Guiness Book of World Records because he has worn maroon and gold longer than anyone. Coach Griak has been like a father figure to so many of us. We love you Roy.

John Kromer

BSB Accounting 1984

U of M 1981-1984

Big 10 Steeplechase Champ

Mike Linnemann

***Coach Griak:** Mike was a real good intermediate-hurdler for the Gophers. He is a great supporter of the program; he sends a check every month and has for years.*

We all have similar stories about Roy. We've all been stopped by Roy after a shower, giving his little motivational talk. We have that as a binding element not unlike Hollywood icons that can say, "We shook Frank Sinatra's hand. It's a measure of brotherhood, admiration and respect." Our version is shorter, "We all knew Roy." It's a testament to his longevity and dedication to the program. I can instantly strike up a conversation with a hurdler from 1972 and have an instant bond beyond our letterman's jackets and our times, sweat and blood given. Roy is our connective fiber. I find it exhilarating to see the same nods when we speak of our legendary coach. Some things change, Roy never does. Men of his caliber don't exist anymore.

I remember being with Roy at a local Division III meet at Gustavus. I used it as a warm up to run some events I didn't normally do. I recall it being windy, as a tornado some years prior removed the majority of trees. I was being a bit apprehensive about running three or four non-hurdling events at a meet that "didn't matter." Right before my 200-meter race, I noticed I had an absurdly fast seed time given by Phil Lundin. I talked to the starter briefly confirming my lane and then noticed that Roy was motioning me over. He was a man of very few words to me, perhaps the snooty nose attitude of 400-hurdles gave me a pass, an unmentioned respect that I wasn't there to mess around. As I walked the thirty or so yards over to Roy, his normal face of stability, of nonchalance, of experience of seeing everything in track, was very stern and serious. I thought to myself, maybe I was in the wrong heat or perhaps I not entered properly. It was nothing of the sort.

Roy simply said, "Gol dang it, get out hard and beat those dang MIAC kids. You're here, you might as well. I know you can." The verbiage is paraphrased, clearly, as I was terrified at what a venerable coach could offer me besides fear. He then motioned me away and my race started shortly thereafter. I won that race. Something clicked. I had a cataclysm for my running career. The 4x400 I actually anchored, starting forty meters behind first place and won that too. Roy said nothing after the relay. He just stood calmly while I changed my shoes. He had said more than enough, and he knew it. I felt that day was the day I started offering leadership to the team, despite not even being a captain. Roy wasn't at every race, but I darn well encouraged fellow relay runners like he was. I'd like to think it mattered when we won the Big Ten championship in 2009 as every member contributed, even Roy.

The second story I have is an ongoing narrative dealing with wealth. I am not a rich man. My parents are teachers and I have no living grandparents. Their lives were defined by cancer, by accidents and misfortune leaving no estates. I'm largely on my own for financial matters but when Roy sends me a letter asking for me to donate, I do. The Lake Wobegon upbringing I had in helping your neighbor is a very real incentive for me. Things you believe in, you have to support. I can't make a $10,000 gift or even a $1000 gift yet. I'm only twenty-seven years old. I still have time to contribute in a greater sense. To appease my inner turmoil of contributing something, I'm active in mentoring graduating seniors into the workforce and into being active alumni members. It's volunteering in the greatest sense, but it still falls short. So, what I do is send a monthly donation to Roy Griak and the scholarship fund. It's not much but it's something. Every month, Roy sends me a personal letter. There is no reason he needs to do this. I've even told the fundraising staff and Roy himself that one letter a year is more than enough, but he insists and ushers me away. Donating back to the program is deeply enriching to me now as Roy takes time out of every month to write an anecdote, a small thank you, or even a team update. Caring about his lifelong passion is deeply enriching to him. I'll carry that with me though life and I'll hound other members who feel a donation is outside their ability. If Roy can contribute day in and day out, there's no reason we can't do something, anything, no matter how small.

Mike Linnemann

CLA '07

MA '12

Hurdles, Sprints '09

Jay Mountain

Coach Griak: *Jay was a tough rascal. He ran both cross country and track for the Gophers and was always doing something mischievous.*

Coach Griak had a lasting impact on me and all of the people that know him...

I was a walk-on for the U of M track and field team in 1977 and competed for the U and Coach Griak from 1977-1981. He always will be Coach to me; not Roy, not Coach Griak...just Coach. He always carried himself with dignity, grace and class...always. I never heard him use a single curse word in all the years that I have known him. Dang, darn, gol dang it, gosh darn it...but never a curse word. I can assure you that during my tenure at the U he had plenty of opportunities to use curse words, but he never did. I recall a meet in Georgia where we were at a nice hotel and I happened to be in the hotel bar with a drink in my hand talking with a very nice young woman after curfew prior to a meet. Coach just walked up to us both and stated, “Miss, I am sorry, but this gentleman has to compete in a track meet in the morning and it is well past his curfew,” and then he just grabbed my drink and said, “Gol dang it Jay, go to your room and go to bed!” He never mentioned the incident the next day.

The influence that he had on me was in how he carried himself. Everyone that knows him respects him. He treated every athlete and every person with the same level of dignity and respect. I have run into him over the years and he always remembered my name and greeted me with his trademark infectious enthusiasm. I have introduced him to many people over the years and he has always greeted them with that same enthusiasm...a strong handshake, a smile, and a warm greeting. I feel very fortunate to have had the opportunity to compete for and become friends with our legendary and much beloved Coach!

Thanks Coach!

John (Jay) Mountain

U of M Track Athlete 1977-1981

Lloyd Ness

Coach Griak: *Lloyd was a tenacious, energetic Gopher runner. He had no leg speed but he was gutty. I put Lloyd and John Idstrom through a training program that simulated the altitude they would face in the national meet at Brighan Young. They both placed in the 10,000 meter. Lloyd's daughter now runs for the Gophers.*

My story is about Coach Griak's honesty. It was a week before the Big Ten Meet and we had a two mile time trial. I ran 9:44. This was a time I had run as a sophomore in high school. I went to Coach Griak and said, “I have been running eighty to ninety miles a week and doing all of your workouts. I can't figure out why I am not running better.”

Coach put his arm around my shoulder and walked me down the track. Then he said, “Lloyd, Gol dang it, you're just too Gol dang fat.” Now this was not the nurturing response I was looking for but Coach was just being honest. That week I lost six pounds and I placed tenth at the Big Tens. Coach could have put it a number of different ways but being blatantly honest worked best for me.

Transfering to the University was one of the best things I ever did. I found my major. I found lifelong friends. I found a Coach that would be blatantly honest but would also buy us hats and gloves on the first cold day of cross country. I found a Coach that would put his arm around me and give me a hug when I needed it.

To this day, every time I get up to 146 pounds I can hear Coach Griak say, Gol dang it Lloyd you're just too Gol dang fat.”Thanks Coach.

Lloyd Ness 1982

Gopher 10,000 meter All-American

Lloyd Ness

"Malo po malo"

A Collection of Roy Griak Tributes

"Malo po malo" (Serbian for "Little by little")
{this phrase is found on Coach's tombstone}

Jim Brunzell

Coach Griak: *Jim came to Minnesota from White Bear Lake as a football player. He had been a Minnesota state champion in the high jump and he became a good collegiate high jumper (6' 6") for the Gophers. He later became a professional wrestler and teamed with Greg Gagne.*

Baton Rouge, Louisiana - 1969 Track Trip

I was a walk-on football player from White Bear Lake. I also tried walking onto the Gophers track team, as a high-jumper. During the indoor season, I placed in a number of meets so Coach Griak asked me if I'd like to go on the spring trip to LSU, in Baton Rouge, Louisiana. I was thrilled! Tim Heikelia was the number one jumper, and I was second. We flew to New Orleans and bussed to Baton Rouge, some eighty miles. The weather that week was wonderful, in the 70's. Quite a change from the March snowstorms we usually endured in Minnesota. The team had a great week of training, and finished reasonably well, considering the speed of the fleet southern schools present. After the meet, we bussed back to New Orleans, and checked into the "Warwick Hotel," a stone's throw away from the infamous "Bourbon Street." After a team dinner, Coach addressed us. He told us we represented the University of Minnesota, and to conduct ourselves accordingly. He wanted us to behave like gentlemen, and be back for a midnight bed check!

I believe our group was small, about ten or twelve. The night was pleasant, and "Bourbon Street" was alive with thousands of fun-loving, all-aged revelers! For the most part, out team members were real reserved and studious, except for me, the walk-on high-jumper, and my fellow sophomore, pole-vaulter Jimmy Rutz from St. Louis Park High. We decided to take full advantage of this once in a lifetime opportunity. On "Bourbon Street," there really isn't a drinking age minimum, so we indulged in a few "Hurricanes," beer, and little bottle of "Southern Comfort" that a "pretty young thing" gave us. As the night progressed, we flowed with the crowd like a river of happy beings, singing and laughing with not a care in the world! Time stood still, we thought, but as we turned a corner, singing the Minnesota Rouser, arm-in-arm with a couple of co-eds, we ran straight into an irate, and I mean irate, Coach Roy Griak! It was 3:00 a.m. and we were the only two of the team members not tucked into bed! Coach was straight-forward in scolding us and guided us back to the Warwick. As I remember, Jimmy Rutz and I were still happy when we crawled in our beds!

In what seemed like a minute or two, I was awakened by a stern knocking on my door. It was

5:45 a.m., and as I opened the door, Coach was with Jimmy Rutz and told me to get ready to run! I stumbled getting my Adidas on, as Roy led us outside to a huge circular paved mall. Jim and I were instructed to run, one to the north and one to the south. It was a foggy morning, with a little dew on the grass as Jim and I passed each other, still amused from our little "escapade in the French Quarter." After ten or so minutes, neither of us was smiling or amused anymore. Coach continued to interject these words, "Keep running…don't stop!" This coaching lasted for thirty-some minutes, resulting in both Rutz and me struggling to stand upright, while upchucking our stomach's contents from our indulging a few hours earlier!

With hands on our knees, somewhat gasping for air, Coach Griak stated to us, as far as he was concerned, the subject of our behavior was over! He felt we had learned our lesson, while he made known to us how disappointed he was in the adolescent behavior that we exhibited. He told us to go shower and get ready for the bus ride to the airport. As lousy as I felt from the drinking, I was really sick about how I let Coach down. Here he had given me an opportunity to make a track team spring trip, and I wasn't even on scholarship. Boy, what a knucklehead! While we were flying home, through an absolutely terrifying, turbulent flight, I agonized over the thought that Coach Griak would spill the beans to Coach Murray Warmath, the legendary head football coach of the "Golden Gophers!" I couldn't fathom the distress awaiting me if Coach Warmath found out about my indiscretion!

A few weeks later, spring football practice started and I was elated there wasn't a hint of our trip mentioned by anyone, least of all Coach Warmath. It's been forty-five years since that track trip to Louisiana. In those years, friends have asked me, "Who was the best Coach you ever had?" Without a doubt, Roy Griak was the best I ever competed for. Not only did he know his stuff, but he fathered, mentored, tutored, and loved all the athletes he coached. He got the best from all his athletes, because he treated us all the same – with respect and dignity. He respected our individualism, while expecting our full dedication to deliver our best performance every time we competed. He genuinely cared for all his students, and made them feel they could come to him with any problem, big or small! In the past several years, I've visited Coach regularly at his Bierman Building office. He's had some health issues, but is still sharp as a tack! He always greets me with a smile, and I humor him with my Warmath stories. He has a warm, comforting presence, which reminds me what a wonderful person he's been, and a huge blessing to all who have known him! God bless you, Roy! Thanks for everything you've done for so many! With much love and admiration!

Sincerely,

Jim (Brunzy) Brunzell – Track '69 and '70

Jim Day

Coach Griak: *Jim was a Gopher distance runner when I arrived as Coach in 1963. A young man who got the most out of his ability. Jim remains a very good friend of the program.*

Congratulations on your fifty years of active involvement with the Gopher cross country and track teams.

When I go to track events or your Bierman office and even Gopher basketball games, I always anticipate seeking you out to chat and feel your warm greeting. Thanks for making me feel welcome in your busy world. I like being around to hear your stories.

For decades, I've regretted that your first year as the Gopher's coach was my last year of eligibility. I missed out on a great deal of quality training and personal development.

Five U C-C Men in NCAA Today

by PAUL KLEYMAN

A team of five Gophers will be among approximately 250 starters in the 1963 NCAA Cross Country Championship at East Lansing, Mich., today.

The quint, Captain Jim Day, juniors Ray Miller and Norris Peterson and sophomores Mike Elwell and Wayne Triebwasser, has a good chance of finishing in the top 12 or 13 of the 49 teams entered, said Minnesota Coach Roy Griak.

SAN JOSE STATE, defending NCAA champion, and Notre Dame are co-favorites for the '63 crown. Villanova, Kansas, Oregon and Missouri are highly rated for top places in the meet.

Minnesota will be joined by Michigan State, Big Ten champion, and Wisconsin, who edged the Gophers by four points and took second place in the conference meet at Champaign, Ill., Nov. 11, as Big Ten entrants.

The Minnesota harriers will be running for revenge against the Badgers, who have downed the Gophers twice this season (a dual meet, Oct. 5, and the Big Ten meet). A deciding factor in today's race, however, may be the fact that Ray Miller, whose cold probably cost the Gopher squad second place in the conference, is in perfect health and has looked "very good" in practice this week, stated Griak.

THE MINNESOTA pilot listed several top propects for individual honors. The Gopher's "big three," Day, Miller, and Peterson, could finish in the first 15 to 20 places, he said.

The favorites include Paul Acervedo, Kansas senior, Frank Carver of Notre Dame, Oregon's Clayton Steinke, John Camian, of Kentucky State Teachers College. 12 of the top independent entries in the race are: Allen Carius Illinois junior and Big Ten champion, Michigan State's Richard Sharkey, Victor Zwalak of Villanova and Julio Marin, Southern California senior and 1963 NCAA three and six-mile champion. Griak declined to pick a favorite, stating that any one of them could win the race.

The Gopher C-C men did "much better than I expected," during the season, said Griak. The squad finished the season with a 4-1 record., and was third in the Big Ten.

THE TEAM will lose only one senior from the traveling squad, Jim Day. Jerry Smith, a member of the varsity squad, will also graduate.

GOPHER CAPTAIN JIM DAY AND COACH ROY GRIAK
Day and four teammates will race in NCAA meet today

News Article "5 U CC Men in NCAA Today"

My running pretty much ended after graduation. Then after three plus decades away from running I picked it up again and in my early 60's entered your Meet of Miles. I remember during my warm up, which from your coaching eye seemed aggressive for my age, you cared enough to tell me to, "Save something for the race."

I remember when you were frustrated with the U of M construction department's price to build an announcer booth / storage structure beside the track. You had a great solution. We drew up some plans, got the materials and over a weekend on the QT we constructed it ourselves. As I remember, you took some heat for that but the building persevered.

Roy, fifty years is an exceptional milestone to celebrate. I'm happy for you and with your remarkable career.

Jim Day

(Minnesota CC & Track 1960-1964)

Arthur Hopp

***Coach Griak:** Arthur was one of the first athletes I worked with as a coach. He was on the team at Nicollet High School in my first year of teaching and coaching.*

Sorry that I cannot attend Roy's celebration on the 26th (Sept. 2013), but I would like to give you a few insights into Roy's early career. It was in the fall of 1950 that I was a senior at Nicollet High School in southern Minnesota. That was Roy's first year of coaching after graduating from the U of M. At Nicollet we played six-man football and I'm sure Roy had to go to the U of M sports library to find information about six-man football back then. At Nicollet he was a coach for all sports, which included football, basketball and baseball. He introduced track to us that year.

To give you an idea of how small our school was, sometimes at practice there would not be enough guys that showed up to have an offense and a defense on the field at the same time. Roy's sports records that first year of coaching were: Football: 1 and 6, Basketball: 6 and 19. The high school annual had to go to press before the end of baseball and track season so I do not recall those standings.

Roy, I will always remember that at the end of football practice you would have us run several laps around the field and that you would give us a one lap head start and then you would run backwards and beat us to the finish. Thanks, and the best to you.

Arthur Hopp

Athlete at Nicollet H.S. (1950)

(Coach's first H.S. job)

Margo Morris

***Coach Griak:** She is Chris' sister. She was a St. Louis Park student. Steve Griak bought Chris and Margo's childhood home just off Lake Calhoun. Their mother owned a grocery store near Lake and Hennepin for many years.*

I never understood the game of football, I couldn't hit a baseball, Karen Holt beat me in the annual Brookside running race in sixth grade, and my idea of incredible luck was not being forced to take any physical education classes at the U of M. So I've been reflecting and thinking about how on earth got to know and love Coach Griak?

My first memories were in St. Louis Park Junior High School where he would patrol the halls in the morning and give the boys a lot of grief if they were silly enough to share a locker with a girl. That marked the boys as a "wuss" for sure. So as he stalked the halls eyeballing what was going on with a whistle around his neck and a clipboard, the boys tried slyly to close their lockers so he wouldn't see their girlfriend's sweater hanging inside. Of course we girls loved putting all of our stuff in there to make our mark. Besides, most of us had a crush on the Coach anyway whether we realized it or not.

Mr. Griak, as I called him "back in the day," was Mr. Park High. He was a fixture, an icon and, yes, a character. Kids love a man like Griak. When my brother Chris made the track team my sports antennae perked up. I loved watching my brother run track. I loved watching him improve and grow stronger and more confident. I knew only Coach Griak could make that happen. We connected in a personal way too. Roy's mom was a customer at our independent grocery store, Morris and Christie, on 31st and Hennepin. She and my mom got to know each other while chatting in the produce department and, through that connection, my mother learned we shared the same religious faith as the Griak family. And, if that wasn't enough, Mother Griak came from the area of Minnesota where my mom was born, the Duluth/Hibbing/Gary area. When my mother decided to sell our house on Abbott in Minneapolis (after Chris moved to Australia and I got married), Roy's brother Steve and his wife bought it. That home, near Lake Calhoun, was our favorite house and both my brother and I drove by it for many years. Often, and without warning, we would knock on the door and usually get invited for a tour of the house as well as hear the latest news about Roy and the whole family.

Staying in touch with Roy over the years has been fun. Christmas cards, phone calls, visits (not to mention that he was one of the star attractions at our fiftieth St. Louis Park reunion)! When he became cross country and track and field coach at the U of M, I was so proud and so happy for him. I still have my Coach Griak tee shirt from years ago, I supported the foundation and Roy always has thanked me for it.

So I think it's fair to say that my connection with Roy is all about sports after all. Through Roy, my brother's experiences on the Park High track team, and my Greek Heritage I learned to appreciate and love that ancient sport. I'm sure if Roy were around in 490 B.C. Phidippides would have not dropped dead after running twenty-six miles from the city of Marathon to warn the Athenians of the approaching invasion by the Persians. Poor, exhausted Phidippides! Were he under the watchful eye of Coach Griak, he could have lived to tell the tale himself and complete a victory lap to boot!

Coach Griak, Mr. Griak, Roy – I send you hugs, and filakia. To a great coach, a wonderful teacher, a great dancer, and a dear friend.

Margo Morris

(St. Louis Park friend)

Joe Lane

Coach Griak: *Joe was recruited as a baseball player but became an excellent Gopher shot putter. His best was 58' 0" in 1966. He was from Proctor, Minnesota. Joe coached at Minnetonka for a long time.*

I owe so much to Coach it is amazing! In 1964-65, as part of my physical education major, I was enrolled in a track and field class taught by Coach Griak. I was a skinny 175 pound kid in the class, but he apparently saw some potential in me. He asked about my background, and I pointed out that after graduating from Proctor High School, I was on the U of M baseball team for two years and an arm injury was forcing me to give up baseball. He kept encouraging me to try track and field as a shot-putter for the Gopher track and field team. We both knew that I had a lot of work to do to compete at the Big Ten level. Because he was there for me in so many ways, in teaching me proper technique and laying out a great strength training program, I was able to be fourth in the Big Ten my first year. In my second and final year, I went on to be runner-up in the Big Ten and set some U of M records. Our team, which consisted of many walk-on athletes with stories similar to mine, went on to be a runner-up in the Big Ten Conference meet.

Coach Griak's leadership and guidance has led me to become a hall of fame track coach at Minnetonka High School. None of this would have happened

Joe Lane – *Minneapolis Star* photo by Russell Bull

without his encouragement, support, and caring for me as an individual over the years. I owe much of my love for track and field to his mentorship and example. I am so lucky to have had a man of his caliber being a positive role-model in my life.

Ever Grateful,

Joe Lane

U of M Track

1965-1967

Chuck Morrow

***Coach Griak:** He was an excellent pole vaulter from Montgomery, Minnesota who was the U of M record holder at one time. He and his brothers were all pole vaulters. He was the state champion in 1959. His brother, Stan, had won state championships from 1954-1956 and his brother, Dick, won state championships in 1958 and 1960. All three brothers lettered at the University of Minnesota. Chuck still supports the Gopher program.*

Roy did not coach me so I don't have "coaching" or "traveling" stories like I do about Coach Kelly. But he was very good to me (and still is) while I was finishing up my degree. I can't imagine saying anything that has not been said many times before but I will give it a shot.

My first close association with Roy took place shortly after he was chosen to replace Jim Kelly. Coach Kelly retired in the spring of 1963 and left for California shortly after the Big Ten Outdoor Track meet had been completed that spring. Roy and Bob Anderson (Jim Kelly's assistant coach) escorted Ray Miller and me to the NCAA Meet that was held in Albuquerque. Bob had married an Albuquerque native and that turned out to be fantastic for us because he knew the area quite well. We did a lot of the things that "tourists" do when in New Mexico and one trip took us to the Isleta Pueblo. I remember that well because Roy made a comment something like this: "Maybe marrying someone from this village would make a lot of sense because the women that have been raised here would probably be less demanding than those that were raised in the Twin Cities." Maybe those words meant more to me that one might imagine because I ended up teaching on the Santo Domingo Reservation (about thirty miles out of Albuquerque) and was able to steal one of their young ladies. Roy was more than "great" in my eyes because he extended my scholarship one additional year even though my eligibility had ended in the spring of '63. I did not, of course, appreciate that "gift" until I got older but it was something that he did not need to do. I also remember him saying something about his first job in Nicollet, Minnesota. Roy had graduated from the "U" and found that jobs were not that easy to find. Well, Roy did get an offer from the Nicollet Superintendent so he drove down to take a look at the town. He told me that he thought that maybe, "Nicollet might have been the end of the world," but he needed a paycheck so he accepted the offer. However, he found out that, "Nicollet was definitely the end of the world when he brought his wife to town" later that summer. Roy did not, of course, spend much time in a small town and Gopher track and field athletes were the benefactors due to his coaching ability and his organizational skills. Jim Kelly was a legendary coach but people soon realized that the correct man had been hired as a replacement and Roy has done a fabulous job for the University of Minnesota, the people of the state of Minnesota and especially for the "lucky' young men who competed for him.

Chuck Morrow

1963 U of M

Keith Ottoson

Coach Griak: *Keith is a loyal supporter of the program. He had limited talent as a Gopher runner but was always very enthusiastic. He is a wonderful person.*

I was very fortunate to run cross-country and track at the University of Minnesota from 1969-1972, my sophomore through senior years. My freshman year I ran at Anoka-Ramsey Community College, and when I decided to transfer, my coach, Ralph G. Powell, gave Coach Griak a call asking if I could be associated with the program as a manager or in some such capacity. I met Coach Griak, and he said, "Why don't you come out and run with us?" I thought I had died and gone to heaven.

I was awed and amazed. My city conference rivals (actually, they were miles ahead of me in talent and success), Greg Nelson and Carter Holmes were there, as well as Captain Kelly, Don Timm, Terry Thomas, John Hopko, Gene Daly, Tom Page, Mike Hanley, and a couple of other new guys – Mike Lawless and some kid from Proctor, Garry something or other. I had never worked so hard before (or probably since) than I did that September. I recall having to pull my car over while driving home because salt sweat had covered my glasses so that I couldn't see out of them.

At the end of the fall we (they) won the Big 10 Championship and did well at Nationals. I still remember Tom Page being mad at NCAA Champ UTEP having all those "old foreign" guys, and this was before the big influx of runners from Kenya.

The indoor season came. I ran intervals with seventy second quarters knowing that our group of seven 4:07 or better milers would blow past me after that, but having the intense joy of hanging on as long as I could. I improved my two-mile time by over a minute at the Northwest Open. In the spring I had a little difficulty finding a niche but just kept running and running. Junior and senior years I picked up steady training partners and friends in Bill Miles (who went on to a stellar coaching career at Cretin-Durham Hall and Wayzata), Garrett Tomczak, and Tim Wilhelmson (long-time coach at Mahtomedi).

I found a niche. I couldn't go fast, but I could go long. During the spring of my senior year, Coach Griak got me into the Drake Relays Marathon, and I got to wear Maroon and Gold for my only time. Northwestern's best runner was also in the race, and I heard over my shoulder as I went past him at about the twenty-mile mark, "Who was that?" The guy he was running with replied, "I don't know, but I recognize the colors." As I approached the stadium, Jack Bachelor and Frank Shorter were taking a warm-down from their races, and I yelled out to ask them how it went. I like to think that my cool and calm demeanor near the end of that grueling event is what caused them to decide to move up to running the marathon and Olympic success. Coach Griak and I talked after the race, and he couldn't think of anyone else who had run the marathon while on the team (probably because no one was that dumb), so I got a school record.

Meanwhile, that kid from Proctor continued to develop and grow (I won't take credit for his success like I just did for Frank Shorter). I'm proud to say that Garry Bjorklund has used me as a positive example in speeches he has given. I consider him a friend to this day, as I do with that whole group I met during those magical three years that all began with Coach Griak looking me in the eye and saying, "Why don't you come run with us?"

Keith Ottoson

U of M athlete (1972)

Coach Griak's Gopher All-Americans, Big Ten Champions and NCAA Champions

Cross Country All-Americans Coached by Roy Griak

1969 Garry Bjorklund
1971 Garry Bjorklund
1976 Steve Plasencia
1978 Steve Plasencia
1978 Steve Plasencia (USTFF)
1978 Gerald Metzler (USTFF)
1981 Lloyd Ness
1981 Lloyd Ness (USTFF)
1981 Dave Morrison (USTFF)
1982 Dave Morrison
1984 Dave Morrison

Track and Field Outdoor All-Americans Coached by Roy Griak

1967 Tom Heinonen (Six Mile)
1968 Steve Hoag (10,000m)
1970 Garry Bjorklund (Three Mile)
1971 Garry Bjorklund (Six Mile)
1971 Tim Heikkila (High Jump)
1971 Don Timm (Steeplechase)
1974 Dennis Fee (Six Mile)
1976 Steve Plasencia (5,000m)
1977 Steve Plasencia (5,000m)
1978 Gerald Metzler (1,500m)
1982 John Idstrom (10,000m)
1982 Lloyd Ness (10,000m)
1984 Ron Backes (Shot Put)
1985 Ron Backes (Shot Put)
1985 Dave Morrison (10,000m)
1986 Ron Backes (Shot Put)
1990 Carson Hoeft (1,500m)
1991 Chris Murrell (High Jump)
1991 Mark Lacy (Shot Put)
1992 Chris Murrell (High Jump)
1992 Mark Lacy (Shot Put)
1993 Martin Eriksson (Pole Vault)
1993 Chris Murrell (High Jump)
1994 Chris Brinkworth (Shot Put)
1995 Tye Harvey (Pole Vault)
1995 Keita Cline (Long Jump)
1995 Chris Brinkworth (Shot Put)
1995 Chris Brinkworth (Discus)
1996 Paul Michalek (1,500m)

Track and Field Indoor All-Americans Coached by Roy Griak

1970 Garry Bjorklund (Two Mile)
1975 Glen Bullick (Pole Vault)
1985 Ron Backes (Shot Put)
1986 Ron Backes (Shot Put)
1992 Chad Goldstein (Shot Put)
1993 Martin Eriksson (Pole Vault)
1993 Chris Murrell (High Jump)
1994 Martin Eriksson (Pole Vault)
1995 Keita Cline (Triple Jump)

Big Ten Cross Country Champions Coached by Roy Griak

1969 Garry Bjorklund
1970 Garry Bjorklund
1971 Garry Bjorklund

NCAA Track and Field Champions Coached by Roy Griak

1971 Garry Bjorklund (6 Mile) (Outdoor)
1986 Ron Backes (Shot Put) (Indoor)
1993 Martin Erickson (Pole Vault) (Indoor)

Minnesota Big Ten Track and Field Champions Coached by Roy Griak

Indoor

1963 Dale Lamski (70 Yard HH)
1964 Norris Peterson (2 Mile)
1965 Norris Peterson (2 Mile)
1965 Tom Barnes (Shot Put)
1966 Tom Stuart (High Jump)
1967 Hubie Bryant (60 Yard Dash)
1968 Richard Simonsen (300 Yard Dash)
1969 Steve Hoag (2 Mile)
1970 Garry Bjorklund (2 Mile)
1971 Garry Bjorklund (2 Mile)
1972 Garry Bjorklund (3 Mile)
1972 Colin Anderson (Shot Put)
1973 Glen Bullick (Pole Vault)
1983 Mike Gebeke (1,000 Yards)
1985 Ron Backes (Shot Put)
1986 Ron Backes (Shot Put)
1986 Brian Schmit (1,000 Meters)
1988 Mike Vukovich (High Jump)
1990 Chris Murrell (High Jump)
1991 Mark Lacy (Shot Put)
1992 Keita Cline (Triple Jump)
1993 Matt Burns (High Jump)
1993 Martin Erickson (Pole Vault)
1994 Omar Douglas (55 Meter Dash)
1994 Noris Williams (600 Meter Dash)
1994 Keita Cline (Triple Jump)
1995 Keita Cline (Long Jump)
1995 Keita Cline (Triple Jump)
1996 Adrian Ellis (Triple Jump)
1996 Paul Michalek (800 Meters)
1996 Chris Darkins (55 Meter Dash)

Outdoor

1963 Chuck Morrow (Pole Vault)
1965 Norris Peterson (2 Mile)
1965 Tom Barnes (Shot Put)
1967 Tom Heinonen (3 Mile)
1968 Hubie Bryant (220 Yard Dash)
1968 Rich Landwehr (660 Yard Dash)
1969 Tim Heikkila (High Jump)
1970 Garry Bjorklund (Mile)
1970 Garry Bjorklund (3 Mile)
1971 Garry Bjorklund (3 Mile)
1971 Don Timm (Steeplechase)
1972 Colin Anderson (Shot Put)
1973 Dennis Fee (6 Mile)
1974 Garry Bjorklund (3 Mile)
1975 Glen Bullick (Pole Vault)
1982 John Idstrom (10,000 Meters)
1984 Mike Moran (800 Meters)
1984 John Krohmer (Steeplechase)
1984 Ron Backes (Shot Put)
1985 Ron Backes (Shot Put)
1986 Ron Backes (Discus)
1986 Ron Backes (Shot Put)
1988 Mike Vukovich (High Jump)
1992 Chris Murrell (High Jump)
1993 Chad Goldstein (Shot Put)
1994 Matt Burns (High Jump)
1994 Chris Brinkworth (Discus)
1995 Keita Cline (Long Jump)
1995 Chris Brinkworth (Shot Put)
1996 4 X 100 Meter Relay (Eric Stommes, Adrian Ellis, Tim Van Voorhis, Scott Beadle)
1996 Vesa Rantanen (Pole Vault)
1996 Jason Schlueter (Discus)

"My Athletes Are My Heroes"

A Collection of Roy Griak Tributes

Coach does not forget his athletes and friends. He had complete loyalty to anyone associated with the University of Minnesota or St. Louis Park High School.

Orv Bies

Coach Griak: *Orv coached at Hibbing when I was at St. Louis Park. I have great respect for him and his coaching. He is one of the better coaches this state has ever produced. He later coached at St. Louis Park. Orv was the executive director of the Minnesota State High School League from 1985-1988.*

Dear Friend Roy,

My good friend and old neighbor Don Timm recently visited with me about his almost daily relationship with you, his coach. Don's enthusiasm alerted me to your closing remarks to me as you concluded your recent phone call, "I truly care about you, Orv."

Roy, I care about you, too. I am privileged that I am included in your thoughts and fond memories and your unending circle of friends.

In my effort to express my appreciation to you for our long friendship, I have searched my mind for that special moment when we first met. Undoubtedly it was related to our common bond of track and field. I still recall being given an information sheet at the first track and field meet at the Lewis Relays in Eveleth. Under the records they listed a distance relay and your name was listed with teammates from a Duluth school (Morgan Park). That had to be 1950. Three or four years later I was appointed the head track coach at Hibbing and I thought I should be meeting with some gung-ho high school coaches and Coach Jim Kelley regarding the status of track and field in Minnesota. Or maybe we met as coaches at one of Coach Kelly's Outstate Indoor Track Meets conducted the last week of March each year. I am not sure about when or where we shook hands for the first time. I do recall that out of that first meeting I finagled an annual invitation for a long bus ride to participate each April in the Park Relays and your 341.6 yd. track. It was a wonderful opportunity for my athletes. It really does not matter very much as to when or where or how we met but that it did happen so that I am able to sincerely state, "I AM FOREVER GRATEFUL TO BE YOUR FRIEND."

I enjoyed my years at St. Louis Park and having the opportunities for our families to meet. I enjoyed being able to serve as an official at your meets at the U of M and often times just exchanging thoughts and concerns about our favorite athletic activity.

I wish all of everything good for you, Roy. May our GOD pour out his rich blessings on you and me in the closing years for each of us.

Stay in touch, old friend...Orv Bies

St. Louis Park

Al Buehler

Coach Griak: *Along with Joe Vigil, Al is my best coaching friend. He coached at Duke for as long as I was at Minnesota.*

We were United States Olympic team coaches in 1972 (Munich) and 1984 (Los Angeles). Roy is my coaching brother in track and field. My wife, Delaina, said that, "We think the world of you Roy, we love you." When Roy would come to visit us in Durham, North Carolina he would help me plant my flowers. Roy is "giving, helpful, kind and loving."

Al and Delaina Buehler

Duke University

Burt Ewing

Coach Griak: *A true friend of the program. He ran for the University of Minnesota.*

Coach Griak…immediately impressed me as a warm human being who very enthusiastically loved our sport. He made a real effort to connect with the people he worked with and I think this was a big part of his ability to motivate his athletes.

I was amazed at how unflappable Coach Griak was in dealing with a problem that he'd likely never remotely considered when he accepted the job at Minnesota. He was clear-headed, calm, supportive and effective as he just did his job, no matter what transpired during what seemed to be just another of his coaching days. Pretty amazing guy!

While my life has been busy with tons of stuff unrelated to track and field, my path has crossed with that of Coach Griak many times over the years since our first times together. Most recently, these occasions have involved connections at state meets or other occasions where track people get together. Each time, Coach knows exactly who I am (perhaps young fools make strong impressions?), asks after my family members and behaves, as always, as the true gentleman that he is.

Coach Roy Griak is an easy guy to love!

Burt Ewing

U of M athlete 1963

Jim Hancock

Coach Griak: *I never got to coach him as he ran for Al Haley at Minneapolis Southwest but he is a true friend. He ran at the University just after I graduated.*

Memories of Coach Griak before he was "Coach."

My memories of Roy Griak date back to his days as a graduate student in physical education. I was a 1949 U of M freshman from Minneapolis Southwest High School running cross country and track (2 mile). Roy recruited Dennis Hanson from St. James and me as subjects for his master's thesis. I was state cross country record holder and Dennis was state mile record holder.

Roy was studying the effects of running on a treadmill after filling our stomachs by drinking up to several liters of water. This involved many adventurous trips to the old Memorial Stadium Physiology Lab after workouts. Jim Kelly was coach and Roy was his assistant coach. I was then Captain of the U of M cross country team and the following year Dennis Hanson was Captain of both cross country and track and field.

My association with track and field continued for many years officiating for home meets.

It has always been a great pleasure to return to U of M events and have the opportunity to talk to Roy and teammates.

Jim Hancock, U of M

CC and Track, 1949-1953

Carter Holmes

Coach Griak: *Carter is a consummate track and field athlete who has continued to compete and wants to excel no matter what age category. He was an excellent Gopher steeplechaser and a member of the 1969 Big Ten Championship CC team. He is a devoted Gopher supporter. Carter is a man with a lot of intestinal fortitude who possesses more courage and determination than most people. You have to love him.*

During the fall of 1967 was the first time I met and spoke to Coach. He was recruiting another Washburn High School runner (Greg Nelson). Well, Coach spoke to me about attending THE University of Minnesota and running track and cross country for the Gophers. Coach also gave me a few things I should do to become a better runner!

Carter Holmes #433 in historic mile

That was the start of Roy coaching me. The next spring I decided I was going to be a Gopher and he coached me during my four years at the U. After graduating I still was racing and from time to time he would give me some pointers. He continued to help me and coach me until 2009 when I became disabled. Since then he has called me from time to time to check on me and see if things are OK. In a nutshell that covers forty-six years of Roy coaching me. Thank you, Roy!

Carter Holmes

U of Minnesota 1968-1972

{Author's note: Carter's sense of humor is second to none as evidenced by his narrow defeat when Roger Bannister elbowed him and went on to break the 4:00 mile.}

Dan Humes

Coach Griak: *Dan Humes is a good friend and supporter of our program. He ran at Owatona High School and then at Minnesota. He was a very good half-miler. Whatever he had he extended to the best of his ability.*

Coach Griak was a surrogate father to me because I lost my father during my freshman year at Minnesota. Coach not only taught me life lessons while I was a Gopher athlete but he has followed up on me and his athletes over the years since graduation. He enhanced my life.

Dan Humes

U of Minnesota 800 meters runner mid-1970s

Tom and Donna Maas

Coach Griak: *They are the parents of Brian Maas who ran 800-meters for the Gophers. Donna Maas still gives me sweet beets. They are very nice people.*

Coach Roy Griak came into our lives in 1980. Our son, Brian Maas was a student at Pacelli High School in Austin, Minnesota and ran cross country and track for Pacelli. He won the state title in the 800 in his junior and senior year at Pacelli.

Trackster roommates – Brian Maas, Dan Roche, Dave Morrison, Brian Schmit and John Kromer

Coach Griak came to our home on several occasions and recruited Brian to attend the University of Minnesota to participate in the track and field program. From the first time we met Coach Griak he was a most likable person, considerate, and made us feel so comfortable in his presence. That started a long-time friendship! In the years from 1980-1985 we had many wonderful memories of attending the "meets," visiting with Roy, and most of all the "potluck suppers" at the guy's apartment and the Coach always came. One of his favorites was my pickled beets which I made from farm fresh beets. As the years passed when Brian saw Roy he would say, "Do you have any of your Mom's beets – dang they are so good**?"**

A quote from Flavia:

Some people come into our lives – leave footprints on our hearts, and we are never, ever the same. Hugs and Blessings Coach,

Tom & Donna Maas

Parents of U of M athlete Brian Maas 1980-85

Joel Maturi

Coach Griak: *Joel originally coached at the Madison Edgewood High School in Wisconsin. He was inducted into the Wisconsin Basketball Coaches Hall of Fame in 1992. He served as Associate Athletic Director at the University of Wisconsin (Madison) from 1987-1996 and then was Athletic Director at the University of Denver (1996-1998) and at Miami of Ohio (1998-2002) before becoming Athletic Director at the University of Minnesota (2002-2012). He was a real administrator and helped all the Gopher sports in the women's and men's programs. I called him "Mr. Fixit." He graduated from the University of Notre Dame. No one in my tenure cared more for all the athletes and all the programs. The football field in his hometown of Chisholm, Minnesota was renamed the Joel Maturi Field in 2012.*

Thank you for including me in gathering some stories/memories of Coach Griak. Interestingly I knew of Coach since I was a high school student-athlete in Chisholm as one of my teammates and classmates, threw for Coach. He had great stories and memories of those days. Then, when I was an Assistant Athletic Director at Wisconsin, Martin Smith, then the cross country coach and the distance track coach was actually in the "mix" to replace Coach Griak upon his retirement. I oversaw Martin at that time and we chatted about the legend, Roy Griak.

Upon my arrival to the University in 2002 it was no secret that we were projected to be $31 million in debt within seven years. One of the many recommendations made to me was to eliminate the salary that the department was providing Coach. I said no then and did so for the ten years that I served as Athletics Director. That small investment I made has paid dividends many times over as Coach has raised over a million dollars. He had engaged the track and field community who have responded to improve the locker room, endow scholarships and improve the welfare of our young men now wearing the maroon and gold.

But Roy is not just about the money. He has always been about the "kids." To this day he continues to mentor the young and many of us not so young. Never shy to voice an opinion to someone who should be doing better, Coach is about being a Gopher and for all of us to be as good as we can be. He has been a mentor and a role model for many – and a special friend.

Joel Maturi

I had ten wonderful years as the Director of Athletics at the University of Minnesota and few supported me more than Roy Griak – I will be forever grateful.

Thanks, Coach, YOU are Minnesota!

Joel Maturi

U of M Athletic Director

Tom Moe

Coach Griak: *Tom Moe was the Interim Athletic Director at Minnesota for several years before Joel Maturi became the A.D. He was a star end on the Gopher football team and is a very loyal Gopher.*

My involvement with Roy Griak primarily occurred during the period I served as the Interim Director of Men's Athletics at the University of Minnesota (12/99-12/02). During that time, Roy was technically serving as Administrative Assistant to the Men's Track and Field and Cross Country programs but, as far as I was concerned, his role was much more significant. Even though I had known Roy for many years prior to the period I served as the Interim Director, it was during that time that I learned, first hand, what Roy Griak was all about. In short, he was the epitome of the word "loyal" and, even though his background in athletics was principally acquired in the sports of track and field and cross country, he was a tireless and enthusiastic supporter of the entire University of Minnesota Athletics Program. In addition, he was obviously loved and admired by his fellow coaches, his former athletes, the staff and others throughout the University community with whom he had associated over the years.

I have never heard anyone say an unkind word about Roy Griak nor have I ever heard Roy Griak say an unkind word about anyone. On the contrary, his comments were unfailingly positive. He is, and always has been, a tremendous credit to the University, and the University is a better place for having had Roy in its midst all these years.

On a personal note, I came away from my

experience in the University's Athletic Department with many fond memories, strong friendships and exposure to good, solid, selfless, committed people. Roy Griak is in all three categories.

Tom Moe, U of M Interim Director of Men's Athletics, 1999-2002

Jo Nielsen

***Coach Griak:** Jo is the widow of Jim Nielsen. Jim was a hurdler and my teammate at Minnesota. Jim was from Minneapolis Roosevelt. The Nielsen's donated $100,000 to help get the endowment fund off the ground. Teammates Dick Kilty also donated $100,000. They are very generous friends.*

My husband, Jim, and Roy Griak were teammates on the 1948-50 track team. For some in the group, Gopher track was postwar or post-service experience of the first order, all under the direction of coach Jim Kelly. For everyone involved it was a memorable time. Among their notable events they won the Big Ten (actually Big Nine) Outdoor Championship in 1949 and the NCAA outdoors National Championship in 1948.

In a memo Jim wrote to the team for their fifty year reunion in 1997 he remembers, "Watching 'Bugsy' Griak sip mineral oil at the Florida relays." Jim and Roy maintained a close friendship up until Jim's death in 2005 and Roy remains a special friend to this day.

Joanna B. Nielsen, Wife of 1947-1950 U of M teammate

Tom Page

***Coach Griak:** Tom Page had a wealth of talent. He had many interests like cars and skiing and he didn't like track but he was one tough cross country runner and he always had a smile on his face. He was a state champion in cross country and was one of our top runners at the University. Tom was a member of the 1969 Big Ten Championship CC team.*

Coach Griak was one of a kind. I remember the summer pre-season cross country workouts at Lake Calhoun. We would start our run from Thomas Beach on the south side of Calhoun and while we were out for our run, Coach would go over to Lake Harriet and get spring water for us. He would mix in some powder and make an orange drink for us. We sure looked forward to that.

I'll never forget the look on Coach's face when I showed up early one morning to Thomas Beach, drove my Jeep across the beach, into the water, and back up to the parking lot. Coach and the whole team just looked at me and laughed. We created a lot of good memories in those summer workouts.

Coach was always there for us - win or lose. He would put his arm around you and give you a big hug.

When I was inducted into the Edina Hall of Fame, Coach showed up for the ceremony. He would always go out of his way to show support. Yes, we were dedicated to him but more than anyone could imagine, he was dedicated to us! He was more than a coach, he was a GOOD FRIEND!!!

Tom Page

University of Minnesota CC 1967-70

Tom Page in 2015 with Garry Bjorklund on his right and Don Timm on his left - 46 years after they were the top three finishers in the Big Ten CC Meet

Norris Peterson

Coach Griak: *Norris was a determined runner who became a Big Ten Champion. He was from the Dakotas. Norris helped to establish Minnesota's running program. He was the leader of the 1964 cross country team that won the Big Ten title. Norris was very tough.*

I had the privilege to run for Roy for the first two years when he became head coach at Minnesota. He exemplified the ideal role model then, as I am sure he did for all those athletes who were to follow. He had a great impact on my life and I am sure the lives of so many after our era. There are only a handful of people who have a major influence on our character, values, and ethics. Roy was definitely one of that select few for me.

During spring break, we went to Tulsa one year and Albuquerque the second year – by bus. That is a good long way to be cooped up with a bunch of overly active, high energy guys. It was on the edge of being a mobile cage at the zoo. The most sought after spot was the overhead luggage rack – there you could stretch out and have a balcony view of the action. And Albuquerque, of course, is at an altitude of 5,300 feet. We had no time to acclimatize to the elevation. It was exhausting working out and particularly racing after a week of twice-a-day training. This bordered on cruel and unusual and I heard that he went easier on guys that came after us.

Norris Peterson

When Coach was asked by reporters (and whoever else asked) about what he had done, he always passed it off as, "He had done nothing, the kids did it all." For someone who "did nothing" he has sure accomplished a lot and impacted a lot of lives.

Norris Peterson U of M athlete, 1963-64

Steve Plasencia

Coach Griak: *Steve ran at Cooper High School. His coach there, Jim Fischer, did a great job grooming him as a distance runner. Steve had great ability and was a tenacious runner. He was a Gopher All-American and an Olympian.*

My path to the U of M program was probably typical of many who were on the team...a Minnesota high school product who Roy recruited with his fatherly caring manner. After arriving at "the U," Roy was a natural at guiding young men through their first experience away from home, all the while imparting sound values with a dose of gentle wit. Sprinkling in a joke here, and a prod there, Coach had a good way of getting his message across.

Steve Plasencia and Coach

Roy was also a "second parent," particularly for those athletes who were a long way from home. One teammate I remember fondly was a young man by the name of John Griffin, who began his college career at Wayne State in Detroit and later transferred to Minnesota. We all called him "Mo Town" for an obvious reason. Mo Town was a free spirit, a dedicated runner, somewhere between man number five and nine on the cross country roster. Late October or early November of 1978, Roy's "little pumpkins" were primed and ready for a Big Ten Cross Country Championship. Griffin had made the team, and like all the rest was nervous and keyed up for the race held at Purdue. To the course as a team, warm-up together, spikes on, to the starting line. The starter called for sweats off and all the runners begin that last minute ritual of "peeling off the sweats." That is when John discovered somehow that he had forgotten to put running shorts on under his sweat bottoms. All he was wearing under the sweatpants was a jock strap! A buzz went through the line of the Minnesota runners at the starting line… "Mo Town forgot to put on shorts!" The word got to Coach but what could be done? Fortunately, he was also dressed in team sweats on the course that day, and came up with a solution. To the bushes near the starting line Mo Town and Coach rushed. There, thirty meters from the crowded race start, the exchange was made. Now it was Roy who had only a jock strap on under his sweats. Thus the fodder for hundreds of future laughs was in place. We all knew Roy would give the shirt off his back for his athletes; that day we learned he would go a step further! Sadly, John Griffin died years after leaving Minnesota in a motor scooter accident. John was in the "Peace Corp" in South America.

Steve Plasencia, U of M runner, Present Gopher Coach

Deanne Richardson

Coach Griak: *He is a very nice gentleman and an astute teacher of physical education. He left a big hole in the department when he left the University of Minnesota for the University of Oregon.*

It is indeed a pleasure for me to send congratulations to Roy Griak for his fiftieth anniversary at the U of M. I first met Roy as a graduate student at the U about 1963, the year I first taught at the U. After finishing his master's degree he was employed at the U as part of the athletic faculty. He became head track coach and under his leadership the U won the Big Ten Track and Field championship in 1968. The U has been most fortunate to have Roy Griak all these years. I wish him well. Congratulations to Roy! Little did I know in the 1960's that forty-five years later, my grandson, Andy Richardson, would be running as a Gopher track and field athlete. I am grateful to Roy for all he has done for my grandson, as well as for the University.

Deanne Richardson

Go Gophers!

Deane E. Richardson, Age 95

Chair of Men's Phy Ed 1963-1970 Cooke Hall

Marc Ryan

Coach Griak: *He is an Associate Athletic Director at the University and a man of great integrity. Marc is a devoted family man. His son is an excellent basketball player and quarterback in football. Marc ran the mile at Moorhead State. He is a good man and a good friend. Marc is very interested in track and field. His wife Dianne is always sending me cookies. When I first experienced heart problems she helped me to the bus at Penn State. She is a sweet lady.*

It is a tremendous honor to have the opportunity to write about the legendary Roy Griak.

There are so many great stories to tell, but honestly what I personally enjoy most of all is when Coach makes that short walk down the hallway in the Bierman Building, there is a knock on my door and I look up and it's Coach. No matter how busy things are, there is ALWAYS time for Coach Griak and those talks are always very, very impactful AND special!

It's incredible to think of just how many lives Coach has impacted during his long and illustrious career. He has touched the lives of thousands of student-athletes, many fellow staff members and colleagues in the coaching profession, not to mention officials and fans not only in the USA, but from around the world.

I don't think I've ever met an individual who bleeds Maroon and Gold more than Coach – not just for Gopher men's cross country / track and field, but for ALL Gopher sports. He is a loyal and dedicated Golden Gopher!

When all is said and done it goes without saying that Coach Griak is the HEART AND SOUL of the Gopher men's cross country / track and field program. He ALWAYS has been and ALWAYS will be.

Congrats Coach on an absolutely amazing fifty years of service to the University of Minnesota!

You are the best. Go Gophers!

Marc Ryan

U of M Associate Director of Athletics

Marc Ryan – U of M Senior Associate Athletic Director

Sue Shelkey

Coach Griak: *Sue was a girlfriend of Joe Nabbefeld. She helped me prior to the Big Ten Outdoor Championship held at Minnesota in 1982. She painted every hurdle.*

I met Coach Griak in the late 1970's. I was a friend of one of his cross country and track runners and I immediately developed a respect for this tall, lanky and friendly man. Creating a successful running program at the U was only one aspect of his many accomplishments. His character was another story. I saw coach as funny, goofy, caring, thoughtful, good natured and kind. His dedication to the program and to his runners was, and still is, mind boggling. Without a doubt, he put a new definition to the word "dedication." For me his quirky kindnesses were what led to a lasting friendship. One year, the nationals were in Austin, Texas. (I hope I have this right?!) I was working in San Diego at the time and flew over to attend the meet. Coach Griak was the one who picked me up at the airport! Geez, I hardly knew the guy! That blew me away!

There was the year when Big 10 Championships were at the U (I hope I have this right, too?!) and Coach had people scurrying all over the place doing this and that to have the track and field complex in perfect condition. He asked at one point, "Sue what are you doing this weekend?" Well, I spent the next three days painting each and every one of the hurdles on the track. My helper: Coach Griak!

And so, many years have passed and I have always kept in touch with Roy. At first, just Christmas cards, but then I would stop in to see him with my family on our way to Wisconsin from Montana. He would open his arms and his lap to these two little toe-headed girls who repeatedly would ask, "Can we go see Coach Roy this year?" My oldest daughter has great memories to this day of wandering around his office, looking at all of the photos of accomplished athletes on the walls and the many plaques scattered about and asking Coach non-stop questions. The younger daughter would just tell me afterwards, "Coach Roy has a messy office." Occasionally, we would go out for lunch at Pontillos before parting ways. Coach, Kirsa wanted me to tell you thank you for the tour of the new athletic facility years ago when she was embarking up on her soccer career at Macalester. We knew that you were recovering from a recent surgery, and were in pain a bit, but you insisted on walking the halls anyway. She also mentioned that she still has the Olympic patch that you gave her when she was about six years old.

Thus, I don't have the stories that were created on the track or the bus, at the team dinners or the team meetings. I saw what kind of a person Coach Griak was in a different light. Heck, I don't even know if he was organized or tough or even a runner himself!?!? I just know that he was and is a good friend, a good man. He has shaped the lives of many men and women over fifty years, and, indeed, I am proud and happy to know him!

I feel privileged to be part of these many, many names. Lots of nostalgia here for you, Coach!

Love you,

Sue Downey Shelkey

(friend of Joe Nabbelfeld, late 1970's who became a permanent friend)

Bill Smith

Coach Griak: *Bill was a Gopher middle-distance runner from Illinois with better than average ability. He was a good student who remains a devoted friend. Bill runs the Snotty Nose Tough Golf Tournament for me each year.*

I had many coaches in my athletic career. Some of them were very good. In fact, I was blessed to be around a number of exceptional coaches. At best, however, they were temporary presences. Today when I refer to Coach, it references only one person…Coach Roy Griak.

I met Coach Griak forty-two years ago in the spring of 1971. At the time, I could have never imagined it would mark the beginning of a lifelong relationship. My initial meeting with Coach was in the spring of my senior year in high school where like most aspiring athletes, I was hoping to perform well enough to catch someone's interest and win a college scholarship. My high school coach, who had grown up in Pipestone, Minnesota, somehow coaxed Coach Griak to come to Chicago to watch an indoor track meet at Proviso West High School where I was competing. My most vivid memory of that first meeting was his physical presence. Hardly imposing, he was tall and gangly, a very fit "Icabod Crane" physique. (At the time my Mom commented he looked striking and to this day my wife still says he is handsome). When I met him he shook my hand, we talked and then he said, "Bill, walk over here with me." He promptly proceeded to drape his arm over my shoulders and swept me along to the stands to talk. My whopping ninety-five-pound frame virtually disappeared under his long arm. Over the years I would come to cherish the safety and the reassuring strength of that embrace. It communicated with complete certainty that I am here for you without judgment or conditions…and he always was. After exhausting workouts when I wondered if I could walk back to the dorm that arm would wrap around my shoulders as I walked back to the locker room congratulating me on a good practice and reminding me to study and get a good night of sleep. After successes when he would drape that arm around me and tell me to keep working hard and that my goals were within reach. After failures like my injury plagued sophomore cross country season when I finished second to last in the Big Ten Cross Country Meet, that protective arm let me know things would be better. He was also there thirty-five years later with that same embrace as we walked to Dinkytown for lunch to reminisce about old times and discuss the current state of affairs. That long arm over my shoulder translated one thing…You're important to me. I wasn't the best runner that ever attended the U of M, not even close, but Coach always made me feel like I was.

Of course we all had our favorite "Coach" stories. The track and cross country teams were a fabulous place for mischief which should come as no surprise given you had thirty-plus 18-22 year olds together with limited supervision. Spring was always marked by the start of the relay circuit. We would work our way north moving from Texas Relays to Kansas Relays to Drake Relays on successive weekends. There is a long list of stories that emerged from those trips. Typically, the meets lasted three or four days and presented way too much free time. My favorite of the three meets was always the Kansas Relays. Great campus and great meet. I even got to see Jim Ryun run the mile one year which I will never forget. (At the time I had no way of knowing that both of our children would ultimately attend and graduate from KU). Back then we always stayed at Sigma Nu Fraternity as hotel rooms were at a premium. It was a big old Victorian home that had once been the Kansas Governors' mansion. We slept in a bunk room with about fourteen beds in it, something akin to an army barracks with Coach sleeping in the same room right by the door. The house stood on top of a large hill that overlooked the campus. Up on the roof of the house was a "widow's walk" similar to the architecture you see along the east coast shoreline. You could get up to the "widows walk" through a trap door to the roof. Several fraternity brothers led us up the first time. As we were "oohing and aahing" they suggested that we come back that evening saying, "The view is even better then." We agreed to rendezvous with them that night up on the roof. As we arrived we noticed a series of painted lines and shoe outlines on the "widows walk" floor. Etched in chalk next to the lines were the names of sororities located down the hill. Some of the lines were marked front door, some were marked back door and some were marked parking lot. The frat brothers were equipped with strips of surgical hose, a square of canvas and water balloons. They quickly fashioned a large sling shot out of the hose and canvas and loaded the balloons. With each brother holding one side of the slingshot and their foot on the shoe outline they pulled the square loaded with the balloon back to a designated line on the floor for a particular sorority and yelled fire. Off went the balloon arching perfectly towards the front door of the sorority where two girls dressed in formals were being picked up by their dates. Thank God they were not direct hits as I am sure it could have killed someone but they did burst and soaked all four. They all promptly turned and flashed an inappropriate gesture up the hill knowing exactly where the balloons came from. Obviously this was not the first incident. I have often wondered if Sigma Nu was an engineering fraternity because these guys were deadly accurate and for the next thirty minutes we watched them demonstrate their expertise as they pummeled sororities down the hill. It was all going along fine until we noticed this maroon clad guy looking up from the ground below, arms folded and clearly not happy…Coach! The next morning all he said was "no more" and then asked how many we hit?

Coach could join in the mischief, too. At the Northwest Open we pulled off the prank of all time. On campus at the time you could hire a person to shove a shaving cream pie in someone's face. I think it was called "Pie Kill." We all knew Colin Anderson was going to win the shot put handily and it was always fun to pick on the "Big Guy." We hired "Pie Kill" and planned to have the "surprise" delivered right when Colin was on the award stand in front of the entire audience. Once the pie was delivered the person was to run to the door on Washington Avenue side of the Field House, exit and escape down the street. Coach got wind of the prank and there he was sitting with all of us in the front row of the stands as Colin received his first place award. Colin was hamming it up thinking all of us were there to see him get his award. All at once the "pie man" dashed to the stand and planted the pie right in Colin's face. We were in hysterics and all would have ended there, however, as the "pie man" raced to the door there was a small snafu. Someone had locked the door. Now, Colin was big but he was also fast and that guy never had a chance. Colin caught him, hoisted him over his head and returned to the victory stand with shaving cream streaming down his face and "pie man" hoisted high. We were rolling in the aisles and Coach was right there with us.

There are more stories than I can probably remember and no doubt most have probably become tall tales over time, however; one final remembrance I know is accurate. My parents were visiting in 2003 and I commented to Coach that they would be in town. I don't remember if they asked if they could have lunch with Coach or if Coach asked if he could have lunch with them. Ultimately it did get organized and all of us ended up together for lunch in Dinkytown. My father went to the U of M for one year on a football scholarship and sustained an injury that ended his playing days. He finished his degree at Northern Illinois. The one year though roughly coincided with Coach's time at the "U." I sat and listened to the two of them telling stories about Fortune Gordien, Leo Nomellini and other great players from the post WWII Bernie Bierman teams. They were like two little kids swapping story after story. I wish I had recorded them. After we said good-bye to Coach I commented to my Dad how lucky I was to have run for Coach and what a great teacher he was. My dad quickly corrected me saying, "What do you mean was? He's still teaching you! Look at how he is showing you that after you retire you can still contribute and be fully engaged in the things you love to do." My dad was spot on.

In this age of college athletics with all the distractions that accompany Division 1 sports it is hard to imagine anyone at any University who can claim five decades of successfully shaping young people with never a single indiscretion. Over the years as conversations with friends and colleagues have drifted to sharing stories about our younger years inevitably I include I had the privilege to run at the "U." It usually solicits comments of, "Wow, that must have been special."I always tell them it wasn't the running memories that I hold onto but the forty year relationship with a man we all call Coach. Many of those friends were Division 1 athletes and they never even mention their coaches. Sad for in retrospect the running part was really inconsequential. It was Coach who was and still is special.

Bill Smith

Pat "Tish" Torchia

***Coach Griak:** Mike has wonderful parents. His father is the head of orthopedic surgery at the Mayo Clinic. His mother (Pat or Tish) was a great cross country skier and runner. She is a very energetic, gracious and beautiful lady who is enthusiastic about everything her family does. She volunteers for many organizations in Rochester, including a prison ministry. All of Mike's siblings are great students.*

Roy Griak…a legend, a coach, but more importantly, a wonderful friend.

As a parent, one is always "in tune" to how others relate to your own children. My husband and I have been blessed with five children, all of which, have in one-way or another, had personal contact with Roy Griak…all of which, LOVE Roy!… as a parent I have "felt" this magnetic draw between my kids and Roy, and it warms my heart!

Our oldest, Mike, was lucky enough to run for the University of Minnesota (2007-2012). I would often hear of his many interactions with Roy, be they in the locker room, his office or on the course. Never was there ANYTHING but the greatest of respect, admiration and genuine love for this man, who our son reverently called "Coach."

Next in line is a daughter, Katy. Though she did not run for the U of M, that never stopped Roy from asking me how she was faring in her own cross country and track seasons. That meant the world to Katy!

Our third child, Kelsey, was fortunate to participate in a summer running camp offered at the U. She came away starry eyed at having met an Octogenarian who could outdo her in her daily "sit ups." Yes, Roy!

Our last girl, Sarah, recently transferred to the University of Minnesota where she has had the good fortune to "run into" and occasionally visit with Roy. Never has she walked away without a smile on her face and a good piece of advice tucked away into her head.

Our youngest, Ian, is now a junior in high school. A gifted runner, like his older brother, he has had numerous opportunities to participate in the Griak Invitational throughout his running seasons. Prior to running cross country, he was (and continues to be!) his older brother's greatest fan. Seeing Ian riding in Roy's cart at the Griak Invitational as they both raced around to "watch Mike!" was simply joyful. Roy and Ian have developed a very special relationship during these past six years. Roy's support of Ian via phone calls and occasional notes (during an injury prone high school career) has been uplifting and so very much appreciated by Ian.

My husband, Mike, and I have had the great opportunity and honor of being with Roy during some of his more recent medical "journeys." Regardless of where we are when we say "good-bye," we all know that we have been given a "gift" in the friend we call "Roy."

We LOVE you, Roy!

Hugs and blessings,

Mike, Tish, Mike, Katy, Kelsey, Sarah and Ian Torchia

(parents of Mike Torchia, U of M athlete)

Ed Twomey

***Coach Griak:** Ed was a terrific student. He was a good runner who ran more with his brains than with his legs. He was driven to succeed. He was an 880-yard runner for the 1968 Big Ten Champion Gopher Track and Field team and an excellent cross country runner.*

I too was shaped in positive ways by Roy, and, as a result, have kept in fairly close contact with him over the years.

My admiration for Roy as a coach was only

exceeded by my admiration for him as a person. I think that the following succinctly sums up that admiration: for a very long time Roy had been in the top five of the most admired persons I have had the pleasure of personally knowing.

One of the personal things I treasure about Roy is how he came to know my mother well while I ran and then when Bill ran. But more importantly, after we both had left the U, he continued to stay in contact with "Katie" as she suffered her long, slow decline due to Parkinsons. He kept asking me about her even after she moved from Minneapolis to Eugene to live close to my sister Cathie.

A couple random thoughts:

Best Track/CC Moment: Winning the 1968 Big Ten Outdoor

Worst Track/CC Moment: Finishing second in the 1968 Big Ten Cross-Country

I also copied a picture that I had forgotten about – the 1968 Big Ten Indoor Champions at Columbus, Ohio where I had the privilege (as well as other medal winners) of receiving their award from none other than Jesse Owens. A real highlight!

Ed Twomey

(1966-1969 Track & CC, U of M)

A Buckeye and a Gopher – Jesse Owens greeting Ed Twomey.

Larry Wieczorek

***Coach Griak:** I respected him as a great runner at Iowa and later as the Iowa coach. We had a good rivalry between Minnesota and Iowa. Larry is a nice man.*

When I was running at Iowa, we won the Big Ten Track and Field Championship in 1967 but then Minnesota won in 1968 in my last year of competition. Minnesota and Iowa have had a good rivalry in cross country and track and field since the days of Francis Ctezmeyer and Jim Kelly and that rivalry still continues. My relationship with Coach Griak developed into a great friendship after my competitive days. Roy Griak is, "One of the most prominent, popular, beloved and revered coaches in the country. Coach Griak loved his athletes and they loved him."

Larry Wieczorek

University of Iowa

Darold "Deb" Wold

***Coach Griak:** I worked with Deb from 1959 until I left for the University. He was an outstanding teacher in physical education and also in social studies. Deb taught from 1959-1991 and is still active in organizing the St. Louis Park Hall of Fame. He assisted Lloyd Holm in basketball and later worked with the girls' basketball team that won state titles in 1986 and 1990. Both he and Lloyd Holm are members of the St. Louis Park Hall of Fame. {Author's note: Coach did not mention that he was in the initial Hall of Fame class of 2005 at Park}*

I first met Roy Griak in 1959 as a teacher and coach at Central Jr. High School in St. Louis Park. It did not take long for me to realize that Roy had qualities that made him a very special coach and person. A few of my observations are: (1st) Roy had the ability to recognize talent. Teaching physical education at the junior high school, he identified individuals with talent, encouraged them to try the sport, got them "hooked" early and the rest is history! (2nd) He was organized. Each practice was carefully and thoroughly planned which hastened the development of each athlete. (3rd) He loved his sport and his dedication and work ethic carried over to the athletes which helped build such outstanding teams. (4th) The bond that developed between Roy and his athletes was remarkable. Of all the sports at St. Louis Park High School, the track and field / cross country athletes have the strongest friendships and a tremendous respect and love for their coach.

My favorite Roy Griak story involves Mike Gillham. Roy had added the 440 to Mike's events. I was working the finish line the first time Roy had Mike run the event. Mike took off at a blistering pace and as he was entering the third curve, one of the opposition coaches yelled out, "He's going to die.!" Instead, Mike just got stronger and shattered the opposition. Roy had him ready!

{Author's note: Mike Gillham twice won the Minnesota state title in the 440-yard dash}

Darold "Deb" Wold

St. Louis Park

Coach Griak Has Created a Lasting Legacy

A Collection of Roy Griak Tributes

LeRoy (Andy) Anderson

***Coach Griak:** He was on the Gopher team in 1963 and 1964 and was one of the best low hurdlers in the Big Ten. He was from Hibbing. He remains a true friend to this day.*

I always thought Roy could walk on water! Why not?

--Andy Anderson

Jim Blin

***Coach Griak:** Jim was a high school teammate in basketball at Morgan Park. He was a consummate athlete who wanted to be good at everything. Jim later became a big time basketball official.*

It is great that a book about Roy Griak will be written. Roy was a good friend and a great athlete. I am sending pictures of our basketball and track and field teams from our Morgan Park High School yearbook. {Author's note: These pictures can be found in the chapter entitled *Coach Griak's Schooling and Introduction to Athletics*.}

Jim Blin

(high school classmate)

Jim Bush

***Coach Griak:** Jim Bush coached at UCLA from 1965-1984 and during that time his Trojan teams won five outdoor national championships in track and field. He coached thirty Olympians and is a member of the National Coaches Hall of Fame. We served together on several US teams in international competitions.*

To Roy Griak,

I want to put my feelings down on paper, so you can see how much our friendship means to me. I really got to know you when we were coaches for the largest team to ever go to Europe and Africa. After the trip, which was a disaster (in my mind), I invited you to come and visit at my home at the beach for a couple of weeks. We had a ball, and became "great friends." Not only are you one of the great coaches in the USA, but one of the nicest people I've ever met.

It is an honor to have you as a friend. If I was a young man, what a pleasure it would have been to be coached by you. Roy, you are the "role model" of what a coach should be. You loved your sport and your athletes and they loved you in return! I wish we lived closer, because I would love to spend time with you, talking about track and field and life in general. I don't travel anymore because my feet/legs are almost numb, and I lose my balance often (many falls). My doctor made me get a walker which is used when I visit UCLA. I got knocked out twice, concussions, fractured my right wrist and hand, my arm fractured at the elbow! Cuts and bruises on my legs and arms, etc…I am a mess…but my solid stone head never injured…I keep telling the doctor, there isn't anything up there to injure (haha). Anyway, I'm so proud of you, and wish I could be there to honor you – you are the greatest.

Love you,

Jim Bush

I can no longer write, so my wife typed my letter from the mess I wrote – my fingers are so sore and stiff, my writing is a mess.

{Jim Bush passed away in July of 2017 at the age of 90}

Jim Deane

***Coach Griak:** Jim was an outstanding high school coach at Osseo; one of the best. He coached many of the people I later coached at Minnesota.*

Roy Griak has been one of the most influential coaches in Minnesota history, inspiring those around him, coaches and athletes alike. He set the standard for what it means to be a coach, and I personally have learned much from the "Old Master." All those he coached are fortunate to have learned from the best and I'm lucky to have called Roy a friend for over fifty years.

Jim Deane

(coached at Osseo for 45+ years)

{Jim Deane passed away on September 1, 2015}

Dick DeShriver

***Coach Griak:** Dick was a graduate of Notre Dame and worked on his doctorate at Minnesota. He was a volunteer coach for our Gopher cross country and track and field teams and was a good one. I will forever appreciate what he and Gil Weingarten did for me and the program at Minnesota.*

Roy,

Congratulations, my good friend, on your fifty years of service to the University of Minnesota. Additionally, this would seem to be the appropriate time to recognize the positive impact you have had on the sports of cross country and track and field, not only at the University, but across the state of Minnesota. Much of what I know about coaching cross country and track and field, I learned from you while I served as your assistant from 1965 through 1969. Besides the actual techniques and planning workouts, I also learned from you how to relate to the collegiate student-athletes.

The evening my family and I arrived in Minneapolis to start my graduate studies, I was admitted to the University Hospital and underwent major surgery. It was not a good way to start a new job and I am still grateful to you for your support during that time. I remember that you told me that my job was to get healthy and not worry about anything else.

Of course, the highlight of my coaching days at the U was winning the 1968 Big Ten Outdoor Track and Field Championship at home in Memorial Stadium. One of the pivotal races was the three-mile run when Steve Hoag ran a great race to finish third despite being ill. The second place finisher was Jim Dolan of Michigan. When I was coaching in Pennsylvania, Jim and I were coaching friends and rivals.

Roy, your dedication to the University of Minnesota is truly extraordinary. For that, you will always be remembered.

Go Gophers!

Dick DeSchriver

Minnesota Assistant T & F Coach and Cross Country Coach (1965-1969)

{Author's note: Dick DeSchriver passed away in 2015}

Jack Griffin

Coach Griak: *We coached together on a United States national team. He is still a good friend.*

Roy and I coached together at the 1984 Los Angeles Olympic Games. He was with the men's team and I served on the women's staff. Our schedules left few opportunities to share time or stories, SAD!

I appreciated his friendship and only wish we would have had more opportunities to share our "free time."

Roy was very professional and was well liked by the athletes as well as the coaches.

Over his long and distinguished career he has established a level of coaching for all future coaches to emulate.

Respectfully,

Jack Griffin

1984 US Olympic Coach

Jack Griffin

Dave Griffith

Coach Griak: *Dave is as good a distance coach as there is in the country. He is assisting Phil Lundin at St. Olaf after a very successful coaching and teaching career at Burnsville High School. Dave has a great personality and is a great friend.*

"Quite the gentleman."Those were my mother's words a few hours after Roy sat with my parents thirty-plus years ago at a high school track and field meet on the campus of Hamline University. My parents had driven in from Wecota, SD, to spend a few days with me, and they wanted to watch the competition on the track.

As they sat in the bleachers, Roy walked by, introduced himself, and sat with them for most of the meet. He regaled them with stories of his many entertaining experiences in coaching and teaching. When he heard that Wecota, SD, had fewer than fifty people, there were stories about Nicollet, Minnesota. When asked about the Big Ten, Roy didn't recount his great athletes and teams, he mentioned cannons and a frightened horse at Michigan State. Every time I looked over to see how they were doing, they were laughing at something Roy had said.

My mother, approaching ninety, still remembers Roy and often asks me how he is doing.

Roy Griak – among the best as a coach, gentleman, and raconteur. He makes a lasting impression.

Dave Griffith

Wendell and Nancy Heers

Coach Griak: *Wendell was from Amboy, Minnesota and was an art teacher at St. Louis Park. He later became the Dean of the art school at the University of Michigan. He was a great sculptor. Wendell was not an athlete but he loved the track team at St. Louis Park.*

We taught school at St. Louis Park, Minnesota in the fifties – a very long time ago now. Roy Griak was a bright spot in my day then just as he is now –we see each other at least once a year.

I, Wendel W. Heers, former Sr. High School art teacher at St. Louis Park High School, was employed there from 1950-1961. Roy had another year at St. Louis Park after I left, and at present, I am a practicing artist – primarily sculpture. I am a Professor Emeritus from the School of Art, University of Michigan. I taught there from 1961 thru 1987 with a year off to teach in a German art school, Kunst Akademe, Karlsruhe, Germany – 1986-1987. I came back to Ann Arbor and the University of Michigan in 1987 and retired. I had taught at University of Michigan 25 years.

Roy Griak has been a lifelong friend. I first met Roy and his former wife Rosemary in 1953 when Roy and Rosemary began teaching at St. Louis Park Public School. Roy was assigned to the junior high school level and Rosemary was hired to teach art to seventh graders. They were a very popular couple as they were young and excellent teachers.

We all taught in the same building – a new senior high school was in the process of being built. I went to the new high school to teach. Roy stayed with the junior high school but coached the track and cross-country teams for both junior high and senior high. My teaching facility was on the ground floor and located across the hall from the athletic locker rooms and gyms. Roy would commute to the new building and that is when I remember him, as he would stop in almost every afternoon that the school was in session. Roy was a legend in St. Louis Park. My classes were over, but I often stayed preparing for the next day or whatever had to be done. I was invited to join the faculty of the University of Michigan in the fall of 1960. I was asked to join the art school, but my school principal, Bert Johnson would not release me unless I could provide a replacement with the same degrees that I held and with the same or similar years of experience. I had to say no to the University of Michigan. However, if I would come, the University of Michigan would hold the opening until the next year – which is what happened.

In the spring of 1961, I was asked to join the art school as a Professor of Art at the University of Michigan, which I did. Roy, when he heard I was leaving, came to my classroom and told me he had been interviewed and hired to be the head track and cross country coach at the University of Minnesota, our alma mater. Roy and I graduated in 1950.

I wrote previously that Roy Griak was a legend in St. Louis Park and that he was a first class teacher and an outstanding person to be coaching young people. I often think that my best teaching experiences were during the time Roy and I were at St. Louis Park.

Roy would often stop to see me in Ann Arbor when the University of Minnesota would be having a meet with the University of Michigan. I treasured those visits.

You can take the boy off the farm, but you can never take the farm out of the boy. That is an old adage, but with a lot of truth in it. You can say the same thing about the University of Minnesota and its graduates and of the state of Minnesota as well.

I am probably the oldest person writing a tribute to Roy. I am now eighty-eight years old, but a couple of years younger than Roy. Roy deserves all the accolades that come his way.

Sincerely, Wendel Heers

St. Louis Park Art Teacher, 1950-1961

Bill Huyck

Coach Griak: *Bill coached at Carlton College. He is a true gentleman, generous with his time and a good friend to high school coaches. He conducted the Carlton relays for many years.*

I think it was May, 1971, when Macalester hosted the College Division Outdoors Track and Field Meet. Other than in cross country, few, if any, small college people had ever seen an NCAA Championship; this was foreign territory! Roy was Referee (of all events).

I was Head Field Judge (what at the time was like referee for jumps and throws combined). I think it took him a while to adjust to the often casual, student oriented nature of what many of us in DIV III saw as OK.

For instance, when I arrived the day before the meet started, the eastern coaches were raising hell over the hammer venue. Macalester, of course, had none. Most of us west of the mountains, had never seen one.

So…a concrete pad was put behind home plate and in front of the baseball back stop. Most wild throws would be contained, but it was not as safe as a regular cage. Now, the kicker…if you threw straight ahead, the measurement had to be up and over the mound, giving you an unmeasured advantage over throws toward the foul lines. The New Englanders had fits, but there was no alternative but to throw there for safety.

Roy accepted the inevitable, but perhaps with slight pain. With all entries due in several days before, the day before the meet saw a nice, big kid, in coat and tie, show up, entry sheet in hand, asking when he was to throw the javelin. (He was from Pacific Lutheran in Seattle and had flown out using his own money.) They had never entered an NCAA event before said the athletic director by phone. The athlete's coach was working part time and was not familiar with the regulations. The lad was eligible, had thrown the standard – would we please let him compete, timely entry or not?

Roy, considering the integrity of the National Meet, the necessity for following rules in the NCAA, etc., rightly and understandably ruled against his competing.

Then small college guys on the Games Committee got together and made a pitch for the kid. I was one. He wasn't at fault. There was no "educational" value in punishing the thrower or his school. He would never throw again (a senior) and the college would learn nothing of value; they were not a track and field power and would not be back for years. The part-time coach was a transient anyway. Roy changed his mind. And, if I remember, the boy threw well and scored.

I suspect no anthropologist in Samoa was ever more amazed at quaint, strange, native customs, than Roy Griak was at DIV III mentality that day!

Last, I recall him, too, standing by the hors d'oouvre table at the DIV I Cross Country NCAA's banquet at North Texas State, several years later, watching coaches snarf up some good snacks and then telling him what "lamb fries" or "Rocky Mountain Oysters" really were!

A great coach, a fine man, an asset and credit to Minnesota, the University, and to athletics…Roy Griak!

Sincerely, Bill Huyck (track official)

Steve Kerzie

***Coach Griak:** We were in high school roughly at the same time but he was at Chisholm. He became an athletic director in Gilbert, Minnesota on the Iron Range.*

What a great privilege it is to honor Coach Roy Griak. I'm sure Roy was a Morgan Park, Duluth, Minnesota graduate (I being a Chisholm High School graduate in 1938) and knew of him as an outstanding athlete there.

I was honored to help out occasionally for over forty years at the University of Minnesota track meets and he was always so much fun to work for. He was one of the most respected coaches in the country, always willing to help a young coach or athlete.

My daughter Karen's son Ronald Hoffner ran cross country for the U of M and she respected Roy so much that she would bake, out of respect for him, an Up-North, Minnesota Bo-hunk Poticia for him at Christmas.

As a side note, two of the best coaches I ever knew at the University of Minnesota were Roy Griak and Johnny Kundla.

Sincerely,

Steve Kerzie; Athletic Director, Retired

Gilbert High School

Gilbert, Minnesota

Hassan Mead

***Coach Griak:** Hassan is one of the best distance runners in Gopher history. He won 9 Big Ten titles and was a 9 time All-American. In addition to being an exceptional athlete, Hassan is also a tremendous young man. {Hassan placed ninth in the Rio de Janiero Olympic 5,000 meter run in 2016 with a time of 13:09.81. His time was only 3 seconds slower than the bronze medal winner and just 6 seconds from the gold medal. He presently trains with the Oregon Track Club}*

As many people can attest, Roy Griak was more than your ordinary man. Coach Griak had the kindness to get the best out of people regardless of whether he knew them for hours or for years. It was something about his character, old school, no bullshit, straight to honesty, that people respected and enjoyed about him. I remember my first Coach Griak moment. It was sometime in the fall of 2006 while I was taking an unofficial visit to the University of Minnesota that I met Coach Griak. He shook my hand and asked me how the visit was going but before I could finish telling him that I was about to take a tour of the campus he pointed at my face and said, "what is that on your face?" He was pointing at my facial hair. I stood there not knowing how to respond and before I could get any words out he said, "Shave that off before the visit is over." You have to understand that this was my first meeting with Coach Griak and as a 17-18 year-old I didn't know whether to take Coach Griak seriously and go shave or assume that he was just picking on me and continue the day. That day I got a small taste of what would become a great friendship and I wish that more people in my generation and the generation after me had the opportunity to interact with him and to listen to the countless stories he told. If I could capture in one sentence what Coach Griak meant to me, and to many of my teammates, we would all agree that Coach Griak was a walking encyclopedia on track and life.

Hassan Mead

University of Minnesota

Cross Country and Track 2007-2012

Bruce Mortensen

***Coach Griak:** Bruce was a state champion miler at St. Louis Park in 1961 and 1962. He won an NCAA steeplechase title at Oregon in 1965 and is an Oregon fan who sticks up for the University of Minnesota. I remember "Weebie" running the anchor leg in the mile relay in 1962 and passing a Northfield runner who had run 49.9 in the open quarter. Bruce passed him on the backstretch and then held him off for the victory. I was in the stands but ended up in the middle of the field at Memorial Stadium jumping up and down. Bruce had about a two-foot stride but he was so tough. He is a loyal friend.*

I knew Roy as a gym instructor at St. Louis Park where every spring we had to run a 440 for time as part of our grade. As a freshman I was in a group that included Wally Hlavac who had lettered in cross-country the previous fall. Although I had done no running, I almost beat Wally as he just passed me at the finish and my time was sixty-two seconds. I'll always remember as we walked back to the school Roy coming up behind me and asking what I was doing the next fall. I told him I had a paper route and he encouraged me to come out for cross-country instead. Thus started an activity that I have loved and has been the major part of my life ever since.

My other fun story is about the train trip Roy, Lefty Wright, and I took to the NCAA championships in June 1962. My graduation present from my parents was a trip via train to the meet which was to be held in Eugene for the first time. I had decided to go to Oregon although I had never been there (smart planning???). At Park the team always gave a gift to the coaches at the end of the season and I led a drive to raise money to send Roy and Lefty to the meet. We took what can only be called the milk run as the train stopped at any town of moderate size and unloaded and loaded milk cans which resulted in a long trip to Eugene. I just remember the fun we had going back and forth with Roy leading the way in interactions with other passengers and train staff – it felt like a moving party. In Eugene, we walked from the station right through downtown with all our luggage and stayed in the dorms. That was when I first met Bowerman and Roy was right by my side as an advocate. Imagine having had the opportunity to run for such legends.

Sincerely,

Bruce Mortenson

St. Louis Park High School

Bruce Mortenson – 1962 Minnesota State T & F Meet at Memorial Stadium – Bruce and teammate John Valentine finished 1-2

Inga and Harlan Nelson

Coach Griak: *The Nelson's were from Fergus Falls. Inga taught physical education at St. Louis Park and was a great swimming coach. We are really good friends.*

What a special friend you have been to us! Now when we think of St. Louis Park days (1956-59) we remember how much fun they were. Remember Elsie coming in late, and the fire drill that Cliff Bohmbach's class missed, and you taking off after two boys trying to skip school. (They should have remembered you were a track specialist). Of course there is more. Our department's Christmas celebration was super. Do you recall those good Swedish pancakes before school? We would love to do that again. Remember how awful we thought that "ELVIS" music was that the kids loved listening to during lunch break? Now we love it! We so admire what you have accomplished in your lifetime. You are the best! We still love you.

Hugs to you,

Inga and Harlan Nelson

St. Louis Park

1956-1959

Phy Ed co-worker

Paul Noreen

***Coach Griak:** Paul ran for Jim Kelly at Minnesota. He later coached at Hopkins High School. Paul continued to compete for a long time after college. Paul has passed away.*

I first met Roy Griak when I became cross country coach and assistant track coach at Hopkins High School. Roy was then head track and cross country coach at St. Louis Park. I soon found out about Roy's earliest successes at Park. Roy's assistants were Bill Torp and Eugene (Lefty) Wright. They formed what I still believe was the best high school coaching staff I have ever seen. I especially appreciated Roy's coaching of a series of distance runners that dominated the Lake Conference. Roy, along with Ed Hendrickson of Embarrass and later, Edina and Al Halley of Southwest were unparalleled. When Roy became track coach at the University of Minnesota following my college coach, Jim Kelly, I knew Minnesota track and cross country were in good hands. Roy's service to track and cross country in Minnesota is legendary.

Paul Noreen

Don Prielipp

***Coach Griak:** Don was a teammate at the University. He ran the 440-yard dash. He roomed with me and my brother Steve. We were good buddies. He was a forestry student.*

'48 Acquaintance, '49 Teammates, '50 Big Ten Champions

'51... Admirer for life, A lifelong friend

Don Prielipp, U of M teammate 1949-1950

Jo Rider

***Coach Griak:** Jo is more than my secretary, she is a devoted friend. Jo is well organized. She is two steps ahead in all that she does. She covers things before I even ask for help.*

The other day someone came into my office and called me Josephine. That was what Coach Griak had called me and it reminded me of how much I miss him.

Coach had a habit of tapping his ring on the counter outside my office as he was coming to work each day. I always knew it was Roy before he even arrived. He always said, "How did you know it was me?" I sure miss hearing that tapping each day, and I miss Roy.

Jo Rider

Administrative Specialist

Men's Cross Country / Track and Field and Men's and Women's Golf

University of Minnesota

Don Schimmel

***Coach Griak:** Don ran at St. Louis Park. His brother Bill was a teammate at Minnesota and a very good friend. Bill talked very fast. He was an enthusiastic half-miler. Bill was one of the better half-milers in the Big Ten. He usually anchored the 4 X 880 relay and I ran the third leg. Bill attended Minneapolis Roosevelt.*

In looking back a few years ago, I had the good fortune to meet Roy Griak when he was a student at the University of Minnesota. I believe it was in 1949, when he was a member of the Gopher track and cross country teams, along with my brother, Bill. Needless to say, they both loved to run.

I was a student at St. Louis Park High School, and I also loved to run. Unfortunately, my high school did not have a track, so if I wanted to compete with other runners, I felt it was necessary to find a track where I could work out. The obvious place was the U of M, with its cinder track in Memorial Stadium. And one of my fondest memories was having the good fortune to work out with Roy, at least on a few occasions. I can specifically recall running with (behind) him, probably in a workout 660. And if my memory serves me correctly, I seem to recall that Roy was ever-so-slightly "bow-legged." I guess I wouldn't want to swear that my memory serves me well, but that is my recollection, not that it really makes any difference, of course.

Shortly after I graduated from Park in 1951, Roy joined the faculty at Park, and one of the first things he did was to establish a cross country team at the high school, and he was also an assistant to Head Coach, Jerry Krueger, in the spring of 1952, and subsequently Head Track Coach. It is no surprise that, shortly after his arrival, the high school constructed a cinder track around the football field, and the rest is history – so to speak.

But my best memory of Roy was in 1952 when I joined Roy and several other friends on a "senior men's" recreational basketball team in St. Louis Park, called the Park Merchants. And lo and behold, our team won the recreational title during that 1952-53 season. Needless to say, Roy's outstanding competitiveness and athleticism came through in basketball, just as it did in track and cross country. I was thankful I was on his team and not playing against him. Looking back, I treasure that time when I had the pleasure to get to know Roy a little better.

After spending 2 years in the U.S. Army from 1953 to 1955, I returned to the U of M, and was a member of the track team at the U of M, coached by Jim Kelly. I graduated in 1958. I will always treasure the opportunity to get to know Roy and to learn from him. I should also mention that, although Roy served our country in the South Pacific during WWII, he was always very modest about it, just as he has been with all of his successes in athletics and life.

I want to add my sincere thanks and appreciation to Roy for his great contributions to athletics at St. Louis Park and the University of Minnesota, as well as to his friendship over the years. Roy is the kind of person who helped make the United States a great country. Thanks, Roy Griak, and many more years of good health!

Don Schimmel

(St. Louis Park 1951 grad, U of M runner 1957, 1958)

Bill Spehar

Coach Griak: *Bill was a classmate at Stowe Elementary School. We were teammates on the basketball team. He was a skinny little guy. He was later employed as a social worker in the Duluth Court House. He rode the bus from Gary to Duluth with my mother and visited with her all the way to their jobs each day. He is a good man, just super!*

Congratulations Roy on the celebration of your long and very successful and honorable service with the University of Minnesota.

You have gone a long way since our time at Stowe Elementary School in Gary – New Duluth. My memory takes me back to the sixth grade when we played fast pitch diamond ball with our friends George Olbin, Al Andrieko, Ray Galiniski and others. You were an important cog in our success then, as you are now at the University – what a life, what a career you carved out for yourself. God bless you, Coach, and may life continue to be kind to you.

Bill Spehar

(grade school classmate, teammate of Coach Griak)

Hans Storvick

Coach Griak: *He was not a graceful runner because he was so tall but he had the drive and passion to get the job done. I didn't see it coming but he won the Big Ten Outdoor 800-meter race in 2008. He was from Mankato East. His parents were great supporters of Hans and of our program at Minnesota. Hans is a great kid.*

There is just no way to be fully able to describe the impact this man has made on the University of Minnesota track and field, the Minnesota running community, as well as me individually. From the minute I stepped onto the University of Minnesota campus and was introduced to him, I immediately did everything I could to consume as much knowledge and advice from him, both in track and in my personal life. I never missed an opportunity to discuss a previous race with him, ways to improve future races, or a discussion about my future.

I think the one thing that has stuck out to me about Roy, ever since I met him and have built this incredible friendship that I continue to have with him today, was the way he would bring a room to silence when he entered it. He had that ability that when he talked, everyone made sure they listened, and took it all in. People knew there was either something to be learned, a great story to be told, or that he was telling any one of his many immensely funny jokes.

No place was this way of bringing silence to a room more noticeable than at every Big Ten meet he attended while I was competing at Minnesota. We would always have a pre-meet team dinner where our final pre-meet preparations were discussed. While Coach Lundin and Coach Plasencia's pre-meet speeches would begin to get the juices flowing for the upcoming Big Ten meet it was always Roy's speeches that everyone awaited. He didn't even need to say much. His speech would just radiate this impeccable energy. It would make you feel like you were ready to run through a brick wall for him, your teammates, the other coaches, the school, and that you were going to find ten extra gears in your races. He knew just exactly what to say in the smallest amount of words, and no matter what it was, there was absolute silence from all others when he stated them. That energy, like I stated, would just radiate throughout the room. I will never forget the feeling I would have after each one of his speeches. It has stuck with me to this day.

I just want to say thank you Roy, for everything you have done for me, my family, and this great university. You taught me what it is like to bleed maroon and gold, to give back to the university that has given me so much, so that those future Golden Gophers can receive the same great opportunities I was able to enjoy. I know I will never be able to give the amount of service you have given this university, but I am going to shoot for the highest bar possible, the one that you have set!

Hans Storvick

U of M runner 800 meters (2005-2008)

Paul Thornton

Coach Griak: *Paul is the current sprint coach at Minnesota and a real student of the game. He is an outstanding recruiter; a real bloodhound. He knows what he is doing.*

My first memory of Roy Griak.....When I was at Northfield Senior High, we attended the University of Minnesota Indoor high school track and field meets. Being a high school kid, coming to the University was a highlight of the year. During that time period, Roy hosted a meet for "Outstate Minnesota" schools and one for "Metro" schools. Northfield competed in the "Outstate" portion of the meet so we competed with schools more our size.

At that time, teams would show up to the meet and Roy would make the heats and sections up on the spot, and still find a way to to time the meet without the help of a fully automatic timing device. He called all the 1600 meter runners to the staging area to begin the making of the sections. He asked all the young runners if they wanted to be in the SLOW section of the 1600 meters. Nobody volunteered to run in the SLOW section. He looked around at the group and, without hesitation, picked me out of the group and began to make the SLOW section of 1600 meters.

Paul Thornton

Associate Head Track and Field Coach

University of Minnesota

Don Woodley

Coach Griak: *Don was a very gifted distance runner. He was one of the better athletes from the city conference. He was a teammate at the University of Minnesota.*

We met on the U of M track team when I was a freshman and (1947-49) sophomore trying out for the team and I believe Roy had just transferred from Duluth.

We immediately clicked as good friends and have maintained that ever since. Unfortunately for this relationship I had to quit the team since I transferred to pre-med and subsequently to medical school.

We have maintained contact and our friendship ever since and I am so pleased to see this honoring of him and his loyalty to the U of M.

I could write pages and pages about all his good qualities and his devotion to his team, the athletes, and the U of M. I will cut it short since I am sure hundreds of others are doing the same.

In my experience as a practicing physician and the first medical director of the Blue Cross-Blue Shield of Minnesota and in all my eighty-three years, I simply have never met a nicer all-around person. We all love Roy for these qualities and his devotion to the U of M. Congratulations Roy.

Sincerely,

Don Woodley, M.D

U of M teammate 1947-1948

Darrell Zimmerman

Coach Griak: *Darrell coached in southern Minnesota for many years and then became a legend coaching cross country and track and field in California. He had many outstanding high school teams. I hear from him every Christmas and he still contributes to the scholarship program. A wonderful guy.*

I first met Roy at St. Louis Park when I was at Farmington 1955-59 coaching football and track. Like Roy, I had been in the service. I was in the Navy during WWII (1945-46).

I attended San Diego State University (1946-1950) and participated in track and field and football for four years. Later I coached at six high schools and four colleges.

I saw Roy at NCAA meets for years even after I left college coaching. Also at Olympics and World Championships all over world.

Roy did so much for track and field at the U of M. He was one of the best NCAA coaches in his days at Minnesota. No Joke. He has been a life-long friend in my thirty years in track and field. I have supported his scholarship at Minnesota for years.

I knew Jim Kelly, Roy Griak's predecessor as head track coach at Minnesota, from my twelve years coaching in Minnesota. Jim let my athletes work out indoors during my four years at Farmington. My Valparaiso cross country teams were the number one private college teams in the NCAA from 1963-1965. I was inducted into the Valparaiso Hall of Fame.

I also coached at the University of the Pacific and was still coaching at the age of seventy in Oregon. I coached sprints, hurdles and relays.

I thank God that Roy Griak came into my life. We both enjoyed coaching track and field for many decades.

Roy was a very good coach and did so much for sport on the national level. He was one of the best in my book on NCAA level.

I am 86 years old and am thankful God gave me the gift to coach.

Darrell Zimmerman

Rival coach,

Farmington HS, Valparaiso

The Final Lap of a Life Well Lived

Don Timm

Lindsay Nielsen in the blocks

Lasting Legacy

Coach Griak treated his athletes as if they were his own sons (or daughters). He encouraged and inspired us to strive not only to reach our potential as athletes but also to become good people, good citizens and good sons (daughters) to our parents. In addition to the thousands of young men he worked with during his lengthy career he also coached a number of women including co-author, Lindsay Nielsen.

Coach was not forceful or pushy but he was a gentle and quiet presence in the lives of thousands of his young athletes. He did not tell us what we had to do with our lives but he directed us by his own example with his truisms and with fatherly advice when we needed it. He taught us never to be boastful but at the same time instilled in us a quiet confidence in our abilities and pride in the accomplishments we made as individuals and, especially, as a team. Coach valued us as individuals but by encouraging each of us to work hard, compete to the best of our ability and respect each other he taught us how to blend ourselves into a team. Those who competed for Coach understood what it meant when he said, "It's not I, it's we."

No matter how successful we became Coach was there to remind us that fame was fleeting and to, "Never forget where we came from."He told us that how we behaved as we represented the University of Minnesota was a part of who had come before us and who would be on the team after we had left. His love of the University and of the state of Minnesota, enhanced rather than dulled by nearly two decades since his time as a Gopher athlete when I ran on his teams in the late 1960s and

The best dressed coach in the Big Ten

early 1970s, shown through to his athletes and became our love also. Without Coach verbalizing it, we knew that representing the University of Minnesota was a privilege and his pride became our pride. Coach Griak's concern for his athletes was not directly related to their athletic success. Instead, Coach would usually spend more time with the athlete who had struggled or come short of their goal rather than showering attention on the athlete who had excelled. A few gentle words of encouragement from Coach Griak has reduced the sting of defeat, placed the competition in perspective and instilled hope to countless numbers of discouraged athletes. We all knew that, even though Coach was always busy, he was there to help, advise and console us if we turned to him. For those young men who were too stubborn or too wise in the ways of the world at the age of twenty to seek help, Coach would find ways to break through their shell while respecting their independence. Coach was a good listener. He said that he always kept his locker with the team, not because he was spying on the athletes but because he was learning so that he could better understand their problems. Coach said that his athletes were his family. Concerning his occupation as a teacher and coach he said, "You have to be prepared for every practice. I spent seven days a week thinking about the young punks on my team. That takes a lot of time but it was worth it. There is nothing more valuablc than timc and the present moment. I don't always remember how fast they ran or how high or how far they jumped or threw, but I remember them as people. I remember them as individuals. I remember their attitude and what they stood for. If you love what you are doing it is not a job. It is time well spent. You have to care about every kid and encourage each one to do their best."

A moment of relaxation

Coach's highest praise was often saved for those who worked the hardest to get the most out of their abilities or maybe even achieved beyond their abilities. He selflessly took no credit for their successes,

Coach Griak with future coach Steve Plasencia "following in his footsteps"

whether at the top of the conference or just personal bests, but he cherished them as much as the athlete did. Coach Griak summarized his philosophy on coaching and on life when he said, "My whole life has been motivated by being a giver, not a receiver but I have learned that because of that attitude, I have received more than I have given. When you are a teacher you give the best you have to your students and what you get in return is the satisfaction of seeing what they accomplish."

The Final Lap

On September 26, 2013, Coach was just a few days away from his ninety-first birthday (Oct. 5, 1923) when he was the guest of honor at a celebration commemorating his fiftieth year as an employee at the University of Minnesota. He had served faithfully under ten athletic directors. Starting with Marsh Ryman when Coach was hired on July 1, 1963, Coach also served under the athletic directorships of Paul Giel, Holger Christiansen (interim), Rick Bay, Dan Meinert (interim), McKinley Boston, Mark Dienhart, Tom Moe, Joel Maturi and Norwood Teague. At the 2013 celebration, Coach told an audience of former and current athletes, co-workers, family and friends that he had enjoyed coaching so much that he had never really seen it as a job. He said it had really been fun.

Enjoying the day with a fellow coach

He told us that someday, maybe in about twenty years, he would quit and get a real job. Although his remark drew laughter from the audience, I think that many of us believed that Coach indeed would go on forever. I believe that Coach now has that job and that there are angels who are lifting their knees, keeping their shoulders square and driving with their arms better than ever before!

In recent years there were indications that Coach's physical abilities had diminished. There had been operations to replace both hips and both knees. Coach had congestive heart failure and used a pace maker. He had fainting spells. He had a persistent burning (neuropathy) in his foot following one of the surgeries. Because of severe bursitis he had difficulty raising his right arm to trim his rose bushes or even to sign his name. He reluctantly turned the mowing of the grass and the raking of leaves at his home to others. I don't know if the countless athletes and coaches who asked him for his signature realized how difficult it was for him to sign his name or even to give them a hug as they had their picture taken with him.

Griak Invitational participant Amanda Anderson and Coach

Even though writing was painful, in the last months of his life, Coach wrote over nine hundred personal notes to his athletes and friends and anyone who had given money to his endowment fund. There were frequent visits to his doctors and a number of trips to the Mayo Clinic to see specialists. However, Coach continued to work, to raise money for U of M athletes through his endowment fund, to support all the Gopher athletes and teams, to dispense sage advice, to keep in touch with his athletes and friends by making many phone calls and visits each day and to plan for the future.

It was evident that Coach was tiring and that he was no longer able to physically do the things he had done for so long. Certainly he was not as fit and strong as he had been when he ran for the University in the late 1940s after serving in WW II. He was no longer able to walk so fast through an airport that his athletes had to jog to keep up with him as we had done when I ran for him in the early 1970s. Coach was no longer running as he had done for decades. He was no longer able to challenge the top athlete at a local high school to a sit up contest because the student was scoffing at an "old man" and then have the young man begging for mercy as Coach had done when he was eighty-four. Coach no

"Leading the pack on the Bierman track" at age 56 in 1979

Directing fans on the golf course at the Griak Invitational

2015 Gopher CC and T & F Captain Blayne Dulian and Coach

longer ran stadium steps. He began to accept a chair and sit down at track meets whereas he had usually been in constant motion, putting in more miles at a track meet than his distance runners. He began to allow others to help him. One of the most difficult tasks I was asked to help with at his home was to cut up and discard a maroon cushioned mat that I knew had been Coach's exercise mat for many years.

Coach's love of sport never faded. He could never pass a golf course without commenting on what a nice cross country course it would make. However, his physical limitations and age could not keep pace with his very active and youthful mind. When he talked with today's Gopher athletes or high school athletes or to the young boys who lived next door to his Plymouth home there was none of the generation gap normally found when nonagenarian (octogenarian sounds better but Coach was in his nineties) meets youth. Instead, youthful athletes and would be athletes sought out and respected his advice, eagerly listened to his stories and took his adages to heart. He maintained a strong rapport with the Gopher athletes and high school athletes even two decades after his "retirement" from active coaching in 1996. When asked about the athletes of today compared to athletes when he started coaching he said, "The athletes today are the same and have the same problems they always did: school work, coming to practice on time, doing their level best. Years ago we didn't have computers and ipods and this other garbage but the problems were still the same. Hope for the best - give your best - be snotty nosed tough." At his celebration in 2013 Coach told the athletes who had assembled to honor him, "It's about you, not me. The kids did all the work. The University gave me a good life - not with riches or money - I love to coach and teach - I love to help people."

While visiting Coach at North Memorial Hospital numerous times during his twelve day stay there in December of 2014 I witnessed another example of Coach at his best. Although he had been confined to the same room for one and one-half weeks and had great concerns about his health, Coach demonstrated great patience, politeness and cheerfulness to those who cared for him. Coach told me that he was not sleeping well and that he was awakened at all hours of the night for medications, shots and numerous tests. When he could sleep it was often during the day. I sometimes would visit him and he would be asleep. I recall that on one occasion when I was there a nurse awakened him to administer a shot. She first called his name and when that didn't awaken him she knocked on the table resting on the bed in front of him. Even before opening his eyes, Coach smiled. I remember one young lady who came into the room and asked if it was alright for her to do some housekeeping tasks. As she was doing the chores Coach asked her, "How are you doing today?"

This concern for others was a cornerstone of Coach's life. He was finally discharged from the hospital just in time to be at home for Christmas. To say that he was anxious to go home would be an understatement. He needed a ride and called me at 9:00 a.m. on December 23rd to tell me to be ready for his next call. He called again at 11:00 a.m. to say that the attendants had so far done nothing to prepare him for his release. He called again at 3:00 p.m. to say that he had been told he would be discharged in an hour and that I should come to get him. Coach said that he would be waiting for me at the emergency entrance to the hospital.

When I arrived in front of the hospital Coach was nowhere in sight. I waited a few minutes and then left my car in a no parking zone and ran into the hospital. I asked the lady at the information desk if she knew anything about Coach Griak's discharge from the hospital. She called his room and Coach answered the phone. He said that nothing had happened so far but that I should come up to the room. I went back to my car, parked it legally several blocks away and raced back to the hospital. When I got to Coach's room on the sixth floor, he was sitting on his bed and was still in a hospital gown. Nothing had been done to prepare him for his release. I think that at that point Coach would have been happy to flee the hospital half naked just to get out. The nurse in charge assured Coach that he would be sent home immediately. He helped Coach get dressed and pack his things. He told me to get the car and that he would have Coach in a wheelchair at the emergency entrance in fifteen minutes. I raced back to get the car and was at the entrance in twelve minutes. Coach was not there nor was there any sign of the nurse I had talked to. When Coach finally did arrive it was nearly 6:00 p.m. Once the nurse had helped me get him into my car Coach thanked the nurse for all of his help. Then his parting comment to me concerning this ordeal was, "Let's go and don't stop for anything." After experiencing a day that would have tried the patience of a saint, Coach spent the ride home talking about how great it was to be out of the hospital and how beautiful the Christmas lights were along the route. Coach Griak made it home in time for Christmas of 2014. It would be his last Christmas on earth.

On Monday evening, March 2, 2015, Coach called to see how I was doing. When I asked him how he was doing he said, "Fine...oh, not so good." He then told me that he had fallen during the night on Sunday. He had hurt his ribs. However, he said that he had gone into the University on Monday because, "I had to congratulate the track team on their Big Ten performance." He said he would probably be staying home on Tuesday. Two weeks later Coach had another fall. He called on March 19th to say that he had fallen during the night. He had gouged his back and had a black eye. His neighbor, Paul Rebehn, had been called to come over and help Coach get back into bed. When Coach called he asked if I would drive him to the University campus on Saturday so that he could see the high school meet at the field house.

Although he was still sore from his fall, Coach had a list of things he wanted to accomplish that Saturday. He asked if I would take him to his barber so that he could get a haircut. Coach told me that he had been going to the same barber, Dennis Anderson, for as long as he had been at the University. There was a steep and rickety stairway leading up to the second story barbershop on Fourth Street in Dinkytown. I

Coach and his barber

believe that Coach not only wanted his hair cut but he wanted to see his barber and to thank him for doing such a good job for so many years. After safely helping Coach descend the stairs to the street level the next stop was the field house. We were able to limit Coach's steps and get him close to the field house by using the back door.

As we pounded on the back door of the field house until someone finally came to let him in I was reminded of a time when I was riding in a golf cart with Coach at the Griak Invitational Cross Country Meet and he stopped at the equipment shed at the back of the course to use the bathroom. The door to the shed had closed behind him and we were locked out. Many runners doing their warmup had ignored the appeal of the most famous Coach in the state until someone finally let us back into the meet. I realized that one of the reasons Coach had wanted to go to the field house was so that he could see the trainer about the wound on his back. The trainer put a dressing on Coach's back and told him to stay home until his doctor appointment the following Tuesday.

Then Coach sat and watched the high school competition. I believe that this was the last meet that Coach saw in person although he later watched a number of meets on television. The total number of meets Coach witnessed during his lifetime would require a computer to calculate. One of the real positives on Saturday March 21st (2015) was the many individuals who came over to greet Coach. There were also several entire high school teams that filed by to say hello. Coach shook hands with every athlete and made each feel that they were the one who was being honored. Coach was also able to see several of his former athletes: Tom Bracher, Steve Hoag, David Sharp and Jeff Renlund as well as some of the meet officials he had worked with for many years: Jack Mayeron, Dan Dornfeld, Greg and Theresa Utecht and his secretary, Jo Rider.

The black eye is evident in pictures taken during Coach's last visit to the U of M field house. I think that Coach felt good about seeing people and being seen. He seemed to thrive on those contacts. As he had done throughout his coaching career, on what turned out to be his last track meet in the field house, Coach was one of the last people to leave the building as evidenced by the picture of him with his friend and Gopher administrative specialist Jo Rider.

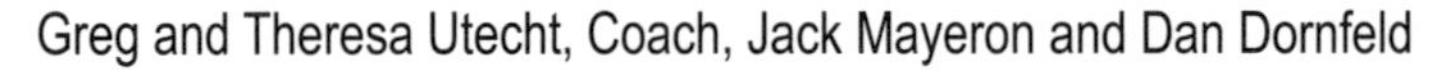
Greg and Theresa Utecht, Coach, Jack Mayeron and Dan Dornfeld

Jo Rider and Coach – May 21, 2015

At the end of March, 2015, I witnessed a repeat of Coach Griak's patience and gentle spirit and also saw that he had lost none of his fire. I had driven him to his clinic in St. Louis Park for a 3:30 appointment. He had numerous medical issues and he had asked his son, Jason, and me to accompany him into the examination room to take notes. Coach had swelling and pain in the calves of his legs. There was a fear that he might have a blood clot. The severe wound on his back was healing but was still a concern. Coach was not sleeping well at night. Although he was in obvious pain he calmly answered the nurse's questions and then waited for an hour in the examination room before the doctor arrived. It was a doctor he had not seen before and when she finally did arrive and announced that she could only give him a few minutes he calmly but firmly told her that he did not appreciate her attitude as he had a legitimate need for medical assistance.

Coach Griak may have been ninety-one but he refused to be pushed around. By the time that he was sent to North Memorial Hospital for an ultrasound that evening it was nearly 6:00 p.m. At the hospital there was another interminable wait at the registration desk. After answering countless questions again about his insurance, date of birth, occupation, address, phone number, etc., he was given the OK to follow the receptionist to the area where the ultrasound would be administered. On the way Coach asked the receptionist, "How are you today?" The ultrasound showed that there was no blood clot. He also obtained a doctor's note stating that he would have to delay the cruise he had already booked for the next week. Coach never did take that cruise.

On April 27, 2015, Coach was returning home from work and had another fall. This time he was about to enter his house from the garage when he lost his balance and fell. He hit his head on the concrete and also cracked a rib. Coach lost a great deal of blood and was rushed to North Memorial Hospital in Robbinsdale. This was the hospital he had "fled" at Christmas time four months earlier. Although he had spent six hours in the emergency room during the night and placed in the trauma unit the next morning, he was already asking for his calendar and was planning his week. Coach had had some fluid drained from his lungs. When my wife and I visited him he was groggy from the pain killers but his memory was good. He recognized me immediately and called Bonnie by her name when he saw her. He was alert enough to be watching a Gopher softball game on television and to comment on what a good pitcher the Gophers had. He also speculated on a recent proposal to possibly place the new Gopher track on the University of Minnesota Golf Course. It was evident that he was really mad that he had fallen again. Coach was black and blue all over and his doctors said that his congestive heart failure was worsening and that he had liver problems too. It was decided that Coach would be moved to a rehabilitation facility to recuperate.

Coach was moved to room 253 in the Hillcrest of Wayzata Golden Living Center. When my wife and I visited him on Sunday May 3rd he was sleeping so we left him a note. He called that evening to thank us for coming and to ask why we hadn't awakened him. Although he had many personal concerns Coach also asked if there was anything he could do for me. Thinking about others and doing for others was a Coach Griak trademark. Two days later I sat with Coach for one and one-half hours as he slept. After a nurse woke him to give him his medications we had a very good conversation. We exchanged stories and Coach asked if I would begin reading this book to him. He enjoyed listening and offering commentary on what I had written. He particularly liked the part where historical events were matched with what was happening in his life at that time. Coach also enjoyed looking at the pictures that had been selected for the book. Together, we had decided that he would make a personal comment on each of the people who had submitted a letter containing a memory about their relationship with him.

Although he was now in the rehab center, he wanted to continue this process. He said that it was good medicine to recall these people and the events they had related in their letters. The comments are now found in this book and are written just before the letters themselves. These direct quotes are preceded by a bold faced Coach Griak. Most of the comments were made in the last three months of Coach's life. Often, the mere mention of the name of one of his athletes or friends would cause him to smile and the sparkle would return to his eyes. The last of these comments was recorded on May 11th, roughly a month before his death.

In a conversation with Coach in the second week of May 2015, he had talked about some of the songs he recalled from the 1940's. The next day I brought him a CD containing popular songs from the World War II era and a machine that he could use to play them. He said that the songs brought back many memories. Some of the songs he particularly liked were: Boogie Woogie Bugle Boy by the Andrews Sisters, I'll Be With You in Apple Blossom Time by the Andrews Sisters and Sentimental Journey sung by Doris Day and backed up by the Les Brown Orchestra. In addition to their optimistic songs, perhaps knowing that Patty, Maxene and La-Verne Andrews were from Minnesota may have reminded Coach of his home during the time he was in the South Pacific during WW II.

I mentioned that our daughter, Liz, often did performances at retirement homes where she would sing show tunes and popular music from the 1930s, 1940s and 1950s. Coach said that he would like to hear her sing. The very next day, May 13th, Liz came to the rehab center and gave a performance for Coach. There was a lounge with an old piano next to Coach's room and Liz played the piano there and sang for an audience that included just Coach, his son Jason, my wife and me. Although Coach was very tired, he enjoyed the music and he especially appreciated the last song Liz sang, "You'll Never Walk Alone."

Kay Richardson, Coach and grandson Vincent

On May 16, 2015, I visited Coach at the Golden Living Center in Wayzata and sat with him as he had his lunch. It was difficult to contemplate aiding a man who had been such a strong and powerful influence in my life. I struggled with how much assistance to give Coach without invading his independence. When he asked for help with a glass of water I told him that I was sorry that it was not water from the pump at Lake Harriet. I asked him how many gallons of water he had pumped for his cross country runners from that pump. He laughed. I told him that it would have had to have been a lake or maybe an ocean.

Two days later at breakfast, a nurse came to the table and wanted to draw blood. With a twinkle in his eyes that had been missing for a few days he replied, "What if I say no?" He would often tease the men seated at his table asking them how they were going to have their steak dinner prepared. There was no steak on the menu. At lunch three days later, Coach asked the nurse if he was getting better. She said yes. Everyone hoped that this was true and that he was improving. Coach was hopeful and anxious to be released so that he could be in his own home. As he was having great difficulty sleeping, his sons Seth and Jason, and several athletes and friends had alternated spending nights sleeping on a cot next to Coach so that he would not be alone.

On May 27th, as I prepared to leave room 253 at the rehab center where Coach had been for roughly a month, he motioned that I come closer to his bed and he whispered, "You are my salvation." I am sure he said the same thing to many others. I told him, "Coach, that has already been taken care of." He replied, "I meant in this life." As I was driving home I thought, as I had done so often in the preceding weeks, what a blessing it was to have had such a wonderful man as my Coach, mentor and friend.

Coach getting water from the pump at Lake Harriet

On May 30, 2015, Coach was still at the rehabilitation center but he had been given hope that he might be allowed to go home soon. Gene Daly and I, both members of the 1969 Big Ten Champion CC team, spent several hours reminiscing with our Coach. Gene, who had come from his home in Franklin, Tennessee, was in the Twin Cities to attend Coach's Snotty Nose Tough Golf Tournament but more importantly to visit Coach. When speaking of his athletes Coach told us, "You guys have given me so much to live for that it keeps me going. It is a feeling that can't be bought. You guys are the driving force in my life."

On May 31st, 2015, Coach called late in the evening to ask whether I would come to visit him. I found him sitting alone in the cafeteria. He wanted to talk about his days as a student in Gary - New Duluth. He said that he hadn't thought of those days for decades but he remembered that his kindergarden teacher was Mrs. Dahl. He remembered that once he got into big trouble with her. The class was playing a game and Coach had hit another student in the stomach. Mrs. Dahl chased him and he hid under a stack of chairs in the corner of the room. The teacher began to pull at the chairs and Coach held them back. Finally, he was extricated from the chairs and sent to the office. Coach remembers that the secretary was named Mrs. Riley and that she gave him a candy kiss and told him to go back to class.

Coach also recalled a teacher named Nona Rich who he said was about three and a half feet tall but that she was very good to the students. Another kind teacher was his English teacher, Mrs. Craig. His math teacher was Mrs. Foster. Coach said that the toughest teacher he had was his penmanship teacher, Mrs. Foyan. She would slap students with a ruler and pull their hair if they misbehaved. Coach remembered one student who was always in trouble with Mrs. Foyan. This was an Italian boy named Carlo Francisco. Mrs. Foyan kept track of demerits and when a student reached the number forty-eight they received an "F" in conduct. Coach said that Carlo would get to forty-eight in about a week. His favorite trick was to take the hair of the girl who sat in front of him and dunk it in the inkwell. Coach said that Carlo was still living in Duluth and that he once owned a boat company.

Still reminiscing about his youth, Coach remembered that he was sweet on a little girl named Anderson in his class. He eventually got a job working at the lumber company owned by her father. Coach was unhappy that he could not remember the first name of the girl but he said that she always sat in the first chair of the first row. He was usually in the first row also but further back. Coach said that whenever he had a piece of candy he would drop it off at her desk on the way by. Coach then admitted, "I was a big time operator."

During the summer months, Coach held three jobs. He would get up early and would help Otto, the milkman, deliver milk. For his efforts he would get a small carton of orange juice. Then he would deliver his newspapers. His route eventually climbed to about one hundred and twenty papers. Thoughts of delivering papers led Coach to recall a side story. He had a wagon that he sometimes used on his paper route. He said that one night his father told him to get the wagon and accompany him to a vacant building in their neighborhood. Coach said that there was an ancient bathtub in an upstairs room of the building and that his dad disconnected the plumbing and then had Coach help him drag the tub down the stairs and onto the wagon so that they could bring it home with them. Coach said that he could still envision that big bathtub on his little wagon as he and his dad lugged it home. That bathtub remained in the Griak home for many years. Returning to the story of his summer jobs Coach related that after delivering his papers, he would work all day at the lumber company for $1.00 a day. He said, "I had a pretty ambitious summer schedule."Coach had known hard work from an early age. Throughout his life, he demanded it of himself and he encouraged and admired it in his student-athletes.

Coach recalled that when he was in the tenth grade at Morgan Park High School he entered a contest sponsored by the Duluth News Tribune and that he won a trip to Chicago. He stayed in Chicago two days and one night. He got to go to Wrigley Field one of the days to watch the Cubs. He would have preferred to watch his favorite team, the Detroit Tigers. He remembers the ivy growing on the outfield walls at Wrigley Field. The other day of his trip he was taken to a slaughter house. He remembers watching one worker who did nothing all day but slit the throats of pigs as they came down an aisle. He also watched a big man with a sledge hammer who did nothing all day but hit cows between the eyes. As a young boy Coach said that he already knew that when he grew up he did not want to do either of those jobs for a living.

On June 1st, Coach made an appearance at his fund raiser and golf tournament. It is called the Snotty Nose Tough Golf Open and Bike Ride. He was there for about forty-five minutes and addressed the crowd by microphone from his car. It was the first time in months that many of his athletes had seen Coach and, sadly, for many it would be the last. Kay Richardson had driven him there from the rehab center. Later that day,

"Snotty Nose Tough" fund raiser in 2015

a family meeting was held with the doctors and staff to discuss whether Coach would be allowed to go home in the near future.

It had been decided that Coach would be sent home on Friday, June 19th of 2015. He would have 24-hour nursing care in his own home. He was definitely more mobile than he had been in weeks and he would often do modified exercises in preparation for his long awaited return home. His spirits were quite good and his memory was sharp. On his last day at Hillcrest of Wayzata (June 18, 2015), Garry Bjorklund and I sat with Coach in the entry lounge of the facility. Garry was in town from Fort Collins, Colorado to see Coach and then to attend the festivities surrounding Grandma's Marathon in Duluth. The half-marathon at Grandma's is named for Garry. Garry had grown up in Twig, Minnesota, not too far from Coach's boyhood home in Gary - New Duluth. He had been Coach's most decorated distance runner. Our time with Coach that day was priceless. We both realized that Coach was saying good-bye to us. He was so open with his declaration of love and thanks for the people in his life. Garry and I agreed that we had been richly blessed to not only have run for Coach but to have his love and respect.

June 20th, 2015 was Coach's first full day in nearly two months where he had not been either hospitalized or in the rehab center. That day, while visiting Coach in his Plymouth home for the first time since late April, we watched a replay of the NCAA Track and Field Meet. He had been disappointed that he had not been able to watch it live while in the rehab center but Kay had recorded it so that he could watch it when he returned home. As he had always done, he critiqued each event applauding the performances of the athletes and noting flaws that, if corrected, may have allowed them to perform even better.

In late June, although I had not been told this I realized that Coach was in hospice care in his own home. His care givers, Jina and Eunice were very pleasant, competent, patient and caring. Years ago, Coach had asked Tom Stuart to officiate at his funeral. Tom is a retired minister and had also been a Gopher Big Ten Champion high jumper for Coach in 1966. Although he said it was a great honor, this was an honor that Tom did not wish to fulfill soon. On June 30th, 2015 I wrote to Tom that the day before Coach had told Jina and me that he wanted to go to heaven with us. I told him, "Coach, that is a promise we have been given." Coach seemed to be most peaceful when he was holding the hand of a family member or friend. The spark had faded from his eyes and he seemed to be slipping more each day. Kay, Seth and Monica, Jason and Nikki graciously allowed many athletes and friends to visit Coach, thank him and say their good-byes. He was having more trouble hearing and speaking. He had always talked softly but his voice was becoming even less audible. The evening of Monday July 6th, 2015, Seth called and said that I should come to the house soon as they thought that Coach was nearing the end of his life. He was sitting in his wheel chair which had been pushed right up to the sliding glass door leading from the dining room onto the deck. Just outside the glass door was a large pot of flowers my wife had sent. Coach had wanted to see Bonnie's garden but this was the best we could do. He spent much of the evening sitting and looking at the flowers and talking with Kay, Seth & Monica, Jason & Nikki, his grandson Vincent, and me. For a time, I held his hand and talked to him, saying the things I had told him so often in the last few months. (Thanks for all that you have done for me Coach, God bless you Coach, I love you Coach). He heard me but had difficulty talking. He did say that he loved me too. Those were the last words I heard from him. Coach was bedridden after that evening and died on Thursday July 9th, 2015.

This book has been a work in progress for several years. It has been an ongoing collaboration with Coach as there were always new stories or requests for Coach to clarify or enhance a story. I felt that I would never finish the story of Coach's life because new episodes continued to surface each time I visited. With Coach's death on July 9th, 2015 the first hand opportunities ceased and it was time to write the final chapter of his amazing life.

Tomstone

Final Thoughts on a Life Well Lived

In the last months of Coach's life, I witnessed many examples of his indomitable spirit, positive attitude, sense of humor and love of life. It troubled him that his body was failing and that he could no longer do the things he had always done and that he so longed to do again. We often

Reverse side of tombstone

talked about the human condition of looking back at what we once could do rather than fully appreciating what we are still able to do. Although Coach was physically slowing down from a pace that had amazed most people, his mind was still sharp and his memory clear. As I sat visiting with him at breakfast in the rehab center the morning of June 3rd, 2015 a young woman came to the table and said that she was the occupational therapist. She told Coach that it was time for his therapy. Coach asked if I would accompany him to the session. He was in a wheel chair and had a tube going to his nostrils from a portable supply of oxygen. The therapist asked him to stand and to exercise what appeared to be a hand bicycle placed on the table in front of him. With effort, Coach propelled this machine for ten minutes. Several times the young woman reminded him that he would need to keep his head up so that he would receive the right amount of oxygen. When he was finished, she asked how he was feeling. He replied, "I'm tired. What kind of recovery do I get, a 110 jog?" Then he said to the young woman, who was not familiar with his spunky playfulness, "Now, I expect that you could do this too and keep your gol dang head up."

On another visit to room 253 at the Golden Living Center in Wayzata, I was talking with Coach when a staff person came into the room. This was not unusual as there were nurses, attendants and doctors coming in at all times of the day, and according to Coach, at all times of the night too. This particular staffer introduced himself as the staff psychologist and asked if there was anything that Coach wanted to tell him. Coach immediately replied, "Yes, don't let the door hit you in the ass on your way out."

With the lack of privacy, the constant interruptions and all the indignities of being ninety-one and in need of help for some of the basics of life, Coach never gave up hope, never lost his sense of humor and never surrendered to despair. He retained a very active and positive mind in a body that was failing him. Seeing that decline in recent years and especially during the last months of Coach's life was very difficult but I also witnessed Coach using those last months to continue teaching those around him. His frailty did not turn to anger. Instead, Coach used his last months and days to thank, laud and encourage the people in his life. I saw him do this with family members, attendants, nurses, home care workers and the long line of athletes, neighbors, co-workers and friends who came to spend time with him. For those who may not have been able to see Coach in his last weeks I think I know what he would have said to you if he had been given the chance. He said it to me and I heard him say it to many others. "Do you have any idea how much I love you and how much you have added to my life?"

"They are not dead who live
in hearts
they leave behind:
In those whom they have
blessed
they live a life again."
from "They Softly Walk" by
Hugh Robert Orr

Moment of Silence
In Memorium
Roy Griak 1923-2015
Twin City Federal Stadium

Observations of Coach's Last Days

Lindsay Nielsen

Lindsay Nielsen

"We make a living by what we get,
but we make a life by
what we give."

Winston Churchill

It's been said that people die like they live. Not their idealized life. Not their edited life. Their true life, their heart and soul life. Coach Griak died at the age of 91, surrounded by people he loved and who loved him back. He worked hard to keep death waiting because he wasn't done living. When he was in the Golden Living Rehabilitation Center in Wayzata, days before he went home to die, I asked him how he felt about his impending death, asked him if he felt ready. He said, "Today we had a conversation we've never been able to have before, and that alone makes today worth it. I still look forward to seeing people and I know there are more important moments to be had with family and friends; so today I'm not ready to let go. I may feel differently tomorrow but today, death can just dang well wait."

Many people who have lived long lives are lonely in their last years. This was not true for Coach. People continued to seek him out as he got older, and in his final months, no distance was too far, no inconvenience seemed too great for friends, former athletes, neighbors and colleagues. People wanted to help, wanted to honor him, but mainly, people wanted more time with him. Aging and failing health can defeat even the strongest resolve to stay generous and loving, to not become self-centered while battling hardships, but Coach, right to the very end, remained genuinely interested in other people and more focused on them than his own concerns. Not a month went by when I didn't get a phone call from him. He often got my voicemail and he would leave me a message telling me he loved me and that I was wonderful. Now who wouldn't be uplifted by that message? I didn't realize until much later in our relationship that I was on a long list of people he regularly contacted.

During one of our visits at the transitional rehabilitation center, he called over an aide who worked with him to introduce us. He told us that he had been thinking that we would like to know each other. And he was right. She was an interesting and dedicated person. There is a Greek saying; "Society grows great when old men plant trees whose shade they know they shall never sit in." Coach never stopped planting seeds.

Former athletes came in with their families in tow. The parents had their own relationships with Coach. Some of the athletes were young women who were primarily coached by Don Timm. Coach Griak had made time to go to their cross country and track meets, be part of their village that encouraged them through both tough and glorious times, and they in turn made time for him.

I remember the last time he met with my youngest son and me. Maliq was a sophomore at Berkeley and Coach asked him questions about how his crew team trained. He pointed out the similarities between Crew and Cross Country, took notes and filed them. At the end of our time together, Coach very sternly instructed him to make sure that his college work would enable him to get a job that paid well enough to support himself right out of the gate, because his parents were sacrificing to send him to college. Furthermore, no matter how old he was, no matter what he was doing, no matter where he was living, he should call his mother. Often.

Coach once told me, "Everyone struggles with successes and failures, and sport is a vehicle for teaching and learning resilience, values, and for learning about how to have and maintain relationships. It's nice to be able to work with people in sport, but it's very complicated. It's not something like 2 plus 2 equals 4. The team is a wheel, the coach is the hub. You have to be the glue for sixty some guys, and every one of them is different. You have to put the pieces in the right places. Find out who they are and then let them know where you're coming from. Have discipline, expect a lot, but do it with love. If you can do that, be the hub in that way, then they become their own hubs, who coach and mentor others who become hubs and on it goes."

Coach Griak lived his life in service of others. He worked tirelessly with his athletes, his colleagues, and the University of Minnesota programs. He never avoided the manual labor that accompanied practice and races.

He surrounded himself with good people he inspired to become better people. He coached, befriended, mentored and worked with people who now also live their lives in service of others. He often said that during the last 15 years of his life he had been able to really connect with family and friends and this meant so much to him. It meant so much to the rest of us too.

Coach driving a golf cart at the Griak Invitational Cross Country Meet

"Everyone must leave something behind when he dies, my grandfather said. A child or a book or a painting or a house or a wall built or a pair of shoes made. Or a garden planted. Something your hand touched some way so your soul has somewhere to go when you die, and when people look at that tree or that flower you planted, you're there. It doesn't matter what you do, he said, so as long as you change something from the way it was before you touched it into something that's like you after you take your hands away."

Ray Bradbury, Fahrenheit 451

Those Who Were Coached / Influenced by Coach Griak and Became Coaches Themselves

Incomplete list

Colin Anderson
Dave Atkinson
Ron Backes
Garry Bjorklund
Hubie Bryant
Dave Casale
Dave Chatelaine
Tom Christenson
Jim Day
Matt Ferry
Ryan Ford
Jason Griak
Seth Griak
Ben Grokett
Chris Harder
Tom Heinonen
Steve Hoag
Carson Hoeft
Steve Holl
Carter Holmes
Roland Jarvi
Jared Johnson
Rick Kleyman
Joe Lane
Wayne Larson
Mike Lawless
Steve Leuer
Phil Lundin
Rob Lyden
Gerald Metzler
Bill Miles (National HS CC Coach of the Year - 2014)
Pat Miles
Rob Miller
Kevin Moorhead
Mike Moran
Charles Morrow
Richard Morrow
Bruce Mortenson
John Nauman
Lloyd Ness
Paul Noreen
Steve Plasencia
Joe Plencner
Jeremy Polson
John Purves
Chris Rombaugh
Lynden Reder
Jeff Renlund
Dick Riter
David Sharp
Mike Slack
Bill Smith
Tom Stuart
Howie Sundberg
Paul Thornton
Don Timm
John Trolander
Mike Vuckovich
Bob Wagner
Dan Wicks
Tim Wilhelmson
Eugene "Lefty" Wright

Coach's Impressions Over a Lifetime

1. Cross Country is the best time of the year.

2. Golf Courses should be used for Cross Country competition, NOT golf.

3. Track and Field is special.

4. Don't miss the wonders that surround you.

5. Be enthusiastic, that's the key.

6. Don't expect life to be fair.

7. You are never tired.

8. There is more than one way to skin a cat.

9. Criticize only in private.

10. Be neat.

11. Be on time.

12. Don't miss class.

13. Smile a lot.

14. Don't be afraid to lose.

15. Look people in the eye.

16. Have a firm handshake.

17. Say "thank you" a lot.

18. Take out the garbage without being told.

19. Never forget your mother.

20. Be the first to say, "hello."

21. Never give up on anyone.

22. Respect your elders, teachers, police.

23. Slow dance.

24. Be nice to people because you'll meet them later in life.

25. Lay down on the floor and listen to good music, preferably Shirley Horn.

26. Listen to your athlete.

27. Education 1st; Running 2nd.

28. Athletics should be an educational experience.

29. Appreciate your officials.

30. Every hour of sleep before midnight is worth double the hours after midnight.

31. Beautiful sunsets always remind me of my mother.

32. You're either a pumpkin or a jug head.

33. When I came back from the South Pacific, I wasn't coming back to the United States but to paradise.

34. Go for a walk alone once a week.

35. Strive for excellence, not perfection.

36. Chase your dreams and give it all you've got.

37. There are very few Bruce Mortensons, Steve Hoags, Don Timms, Colin Andersons, Tom Stuarts, Ed Twomeys, and no Garry Bjorklunds.

38. Never, ever look back, especially in the 4 X 100 Relay.

39. Run and finish beyond the finish line.

40. Always think positively about yourself.

41. I appreciate my army buddies more with every passing day, especially my fox hole buddy, Joe Payne.

42. Always put down the toilet seat.

43. Deep appreciation for all my athletes from St. Louis Park; I'll never forget what they did for me.

44. Buddy Edelen came from a fat little kid in St. Louis Park to a world record holder.

45. Teacher first, coach second.

46. Always replace the cap on your toothpaste.

47. Never be the first to let go of a hug, especially if you like them.

Coach Griak Has Altered My Life

A Collection of Roy Griak Tributes

Don Brown

Coach Griak: *He was my first state champion and the first state champion in track and field at St. Louis Park High School when he won the 880-yard dash in 1954. He was a tough little guy and a good friend of Buddy Edelen. Don was enthusiastic about everything he did. He remains a great supporter of the program. He was the longtime announcer for U of M track and field. His famous call was 'Let's bring him around.'*

Story #1:

Do you know how Roy Griak became the coach at St. Louis Park? His first year at Park was the fall of 1952 and the spring of 1953 when he took a teaching job there after being a coach and teacher in Nicollet, Minnesota. At the time, Park's track and field coach was Gerry Krueger. Mr. Krueger was a nice guy who had been at Park seemingly forever. He was the head football coach and had established a good record in that program. As a track coach, he was, as I have said, a very nice guy.

We didn't have a track at Park. In the spring, we'd run around the neighborhood adjacent to the school. Mr. Krueger would tell us to, "Run a block, walk a block." That was pretty much it. You were responsible for your own conditioning. We used the vacant lot next to the locker room for the shot and the discus and for practicing starts and showing off to the girls who would come to watch.

I was a junior in 1952-1953 and had lettered in track the two previous years. I liked to run and was the lead quarter-miler on the team. That spring, we had heard that a former University of Minnesota half-miler was teaching at Park – a Roy Grijak (see below regarding the spelling). Several of us thought that I should talk to him to see if he would come out and help Mr. Krueger coach the team. I had never met Roy up to that time but had seen him around the school.

I spoke with Mr. Krueger and asked him if he would like an assistant. I told him about Mr. Grijak. There was some confusion as to how it was spelled and pronounced. I told Coach Krueger that Mr. Grijak was a former runner at the U of M and asked him if it would be alright if we talked with Roy to see if he would be willing to come out and help the team. It was fine with Coach Krueger.

The next day, I went to Mr. Grijak's classroom. Mr. Grijak was very nice to us and said that he would talk with Mr. Krueger about it. Pending the approval of Coach Krueger, Mr. Grijak said that he would be glad to help us. The next day, he was at practice. That was the beginning of his coaching career at Park. He became the head coach the next year when Coach Krueger resigned the position. Roy went on to become one of the premier coaches in the country.

Story #2:

In the fall of 1953, Roy began his second year at Park. He was one of the assistant football coaches and those of us who were on the football team got to know him pretty well. This was especially true for those of us who had run for him on the track team the previous spring. All of the athletes realized that Roy was a great guy.

In addition to his coaching activities, he was also active with the kids in the high school and was one of the teachers who volunteered to be a supervisor for one of the Hi-Y groups at Park {organization promoting leadership and civic engagement for teenagers}. During my senior year, in the winter of 1953-1954, there was a big leadership conference for all Lake Conference Hi-Y leaders at

Camp Iduhapi in the Loretto / Maple Plain area on Lake Independence.

It was a typical Minnesota winter and the snow was deep and piled high along the roads by the snowplows. By then Roy and I had gotten to know each other pretty well. My dad had let me have the family car to drive out to Iduhapi. Coach was in the car along with my girlfriend and two or three other friends from school.

After the conference ended at about nine p.m., I was driving everyone back home. The car was a 1949 Chrysler with a bench seat in the front. My girlfriend was sitting close to me and Roy was also in the front seat on her right. He always gave his track athletes a bad time about girls so I was on my guard, and on edge, as we pulled out onto a snow and ice covered road bordered with large drifts of fresh snow.

I was driving at a safe speed and we were all talking and joking with Roy. Suddenly, my right wheel got caught in an ice rut and in a second we were careening off the road and into a big snow drift. I recall thinking, "Oh no! Of all times to have something like this happen with Griak in the car!"

I also recall the next words anyone uttered. They were from Roy who said, "Donny Brown. Where did you learn to drive?" It took us quite a while to dig the car out of the snow drift. Luckily, I had a shovel in the trunk. Fortunately, no one was hurt nor was the car damaged. However, for the next ten years, Roy would say, with a twinkle in his eyes and a mischievous smile on his face, "Have you been in any snow drifts lately?" He never let me forget!

Story #3:

One day, during my senior year, I was walking down the hallway at school with my girlfriend. I happened to be holding her hand. The hallway was loaded with sophomores, juniors, seniors and teachers coming and going between classes. Students were opening their lockers, slamming them shut and hurrying along. There was a great deal of noise as friends were talking on the way to their next classes. About twenty feet behind me, Roy had come out of his classroom and he shouted over the noise of all the kids, "Donny Brown, you are either going to be a runner or a lover. Which is it?" I dropped my girlfriend's hand as if it had suddenly warmed up to 212 degrees and I didn't hold a girl's hand for the next twenty years!

Story #4:

Buddy Edelen's life was saved by Roy Griak. Buddy went on from being a great high school runner to being a world-class runner, an Olympian who finished 6th in the Tokyo Games in 1964 and a world record holder in the marathon. In high school, at the University of Minnesota and for many years later we were inseparable friends.

Buddy was a chubby kid as a freshman and sophomore in high school. He was also a hell-raiser. At that time we were in the band together but did not know each other because he played the clarinet and sat across the band room from me. The only reason I knew of him then was that the band instructor was always yelling at him to, "Shut up Ed-lin!" (Buddy's last name was frequently mispronounced).

His mom came to school one day in the late summer of 1953, just before the start of my senior year. It was Buddy's junior year and she told Roy that she was very worried about her son and afraid that he was turning into a juvenile delinquent. Buddy had not been involved in any sports up to that time. She had heard that Roy was starting a cross country team and wondered if he would accept Buddy on the team. Of course, Roy said yes. It began a great world-class career for Buddy and very likely, according to Buddy himself, saved him from jail and a very bad life.

Buddy was a natural runner and before his first cross country year was history he had become one of the top distance runners in the state. He won the Swain Invitational in Duluth and set a course record there. He placed third in the

Minnesota State Cross Country Meet. His physical conditioning improved under Roy's coaching and he left juvenile delinquency behind him.

During track season, Buddy ran the mile and the two mile. He was terrific. Before every meet, the two of us would go off by ourselves to get ready for our respective races and we didn't want anyone else around us. At the Faribault Relays my senior year, I ran the 880 and Buddy ran the mile. I was the State Indoor Champion and was undefeated outdoors. The field of runners for the 880 was excellent with runners from all over the state competing. Buddy also faced an excellent field of runners in the mile.

We found a place to be alone in a concrete picnic shelter about a half mile from the track. It was a raw, spring day, overcast and a bit windy with some rain. However, the track was in great shape and fast.

Buddy and I sat in the shelter and talked about our races and many other things. We probably talked some about girls as well. Buddy's mom had given him some bananas to munch on. We were talking and Buddy was eating a banana when Coach found us. He saw Edelen eating the banana and I think it is the only time I ever saw Roy get mad. Boy, did he get mad! He grabbed the bunch of bananas next to Buddy and slammed them against the concrete wall. SPLAT! He yelled at Buddy, "I hope you puke your guts out while you are running." I sat there in state of shock. I was glad I hadn't eaten any bananas but still tried to look as small as possible. Buddy took off like a shot, running out of the building like the hounds of horror were after him. He had tears streaming from his eyes and down his cheeks as he fled the picnic area. Roy saw what he had done and I think he was shocked himself. He tore after Buddy calling for him to stop. Buddy kept running. Well, Roy was faster than Buddy, he used to run the 880 at the University, and caught up to him. He stopped him, hugged him and apologized. He explained to Buddy that the mile was in thirty minutes that it was not a good idea to eat bananas, which sit heavy in the stomach, so soon before a competition. Buddy was fine after Coach explained that to him. Buddy returned to the shelter where I remained, too scared to move.

Roy told me later, smiling with that determined look of his, "That gol dang Edelen. Eating bananas before he ran and then to top it off he goes out and not only wins the mile, but sets the gol dang meet record too." We both laughed. I also won the 880 and set the record. I ran my race without eating bananas first so suit yourself. Eat them or not.

There are many more stories but in general, Roy has been a lifelong friend of mine, as he has been for many of us. He has unusual and rare leadership qualities which instill in each person a loyalty back to him as well as to yourself. I can still remember my first 440-yard race as a freshman when Roy came up to me to help me set my blocks. He wished me good luck and I was so inspired that I ran like hell and earned not only my fastest time but my first medal. I was so proud of what I had done but mainly I was inspired by Roy and those few words of encouragement spoken to me that did wonders.

Roy switched me to the 880 toward the end of the 1953 season, seeing something in me where he felt that I was better suited for the half-mile. I ran in the district meet and placed fourth in my first 880 race. I was pleased. I knew I could have won the race if I would have just done this or that, or stayed with Larry Klick, the winner from Robbinsdale, just a little longer. I loved the distance and was excited about the next year. I knew I had found my race. Roy knew that well before I did.

I was the announcer at the University of Minnesota for thirty years. I did this because Roy was the coach and out of respect for him. It was out of gratitude for who he was and what he did for me and for so many, many others. I saw him encourage kids to come out for the University team no matter how talented they were. He always gave them a chance and treated everyone, stars, champions, or last-place finishers alike. All received his respect and love.

Throughout my career in athletics, I have run with and against many Olympians, national champions, and other runners of note. Many are my friends. I have never met anyone else who had the qualities of integrity, passion and love for his fellow man that Roy Griak demonstrated. It has been a privilege and an honor for me to call him my friend.

Don Brown

St. Louis Park athlete 1952-1953, U of M announcer for 30 years

Coach, unidentified man and Dan Brown in 1996

Jim Fischer

***Coach Griak:** He was an outstanding coach at Cooper High School who helped to develop Steve Plasencia as a runner. He is a good friend who coached at the University of Delaware until they dropped the program.*

Coach Griak has been a huge influence on my life. His letters on my behalf or the mention of a connection to him gave me instant credibility. I did not run at the University of Minnesota. I watched and participated in collegiate meets in the field house and at the outdoor track, brought high school athletes to participate, worked at various indoor, outdoor, and summer meets, including the Big Ten Championships, and even took his track and field class. I thoroughly enjoyed his organization and enthusiasm for cross country and track and field.

Coach gave me the opportunity to assist him during one indoor track and field season. I learned so much about workouts, the level of work that was expected from athletes, and philosophy. The after-practice runs with the coaching staff along the river road were great times for talking. This was truly a growing experience in my coaching maturation.

Through all of the years that have followed, he has been supportive of my career. We have talked on the phone and seen each other from time to time at meets, meetings, conventions, and in his office. He has encouraged me and given thoughtful knowledge of training and opportunity through my eleven years of coaching in high schools and thirty-two years at the collegiate level. His support has been especially important during the time when the men's cross country and track and field program at the University of Delaware was shut down.

The other things I remember…

Roy's jokes – He always had a few in every setting. I was envious as I could never tell a joke.

The indoor track was always busy and dust was everywhere.

The organization of high school meets was unique with the great on-the-fly organizations (before computers) and everyone participating in a timely manner, including two heats of the 400 meter on the track at the same time.

Coach Griak was a mentor to me, whether he knew it or not. I am very grateful for the time and effort he took to make sure that I found some measure of success in the career I have enjoyed.

Jim Fischer

Cooper High School, University of Minnesota, Concordia College,

University of Delaware

Mike Gebeke

Coach Griak: *Mike was a huge talent with a big heart. He is an outstanding human being devoted to the University: a true Gopher. Mike was a tremendous miler.*

During the winter of my senior year of high school in 1979, I had received some recruiting interest from a few Division I schools. I took official visits to Missouri, Colorado, and the United States Military Academy, but do not recall if I took an official visit to Minnesota. Coach Griak called me a few times, and I do remember meeting him in his office and walking to lunch at Vescio's in Dinkytown. I guess that was my "official" visit!

By late February, I was still competing in nordic skiing but had not run a step all winter. I was anxious to move higher on Coach Griak's radar screen, so I decided to run the mile at an all-comers meet being held at the U of M. To my surprise, I was placed in a heat with Steve Plasencia, the Gopher All-American who had recently completed his eligibility and was there to run a time trial. I recall that Steve clocked around 4:12 running by himself, but pulled me along to a 4:19. Immediately following the race, Coach Griak came over and asked me twice, "Do you really love to run?" He then proceeded to offer me a scholarship. I think he was expecting me to commit to the Gophers on the spot. Instead, I thanked him and told him I would make my decision by national signing day in early March.

When signing day arrived, I had narrowed my choices to Minnesota and Missouri without a clear winner. I deliberated all day, doing pros and cons and weighing the rankings on paper. I was leaning toward "the U" but could not make a final decision. Immediately following track practice that afternoon, my father showed up at our high school locker room. He had come to tell me that I needed to get home right away because Coach Griak was sitting in our living room. This was in an era before cell phones and texting. He had come to our house with a National Letter of Intent and a pen in hand!

When I arrived home, there was Coach Griak enjoying a ham sandwich and a glass of milk my mother had prepared for him. I don't know about you, but at eighteen years of age, I was not going to look Coach Griak in the eye and say, "No thanks," so I signed with Minnesota that day and have never regretted the decision. Little did I know at the moment what an impact Coach Griak would have on my life. As a coach, he was endlessly positive and encouraging. As a mentor, he offered great perspective on many life topics.

I am privileged to have run for Coach Roy Griak and to represent the University of Minnesota. More importantly, I am honored to have Coach Griak as my longtime friend.

Mike Gebeke, Gopher Middle Distance Runner 1983

Mike Gebeke wearing the Sub-4 uniform; the other three Gopher runners are L-R: Brian Schmit, Mike Moran and Dave Casale Coach gave Brian Schmit credit for naming the "Snotty Nose Tough" Golf Tournament

Tim Heikkila

Coach Griak: *Tim was a great athlete from Superior High School (Wisconsin). When I first saw him I thought, "What a talent." He would have been a great decathlete because he was not only a tremendous high jumper but he had very good leg speed and was a great hurdler. He was Minnesota's first seven-foot high jumper and he and Pat Matzdorf of Wisconsin were at one time rated one-two in the world. Tim's mother was an unbelievable bowler.*

Thank you Coach. My Minnesota Gopher Hall of Fame Award in 2007 would not have been possible without you.

Tim Heikkila

Gopher Track and Field 1967-1971

John Hopko

Coach Griak: *John Hopko was always ready to compete, no matter what the competition. He would always give you 100%. John ran at Robbinsdale before coming to the University. John was a member of the 1969 Big Ten Championship Cross Country Team.*

Coach,

The experience I had competing at the University and being part of your talented teams speaks for itself. The influence that you and that part of my life had on me is something that I will cherish for the rest of my life. Hardly a day goes by that I don't reflect on that time period.

However, this letter is about an impact you had on my life which you probably didn't realize. In 1970, my sophomore year, I asked if you could get me a job at the University Golf Course. My thought was that I could make some money and also play lots of golf. I loved the game and could also save the $1.55 it cost to play 18 holes at the time. You got me a job working for Russ Adams. He was also very kind and helpful to me. That job in 1970 was the start of a 43-year career in the turf industry. I am so passionate about my work just as you are about yours. That job allowed me to go on and graduate from Penn State University in Turfgrass Management. Their program is considered the best in the country. I was able to become a golf course superintendent, work for Northrup King Seed Company and start a business that specialized in athletics fields and golf courses. For 31 years, I have been "running" the business that I love.

It is even more gratifying that my son, Andy, got to be around you while running. He worked at the U of M course and will be taking over the business in the near future. Like you, I hope to be involved as long as my body allows.

I remember my first workout at Thomas Beach on Lake Calhoun. You told us that we would be running three lakes. I asked Steve Hoag how far that would be. He said, "About ten or eleven miles." I had never run more than seven miles at one time. Although I wasn't sure that I would make it, I did. For my first race, I showed up without spikes because I had always run barefoot at Robbinsdale. You told me, "Not at the University of Minnesota."

The hard work, discipline and intense competition day in and day out not only made me a better runner but was also the perfect preparation for being in business. I have great respect and admiration for you and what you have done for the U of M track and cross country programs.

From the bottom of my heart, I wish you all the best. Thanks for all the memories.

"Johnny Hopko" (as you so often called me)

U of M runner 1968-1970

Jack Mayeron

Coach Griak: *Jack was a student at St. Louis Park. However, he ran for Orv Bies. He works now for Barnett Chrysler. Jack is what you call a track enthusiast and is really a good person. He is in charge of the indoor high school meet at the field house. Jack coaches a club team and has for a long time.*

Having grown up in North Minneapolis without a father, I arrived at St. Louis Park in my junior year as a rather shy, awkward 15-year-old. In fact, I was such a geeky kid that in my sophomore year at Minneapolis North, when I won the gym class 100-yard dash, my gym teacher made us run the race again, saying that I must have gotten a jump on the other students.

At St. Louis Park, I was encouraged to go to the sign-up meeting for the track team and had my first encounter with Coach Roy Griak. He somehow was both terrifying and charismatic and I knew that I would do whatever it took to be a part of that team. I thought my efforts at practice had been noticed and rewarded when I was given a spot on the eight-man mile relay team. Many years later, I understood how many runners are needed for an all-relay meet, but at the time I felt valued and important. This was a new experience for me.

While I was never a major contributor to the St. Louis Park track team, I did run on relays that had success and occasionally scored a point or two in open events. Much more importantly, I gained friends and self-confidence and, in the process, a lifelong appreciation for our sport that led to a coaching career, a full drawer of 10K and marathon T-shirts and now lots of weekends spent officiating track meets.

One of the meets I officiate each year is a favorite project of Coach Griak's: It is the indoor high school meet. I was extremely honored when Coach Griak called me three years ago and asked for my help in managing the meet. I got to the field house at 7:00 a.m., thinking I would get things set up, only to find that Coach Griak was already there and working. As we were putting the finishing touches on the venue, I was at one end of the field house and Coach Griak called to me at the other end. I didn't hear him at first and so he yelled, "Jack!" This time I not only heard him but I did exactly what I had done when he hollered at me fifty years ago. I started running!

I am very grateful for the opportunity to continue to interact with Coach Griak for all of these years and hopefully have been able, in some small way, to let him know how much he did to change my life by changing the way I thought about myself.

Jack Mayeron

St. Louis Park athlete, Track Official

Coach and Jack Mayeron

Bill Miles

Coach Griak: *He is a student of the game. Bill had just average talent as a Gopher runner but he is a great person. He became a very enthusiastic coach. He has a nice way about him and he has developed the best program in the state of Minnesota at Wayzata.*

{Bill Miles coached his final season at Wayzata in 2014 where his boys' cross country team had both the individual and team champion in the Minnesota State Meet. He was named the 2014 National High School Cross Country Coach of the Year.}

Roy Griak has impacted my life in so many ways. When I began running, I had no clue who Coach Griak was, but my running experience was touched by him, nonetheless. My first track races were in my sophomore year running at all-comers races in the U of M field house in a meet put on and administered by Coach Griak. A year later, I won my first track invitational in the Private School Indoor Meet, again put on by Coach Griak.

In the fall of my senior year, I had the opportunity to run in the Early Bird Meet at Lake Nokomis in a meet put on by Coach Griak. It was a treat, as a Catholic school runner, to be allowed to compete in season with the best public school runners.

I was just one of thousands of high school athletes who were given competitive opportunities because Coach Griak provided them. I found out later that these were not duties he was expected to provide or paid to provide as head coach of the University of Minnesota team.

Later, as an adult, it became obvious to me from watching Coach at these events that he loved the sport and loved watching kids compete – all kids, not just the stars. He was a head coach at a Big Ten University, but he was still the physical-education teacher finding joy in helping beginning runners.

I benefitted from these opportunities both as a runner and later as a coach. Before I knew who he was, he was giving me chances. Later, when I knew who he was, he was a role model for me to emulate.

As an average high school runner, I was not recruited to run in college. I knew that I was going to the University of Minnesota and wanted to continue running. Early in the summer after my graduation from high school, I got up the courage to call Coach Griak at his office and ask if it was possible to run for the Gophers. He said that if I was willing to work hard that I was welcome to join the team. He sent me a packet of information and weekly workout report forms to send in. I was ecstatic that I was going to be able to run in college with the Gophers. Coach Griak's willingness to accept slow walk-ons allowed me to stay connected to the sport. It allowed me to observe how elite coaches and elite athletes prepared, trained and competed. That experience fanned my interest in coaching and later in teaching. It set my life on a trajectory that led to a career of over forty years. Again, it was Coach Griak's love of sport and inclusive nature that touched my life.

After one year of running at Minnesota, I had the opportunity to become a head coach at Cretin High School. When I spoke to Coach Griak, he wished me the best and told me that I could count on his support if I ever needed help. That was exactly what I needed to hear.

If he had been an elitist, interested only in winning meets and working with the most talented athletes, which is the path that most major college coaches take, my life would have been different - - - less. Because Coach opened the door for me, I was able to find a path in life that has brought me great joy.

Sincerely,

Bill Miles

Coach and Bill Miles at the field house

Herb Nichols

Coach Griak: *Herb did not have much talent but he had a great desire to compete and to do well. Herb was proud to be a Gopher runner and is still a supporter of the program. He is just an exceptional young man.*

I ran on the cross country and track teams at the University in the mid-1970s. I graduated in 1976. I think there was one season when we were both on the team at the same time, but by then you (Don Timm) had already won the Big Ten steeplechase and I think you and Garry Bjorklund were preparing for the Olympic Trials. At any rate, as a runner who had come to the University without a scholarship or any fanfare, you had succeeded beyond the wildest dreams of the average walk-on, and as a result, I looked up to you as an example of what was possible for individuals such as me. The reason I mention this is that I think you must have some of the same sense of appreciation as I do for Coach's willingness not only to permit, but to encourage individuals like us to participate in a varsity sport at a Big Ten university. During my career at the U, I never succeeded in any way which remotely approached your success, but the fact is that I still run almost every day of my life as a result of Coach's commitment to me.

When we leave high school, we all have some talent which we bring to a place like the University. We know our experience there will be forged into a fundamental part of our adult identities that we will carry with us for the rest of our lives. For me, that was the study of mathematics. However, we also hope to discover some part of ourselves which we didn't expect and which can be as important to us as what we had expected. For me, that was running. I know that Coach realized how much he has meant to generations of people like me whose best time was a 4:48 mile in practice, but I hope he also realizes what a great teacher he has been and how important his teaching was to so many of us. When you come to a place like the University of Minnesota, you are exposed to remarkable teachers who make us what we are for the rest of our adult lives. Coach was my best teacher.

Herb Nichols

U of M athlete 1976

Arthur Patterson

Coach Griak: *"Archie" was a very gifted runner. His feet were never on the ground for very long. He was one of the people who made our program at St. Louis Park so strong. He had wonderful running technique. {Author's note: As Coach talked of "Archie" Patterson's running technique 56 years after he had won the Minnesota State Meet 880 title in 1958, Coach almost drooled at the memory of such a "beautiful runner."}*

MY HERO

Coach Griak

This story begins one weekend in the winter of 1953. I was thirteen years-old and this day would alter the rest of my life for the next 60 years. I seem to have been in constant trouble and on this particular weekend I was with three others who were invited to spend a weekend at a cabin on Green Lake in Spicer, Minnesota. After a long day ice fishing and skating, the four of us decided to walk the short distance into Spicer. There was a drug store in town and, as we were about to pass it, a customer pulled up in front of the store. Leaving the car running, the customer went inside. The car was just too tempting for four very stupid young boys to pass. Needless to say, these four stupid boys piled into the car and sped out of town. Once out of town, panic set in and it wasn't long before the car was in the ditch and we were in the woods and headed back to the cabin. At 3:00 a.m., the entire cabin was surrounded by Sheriff's officers and everyone inside was arrested. I don't know any details but, later the next day, we were returned to our parents in St. Louis Park. The next day, the day my life began, I was in my home room class at school and was instructed to report to the principal's office. I had no idea what might be coming. It turned out that the principal and my mother were grade school classmates in St. Cloud, Minnesota. He explained to me that she had been to his office and had told him the entire story. Next to the closed door of his office was a long paddle. He explained that I had a choice to make between the paddle or reporting to the boys' locker room for an opportunity to meet someone that would most certainly change my life. On a bench in his usual sweat clothes was Roy Griak. In front of him was a stack of books from the school library. He said, "Archie, sit down, shut up, and listen." My mother had to have spoken to him also as no other person had ever called me Archie. For over an hour he read to me from the many books. Some of it was poetry, some were short stories and others were famous quotes. All of his selections were about mothers, fathers, honor, dedication, respect and hard work. By the time he was finished, there were tears streaming down both of our faces. He then turned to me and said, "Archie, from this day until you graduate form this school you will report to the track and you will run and run hard and fast until I tell you to stop." By 1958, my teammates and I had won the first two Minnesota State Championships in the 100-year history of St. Louis Park High School. One was in cross country and one was in track and field.

Coach, without a question, saved my life. Coach to this day will call just to talk and just to see that we are all OK. Coach was the first person to visit my wife, Mary, when she was in the hospital for a bone marrow transplant as part of her breast cancer treatment. When my father was near death, Coach asked if he could talk to my dad. He wanted to let him know how honored he was to have coached such a fine boy.

Coach to this day has never told me to STOP.

Archie Patterson

St. Louis Park CC & Track and Field

University of Minnesota 1959-1960

Coach, Tim Kiernan and Arthur Patterson in 1998 – 40 years after "Archie" won the State 880

Lynden Reder

Coach Griak: *Lynden is an outstanding teacher who is probably one of the very best throws coaches in the country. We are lucky to have him at the University. He is the most knowledgeable throws coach I know. He is also a topnotch recruiter.*

For Roy:

July 22nd, at noon, we said our final goodbyes to a great man from a great generation, to quote Steve Plasencia.

A solid percentage of my facebook friends knew Roy Griak in some capacity or at least they knew 'of' him. Maybe they competed at the University of Minnesota in one of the six decades Roy's career touched. Maybe they coached with or against Roy. Maybe they ran at the cross country race named in his honor, or were on an opposing team way back when. Maybe they've only seen his name on the occasional facebook post from me or others over the years.

Either way, I think it is safe to say that if you knew him, you count yourself lucky. If you didn't know him, I sure wish you had.

Roy had a modesty and kindness about him that was infectious. He had a gentle soul, a kind heart, a sharp wit, and like so many have said, a way about him that made you feel important and valued and loved.

For a more complete bio of Roy there are certainly better sources than this post will provide, but in short, Roy grew up in Duluth, Minnesota...lost his father when he was 16, was the oldest of four siblings and was raised in the 1930s by a single mother he adored. He graduated from high school and promptly shipped off to fight in the South Pacific in World War II. His return home he called a return to paradise.

A talented high school athlete, he decided to continue his running at the University of Minnesota. He went on to earn both his undergrad and graduate degrees from the U. In what must be unprecedented service, he then dedicated 52 years of his life to the school, but more importantly, to the people he held so dear.

Roy coached at the U from the early 1960s until the mid-1990s after a successful decade as a high school teacher and coach. He was on some Olympic coaching staffs and had countless NCAA All-Americans in track and cross country. He had teams and individuals win Big Ten titles. He is in about every hall of fame possible. He coached nearly every event in both the field and on the track as this was back when a college track team had one paid coach.

He spent Sundays in the office handwriting workouts for each guy – at least for the three decades or so that he coached until computers came around. The team took buses and trains to meets. There was no internet to plan travel or read hotel reviews. He relied on simple tools like a catalog he would eventually give to me as a gift, a bible-sized book of hotel names and phone numbers for cities around the U.S. He figured it would come in pretty handy as I took on the task of booking rooms myself. I politely explained the wonders of Google, but accepted the catalog just the same.

Roy lined many cinder tracks, raked many pits, patted many backs, wiped many tears and kicked many butts that needed to be kicked. He coached some great teams and some terrible teams. He saw the best in people, but wasn't blind to jerks. He knew a jerk when he saw one and, although he didn't treat these folks much different, he was careful to keep them at "arms- length".

He cared deeply for his athletes. He cared deeply for the coaching staff at the U and was loyal to them to a fault.

After he retired from coaching, he stayed on with the track program and worked in several roles including raising money, organizing meets, stuffing envelopes, you name it. I think he was most proud of the millions of dollars he raised to endow track and field scholarships for the U. I know from my time sitting only a few feet from his side, that he delighted in writing the handwritten notes to hundreds of alums and supporters of our program and was thrilled when the donations came in. The small gifts meant as much, if not more, than the big ones. The same stood for the gifts from the modestly talented alums compared to gifts from those who were on big scholarships. He mentioned alums who had earned big scholarships over their years at Minnesota and had been provided tremendous resources and a quality degree…and when they failed to donate to the program it clawed at Roy. Alternatively, when former walk-ons, who earned no scholarship and never made a Big Ten final but were positive and on time and great kids would send a small gift it would choke Roy up. That kid was now maybe fifty years old and would likely take a bullet for Roy if he asked, so sending twenty bucks seemed like a no-brainer.

He had a soft spot for less talented kids…I remember once riding on the golf cart with him picking up after the 'Roy Griak Invitational' cross country race and there was a young girl struggling and trailing badly at the back of the pack. She was fighting to even finish the race and Roy had me stop the cart and we stood and cheered her on. No one was around and the girl probably didn't even know who Roy was, but he commented that 'those little duffers, out there trying their hearts out…that is what it is all about.' I think those kids impressed him more than the talented ones. He was about heart and passion and grit. He had no room for ego or laziness or bullshit.

One of the great honors of my life has been to share an office with Roy for the last seven years. It was, at times, like sharing a bedroom with your grandpa. That is to say, it was a mixed bag. He would share stories from the war…from former races he had run or coached or witnessed. He had frequent visitors of all ages. He would often randomly launch into deep thoughts about life and family and fate. Many of those times I would be in the middle of an email or writing training or researching a recruit. I was, I guess, working. But I was quick to roll away from my desk and focus on what he had to say, as hard as it was at times. My work, I knew, was trivial compared to this relationship. It was trivial compared to what Roy had to share. These moments are what I will cherish most and I'm glad I rolled away from my desk all the times that I did. In the end, the emails were worthless and Roy's stories were priceless. It is as simple as that.

There were, though, other roommate issues. Namely, peaches. Oh man, no one in history has heard a sound as disgusting as Roy Griak eating a peach. Hunched over his waste basket for the juice to spray and drip and drool. He found a way to do this when the office was otherwise completely silent. It was so bad most of the time that I just got up and left the room until he was done. The other thing, and I suppose we can chalk this up to his age, was the farting. Oh man, that guy could fart. Mostly it happened when he stood up and walked out of the room and I was always amazed at not only the decibel level but also the great duration those farts would last. Ahhhh, sharing an office with a 91-year-old had its highs and lows. I'm here to tell you that it was 99.99% highs.

One great high was hearing Roy's jokes. Most I heard over and over but they stayed funny. One he would tell alums over the phone…'Oh, I'm doing OK I would hear, 'I got my shoulder replaced a few years ago…then my knee…then both hips…but next I'm going to do my pecker.' Usually, he would need to pause for a while as there was laughter at the other end of the phone…then he would close with…'and when I do I'm going to give it a good shellacking!'

Another classic would be when we had a recruit on campus whose mother happened to be pretty attractive. He would charm the recruit and his parents, as he was masterfully known to do…then once they were on their way he would lean in and say, 'I'm not sure what size scholarship you're offering the kid…but the mom is worth a full ride.'

But 'Father Time" is undefeated. Roy began to fail. He would recover, but then fade. Recover. Fade. Like a stock market graph ticking down the last few years showed a slow but consistent decline. When I came back to the University of Minnesota seven years ago, now as a coach instead of as an athlete, Roy worked out nearly every day. He was only 84 you know, so still pretty fit. Fast forward to 91 and I was scared he would die in the office. I feared that he would fall when sitting down in his roller chair…when he arrived each morning he sorta just lined himself up in front of it and then fell into it. I cringed at the thought of him missing the chair. But let me be clear…his body was the only thing that faded.

His mind stayed sharp, and as if compensating, his sweetness, kindness and love seemed to only grow as his body failed. He said, 'I love you,' a lot. He gave sweet advice and seemed to truly cherish each day he had in the office…he cherished those around him that he cared deeply about. He said, 'thank you,' a lot…'thank you for letting me hang around here and get in the way' he would say. We all knew it was us that should be thanking him and so we did.

I took Roy to the hospital on two different occasions. The first was right out of the gate when I was hired. In what must have been my third week or so, Roy complained that he couldn't see out of one eye and felt really out of it. A stroke, I was convinced. Roy was going to die on my watch and it was just my third week. I rushed to the training room and let them know what was happening and to get quick advice. Although the details escape me, I remember pulling up to the Bierman Building in my rusted Honda Civic and taking Roy to the emergency room. It turned out that there was no stroke…just a bad migraine and a night of monitoring. Thank goodness.

The second occasion was at the 2013 Big Ten Championship meet. After a long day at the track I settled into bed. Just then I got a call from one of my athletes…he was having an appendix attack or so we thought. The trainer and I rushed him to the ER where we would spend the next seven hours or so. Somewhere in the middle of all that we started getting calls from Roy. Something was wrong with his heart…he was out of breath…his heart was racing. The trainer advised that he take his beta-blockers and see if he couldn't get calmed down. He couldn't. So, we departed the hospital for the hotel, pulled up to the front door to pick up Roy, who looked like hell mind you, and we returned to the ER, where our same parking spot was awaiting us. The nurses did a double-take that we were back with someone different and kindly offered us some coffee.

The doctor came in. (This memory is burned in my mind.)

For some background, my hammer throwers had finished one-two in the Big Ten earlier that day. One of them, Quentin Mege, had competed with a broken hand and it was widely regarded as what we call in the business…a pretty ballsy performance.

The doctor came in and pulled off Roy's shirt to hook him up to some monitors. It was maybe four a.m. I hadn't seen him shirtless for some time, so it shocked me to see how skinny he had become. I could see every rib. I could see his heart beating out of his chest. My heart broke a little to see him so frail. He looked a little scared. His heart rate was something like 180 beats a minute. Something was really wrong. The doctors and nurses stepped out to discuss and we had a quiet moment alone looking at each other. I was scared and I think he was too. I couldn't stop from watching how fast his heart was pounding and from what seemed like just beneath the surface of his skin. He was white as a ghost.

'You know Lynden' ---he stated, 'What Quentin did today was so special.'

THAT was what he wanted to talk about.

Facing death, at four a.m. in a hospital God knows where, he wanted to talk about the track meet. He wanted to talk about our guys and how proud of them he was. If that doesn't sum up Roy right there I'm not sure what does.

He thanked me and our staff for letting him come to the meet and he was sorry to be such trouble. I dismissed this, as you had to do with some things Roy would say, and said 'We wouldn't have it any other way.' But I think we both knew that if he pulled out of this, it was probably his last Big Ten meet. Between cross country, indoor track and outdoor track, he must have been to about 150 or so…and they are all special events for the athletes and coaches…but this one probably marked the end.

The doctors returned and tried a series of meds to slow down his heart and, after several attempts, it finally took. His monitor dropped from 180 to 90 in what seemed like five seconds. His breathing slowed down and his color returned. He eventually fell asleep and Casey Madden, our trainer, and I were able to return to the hotel at eight a.m. or so. A long night, but a successful one to say the least.

Roy battled back and was eventually back in the office but in my mind that was where the decline picked up steam. Recover. Fade. Recover. Fade.

Eventually, it was clear he was in his final days. I was fortunate to visit him shortly before he died. He had his mind. He was full of love and appreciation and gratefulness. He wept a great deal while we talked, as he did with many of his visitors. I like to think that this was one part sadness but two parts thankfulness for closing his days with thousands of admirers but mostly surrounded by his family and close friends who loved him so.

He wept, and as I rubbed my hands across his back to comfort him, I felt his vertebrae and ribs. He was wearing a maroon Gopher fleece of course. I didn't want him to go, but it was time. I was speechless. I was grateful. I knew that I would never know a man like Roy again. A great man from a great generation. A generation of the 1950s phy-ed style coaches…with high shorts, a whistle and a stop watch. Not paid much, focused on the kids. Teaching lessons reaching beyond those of athletics and into life and family and fate.

As Roy leaves us, I'm sure his modest pay will somehow be swallowed up to cover some needed expense in the arms race, the corporate world of college athletics we now find ourselves in. Millionaire coaches…convict athletes…CEO administrators…multi-million-dollar locker rooms to impress seventeen-year-olds.

It is the turning of a page from one of our great Gopher men to a New World Order of Gopher Athletics. Many of Roy's teams were so bad for so long that he surely would have risked being fired in today's NCAA climate. "On the hot seat" as they say. Can we not see how broken that is?

We are lost.

Roy had it figured out but now he is gone and if he isn't here to show us the way I'm not sure we have someone who can.

I wish I were more like him. I think all of the people that Roy touched over his iconic career learned something from him, and it is our responsibility to take that out into the world the best we can. I do know that I learned a lot form Roy and I'm proud to have called him coach, friend and roommate.

In Roy's honor, I will do the best that I can to carry on who he was and what he represented. I want to try and be just a little more like Roy tomorrow than I was today and a little more the day after that…little by little…'malo po malo,' as he would say in Serbian…but no one will ever hold a candle to Roy Griak.

Salute to a life well lived…our dear friend Roy…

Thank you and goodbye.

Lynden Reder

Officemates Lynden Reder and Coach

Richard Simonsen

***Coach Griak:** Richard was a brilliant student. He was a gifted short sprinter for Minnesota. His life revolved around his intelligence – I think he earned five degrees in four years at Minnesota.*

Where does one start trying to talk about "Coach"? I would like to think I was the first one actively recruited to the U of M track squad after he assumed the role as Head Track and Field Coach in 1963. But I am sure that others would like to make that claim too, so I may have to share that honor with my hand-picked (by Coach) roommate, Tom Stuart. Tom was my roommate for my first year in the United States, my first year in college and my first year in Territorial Hall. I think that Coach felt that Tom was most likely to be able to steer his roommate through the inevitable homesickness and transition to a new chapter in life in a new country. This was the first stroke of kindness with forethought that Coach Griak sent my way.

So let me start with my first contact with Coach in 1963. It's all tied closely to the serendipitous events that led to me coming to the United States. My headmaster (principal) at Portsmouth Grammar School in Portsmouth, England, Dennis Hibbert, met a US Navy Captain, Eric Hopely, at a function in Portsmouth in 1962. Portsmouth was the United Kingdom's Royal Navy homeport and thus, US Naval officers were sometimes stationed there, or across the harbor in Gosport, the headquarters of the submarine flotilla. My headmaster mentioned that he had a boy in school who wanted to go to the US to study dentistry and who happened to be a fast runner. Captain Hopely took it upon himself to write to the track coach at the University of Minnesota, Jim Kelly, for whom he had run before heading off to the US Naval Academy. This was one of those extremely fortuitous times in one's life when a guiding hand (Captain Hopely) does something small (writing to Coach Kelly) to help someone else without being asked, that ends up changing a life.

U of M Track Coach, Jim Kelly, was retiring at the time so he wrote back to Captain Hopely that he was going to leave his letter on the desk of the incoming coach, Roy Griak. That started a correspondence where Captain Hopely and Coach Griak shaped the future of one young, half-English, half-Norwegian, lad whose childhood dream was to come to America. Coach Griak kept all those letters over these years and surprised me with them when he handed me his

"Simonsen" file some years ago.

This is why I stake my claim to being Coach Griak's first recruit to the U of M. The letter from Captain Hopely was on Coach's desk the day he arrived to take up his work as Head Coach at the University of Minnesota. Fortunately for me, Coach wrote back to Captain Hopely and so they began to plot how they could get me to come to Minnesota. For me, it was a no-brainer – I was coming. For Coach Griak, it was a gamble. He was betting on a foreign recruit, sight unseen and a track scholarship to a foreign athlete was quite unusual in the early 1960s. I think it was a first for the U of M.

I took my ACT and SAT tests at a US Air Force base in England (Lakenheath). That turned out to be my first introduction to a multiple-choice test! I apparently scored enough points that Coach was able to get me admitted to the U of M in the fall of 1964. I arrived without family or friends in a foreign environment at the age of exactly nineteen years and two weeks.

I have a very clear impression to this day from early September of 1964 when Coach Griak met me at the Minneapolis / St. Paul airport in his Oldsmobile 88. I had never seen a car so huge! In the passenger seat I looked at the space between us and was in awe at the distance! Coach apparently wanted to impress me right away so rather than taking me to the dormitory at Territorial Hall, he wanted to first show me Southdale Shopping Center, which was new and I believe the first shopping center in the nation. I had never seen anything like it! We stopped at Bridgeman's and Coach wanted to buy me a root beer float. I had no idea what a root beer float was but my English upbringing told me that I should of course accept the offer. Having never had root beer before the taste was to my palate completely disgusting but I forced it down to be polite. I thought it tasted like cough medicine and I have never had a root beer float since!

What a huge transition this was to be with root beer floats being the least of my worries. I was immediately welcomed by being a part of a peer group that took me in as a member of their team, the incoming track and field squad of 1964. Naturally enough, Coach Griak became more than a coach, he became a father-figure to me, alone in a new country at a time when communication to home meant not a tweet, a text message or an email, not even a phone call as that was extremely costly in those days and way out of budget for me. No, communication home in those days was a letter and it would take about three weeks to get a reply. The next opportunity for a visit home for me was not Thanksgiving or Christmas, but the end of the academic year in June.

So my feelings for Coach are more than a coach, more than a mentor, more even than a father-figure. He was the role model that we all looked up to. He was the pusher, the goader, the guider, ready with a hug, a stick, or a kick-in-the-ass, whichever was needed at a particular time. Always stressing that we must hit the books before the track. I will never forget that lesson in life of never letting his personal goals of success for the team on the track become more important than the individual future lives of his charges. It was, "Books first! Workout next!" Always!

From the group of athletes who were freshmen in 1964, three of us went on to professional school in dentistry. Several more followed this course of study in succeeding years too. The "education" we got, however, was more than can be learned in a dental clinic or from our textbooks. The "education" Coach Griak gave us was a never-to-be-forgotten lesson in working hard, running hard, and above all doing the right thing – an invaluable life lesson.

I remember one particular incident when I was feeling down. I had received a letter from my mother saying that she was leaving my father. While I don't remember the exact particulars, I do remember what Coach did to help me overcome that particular hurdle in my life. He invited me to stay at his house overnight in St. Louis Park rather than letting me go back to the dorm. This is where I met and came to know Seth and Jason as small boys. He put me back in a home environment – home cooking and the feeling of family. This small but well-timed gesture was maybe even stretching the NCAA rules of what was allowed – but I will never forget that time, and how that small act of kindness meant perhaps the difference between remaining at the University or allowing sadness and homesickness to win out and returning to Europe.

What greater joy can someone have, Coach, than to have influenced so many lives, in so many ways, over so many years as you have. You are one of a kind. I can't begin to express how much your guidance, your example, your kindness, your sense of ethics, and your judgment meant to me in my most formative years. Here I am now 68 years of age looking to start a new and exciting job in the coming fall based on a University of Minnesota education that I only got thanks to you. I have had a most meaningful and fulfilling career in dentistry, all thanks to the start that you gave me. Your "education" was more than books, more than track and field – it transcended life itself. Thank you is not enough, but it's all I have.

One of my favorite memories was that in 1968, the senior year of the inaugural Griak-recruited team, they helped give Coach his first Big Ten Championship in Track and Field - on the hard cinders of Memorial Stadium no less. I will always remember the team carrying Coach to the water jump and throwing him in! He came out wet from the water, but also wet from the tears of joy we all were sharing at the culmination of a lot of hard work. Who could have thought that Minnesota could beat the powerhouse Michigan team?

I think that we should judge life not by the financial riches one may accumulate but by how many people one manages to help or positively influence. In that respect, Coach Griak is the wealthiest person that I know. His positive influence on the thousands of young men who passed under his tutelage and influence as the Head Track Coach at the University of Minnesota will live on forever because those thousands subsequently passed those same lessons on to thousands of other young men and women – and so it goes on…

The renewal continues throughout the generations, and the world is a better place because of people such as Coach Roy Griak. Self-made billionaire and philanthropist, Jon M. Huntsman, the author of a great little book called *Winners Never Cheat*, once said, "Success is a cooperative effort; it's dependent upon those who stand beside you." Coach Griak is one who stood beside his charges and was a hero, a mentor and a coach to them all at once.

Thanks, Coach! I love you, respect you, and I will always think of you as the major positive influence on my life.

Richard Simonsen

1964-1968 U of M runner

1969 BS and BA, 1971 DDS, 1981 MS, 1981 cert Cardiology

(all from the University of Minnesota)

Tom Stuart

Coach Griak: *Tom is a caring, loving man. He was an excellent student and a great high jumper. J. T. Smith was his high school high jump coach at Breckinridge, Minnesota. Tom became a Gopher Big Ten champion and was a member of the 1968 Track and Field title team. He is also a very nice person. Tom became a minister. {Author's note: Tom Stuart was asked by Coach Griak to be the minister to officiate at Coach's funeral on July 22, 2015}*

There are only a few men, including my own father, who have shaped and impacted my life as deeply as Coach Roy Griak. To begin with, he was the reason that I made one of the most important decisions of my life in where to pursue a higher education. From the moment I met him, I was drawn to his warm, genuine and caring personality. In the spring of 1964, his visit to my home in Breckenridge out in western Minnesota to meet my family and partake in a good-old fried chicken meal, sealed the deal. I will never forget that visit and his pep talk to my high school track team, and he never forgot my Mom's fried chicken which he commented on for years afterward to her delight and mine.

The choice to attend the University of Minnesota, due only to him, in and of itself set the course of my life. As a wet behind the ears freshman, from day one I was enfolded into a close-knit family of young track athletes under the watchful care of "Papa," as sprinter, Hubie Bryant used to call Coach Griak. He even chose Richard Simonsen as my first roommate, a great choice by the way, that led to several more years of dorm life together. As a result of Coach's influence in my life, I was introduced to lifelong friends, engaged in an education that shaped my lifelong profession and ultimately led to meeting my future wife. As an aside, like many of my friends, I tried to avoid introducing any girlfriends to him because he would always drop the line, "That wasn't the same girl I saw you with yesterday." He was even instrumental in helping me to land my first real job after graduation. How does a person measure such an impact?

As a young man, seeking to find myself and a sense of self assurance and belonging, I could not have asked for a better setting in which to grow and develop as a person. Coach was always so encouraging and on many occasions expressed a belief in me that seemed beyond what I deserved. It made me aspire to be the kind of person he expected me to be and as a result, challenged me to be a better man.

My junior year, unbeknownst to me, he nominated me for the "Christian Athlete of the Year" award. When I was chosen for the award and invited to the banquet, I was not only surprised but a bit chagrined because, in reality, I had not yet made a genuine commitment to following Jesus Christ. That event, as much as anything, catalyzed a several year spiritual search that led to a life-changing surrender of my life to Jesus and a call into the ministry.

Over the years, there have been numerous ways he has been an encourager in my life. My senior year, he recommended me as a chaperone to a national publication that took newsboys to Europe which netted me an all-expenses paid trip to Spain and Portugal. He hired me as an assistant track coach a couple of years after my graduation and I thoroughly enjoyed coaching the high jumpers. He was present at my wedding. He frequently invited me to officiate at meets hosted at the U. His yearly notes and cards have always kept me abreast of Gopher track and his life. He personally has phoned me on many occasions just to express his care. His call to check on how I was doing when he heard that I had a bout with thyroid cancer will forever mean more to me than I can express.

Tom Stuart

Coach Griak is an amazing man. Like so many other men whom he has influenced, I can genuinely say who and what I am today would not have been possible without him. I thank God for placing him in my life at such a critical time and for his continued influence right up to the present.

What a gift you have been in my life! Thank you, Roy!

Tom Stuart

Don Timm

(Coach Griak's comments were related to co-author, Lindsay Nielsen)

Coach Griak: *Don Timm is easy for me to talk about. He's more than a former athlete; he's more like a son to me. Don lives his life with an attitude of giving; he's that kind of person. Don's lifestyle is infectious; he inspires other people to be more giving too. I remember when he came into the track office in 1967 and asked if he could join the cross country team. I didn't know if he had talent but I could see that he had a big heart and a strong will. I saw his character every day at practice.*

He was determined, driven and focused. He went from not being able to run in a straight line, to a season where few in the United States could beat him in the steeplechase. Don did more with his talent than any runner I've ever known, missing the Olympic Team in 1976 by .02 second. Don had wonderful parents. His parents seldom missed a meet home or away.

What Don had at home, he passed on to others. Big wheel keep on rolling, hub and spokes, and as many spokes as he lays out become their own wheels. All the athletes he's coached will pass on what he's given them. He's a student, an intellectual, he's forgiving, has a passion for everything, is willing to sacrifice, he cares for others and he's not afraid of getting hurt. Like I said, Don is easy for me to talk about.

When I came to the University of Minnesota in the fall of 1967, I had never met Coach Griak. I remember standing outside of his office at Cooke Hall trying to summon up the courage to knock on the door, introduce myself and ask if I could try out for his team. Although I had high school running credentials far below those of the young men on his team he greeted me warmly, gave me a pair of shoes and practice gear and welcomed me to the team. He was so humble that he referred to himself in the third person. He told me, "Coach Griak will get you a pair of shoes." I wondered at first who he was and when I would meet Coach Griak. In my years as a student-athlete at Minnesota, and in the four decades that have followed, the title "Coach" has taken on a new and, ultimately, respectful meaning.

As a freshman, I was just happy to be a member of the team. At that time, I felt that my biggest claim to fame would be to say that I had changed my socks in the same locker room with Steve Hoag, Ed Twomey, Bob Wagner, Tom Page and the other great Gopher runners. However, under Coach Griak's guidance and encouragement and with a great deal of hard work, I began to develop the ability I had been given. I am proud to have been a member of Minnesota's 1969 Big Ten Cross Country Championship team. Every member of that team was a native Minnesotan and that team remains the most recent Gopher CC team to win a Big Ten championship. We may not have had the most talented team in the conference but Coach Griak had convinced us that we were the toughest. The cold and snow in Bloomington, Indiana that day may have discouraged other teams but Minnesota had been taught by our coach that these were perfect running conditions. I am also very proud to have been a member of the three-man team Coach Griak sent to the 1971 NCAA Track and Field Championships in Seattle, Washington. Minnesota's three-man team of Tim Heikkila (high jump), Garry Bjorklund (6 mile) and Don Timm (steeplechase) scored enough points to place the Gophers ninth in the national meet.

Thanks to Coach Griak, I have tremendous memories of my years at Minnesota. I will never forget long training runs and intervals on the river road with some wonderful teammates; Saturday morning cross country races while wearing maroon and gold at the University Golf Course; running on the 220-yard dirt track in the field house (I can still remember the unique smell and the quantity of dirt and dust that could enter my nostrils and lungs during a workout); participating in the last track meets at old Memorial Stadium; and being so very proud to be a Gopher runner. I owe all of these memories to Coach Griak who was willing to give me a chance to participate. Coach had a way of telling me that, "He had a 98-year-old grandmother who could run faster than me," and make it feel like a hug.

The night before the 1970 Big Ten Conference Cross Country Meet at East Lansing, Michigan, Coach told me that the Michigan State coach, Coach Gibbard, had told him that, "Don Timm doesn't have any ability, but he's just so darn tough." I didn't know if Coach Griak was trying to compliment me, insult me, or just make me mad but I do know that if Coach Gibbard was correct about me being tough, I came upon it naturally. I inherited it from my mother. When I was twelve, my mother had a severe stroke and was paralyzed on the left side of her body. Doctors told her that she would never walk again and might never get out of bed. As I was growing up, I watched my mother prove the doctors wrong as she did walk, drive a car, and do just about anything she set her mind to accomplishing. The lessons I learned about doing the best I could with what I had been given and about never giving up I learned from my mother. Those lessons were reinforced by Coach Griak. When he told me and the other Gopher runners to know what we were going to do when the gun went off, to believe in ourselves, to think positive, to know that, "We were never tired," and to run ten yards beyond the finish line before easing up, I thought he was just trying to get us to become better runners. Now I realize that he was also preparing us for life. While he did make me a better runner, Coach Griak also quietly modeled the type of person I wanted to become.

My years at Minnesota were some of the best times of my life and I am very thankful that I came along when I did. Today the number of athletes that can participate on a team is limited and someone with my high school times would not be allowed on the team. I will forever be grateful to Coach Griak for giving me the chance to develop my talents and to have had the experience of being one of his runners. I am also thankful that Coach's interest in me did not stop when I crossed my last finish line for the Gophers. I feel that Coach has been looking out for me ever since. Solely upon his recommendation, I was offered a teaching and coaching position at Coon Rapids High School in 1973 even though my principal-to-be had never met me and I was never interviewed for the job. I was training in California at the time. I held that teaching job for 38 ½ years. It was there that I met my beautiful wife, Bonnie. As with so many of the special events later in my life, Coach went out of his way to attend our wedding. He continued to have a strong interest in my family and in the high school cross country team I coached through 2014. The 2008 team won the conference and placed seventh in the state meet. Not only was Coach at those meets encouraging my runners but when I asked him if he would speak at our banquet he immediately said yes. At the time, he was no longer coaching the Gopher team but was traveling with them to major meets. It was only after Coach had delivered an inspiring speech to my runners and their parents that I found out that, to speak to us that evening, Coach had missed his first Big Ten Conference Cross Country Championship in over forty years. I was embarrassed but should not have been surprised; Coach never forgot his runners and would do anything for us.

He remains an honored friend and trusted advisor. When I think of the amount of time he has devoted to helping me, and that he has done and continues to do this with countless others, I realize that this is his life and that it has never been a job for him. My debt to Coach Griak can never be repaid no matter how many times I tell him, "Thanks Coach, for all that you have done for me."

Don Timm

Gopher Cross Country and Track 1967-1971

Coach, Don Timm and Garry Bjorklund at the golf course

Joe Vigil

Coach Griak: *Joe is the foremost student of what makes the body function to run faster, better and longer. He is an excellent coach at Adams State (Alamosa, Colorado) and a great friend. He was my assistant when I was the head coach of the 1975 United States Pan American team.*

To my friend, Roy Griak,

Congratulations on fifty years of coaching and service to the University of Minnesota. Roy, I have always admired you because you always did things in coaching for the right reasons. Because of this, you have earned the respect of the national coaching community.

The first time that I met you was in 1973 at the University of Kansas for the Kansas Relays, at their annual banquet. You were invited to give a report of your involvement as a coach at the Munich Olympics. I admired you very much from that day on.

Our next encounter was on the coaching staff for the Pan American Games in Mexico City.

Humorous reminders:

- The bull pinatas
- The flower collected by a staff member

Highlight:

- Ron Ray's victory over Cuban, Alberto Juantorena

From then on…many meets, many dinners and lots of conversation.

Your hospitality at the Roy Griak Invitational Cross Country Meet was unforgettable when my little Adams State College team was victorious over the likes of Penn State, Iowa State, Wisconsin and many others. As were all the clinics and seminars we both attended in the years that followed.

I have treasured our friendship and getting to know you has made me a better person, to which many people would attest. The whole national coaching community has a world of respect for you and your high level of professionalism…Roy, you're the best.

Your friend,

Coach Joe Vigil (Adams State)

Dan Wicks

***Coach Griak:** Dan scored in the shot put for the Gophers when we won the Big Ten Outdoor in 1968 by just one point. He was a glider rather than a spinner in the shot put circle. Dan was mischievous. He and Pat Kelly were always into some shenanigans. Dan got married recently – I hope his wife tones him down.*

Coach, you made my life better. You are the best. Thanks for taking a chance on a skinny kid from South Dakota.

Dan Wicks

Member of the 1968 Big Ten Championship Track and Field Team

Eugene "Lefty" Wright

***Coach Griak:** Lefty was a student at St. Louis Park when I started there. He was on the cross country team. Lefty went to Macalester and later became a history teacher at St. Louis Park. He became my assistant on the track team. Lefty was a good teacher and coach and remains a good friend. He still officiates meets as he has done for years.*

I began teaching at St. Louis Park in 1958 and that year Coach Griak asked me to assist him in the track season. I had graduated from Park the year that Roy arrived. When he first came to St. Louis Park there was no cross country team and there was no track facility. Soon we had a cinder track but because of limited space it measured only 341 yards rather than 440. By 1955 Roy had a Minnesota state championship team in cross country. In 1958 we had St. Louis Park's first state championship in track and field.

Roy, you have played an integral part in my life for over sixty years. It has been a remarkable journey for both of us in coaching, involvement with the Olympic Festival, in International Special Olympics, Race for the Cure and many other endeavors that deal with running.

Your continued faith in me opened opportunities in becoming a track and field official at all levels: the high school, the college and the NCAA. You made me aware of what loyalty means and how it connects us. Many times you stressed to me the need to give back your talents and to help others. It has been a wonderful experience.

Preparedness is the key to success as well as having faith with your principles. Mutual trust and respect are also imperative for success. There is always the need to be humble.

I will always remember the years at St. Louis Park and my work at the University of Minnesota as an official and a meet organizer.

You have my sincere thanks for making me who I am. You have had a lasting impact on so many. You have been an extraordinary mentor. May our journey continue.

Sincerely,

Lefty Wright

{Author's note: Fittingly, two of the initial inductees into the Griak Invitational Hall of Fame in 2015 were Roy Griak and Lefty Wright. Sadly, Lefty passed away just three months and four days after Coach.}

Eulogies for Coach

Andy Bunge & Don Timm

Eulogy

Spoken by Andy Bunge, one of Coach's athletes, at Mount Olivet Lutheran Church at Coach Griak's funeral on July 22, 2015.

My relationship with Roy Griak began in February of 1973. Roy invited me to make a campus visit to the U of M as a potential recruit for the track team. My hosts were John Purves and Tim Oliver. We attended my first Gopher basketball game. The Gophers defeated Michigan State. During this visit I decided to accept a track scholarship.

Coach drove to our farm home in Preston, Minnesota on a snowy March day. He had to park at the end of our driveway and walk up the hill. I can still see him trudging up the driveway in his boots and trench coat carrying his briefcase. My mom and dad prepared a roast beef dinner for his visit. With my family and Roy sitting around the table he stated, "The two most important things in life are your faith and your family." I knew from his visit that he was a man I could run for and signed my letter of intent.

Years later when I would visit Roy he would remind me of the delicious meal he had been served and to greet my mom and dad.

Roy was my father away from home. He cared for all of his student athletes. He wanted us to pursue athletic excellence and to compete at our best. Reflecting back, I believe his ultimate goal for us was to pursue human excellence, to be the best human beings we could be.

Over the years when I would be in a group and would mention that I had competed for the University in track and field during the 1970s someone would say, "You must have been one of Roy's Boys," and I would answer, "Yes, I was," and I was proud of that fact.

I am glad that two of my three children were able to be a part of Roy's life. Jonathan graduated from Luther College but Alison graduated from the University of Minnesota St. Paul campus and Kristin graduated from Augsburg College. Many times during those years they would plan a visit or just drop in to Roy's office and surprise him. He would take them to lunch or just visit and laugh. I'm sure he shared some stories about my school days. He would also play matchmaker with Gopher athletes which was fun. In the spring of 2012 Roy attended Kristin's graduation from Augsburg. That was a special day for our whole family.

I always enjoyed Roy's phone calls. He would say hi and was interested in what I was doing. We would visit about friends and university events. Staying connected was important for both of us. He would close by saying, "Greet your mom and family and I love you."

In closing I would like to read a piece entitled "What Will Matter" by Michael Josephson (reprinted with permission of the Josephson Institute of Ethics).

Ready or not, some day it will all come to an end.

There will be no more sunrises, no minutes, hours or days.

All the things you collected, whether treasured or forgotten, will pass to someone else.

Your wealth, fame and temporal power will shrivel to irrelevance.

It will not matter what you owned or what you were owed.

Your grudges, resentments, frustrations, and jealousies will finally disappear.

So too, your hopes, ambitions, plans and to-do lists will expire.

The wins and losses that once seemed so important will fade away.

It won't matter where you came from or what side of the tracks you lived on at the end.

It won't matter whether you were beautiful or brilliant.

Even your gender and skin color will be irrelevant.

So what will matter? How will the value of your days be measured?

What will matter is not what you bought but what you built,

not what you got but what you gave.

What will matter is not your success but your significance.

What will matter is not what you learned but what you taught.

What will matter is every act of integrity, compassion, courage or sacrifice that enriched, empowered or encouraged others to emulate your example.

What will matter is not your competence but your character.

What will matter is not how many people you knew,

but how many will feel a lasting loss when you are gone.

What will matter is not your memories but your memories of those who loved you.

What will matter is how long you will be remembered, by whom and for what.

Living a life that matters doesn't happen by accident.

It's not a matter of circumstances but of choice.

Choose to live a life that matters.

Eulogy

Spoken by Don Timm, one of Coach's athletes, at Coach Griak's funeral at Mount Olivet Lutheran Church on July 22, 2015.

Speaking for myself, and for many other athletes, I would like to thank the entire Griak family for sharing Coach with us while we competed for him and more recently for giving us the opportunity to visit him, thank him and say our good byes.

Last month when talking to Coach I mentioned that the Bible teaches that the fruits of the Spirit are peace, love, joy, patience, kindness, goodness, gentleness, faithfulness and self-control. I told him, "I have learned a great deal about those things from you." He immediately said, "That's from St. Paul." It is Paul's letter to the Galatians (Chapter 5:22). Coach was not only familiar with the verse but he reflected the traits in his daily life.

Whenever I would telephone Coach I could tell by his enthusiasm and the tone of his voice that he must have been sitting by the phone just waiting for me to call. However, when I would visit him in his office at the University or at his home in Plymouth, his phone would ring every few minutes and the enthusiasm and tone of voice in greeting that caller were the same. Coach had a way of making everyone feel that they were the most important person in his world at that moment.

One Saturday morning last month, I sat with Coach at breakfast at the rehab center. He was having some trouble ordering. The menu listed the choices for Saturday, Sunday and Monday. I noticed that he was looking at Sunday's menu instead of Saturday's. Having so often looked to Coach for direction in the last forty-seven years I found it strange to think of giving him direction but I gently said, "Coach, I think the menu for today is on the other side." He replied, "Don, you always have to plan ahead." ....Although he had been hospitalized or in rehab for many weeks, Coach never lost his sense of humor and he never stopped teaching.

On July 6th, just three days before his death, I sat with Coach and Seth and Jason as Coach looked out at some flowers on the deck of his home. We had a very good conversation. Jason used an application on his phone that allowed him to show his father the house where he had lived in Gary - New Duluth. Coach enjoyed pointing out the location of the Serbian church, the bank, his junior high school and other land marks from his youth. Coach's mind was still sharp and his memories very clear.

Jason brought over a picture of his father posed as a sprinter in the starting blocks. You may have seen this picture at the visitation. He said, "Dad, was this at the University or at Morgan Park?" Coach replied, "Morgan Park." Then Coach, ever the technician, without hesitation said, "The hips are too low; the head is too high."

Coach's phone calls were frequent but never long in duration. He would usually say, "I'm just calling to say hello and to see how you are doing." I knew that he kept the conversations short because he had a long list of people to call each day.

The last recorded message from Coach on my home phone contained just three words. He had called earlier and had left a message that was long enough so that he had been cut off. He immediately called back and said "THANK YOU. BYE." Coach Griak was always big on thank yous.

Today Coach we say GOOD BYE to you and we say thank you.

THANK YOU for your guidance;

THANK YOU for your encouragement;

THANK YOU for the many opportunities you have given us;

THANK YOU for the legacy you have left. Even though this church is filled today, the people here represent only a small fraction of the lives you have touched.

THANK YOU for your friendship.

THANK YOU for your love.

GOD BLESS YOU COACH.... WE LOVE YOU.

In the starting blocks at Morgan Park High School

Contemporary Events from Selected Years in Coach's Life

Don Timm

1923-1924

Roy Grijak was born in Butte, Montana on October 5, 1923 to Milica and Milan Grijak. He was the first of their four children. The following events took place during that first year of his life (1923-1924).

- President Warren G. Harding died and was succeeded by Calvin Coolidge. Nikolai Lenin, the founder of the USSR, died as did architect, Louis Sullivan and former President Woodrow Wilson.
- During a race in Stockholm, Sweden Paavo Nurmi of Finland set a World Record (WR) for the mile at 4:10.4 that would last for 8 years. The Summer Olympic Games were held in Paris in 1924. Two of the Gold Medal winners in track and field (one of the sports Coach would come to love) were Harold Abrahams of Great Britain (GB) who set an Olympic Record (OR) of 10.6 in the 100m and Eric Liddell (GB) who set an (OR) of 47.6 in the 400m. Abrahams and Liddell would become famous again in the film "Chariots of Fire." Paavo Nurmi set Olympic Records of 3:53.6 in the 1,500m and 14:31.2 in the 5,000m while Finnish countryman Ville Ritola set a World Record (WR) of 30:23.2 in the 10,000m and an (OR) of 9:33.6 in the 3,000m steeplechase. Two United States athletes won two Gold Medals: Bud Houser in the Shot (49' 2 1/2") and Disc (151' 4") and Harold Osborn in the High Jump (6" 6") and Decathlon (7711) (WR).

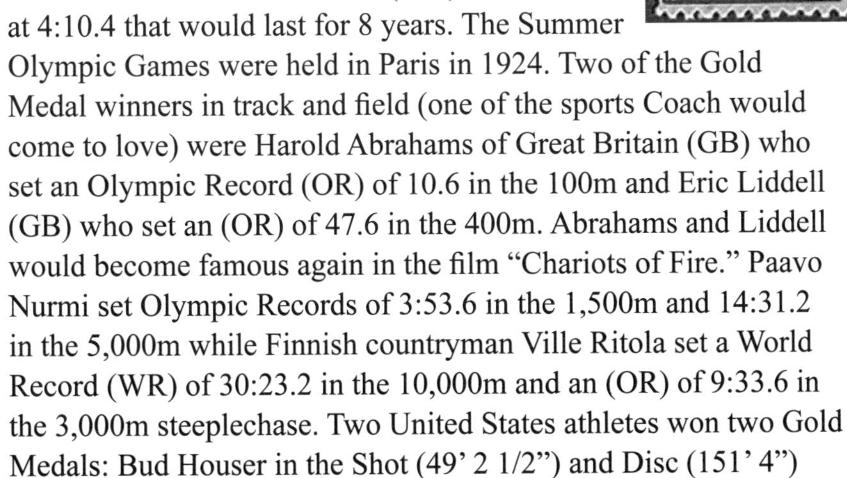

- Adolf Hitler was sentenced to 8 months in Landsberg Prison for his part in the Munich Beer Hall Putsch. While in prison he would write Mein Kampf.
- Calvin Coolidge won the 1924 Presidential election over the Democrat, John W. Davis.
- J. Edgar Hoover was appointed director of what was then called the Bureau of Investigation. It would become the Federal Bureau of Investigation (FBI) and he would lead it until 1972. One of Coach's high hurdlers, Byron Gigler (14.44 in 1965), would later work for the FBI.
- The Notre Dame football team, coached by Knute Rockne, completed an undefeated season in 1923 including an upset win over Army at the Polo Grounds. The Fighting Irish were led by their four horsemen: Leyden, Stuhldreher, Crowley and Miller.
- The first Winter Olympic Games were held in Chamonix, France.
- The 1923 U.S. Lawn Tennis Men's Singles Championship was won by Bill Tilden and the Women's Championship was won by Helen Wills.
- The 1923 U.S. Golf Association Amateur Champion was Bobby Jones.
- The Ford Motor Company produced 2 million cars and the price of

their Model T touring car fell to $290. The cost of a gallon of gasoline varied between 20-25 cents. A pair of children's shoes cost $4.95 at Sears-Roebuck while a girls' coat cost $10.95 (Coach remembered his sisters and many classmates wearing orange welfare coats). A dozen eggs cost 47 cents; a loaf of bread 9 cents (like 30% of the population in 1924 Coach's mother still made her own bread. Coach said that his mother's bread was much better than store bought bread). Butter cost 57 cents / lb. A first class U.S. stamp cost 2 cents.

- Unemployment was 5% in 1924
- In 1924 Secretary of the Interior, Albert B. Fall, was charged with bribery and conspiracy in the Teapot Dome Scandal and was eventually sentenced to a year in prison.
- Clarence Darrow defended Nathan Leopold and Richard Loeb and was able to get them life in prison rather than the death sentence for killing 12 ycar-old Bobby Franks.
- George Gershwin's "Rhapsody in Blue" was introduced.

1932

In 1932, Roy Grijak had his ninth birthday. Presidential elections that year saw Paul von Hindenburg defeat Adolf Hitler in Germany and Franklin D. Roosevelt defeat Herbert Hoover in the United States. The United States, and much of the world, was in the depth of the Great Depression.

- The Bonus Army (17,000 ex-soldiers) marched on Washington, D.C. to ask that their WW I bonus be given them early. They were driven out of Washington. Coach's father, Milan, was a WW I veteran who was also waiting for that bonus.
- Aldous Huxley wrote "Brave New World"
- Johnny Weismuller appeared in his first "Tarzan" movie and Shirley Temple appeared in her first film, "Red-Haired Alibi."
- Popular songs: "Brother, Can You Spare a Dime?" "Night and Day."
- Work began on the Golden Gate Bridge.
- Prohibition (18th Amendment) continued in the United States.
- Amelia Earhart flew solo across the Atlantic Ocean from Newfoundland to Ireland in 13 1/2 hours.
- the Lindbergh baby was kidnapped in Hopewell, New Jersey.
- the Olympic Games were held in Los Angeles. Mildred "Babe" Didrikson won gold medals in the hurdles and javelin and set a world record in the high jump but finished second on misses. Stella Walsh of Poland "won" the 100-meter dash but decades later was discovered to have been male. In 1984 The Olympic Games returned to Los Angeles and Coach Griak was part of the United States coaching staff.

1934

Roy Grijak was eleven in 1934. Franklin Roosevelt was implementing many of his New Deal programs in an effort to help the country out of the Great Depression. Times were hard all over the country and this was the case in Gary-New Duluth, Minnesota for the Grijak family.

- Glenn Cunningham broke the world record for the mile when he ran 4:06.8 at a meet in Princeton, N.J. He broke Jack Lovelock of New Zealand's record of 4:07.6.
- the President of the German Weimar Republic, Paul von Hindenburg, died and was succeeded by Adolph Hitler who assumed the title of Fuhrer.
- The Polish-French scientist, Marie Curie, died.
- In Callendar, Ontario, Canada, the Dionne quintuplets were born.
- "Blue Moon," written by Richard Rodgers and Lorenz Hart was one of the popular songs. Elvis Presley gave it a new rendition in 1956.
- The FBI shot John Dillinger, "Public Enemy Number 1."

- Sadly for Roy Grijak, his favorite team, the Detroit Tigers, was defeated four games to three in the World Series by the gas house gang St. Louis Cardinals led by Dizzy Dean and Pepper Martin.
- Max Baer won the heavyweight title of the world by defeating Primo Carnera. Baer wore the Star of David on his trunks, as he had when he defeated German champion Max Schmeling in 1933. Baer held the world title for 364 days and was the father of Max Baer, Jr. who played Jethro Bodine on the TV program "The Beverly Hillbillies."
- Bonnie Parker and Clyde Barrow were killed in a police ambush in Bienville Parish, Louisiana ending their 21-month crime spree.

1937

Thirteen-year-old Roy Grijak, his mother, Milica, father Milan (Mike), sisters Dolly and Kay and brother, Steve lived in Gary-New Duluth, Minnesota in a house Mike Grijak had built with the bonus for his service with the U.S. Army in WW I. Mike spent most of the last years of his life in a veteran's hospital and died of tuberculosis in 1940 when Coach was a sophomore at Morgan Park High School.

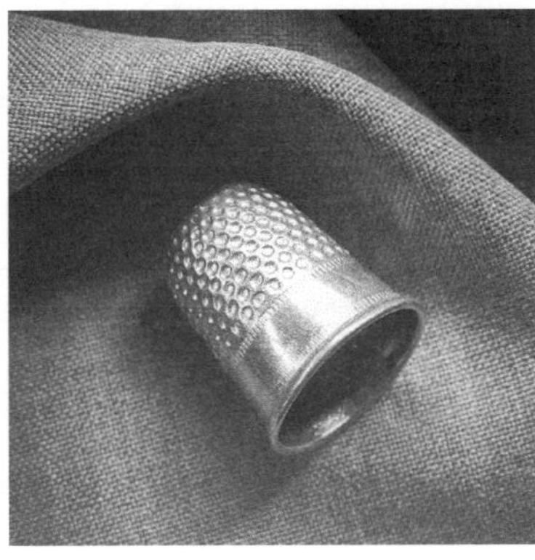

His mother worked as a seamstress to provide for her family. In 1937, Roy was a student at Stowe Junior High School. That year Europe and Asia moved closer to war on a world scale.

- George VI was crowned King of England. His brother, Edward VIII, had abdicated the throne to marry a divorced commoner (Wallis Warfield Simpson).
- As tensions grew in Europe and Asia, Franklin Roosevelt signed a U.S. Neutrality Act.
- Neville Chamberlain became Prime Minister of Great Britain (Stanley Baldwin had retired).
- Prince Konoye was named Japanese Premier and a more aggressive Japanese war policy grew.
- Italy withdrew from the League of Nations. They had invaded Ethiopia in 1935.
- Japanese planes sank the U.S. gunboat "Panay" in Chinese waters.
- Pastor Martin Niemoller was interned in a concentration camp by Adolf Hitler. He was held at Sachenhausen and then at Dachau. Unlike pastor Dietrich Bonhoeffer, who was hanged at Flossenberg in April of 1945, Niemoeller survived the war. (Quote: "First they came to get the Socialists - and I did not speak out because I was not a Socialist. Then they came to get the Trade Unionists - and I did not speak out because I was not a Trade Unionist. Then they came to get the Jews - and I did not speak out because I was not a Jew. Then they came to get me - and there was no one left to speak for me." Martin Niemoller)
- Pablo Picasso painted the mural "Guernica," depicting the Spanish Civil War, for the Paris World's Exhibition.
- John Dos Passos wrote "USA" and John Steinbeck wrote "Of Mice and Men."
- Walt Disney made the film: "Snow White and the Seven Dwarfs."
- Popular songs: "Whistle While You Work" "I've Got My Love to Keep Me Warm."
- Insulin was first used to treat diabetes.

- Wallace Caruthers patented nylon for the Du Pont Company.
- The first jet engine was built by Frank Whittle.
- Amelia Earhardt disappeared while on a flight over the Pacific Ocean.
- The dirigible "Hindenburg" disaster took place at Lakehurst, New Jersey.
- The Golden Gate Bridge opened in San Francisco.
- War Admiral won horse racing's Triple Crown.
- Don Budge won the U.S. Lawn Tennis Association Men's Singles Championship.
- Sydney Wooderson of the United Kingdom broke the World Record in the mile with a time of 4:06.4.

1942

As World War II entered its third year and the United States was entering its first full year of the fight, Roy Grijak graduated from Morgan Park High School. He placed fifth in the 880 in the Minnesota State Track and Field Meet that year. He would soon be in the U. S. Army.

- Gunder Hagg set the World Record for the mile at Gothenburg on July 1 when he ran 4:06.2 only to have fellow Swede Arne Andersson tie the record in Stockholm ten days later. In September, Hagg reclaimed the record in Stockholm when he ran 4:04.6. In July of 1943 Andersson took the record back again by running 4:02.6 in Gothenburg. He beat his own record in July of 1944 by running 4:01.6 at Malmo. Hagg reclaimed the record in Malmo in July 1945 and it was that record that was eclipsed by Roger Bannister when he broke the 4-minute-mile in May of 1954 (3:59.4). John Landy of Australia would lower the mile world record to 3:58 the following month.
- The U.S. government transferred over 100,000 Japanese-Americans from the West Coast to camps in the interior of the country.
- The Bataan Death March took place on the island of Luzon in the Philippines. (Coach would later be part of the American "return" to the Philippines.)
- Major Jimmy Doolittle led a raid of B-25 bombers on Tokyo.
- American forces won the Battles of the Coral Sea and Midway.
- American troops landed in North Africa.
- John Steinbeck wrote "The Moon is Down." and Thornton Wilder won the Pulitzer Prize for drama with "The Skin of Our Teeth."
- Enrico Fermi (Italian scientist who had moved to the United States) split the atom at a laboratory beneath the football stadium at the University of Chicago. The University of Minnesota's Roy Grijak would later compete in the 1948 conference cross country race that started in that football stadium.
- Cornelius Warmerdam of the U.S. established a new pole vault record by vaulting 15' 7 3/4" on May 23, 1942. This record was not broken until 1957.
- "Stars and Stripes," a daily newspaper for U.S. forces in Europe appeared.
- Gasoline, coffee and sugar rationing began in the U.S.

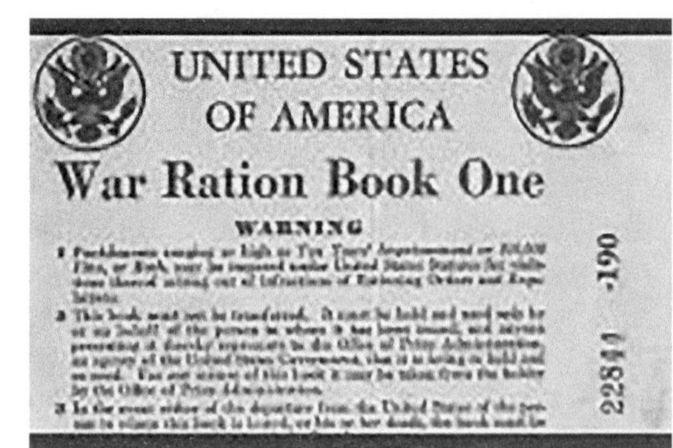

- Popular songs: "White Christmas," "Praise the Lord and Pass the Ammunition"
- Joe Louis knocked out Buddy Baer to retain the World Heavyweight Boxing title.
- A ticket to a movie in the U.S. cost 27 cents

1945

Coach Grijak (Griak) was with the United States Army in the South Pacific. The atomic bombs that were dropped on Hiroshima (Aug. 6th) and Nagasaki (Aug. 9th) led to the surrender of Japan and kept him from likely being part of the invasion forces on the major Japanese islands. Instead he would be part of the occupation forces in Japan. He held the rank of sergeant when he was honorably discharged from the Army. He returned to the United States on February 3, 1946.

- President Franklin D. Roosevelt died on April 12th and was succeeded by President Harry S Truman. Both Mussolini and Hitler died in late April.
- The first atomic bomb was detonated near Alamogordo, New Mexico on July 16th.
- The war ended. Victory in Europe (V-E Day) was May 8, 1945. The surrender of Japan was announced on August 14th and the official signing of the surrender document (Victory in Japan - V-J Day) was September 2, 1945.
- The Nuremberg Trials of Nazi war criminals began.
- The Nobel Peace Prize was awarded to American Secretary of State, Cordell Hull.

1949

Coach Grijak (Griak) was a member of the Gopher's Big Nine Championship Track and Field Team. He was twenty-six years old and soon would graduate from the University of Minnesota and begin to look for employment.

- The Communist People's Republic was proclaimed in China under Mao Tse-tung. the Nationalist forces of Chiang Kai-shek left for Formosa.
- The North Atlantic Treaty was signed in Washington.
- The Berlin blockade was officially lifted. There had been 277,264 flights in the airlift that brought food and supplies into Berlin.
- The German Federal Republic came into being with Bonn as its capital. The Democratic Republic was established in East Germany.
- George Orwell wrote 1984. (By 1984 Coach would have already coached the Gophers for two decades).
- Arthur Miller wrote "Death of a Salesman."
- The U.S.S.R. tested its first atomic bomb.
- The New York Yankees defeated the Brooklyn Dodgers four games to one in the World Series. The Yankees would go on to win five straight World Series titles (1949-1953).

1953

In the spring of 1953 Roy Griak (changed from Grijak) began his coaching career at St. Louis Park High School. The school did not have a 440-yard track.

- Dwight David Eisenhower was inaugurated as President of the United States.
- Jim Thorpe, who had won the decathlon in the 1912 Olympics in Stockholm, died. He was buried in Mauch Chunk, Pennsylvania which is now called Jim Thorpe, Pennsylvania. In the U.S.S.R. Joseph Stalin died.
- Elizabeth II was crowned Queen of England.
- Julius and Ethel Rosenberg were executed after being convicted of being atomic spies.
- The U.S.S.R. detonated a hydrogen bomb.
- Popular songs: "How Much is that Doggie in the Window?" "Stranger in Paradise"
- Edmund Hillary and his Sherpa guide, Tenzing Norgay, became the

first to scale Mt. Everest.

- In baseball the Boston Braves moved to Milwaukee and the St. Louis Browns moved to Baltimore and became the Orioles. For the last half century Boston and St. Louis had had teams in both leagues.
- the New York Yankees won their fifth consecutive World Series by beating the Brooklyn Dodgers four games to two.

1955

Coach Griak's St. Louis Park Orioles won the Minnesota State Cross Country Championship.

- President Eisenhower suffered a heart attack.
- The American Federation of Labor and Congress of Industrial Organization merged under a new president, George Meany.
- Rosa Parks was arrested for challenging the segregated bus system of Montgomery, Alabama. A bus boycott, led by Dr. Martin Luther King, Jr., began which lasted over a year (382 days) before the busses were integrated.
- Popular songs included: "The Yellow Rose of Texas," "Davy Crockett," and "Rock Around the Clock."
- Albert Einstein died.
- The Brooklyn Dodgers defeated the New York Yankees to win their only world championship. "Wait till next year" had become "This Year!"

1961

Coach and his wife Rose-Mary had had their second child, a son named Jason on March 23, 1960. Their first son, Seth, had been born on September 19, 1958. In 1961, Coach Griak led the St. Louis Park Orioles to another Minnesota State Championship in cross country. By this time the world record in the mile had been lowered to 3:57.2 by Derek Ibbotson of the United Kingdom in 1957 and then to 3:54.5 by Herb Elliott of Australia in 1958.

- John Fitzgerald Kennedy became the youngest elected president in U.S. history.
- Unsuccessful invasion of Cuba at the Bay of Pigs by U.S. trained and equipped rebel forces.
- To counter the North Atlantic Treaty Organization (1949), the Soviet Union and its communist allies formed the Warsaw Pact. Its members were: Albania, Bulgaria, Czechoslovakia, East Germany, Hungary, Poland, Romania and the Soviet Union. In East Germany, the Berlin Wall was constructed.
- United Nations President, Dag Hammarskjold, was killed in an airplane crash. He was awarded the Nobel Peace Prize.
- Adolf Eichmann was found guilty of war crimes in a trial held in Israel.
- Ernest Hemingway died. Ty Cobb, "The Georgia Peach" died.
- "Freedom Riders" were attacked in Alabama as they tested the integration of travel facilities.
- The Minnesota Gophers were defeated in the Rose Bowl by the University of Washington 17-7.
- The Washington Senators moved to the Twin Cities and became the Minnesota Twins.
- The National Football League expanded with the addition of Coach Griak's "favorite" team, the Minnesota Vikings.
- Popular songs: "Moon River," "Where the Boys Are," "Love Makes the World Go Round," "Exodus." Film: "Judgement at Nuremberg."
- Alan Shepard made the first United States space flight after the Soviets had sent Yuri Gagarin into orbit.

1963

Coach Roy Griak ended his very successful ten-year career at St. Louis Park High School and became the coach of the Minnesota Golden Gopher Cross Country and Track and Field program. He replaced his former coach, Jim Kelly. Rod Lamski won the Big Ten Indoor 70-yard high hurdles to become Coach Griak's first Big Ten individual champion. In the spring, Chuck Morrow became Coach's first outdoor individual champion when he won the Big Ten outdoor pole vault.

- Winston Churchill became an honorary citizen of the United States.
- There were civil rights demonstrations in Birmingham, Alabama and throughout the South. On August 28, 1963 250,000 people of every race and age marched on Washington, D.C. and gathered at the Lincoln Memorial to hear Dr. Martin Luther King, Jr. give his "I have a dream" speech.
- John Fitzgerald Kennedy was assassinated in Dallas, Texas on Nov. 22.
- Robert Frost and Rogers Hornsby also died.
- Films: The Birds (Alfred Hitchcock) Dr. Strangeglove (Kubrick and Sellers)
- Dr. Michael DeBakey first used an artificial heart to take over the circulation of a patient's blood during surgery.
- Jack Nicklaus won his first Master's Tournament.
- Songs: "I Want to Hold Your Hand" (Beatles) "I Saw Her Standing There" (Beatles)
- Studebaker ended its production of automobiles.
- Zip codes were introduced in the United States.
- Alcatraz federal penitentiary (The Rock) closed.

1964

Coach Griak's cross country team won the Big Ten Championship over perennial favorite Michigan State. It had been fifty years since the Gophers had last won the title.

- Peter Snell of New Zealand (NZ) lowered his own World Record in the mile from 3:54.4 (set in 1962) to 3:54.1 at a meet in Auckland, New Zealand. Michel Jazy of France would lower it to 3:53.6 in 1965. The world record for the mile would next be held by Jim Ryun of the United States who ran 3:51.3 in 1966 and then 3:51.1(set in Bakersfield, California on June 23, 1967)
- Douglass MacArthur, Herbert Hoover and Rachel Carson (Silent Spring) all died.
- A movie ticket cost an average of 93 cents. Gasoline sold for 30 cents a gallon.
- The alleged Gulf of Tonkin incident led to the escalation of the war in Vietnam. Lyndon Baines Johnson was elected President and he signed the Civil Rights Act of 1964.
- The Warren Commission determined that Lee Harvey Oswald was responsible for assassinating President Kennedy.
- Martin Luther KIng, Jr. who had written "Why We Can't Wait" was awarded the Nobel Prize for Peace in Oslo.
- Films: Goldfinger, Mary Poppins. Popular Song: Hello Dolly
- The Olympic Games were held in Tokyo: unheralded Billy Mills of the United States won the 10,000m run; Peter Snell (NZ) won both the 800m and 1,500m.
- Cassius Clay defeated Sonny Liston to win the World Heavyweight Boxing title.
- Sidney Poitier won the Academy Award for Best Actor (Lilies of the

Field).

- Nikita Khruschev was ousted in the Soviet Union and replaced by Communist Party leader Leonid Brezhnev and Prime Minister Alexei Kosygin.
- Nelson Mandela was sentenced to life in prison in South Africa.
- The St. Louis Cardinals defeated the New York Yankees four games to three in the World Series.

1968

Coach Griak's Minnesota Gopher team scored a stunning upset at Memorial Stadium on the University of Minnesota campus in winning the Big Ten Outdoor Track and Field Meet. As proud as he was of his team's accomplishment Coach was even more proud that the Minnesota point scorers in the meet went on to become teachers, ministers, doctors, dentists, lawyers and other professionals. His cross country team had placed a very close second in the Big Ten that fall and then had placed fourth in the NCAA Meet. Steve Hoag made the All-American team in the 10,000m run.

- A gallon of gasoline sold for 34 cents. A cost of a movie ticket averaged $1.31.
- The United States reached its greatest military involvement of ground troops in Vietnam. The North Vietnamese staged the Tet Offensive.
- Mainly because of the division in the United States concerning the war, Lyndon Johnson announced that he would not seek another term as President.
- It was a year of violence in our country as Dr. Martin Luther King, Jr. was killed in Memphis, Tennessee and Senator Robert Kennedy was killed in Los Angeles. The Democratic Party Convention in Chicago also sparked violence as Chicago police used force in an attempt to quiet young people protesting U.S. presence in Vietnam.
- The Olympic Games were held in Mexico City: Bob Beamon (USA) broke the world record in the long jump by nearly two feet as he jumped 29' 1/2." Dick Fosbury won the gold medal in the high jump by "flopping" 7' 4 1/4."

1969

Coach Griak's Minnesota Gopher Cross Country team won the Big Ten title in Bloomington, Indiana. It was Coach's second cross country title in his first seven years at Minnesota. Garry Bjorklund won the Big Ten individual title in cross country (his first of three) and made the All-American team with his sixth place NCAA finish. The Gophers placed seventh in the NCAA Cross Country Meet in Van Cortlandt Park (New York City).

- Richard M. Nixon was inaugurated President of the United States.
- James Earl Ray was sentenced to prison for ninety-nine years for assassinating Martin Luther King, Jr.
- Dwight D. Eisenhower, Ho Chi Minh, Boris Karloff, Jack Kerouac and Judy Garland of Grand Rapids, Minnesota died.
- Senator Edward Kennedy's Presidential hopes ended with the mysterious death of Mary Jo Kopechne at Chappaquiddick in Massachusetts.
- Continued protests in the United States against the war in Vietnam. President Nixon began the Vietnamization program in southeast Asia.
- William Calley went on trial for his involvement in the massacre at Mylai in Vietnam.
- Mario Puzo wrote "The Godfather." Kurt Vonnegut wrote "Slaughterhouse Five."
- Popular films: "Midnight Cowboy," "Easy Rider," "Butch Cassidy and the Sundance Kid," "MASH."

- Woodstock music festival.
- A gallon of gasoline cost 35 cents and a movie ticket averaged $1.42.
- Popular Songs: "Hair," "Aquarius," "In the Year 2525."
- Apollo 11 landed on the surface of the moon. Neil Armstrong walked on the moon.
- The Miracle New York Mets defeated Baltimore to win the World Series.

1972

The Gophers moved from Memorial Stadium to the new Bierman field track. According to the Minnesota Daily, the first intercollegiate track meet on an all Tartan track would be held there on May 1, 1971 against the University of Illinois. However, the track was not fully completed by that date and the meet that day against Illinois was held at Macalester College in St. Paul. The first meet at the Bierman track was run on May 15, 1971 against the University of Iowa. The track was bare as the lanes had not been installed but the Gophers and Hawkeyes did run the meet. The first race on the completed track would not be held until the spring of 1972. Coach Griak was very proud of the new facility. The Olympic Games were held in Munich, West Germany. Coach Griak was a member of the coaching staff for the games. Olympic marathon gold medalist, Frank Shorter, entrusted Coach Griak with supervising the de-fizzed Coca-Cola he drank at the aid stations along the route. Coach Griak was in Munich when terrorists struck the Olympic Village and eventually eleven Israeli athletes / coaches were killed.

Don Timm running on unlined Bierman track

- The last United States ground troops were removed from Vietnam.
- President Nixon and Henry Kissinger went to China and met with Mao Tse-tung and Chinese Premier, Chou En-lai of the People's Republic of China. This led to a softening of relations between the United States and China.

Coach surveying the new Bierman track

- President Nixon met with Leonid Brezhnev in summit talks that were known as SALT (Strategic Arms Limitations Talks).
- Mark Spitz won seven gold medals in swimming at Munich.
- Bobby Fischer beat Boris Spasky to win the World Chess Championship.

- A gallon of gasoline cost 36 cents and a movie ticket averaged $1.70.
- The Oakland Athletics won their first of three straight World Series titles.

1980

Coach Griak entered his third decade at the helm of the Gopher Cross Country and Track and Field teams. His son, Jason, running for St. Louis Park, had placed second in the state 3200-meter run (9:16) in 1979. Coach was selected to be an assistant coach of the U.S. Olympic team that summer. Former Gopher shot putter Colin Anderson qualified for the Olympic team but President Carter decided that the United States would not compete because of the Soviet invasion of Afghanistan. Other athletes who had competed for Coach Griak who actually had Olympic Games experience were Leonard Edelen (1964 marathon); Garry Bjorklund (1976 10,000 meters); Steve Placencia (1988 and 1992 10,000 meters); Ron Backes (1992 Shot Put) and Keita Kline (2000 200 meters - Kline represented the British Virgin Islands).

Jason Griak, Coach and Seth Griak in 1980

- Lech Walesa led the Solidarity union movement in Poland against the communist government.
- Mount St. Helens erupted in Washington State killing thirty-four people.
- Over sixty other countries joined the U.S. in boycotting the Moscow Olympics.
- Ronald Reagan defeated Jimmy Carter in the Presidential election.
- Bjorn Borg of Sweden won his fifth Wimbledon tennis title.
- Japan surpassed the United States in the production of automobiles.
- John Lennon was killed. Other deaths in 1980 included Alfred Hitchcock, Jimmie Durante, Jesse Owens, Mae West, Colonel Harland Sanders and Shah Mohammad Riza Pahlavi.
- The Rubik's Cube, Post-It Notes and the arcade game Pac-Man were introduced.
- The winter Olympic games were held in Lake Placid, New York. Wisconsin speed skater Eric Heiden won gold medals in the 500-meters, 1,000-meters, 1,500-meters, 5,000-meters and 10,000-meter races. His sister Beth won a bronze medal in the 3,000-meter race. The United State Hockey team won the gold medal ("Miracle on Ice").
- A gallon of gasoline cost $1.24 and a movie ticket averaged $2.69.
- The world record for the mile had been lowered from Jim Ryun's 3:51.1 to 3:51.0 by Tanzanian Filbert Bayi in 1975 and to 3:49.4 by New Zealander John Walker later that year and then to 3:49.0 by Sebastian Coe of the United Kingdom in 1979. Starting in 1980 it would be broken four times in the next year by British runners:

Steve Ovett 3:48.8 in 1980; 3:48.53 by Sebastian Coe in 1981; 3:48.40 by Steve Ovett in 1981 and 3:47.33 by Sebastian Coe in Brussels in 1981.

1984

Coach Griak was selected to be on the coaching staff as head manager for the United States Track and Field team for the Los Angeles Olympic Games. His sons, Seth and Jason, accompanied him to Los Angeles. That fall he coached the last of his seven NCAA All-American cross country runners when Dave Morrison placed thirteenth.

- The Union Carbide pesticide disaster in Bhopal, India killed 2,000 people and injured as many as 150,000 others.
- Indian Prime Minister Indira Gandhi was assassinated by two of her own body guards.
- The Soviet Union withdrew from the summer Olympic Games in Los Angeles and other communist bloc countries followed. This was a snub of the United States for the U.S. refusal to compete in Moscow in 1980.
- Carl Lewis duplicated the four gold medals Jesse Owens had won in Berlin in 1936 by winning golds in the same events (100 meters, 200 meters, long jump and 4 x 100 meter relay).
- The Democrats nominated Walter Mondale of Minnesota and Geraldine Ferraro (she became the first female on a major party ticket). The Republicans nominated incumbent President Ronald Reagan and Vice President George H. W. Bush and won in a landslide.
- The winter games were held in Sarajevo, Yugoslavia.
- Apple introduced the user friendly Macintosh personal computer.
- The average cost a gallon of gasoline was $1.21 and a movie ticket averaged $3.36.

1993

Coach Griak entered his thirtieth year as the coach of the Gopher teams. Vesa Rantanen became Coach's second and final NCAA Indoor national champion when he won the pole vault with a height of 18' 2 1/2." Coach's other indoor national champion was Ron Backes who had won in 1986 with a 68' 1 1/4" effort in the shot.

- Noureddine Morceli of Algeria broke Steve Cram's world record in the mile (3:46.32 - 1985) when he ran 3:44.39. That would remain the world record for six years until in 1999 Hicham El Guerrouj of Morocco ran 3:43.13. This remains the world record today.
- William Jefferson Clinton took the oath of office as President of the United States.
- Sprinter Ben Johnson was banned from athletics for life for his use of performance enhancing drugs.
- Israel's (Yitsak Rabin) and the Palestine Liberation Organization's (Yasir Arafat) signed a peace accord on the White House lawn with President Clinton in attendance.
- Liam Neeson starred as Oskar Schindler in the WW II film, Schindler's List.
- Michael Jordan retired from the National Basketball Association.
- Among the deaths in 1993: Thurgood Marshall, Arthur Ashe, Roy Campanella, James Doolittle.

1996

This was Coach Griak's thirty-third and last year of active coaching at the University of Minnesota. He was inducted into the "M" Club Hall of Fame. His last indoor Big Ten champions were crowned that year: Paul Michalek won the 800-meter in 1:51.34; Chris Darkins won the 55-meter dash in 6.24 and Adrian Ellis won the triple jump with a distance of 52' 2". Outdoors that spring Coach had conference champions in the 4 X 100 meter relay (Eric Stommes, Adrian Ellis, Tim Van Voorhis and Scott Beadle) and individual champions in the pole vault (Vesa Rantanen - 17' 10 1/4") and in the discus (Jason Schlueter - 185' 0"). During his coaching career at Minnesota Coach Griak coached a total of sixty-two track and field Big Ten individual champions (thirty-one indoor and thirty-one outdoor plus relay winners). He also coached his twenty-ninth and last outdoor All-American when Paul Michalek ran 3:39.64 to claim sixth in the 1996 NCAA 1,500-meter run. Coach Griak's final indoor All-American was Keita Cline who placed eighth in the 1995 NCAA triple jump with a distance of 52' 9 1/4." Keita was Coach Griak's ninth indoor All-American. Add seven NCAA All-American cross country runners to his thirty-eight track and field All-Americans totals forty-five All-American athletes (plus four more United States Track and Field All-Americans in cross country).

Coach Griak's "M" Club Hall of Fame Pyramid

- The US, USSR, Great Britain, France and China signed a nuclear test ban treaty.
- The Olympic Games in Atlanta, Georgia were disturbed by a bombing in Centennial Park.
- Israel elected Benjamin Netanyahu as their Prime Minister.
- Militant Taliban leaders seized the Afghan capital of Kabul.
- The Republicans nominated Bob Dole and Jack Kemp but the Democrats nominated incumbents Bill Clinton and Al Gore who won the national election.
- Madeline Albright was appointed by President Clinton as the first female Secretary of State.
- Unemployment was 5.4%. A first class stamp cost 32 cents.
- Joel and Ethan Coen (graduates of St. Louis Park High School) wrote, produced and directed the film Fargo.
- Spiro Agnew, Ella Fitzgerald, Gene Kelly and George Burns all died.
- Svetlana Masterkova of Russia broke the world record for the women's mile when she ran 4:12.56 at Zurich, Switzerland.

2013

Coach Griak celebrated his fiftieth year at the University of Minnesota. By this time he had been inducted into numerous halls' of fame including the United States Track and Field and Cross Country Hall of Fame and the U.S. Track Coaches Association Hall of Fame. On September 26th, a banquet held in his honor at the Twin City Federal Bank Stadium on the Minnesota campus. There were accolades from Governor Mark Dayton, St. Paul Mayor Chris Coleman and Minneapolis Mayor, R.T. Rybak. Mayor Rybak proclaimed September 26th ROY GRIAK DAY IN THE CITY OF MINNEAPOLIS. The Gopher band spelled out GRIAK on the football field and then played the Minnesota rouser in his honor. Hundreds of athletes, coaches, staff members and friends joined Coach and his family in the celebration. At the celebration Coach thanked all the people who had come to honor him and prophetically said, "Life is short, some of us may never see each other again." He said, "I appreciate all of you and the smiles and handshakes. You give back to me more than I have given you." Two days later Coach was at the Griak Invitational as he hosted the most prestigious cross country meet in the United States.

Coach Griak Bobblehead

- Alabama defeated Notre Dame in the National Championship football game.
- Lance Armstrong admitted doping during his biking career.
- Former Mayor of Detroit, Kwame Kilpatrick, was convicted of corruption charges. Detroit would later file for bankruptcy.
- Louisville defeated Michigan to win the NCAA Men's Division I Basketball Tournament.
- Two explosions near the finish line of the Boston Marathon killed three people and injured two hundred sixty.
- The Miami Heat defeated the San Antonio Spurs to win the NBA title.
- The Chicago Blackhawks defeated the Boston Bruins to win the Stanley Cup.
- George Zimmerman, who had been charged with the fatal shooting of Treyvon Martin, was acquitted of all charges.
- Target Corporation and the United States Secret Service reported that forty million credit and draft cards were compromised due to a data breach.
- Among the deaths in 2013: Patti Page, Stan Musial, Van Cliburn, Jonathan Winters, Vern Mikkelsen, Lou Brissie (pitcher with the Philadelphia A's and Cleveland Indians who won forty-four major league games between 1947-1953 despite almost losing a leg during his service in WW II - he was one of Coach's favorite ballplayers).

United States T & F and CC Hall of Fame

United States Track & Field Coaches Hall of Fame - 2001

2015

A fall in his garage (after coming home from work at the University) on April 27th led to Coach Griak's hospitalization, many weeks in a rehabilitation center in Wayzata, hospice care in his home and eventual death on July 9, 2015. A visitation on July 21st was followed by Coach's funeral at Mount Olivet in Minneapolis on July 22nd. Tom Stuart, one of Coach's athletes, was the minister who officiated. Among the many people who attended the visitation / funeral were people from all stages of Coach's life: high school classmates, former and current coaches, former and current University athletes and administrators, rival coaches and athletes, neighbors, friends and family. Coach was buried in the Oneota Cemetery in Gary - New Duluth on July 25th.

- Cuba and the United States re-established full diplomatic relations after fifty-four years of hostility between the nations (thus, the U.S. and Cuba had severed relations throughout Coach Griak's entire coaching and administration career at the University). The relations were restored during the presidency of Barack Obama.
- Queen Elizabeth became the longest reigning monarch in British history. She has been the Queen of England ever since Coach started his career at St. Louis Park High School.
- Earthquakes in Nepal led to over nine thousand deaths in Nepal, India, China and Bangladesh.
- The Confederate flag was ordered to be removed from the state capitol in Columbia, South Carolina.
- Among the deaths in the first seven months of 2015: Billy Pierce, Ron Clarke, Minnie Minoso, Al Rosen, Dean Smith, Jerry Tarkanian, Mario Cuomo, Ernie Banks, Coach Roy Griak.

1 Kilometer marker at the Griak Invitational CC Meet

Coach Griak CC Etching at the Griak Invitational

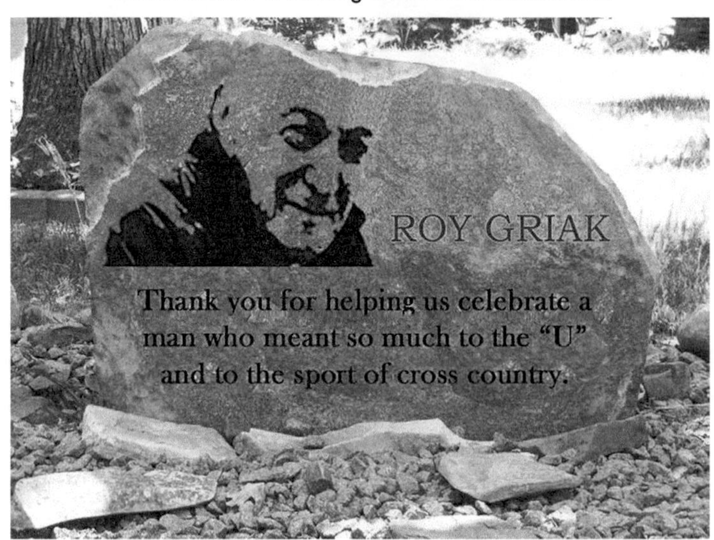

"Well started is only the beginning - - 10 yards beyond the finish line in all that you do."

Coach Griak

Appendix

Coach Griak's St. Louis Park Track and Field Handbook

In a handout given to Oriole track prospects in the early 1960s, Coach Griak justly billed St. Louis Park High School as "the Home of Track Champions." He wrote that "Park has become well known in the state of Minnesota for its fine track teams and our hope is that we can continue to enjoy as much success in the future so that we can keep a track tradition at St. Louis Park." He went on to thank the past team members for making this tradition possible. Coach called Track and Field a fine individual and a great team sport and then went on to list his expectations for those wishing to represent the Orioles in competition.

What is written below are the expectations for high school athletes at St. Louis Park but they could just as well have been written for those collegiate athletes who represented him later at the University of Minnesota. Coach's straight forward requirements about respecting teammates and school and submitting to rigid discipline in striving to maximize one's potential were constants no matter what the age of his athletes.

Coach Griak's St. Louis Park Track and Field Handout

Membership on an athletic squad is one of the most enjoyable and valuable privileges any boy can have. When you make close contacts with your teammates day after day, dressing, training, racing each other, making trips to meets, friendships are made that may never be broken.

If you are to get the most from this team association there are certain matters that you ought to consider. The following suggestions if learned and followed will help you to win: (1) You must live sportsmanship. You won't be very popular, and you will cause your team harm if you are the type of person who crabs about the weather, the coach, the bad start you got, or many other things a poor sport can crab about. Remember, all successful athletes take instruction in good spirit. (2) At the track meet, while waiting for your event, the wise competitor "takes it easy." Do not run around the field trying to see everything that goes on, you will be wasting vast amounts of physical and nervous energy that you will wish to have when your event comes around. Before and during a meet, try to keep calm and unruffled. Sleep all you can, and talk things over with your teammates and coach, but try to avoid any LOUD boisterous rough-house. Most champions are hard-working fellows, not PLAYBOYS. (3) Always finish a race regardless of how much it hurts. Never quit. Break through "Fatigue" and have "guts." Never fall into a set stride and stay there. This is a rut that leads to mental fatigue. Learn to punish yourself when the going is the toughest. Do Not Be Last. Always

1

beat one man of the opposition. Never fall on the ground at the finish of a race. This indicates either a showoff or a boy who is not taking care of himself; it probably means that he is out of condition. Intend to be a leader, not a follower. Remember---you are never tired, very few runners have physical fatigue, its mental fatigue that loses most races.

Never pass a man slowly. Pass him with some "zip." This is good psychology as your opponent will feel that you are fresh and have lots of stuff left.

Keep alert. It is the "alert mind" that wins. Keep thinking! (4) Next, let's consider the bare essentials of training and study the problem from the standpoint of taking care of the body as though it were a machine that we wish to use for some delicate and important work. All of you know athletes who sneer at training rules and still seem to do pretty well. The answer to this is that some boys are born with so much ability that they can waste part of it and still win against boys with less ability. Who knows what these fortunate fellows would be able to do if they cared for themselves properly? Perhaps they would have done twice as well. One never knows what might have been. You don't run the jalopy on water or alcohol; you buy gasoline. Your car runs better with good gas than other varieties. Yet, some of the boys in St. Louis Park and other schools try to make their bodies run on smoke, alcohol, grease, and with as little sleep as possible.

Training is a matter of SELF DISCIPLINE. The boy who really wants to be a fine cross country runner and track man must train for himself. It takes a MAN to be a good athlete.

2

SLEEP

Probably one of the biggest crimes against good body care is the matter of sleep. During sleep the body makes repairs and builds muscle, tendon, bone and nerve. One should establish regular hours for sleep. For a growing boy in athletics (9) nine hours is a safe rule to follow. All members of the St. Louis Park track team must be in bed not later than 10:00 P.M. during the school week. Since sleep is very important not only before the day of competition, but during the week as well, for this reason, I feel that this rule should never be broken. Any team member who finds it necessary to be out later than 10:00 P.M. during the school week should as a matter of courtesy discuss the matter with the coach. For further clarification, the school week includes days Sunday through Friday. Team members should use good common sense in regard to curfew hours on week-ends. The boy who loses sleep, stays out late and insists that he is getting (8) hours of sleep from 12 A.M. to 8:00 A.M. is only fooling himself. Regularity in the time one sleeps is just as important as the length of time one sleeps. ***By the time that I ran for Coach he had further formulated this so that each hour of sleep before midnight was worth twice as much as the value of an hour of sleep after midnight.***

DIET

Probably the next most common body care error involves food. Diet should be a matter of a well-balanced diet by eating a good breakfast, a very light lunch, and a good evening meal. Greasy and fried foods should be especially avoided. Meat should be a part of the diet for the evening meal only. Green and yellow vegetables and all fruits should be a definite part of the

3

diet. Eggs should never be eaten in any fashion prior to hard practice or on the day of competition. They are composed of sulphur base and cause gas to form. This can cause illness, especially when a runner has a nervous stomach.

On the day of competition eat sparingly. Athletes should eat three or four hours before competition if possible. The food eaten immediately before a race just relieves the hunger pangs. A pre-race diet consists of honey, baked potato, dry toast and weak tea with plenty of sugar. These foods in very moderate portions should be sufficient to carry any runner who is in good shape. ***Today, the "plenty of sugar" would be modified or subtracted from the diet.***

Eating between meals is a very bad habit to form. A good athlete in training will limit himself to eating only at meal time. Do not eat before going to bed. If you must have something, eat an orange or an apple. Cake and pie should be eaten in moderation, and do not eat such food in the latter part of the week and never eat to excess at any time.

During your workouts as during competition the water you drink should be sipped, not gulped, and should not be taken in large quantities. When sipped, the cold fluid is warmed before it reaches the digestive tract.

THINK OF WINNING AND IT WILL BE EASIER TO TRAIN. Remember that any slight errors in training may be responsible for the tenths of seconds and fractions of inches that make the difference between winning and losing.

4

SMOKING

Smoking is a difficult subject to discuss because so many boys, girls and parents smoke. However, regardless of what other people do, you should try to find the truth about the effects of smoking on the body. Some of the adverse effects of smoking are: nicotine acts as a depressant on the nerves and the brain, constricts or tightens up blood vessels, and slows and retards the flow of blood to all parts of the body. Thus the supply of oxygen is limited and burning (oxidation) of the food energy is limited. You can't fill your lungs with carbon from burning leaves without interfering with the lungs' function of taking oxygen from the air for the blood. Money spent by some boys for cigarettes would come in handy for other things in high school and college!

A bit of reading by any boy in doubt as to these statements will provide plenty of literature to convince him. SMOKING, OR THE USE OF TOBACCO IN ANY OTHER FORM, WILL NOT BE USED BY ANY ST. LOUIS PARK TRACK TEAM MEMBER, IT HAS NO PLACE IN THE LIFE OF A GOOD ATHLETE. Any boy in athletics who insists in using tobacco is not fooling anyone (coach, teammates, parents) but only fooling himself.

ALCOHOL

There isn't any doubt about the use of alcohol being harmful. People who use it, use it in spite of the fact that they know it is bad. If you are to be a successful athlete, however, you will never, under any circumstances, drink alcoholic beverages.

5

The whole problem of training is just to take care of your body in the same way that you would take care of any fine instrument or other possession. Your body will win you athletic honors, if you care for it properly.

OTHER TRAINING RULES

Never wear your track shoes in the school building. When track shoes are not being worn the shoes should be placed so that the sole of the shoe is always facing the floor.

Always take a shower after practice. A lukewarm shower is best. A hot shower opens the pores too much and brings a feeling of weakness and drowsiness. Don't take a very cold shower, as the shock on the heart is severe. Take a lukewarm shower and gradually cool it off if you like a cold shower.

For daily workouts, time trials, and days of meets, one of the most important items is to be thoroughly warmed up. The idea behind warm ups is to acclimate the physical system of the heart, lungs, and muscular structure to a higher level of locomotion for action. A set rule is that "the runner should run as hard in the latter part of his warm up as he will have to run at any time in the race." An athlete thoroughly warmed up really expends less energy and has less chance of muscle injury. So, take a good warm up.

Keep your equipment clean, especially the supporter and socks. It will help to prevent rashes and inflammation that could remove a boy from training or competition. Take care of your equipment by hanging it in its proper place and return all school equipment after it has been used.

6

For a small fee you are allowed one clean towel for a workout. When you return your dirty towel you will be given a clean one. Under no circumstances should you ever have two clean towels in your possession. ***Apparently this did not pertain to green towels at the University of Minnesota***.

ELIMINATION OF ALL HORSEPLAY IN AND AROUND THE LOCKER ROOMS IS A MUST --- this will prevent many avoidable injuries from occurring.

Immediate treatment of all injuries, NO MATTER HOW SLIGHT.

A continual program of calisthenics should be conducted during the season, with special emphasis on upper body and abdominal work.

ALL TEAM MEMBERS WILL RETURN FROM TRACK MEETS ON TRANSPORTATION PROVIDED FOR THEM BY THE SCHOOL.

Never enter the drying-room unless you are given permission by the coach or under the supervision of the team managers.

KEEP THE FOLLOWING IN MIND

1. Have an ever active willingness to work hard to develop one's track potential to the highest possible degree.
2. Don't think you are good enough to get by with less than your very best; no one ever was or will be that good.
3. The coach's criticism is never personal.
4. Have absolute faith in your own ability to do your best at all times and under all competitive conditions.

7

5. Aim for perfection. Any boy who puts himself in the hands of his coach and sincerely tries to learn and improve is going to benefit from track and field athletics.

<u>THE TRACK MAN'S CREED SHOULD READ LIKE THIS:</u>

1. I will win.
2. If I cannot win, I will be second; If not second, then third.
3. If I cannot be placed at all, I will still do better than ever before.

Sincerely,

Roy Griak, Coach

Eugene Wright, Ass't Coach

St. Louis Park School Song

Park High Loyalty

(Based on Illinois Loyalty - We're Loyal To You, Illinois)

We're loyal to you Park High-------- We're Orange and Black Park High--------

We'll back you to stand 'Gainst the best in the land, For we know you have sand, Park High.

Rah! Rah! So smash the blockade Park High-------- Go crashing ahead Park High------

Our team is our fame protector, Oh! Boys, for we expect a victory from you Park High----

8

About the Authors

DON TIMM is a retired teacher and coach who ran cross country and track for Coach Griak and the Minnesota Gophers from 1967-1971. He lives in Anoka, Minnesota with his wife, Bonnie. They have three grown children, Andy, Liz and Katie.

LINDSAY NIELSEN is a Psychotherapist, Writer and Paralympian. In her 40's, with Coach Griak's help, she broke world records, became a Paralympian, and became the world's first amputee woman to finish an Ironman Triathlon. Lindsay lives in Minneapolis with her husband Jeffrey Hunsberger. They have two grown children, Miles and Maliq and a grandson, Mikah.